LAW AND INTERSYSTEMIC COMMUNICATION

Studies in the Sociology of Law

Series Editor
Alberto Febbrajo, University of Macerata, Italy

Series Advisory Board
André-Jean Arnaud, University of Paris X, France
Alfons Bora, University of Bielefeld, Germany
Denis Galligan, University of Oxford, UK
Karl-Heinz Ladeur, University of Bremen, Germany
Setsuo Miyazawa, University of Waseda, Japan
Jirí Pribán, Cardiff Law School, UK
Darío Rodríguez Mansilla, University Diego Portales, Chile
Wojciech Sadurski, University of Sydney, Australia
András Sajó, Central European University, Hungary
Gunther Teubner, Johann-Wolfgang-Goethe University, Germany
Chris Thornhill, University of Glasgow, UK
David M. Trubek, University of Wisconsin, USA

The objectives of Studies in the Sociology of Law are threefold. Firstly, the series aims to deepen the analysis of the sociolegal problems related to the enlarged European Union and the different paths of its constitutional process and policy. Secondly, it examines the many facets of legal cultures within and outside the European context in comparative perspective and in an open debate with extra European scholarship. Thirdly, it reconsiders the historical legacy of sociolegal thought while dealing with the broader dynamic and the new challenges of contemporary societies.

Law and Intersystemic Communication
Understanding 'Structural Coupling'

Edited by

ALBERTO FEBBRAJO
University of Macerata, Italy

GORM HARSTE
Aarhus University, Denmark

ASHGATE

© Alberto Febbrajo and Gorm Harste 2013

All rights reserved. No part of this publication may be reproduced, stored in a retrieval system or transmitted in any form or by any means, electronic, mechanical, photocopying, recording or otherwise without the prior permission of the publisher.

Alberto Febbrajo and Gorm Harste have asserted their right under the Copyright, Designs and Patents Act, 1988, to be identified as the editors of this work.

Published by
Ashgate Publishing Limited
Wey Court East
Union Road
Farnham
Surrey, GU9 7PT
England

Ashgate Publishing Company
110 Cherry Street
Suite 3-1
Burlington, VT 05401-3818
USA

www.ashgate.com

British Library Cataloguing in Publication Data
Law and intersystemic communication : understanding
  'structural coupling'. -- (Studies in the sociology of law)
  1. Sociological jurisprudence. 2. Legal positivism.
  3. Legal polycentricity.
  I. Series II. Febbrajo, Alberto. III. Harste, Gorm.
  340.1'15-dc23

Library of Congress Cataloging-in-Publication Data
Law and intersystemic communication : understanding structural coupling / by Alberto Febbrajo and Gorm Harste.
    p. cm. -- (Studies in the sociology of law)
    Includes bibliographical references and index.
    ISBN 978-1-4094-2110-8 (hardback) -- ISBN 978-1-4094-2111-5 (ebook)
  1. Law--Social aspects. 2. Sociological jurisprudence. 3. Social systems. I. Febbrajo, Alberto. II. Harste, Gorm.
   K376.L354 2012
   340'.115--dc23
                                                                           2012022209

ISBN 9781409421108 (hbk)
ISBN 9781409421115 (ebk – PDF)
ISBN 9781409471479 (ebk – ePUB)

Printed and bound in Great Britain by the
MPG Books Group, UK.

Contents

List of Figures	*vii*
List of Tables	*ix*
List of Contributors	*xi*

Introduction   1
Alberto Febbrajo

PART I: SOCIOLOGY OF LAW AND THE INTERSYSTEMIC OPENNESS OF LEGAL SYSTEMS

1   The Transplanetary Journey of a Legal Sociologist   17
André-Jean Arnaud

2   The Growth of Legal Transnationalism   31
Roger Cotterrell

3   A Comment   51
Alberto Febbrajo

PART II: SOCIAL COMMUNICATION AND LEGAL REGULATION

4   The Big, Large and Huge Case of State-building: Studying Structural Coupling at the Macro Level   67
Gorm Harste

5   Reflexive Governance in the European Union? An Example of Structural Coupling   97
Julien Broquet

6   Contract as a Form of Intersystemic Communication   129
Niels Åkerstrøm Andersen

7	Functional Differentiation, Financial Instruments and Regulatory Challenges *John Paterson*	155
8	Values as Certain Uncertainties: The Paradox of Value Communication in Organisational Practice *Victoria von Groddeck*	179
9	Moralized Communications and Social Regulation *Diane Laflamme*	197

PART III: BEYOND LEGAL POSITIVISM: NORMS, RIGHTS AND CONSTITUTIONS

10	Making Law Together? On Some Intersystemic Conditions of Judicial Cooperation *Jan Winczorek*	229
11	Rights in Niklas Luhmann's Systems Theory *Pierre Guibentif*	255
12	Jurisprudence and Intersystemic (Mis)communication *Katayoun Baghai*	289
13	Structural Coupling between the Systems of Law and the Media: The Contrasting Examples of Criminal Conviction and Criminal Appeal *Richard Nobles and David Schiff*	317
14	Constituting Constitutions beyond the State: Polycontextural Constitutionalism of the World Society *Lasha Bregvadze*	327
15	Legal Pluralism as a Form of Structural Coupling *Gunther Teubner*	343

Index 361

List of Figures

4.1	Codes, re-entries, and forms functionally differentiated	73
4.2	A methodological construction of the state as an organisation system structurally coupled to functional differentiated systems with forms of re-entered codes	74
6.1	The form of contract	139
6.2	The multiplicity of contract	141
6.3	The contract as structural coupling	142
6.4	Contract vs. functional differentiation	147
7.1	The relationship between a corporate bond and a credit default swap	161
7.2	Systems theory representation of a corporate bond contract	162
7.3	Systems theory representation of a credit default swap contract – version 1	163
7.4	Systems theory representation of a credit default swap contract – version 2	166
7.5	Systems theory perspective on the company interest	168
8.1	The form of observation	181
8.2	First form of research observation	182
8.3	Second form of research observation	184
8.4	Third form of research observation	186
8.5	The uncertainty of heterogeneous expectations	189
8.6	The uncertainty of the organisational identity	191
8.7	The uncertainty of the organisational future	192

List of Tables

0.1	The main steps of Luhmann's theory	6
3.1	Two models of contemporary sociology of law	52
3.2	Classic approaches to sociology of law	56
3.3	Problems of classic and contemporary sociology of law	57
4.1	A system theoretical typology of states (with different degrees of structurally coupled programmes coded in organisational and functional communication systems)	87
6.1	Society's function systems	144
6.2	Poly-contextuality presented as a matrix of observation	145
6.3	Contractual constructions in function systems	149
6.4	Organizational constructions in function systems	150
9.1	Self-constituting systems	199
9.2	The three dimensions of meaning and their double horizon	211
9.3	Morality: Steering at the level of expectations that are expected	221

List of Contributors

Niels Åkerstrøm Andersen is Professor of Political Management at the Department of Management, Politics and Philosophy, Copenhagen Business School, Denmark.

André-Jean Arnaud is Chairholder of the UNESCO/UNITWIN Chair 'Human Rights, Violence: Public Policies and Governance', Universidad Externado de Colombia, Bogotà, and Director of RED&S (Réseau Européen Droit et Société), Fondation Maison des Sciences de l'Homme, Paris, France.

Katayoun Baghai is a post-doctoral fellow at McGill University, Montréal, Canada.

Lasha Bregvadze (MA, LL.M.) is Assistant Professor at the Javakhishvili Tbilisi State University, and Director of the Tsereteli Institute of State and Law, Georgia.

Julien Broquet is a member of the Centre de Recherche sur l'Industrie, les Institutions, et les Systèmes Économiques d'Amiens (CRIISEA) and is teaching Economics at the University of Picardie Jules Verne, France.

Roger Cotterrell is Anniversary Professor of Legal Theory at Queen Mary and Westfield College, University of London, and a Fellow of the British Academy, UK.

Alberto Febbrajo is Professor of Sociology and Anthropology of Law at the University of Macerata, Italy.

Victoria von Groddeck is Assistant Professor in the Institute of Sociology, Ludwig Maximilian University of Munich, Germany. Her research focuses on organisational sociology with a special interest in the coevolution of society and organisations.

Pierre Guibentif is Associate Professor in the Department of Sociology, ISCTE-IUL – Instituto Superior de Ciencias do Trabalho e da Impresa at the Instituto Universitario de Lisboa, Portugal.

Gorm Harste is Associate Professor in the Department of Political Science, Aarhus University, Denmark.

Diane Laflamme, Ph.D. in Applied Human Sciences at the University of Montréal, is now teaching at the University of Québec, Montréal, Canada.

Richard Nobles and **David Schiff** are Professors in the Department of Law at Queen Mary University of London, UK.

John Paterson is Professor of Law in the School of Law and Co-Director of the Centre for Energy Law, University of Aberdeen, UK.

Gunther Teubner, at present Visiting Professor, Den Haag and Tilburg University, is Principal Investigator, the Cluster of Excellence: 'Normative Orders', at the Johann Wolfgang Goethe University, Frankfurt am Main, Germany.

Jan Winczorek is Assistant Professor at the University of Warsaw, Poland.

Introduction

Alberto Febbrajo

The basic intent of the following chapters is to explore not the core of a social system but its borders, not its substantial contents but its channels of communication to and from other systems. In other words, this book is fundamentally oriented not so much to a "functionalism of distinctions" which emphasizes the typical characteristics and the internal coherence of single social systems, but to an emerging "functionalism of links," which stresses the importance of the several bridges which, at various levels, mutually connect the different social systems.

At first sight the functionalism of links seems to be the obvious opposite of the "autopoietic" approach, based on the "self-reference" of social systems. Every social system has to be equipped with mechanisms of inclusion or exclusion. This would require a rigid distinction between the internal and external side of a given social system, between what belongs to the system and what belongs to the environment. The political system has to defend its own borders, accepting what is politically relevant; the legal system, what is legally relevant.

But the refinement of the concept of "autopoiesis," emphasized by social systems theory as the theoretical key for defending the autonomy of functionally differentiated social systems, has underlined that the basic abilities of self-observation and self-delimitation are not necessarily connected with a rigid closure. "The open rests on the closed."[1] A social system, although, or even because, internally regulated by autopoietic mechanisms, can tolerate fluid definitions of its borders, which are operationally closed in relation to their reproduction and cognitively open in relation to their self-correction. For a social system conservatism implies a constant disposition to change.

In this perspective closure and openness may be regarded as the extremes of a *continuum* in which every social system finds different levels of openness or closure towards external influences. It is thus possible to exclude a sharp alternative acceptance/refusal in relation to the highly controversial autopoietic approach.[2]

---

1   "L'ouvert s'appuye le fermé," E. Morin, *La Méthode, vol.1 La Nature de la nature* (Paris: Seuil, 1977).

2   The autopoietic approach, since its introduction in the sociological debate, has been at the center of a wide debate. See, among the first contributions, K. von Bema, "Ein Paradigmawechsel aus dem Geist der Naturwissenshaften: Die Theorien der Selbssteuerung von Systemen (Autopoiesis)," *Journal für Sozialforschung* 31 (1991), 3–24; D. Zolo, "The Epistemological Status of the Theory of Autopoiesis and Its Applications to the Social

Rather, we should count on the fact that its further development can capture the main intersystemic facets presented by social reality. Autopoiesis appears to be an amphibious concept which as such combines, in variable degrees, the ability of social systems to change in order to properly react to external impulses (openness), and the ability to save their own identity and to remain recognizable in spite of the changes occurred (closure).

Starting from these presuppositions, the functionalism of links and the functionalism of distinctions can be considered not as alternative but as potentially complementary hypotheses. If a completely autonomous system, being blind to other systems, were unable to react in the way required for its own survival, a completely open system, being unable to defend its own autonomy, would inevitably be destined to be absorbed by its environment.

These extreme presuppositions could have ideological or Utopian character, as occurs with some current representations of law. On the one hand, unilateral emphasis on the closure of the legal order is normally supported by the internal ideology of legal professionals, who justify their social prestige by representing their technical knowledge as a durable protection of the "neutrality" of legal decisions. On the other, unilateral emphasis on the openness of the legal order is often supported by the Utopian vision of a "direct participation" in legal institutions by social actors, who are convinced of the possibility of influencing these institutions without passing through any intermediate filters.

In an attempt to skip ideological as well as Utopian simplifications, the social systems theory could be used to analyze the different types of closure, or openness, in single social systems. Following its most influential representative, Niklas Luhmann,[3] the basic difference between closure and openness, identity and evolution[4] of social systems could be articulated in a series of symmetric distinctions between abstract and concrete levels (norm and action, rule and decision), which are relevant for the functioning of legal systems. From this point of view, Luhmann's thought is not to be considered a fully fledged theory but the

---

Sciences," in G. Teubner and A. Febbrajo (eds), *State, Law, and Economy as Autopoietic Systems* (Milan: Giuffrè, 1992), 67–124.

3 A realistic interpretation of autopoiesis is explicitly professed by Luhmann himself: "All that matters in the sociological context is whether or not the concept of autopoiesis leads to the formulation of hypotheses, which are fruitful science (and this includes empirically fruitful)" Cf. Luhmann, *Law as a Social System* (Oxford: Oxford University Press, 2004), 83 fn. 17.

4 Evolution, in living organisms as in social systems, is not produced by the iteration of a chain of identical elements, but by the combination of heterogeneous factors. It requires, in Luhmann's approach, constant adaptation to external irritations and increasing ability to react to higher levels of complexity of the environment. Cf. R. Nobles and D. Schiff, "Introduction," in N. Luhmann, *Law as a Social System* (London: Routledge & Kegan Paul, 1985), 8.

product of a sort of autopoietic "way of thinking", based on the internal dynamic of a process of self-reflection which must eventually be continued by its interpreters.[5]

Adopting the same scheme, the evolution of the theory worked out by Luhmann could be reconstructed through four basic steps: the first two predominantly influenced by the intrasystemic perspective typical of the functionalism of differences, and the last two by the intersystemic perspective typical of the functionalism of links. Each step is principally connected with at least one of the fundamental autopoietic moments: selection, stabilization and variation, which guarantee the identity of the system and its ability to change.[6]

In his early works, Luhmann represents the legal system as the sociological and anthropological extension of social structures, suffocated by routine and by the idea that people must act only as others expect them to.[7] In this phase, the sociological, and psychological, concept of *expectation* appears as the essential point of reference for legal structures. Situated at the pre-juridical level of the rules spontaneously produced by individuals in their mutual relationships, this concept is woven by Luhmann into a functional definition of normative systems. Social expectations appear based on criteria of normative resistance to, or of cognitive recognition of, the possibility of delusions created by unexpected behaviors.[8] In terms of a "reduction" of social complexity which limits possible alternatives of actions, social actors can thus rely on a double strategy: either on a self-referential normativity, reacting to violations with sanctions, or on a fact-oriented cognitivity, reacting to delusions with a correction of the expectation.

A further level of self-reflection is reached by Luhmann with the concept of *generalization*. Generalization ensures the gradual transfer of the concrete needs of continuity from single operations to more abstract criteria of regulations.[9] The trend towards generalizations is essential in terms of the "stabilization" of structural expectations. This implies a largely diffused definition of factual regularities, and normative criteria of justification. The fundamental hypothesis is that the autonomy of every social system is better defended by the presence

---

5   In fact, the internal development of the work of each individual author, which normally does not exclude constant adjustments to various external stimuli and influences, can be considered an example of autopoietic maintenance of identity. Therefore interpreters are totally unjustified in treating a largely uncompleted work like Luhmann's as a closed entity.

6   Cf. N. Luhmann, *Law as a Social System* (Oxford: Oxford University Press, 2004), 259.

7   See, among others, N. Luhmann, "Normen in soziologischer perspektive," *Soziale Welt* 20 (1969), 28–48.

8   The reassuring function of social norms, and their ability to reduce an otherwise intolerable complexity, is typical of Gehlen's anthropology, which represents an important but often neglected source of Luhmann's thought. See A. Gehlen, *Man: His Nature and Place in the World* (New York: Columbia University Press, 1988).

9   N. Luhmann, *A Sociological Theory of Law* (London: Routledge & Kegan Paul, 1985),73ff

of a normative area concerning its internal relations. Even within the scientific system, which is typically open to constant changes due to new factual discoveries, the need of normativity is present, basically anchored at the level of widely accepted methodological requirements which can normatively stabilize what is recognized as research and what is not. In particular, in modern societies the process of generalization is accompanied by autonomization of legal systems and the positivity of law. Positive law seems more open than natural law to further evolution because it is dependent not on externally predetermined values but on variable operations oriented, at the same time, to internal technical criteria and to external empirical factors.[10]

With the concept of *procedure*,[11] Luhmann implicitly abandons the analysis of "regulative" rules connected with regularities of single or collective expectations, and enters into the domain of the "constitutive" rules, that is of the meta-rules which regulate, as in a sort of social game, artificial behaviors created within a conventional context.[12] Law itself, being not only a "differentiated," but also a "differentiating" system, is presented as a system which is able to autonomously "constitute" its own criteria of differentiation. In this context, procedures could be interpreted as specific legal games which "constitute" the possibility of a series of acts, unthinkable outside their context. Like social games, procedures can "innovate" and produce uncertain outcomes. Thus they acquire a self-legitimating function because the participants, having taken part in a game, are discredited if they try to discredit its outcome: the loser has only himself to blame for not having played his cards better.[13]

Moreover, procedures appear not only as systems closed by their criteria of relevance (*quod non est in actis non est in mundo*), but also as conventional buffer zones where law is allowed to "learn" from the intersection of internal and external legal cultures, and from the interaction of social actors and legal professionals. In the most important set of procedures of the legal system, the trial, the legal "truth" produced by the sum of its artificial steps, does not necessarily correspond to the truth as it is socially and empirically understood by the single actors. A trial, in other words, constitutes its own roles *and* its own rules. By means of different levels of self-observation, it stipulates how the conflict is going to be resolved and the real influence of the players on its final outcomes.[14]

---

10   N. Luhmann, *A Sociological Theory of Law* (London: Routledge & Kegan Paul, 1985), 159.

11   N. Luhmann, *Legitimation durch Verfahren* (Frankfurt am Main: Suhrkamp, 1969).

12   For the dichotomy regulative vs constitutive rules, cf. J.R. Searle, *The Construction of Social Reality* (Harmondsworth: Penguin, 1995). From a constitutive point of view, the "reification" of social systems theory appears somewhat justified because this theory predetermines, at the same time, its own object and its own borders of relevance.

13   Cf. N. Luhmann, *Legitimation durch Verfahren* (Frankfurt am Main: Suhrkamp, 1983).

14   On these early phases of the development of Luhmann's theory, see Febbrajo, *Funzionalismo strutturale e sociologia del diritto nel pensiero di Niklas Luhmann* (Milan: Giuffrè, 1975).

In the last phase of its development Luhmann's theory concentrates on an autopoietic approach to the intersystemic concept of *communication*.[15] The monadic notion of a system completely unable to communicate, which was one of the most popular symbols of postmodern societies, is set aside by the increasing importance attached to communication processes within and between different systems, which are able to extend the constitutive character of single procedures to the whole society.[16] Law, in particular, translates the relevant conflicts concerning generalized expectations into its own language, settles them and arranges their re-entry in procedures which are part of a self-referential system able to produce and select legal communication. This chain of communicative acts constantly generates new stories, that are open to new developments and are interpreted by sets of meaning typical of the legal system. "Meaningful communication" is presented by Luhmann as "the mode of operation, which produces and reproduces the social system" according to specific codes generally articulated in binary forms.

In this sense, legal system as a closed and specialized system of communication assigns meanings exclusively according to a typical dual code legal/illegal, or lawful/unlawful.[17] Internally, law communicates only about law, but it is also open because it exchanges beyond its borders the meanings developed by mutual intersystemic contacts. This does not exclude the fact that the huge flow of communications thus created can cross other self-referential communications, and in the long run even modify the borders of the different social systems involved. The "autonomy" of political and economic systems, for instance, could transform itself into regulated "heteronomy" since these systems are extensively under the control of legal norms.

In these cases, mutual intersystemic indifference is substituted by a sort of mutual intersystemic communication which encompasses all the three basic moments of the autopoietic process. For Luhmann, in particular, autopoietic coevolution is the product of processes of co-selection, co-stabilization, and co-variation based on the interpenetration of different social systems.[18] Every system "selects" the redundant possibilities of intersystemic communication at its disposal in order to "stabilize" its own borders through filters embedded in a multilevel process of self-observation which allows self-corrections and

---

15 The concept of communication is apparently developed by Luhmann as a response to Habermas. But the convergences between the two authors are reciprocal. Habermas tries to establish inter-subjective criteria of communication, based on a cooperative coordination, which can be considered as a form of intersystemic rationality. For an extensive combination of the autopoietic approach with a theory of communication, see Luhmann, *Social Systems* (Stanford: Stanford University Press, 1995).

16 Cf., for instance, Luhmann, *Die Realität der Massenmedien* (Opladen: Westdeutscher Verlag, 1996).

17 Luhmann, The "Coding of the Legal System", in G. Teubner and A. Febbrajo (eds), *State, Law and Economy as Autopoietic Systems* (Milan: Giuffrè, 1992), 145–86.

18 N. Luhmann, *Law as a Social System* (Oxford: Oxford University Press, 2004), 440ff.

"variations", and the same happens to individuals.[19] The combination of these phases assures at a micro- and a macro-level the mutual exchanges of meanings, which are necessary for coevolution.

It is important here to stress the importance of intersystemic instruments of "structural coupling" which "separate and link system at the same time" as if such a kind of interpenetration could reach the level of intersystemic communication. Indeed, general systems theory being applicable to all systems, contains the possibility of intersystemic connections in a "polycontextural perspective"[20] which could encompass a number of cultural products, such as the university, seen as an institutional connection between research and education, or the contract, seen as a formal connection between law and economy. These instruments appear to be essential elements of intermediation between the two functionalisms, of distinctions and of links, previously mentioned (see Table 0.1).[21]

Table 0.1 The main steps of Luhmann's theory

Conceptual aspects	Functional aspects	Theoretical points of reference
expectation	selection	normative/cognitive
generalization	stabilization	operation/structure
procedure	innovation	certainty/uncertainty
autopoietic communication	coevolution	structural coupling

The functional connection "*autopoietic communication—co-evolution—structural coupling*" is of the utmost importance for understanding the Luhmann's last works. Social systems are in general capable of combining communications coming from different systems on the basis of a common structure which allows them to learn from external stimuli. This means that coevolution does not presuppose a point-

---

19 These moments are not necessarily connected with an intersystemic approach and could also be applied to individuals in a different, both internal and vertical, way. Confucius (Analects) declares that wisdom can be reached by human consciousness through three steps of internal ascesis: "imitation" (which produces social stabilization); "experience" (which produces personal innovation) and "reflection" (i.e. moral selection of what is essential).

20 For an application of this concept, see G. Teubner, "The King's Many Bodies: The Self-deconstruction of Law's Hierarchy," *Law and Society Review* 31 (1997), 763–87.

21 Indeed, the concepts belonging to the typology of the "self" (self-reference, self-observation, self-correction, autopoiesis), are balanced, in Luhmann's theory, by several concepts explicitly based on intersystemic connections (interpenetration, re-entry, structural coupling). This double articulation progressively absorbs the basic antinomy normative vs. cognitive into a sort of "second order" logic.

to-point contact between systems, but simply their coupling through intersystemic structures which can be utilized as a common platform for mutual exchanges of communications.

Furthermore, instruments of structural coupling can overcome the internally linked communications which ensure the maintenance of the identity of social systems by reproducing themselves according to self-produced structural rules (operative closure), and recognizing a limited system's openness to external influences. This means that the concept of structural coupling like the concept of autopoiesis does not suggest any kind of strict separation and isolation, but underlines the disposition of the legal system to defend one's identity in situations in which appear necessary to introduce cognitive processes of self-correction based on intersystemic communication.

In the early stages of social evolution, when societies were differentiated segmentally (tribally), Luhmann only signalizes general mechanisms of structural coupling concerning the direct connections between law and violence. But in modern societies the instruments of structural coupling are highly heterogeneous. In these societies intersystemic communication could require, from a temporal perspective, "synchronicity" between system and environment, that is the instantaneous coupling of their operations.[22] Nevertheless there are cases in which the instruments of structural coupling provided by legal system are too slow for the purposes of other (economic or political) systems, and are thus perceived by decision-makers as practically useless. This can for instance explain the emergence of informal equivalents to a too slow formal justice.

There are also cases in which the mechanisms of structural coupling could exercise different roles. Property, for instance, assumes in a money-based economy a double significance within legal and economic systems because lawyers "are used to treating legal claims arising from property separately from legal claims arising from contract."[23] Payment is quite different when it relates to the economic effects of the reuse of money, or to the legal aspect concerning the situation that the payment can induce.

These ambiguities for Luhmann are controlled by a structural coupling which, as such, respects the identities of the specific systems. If one were to give up the distinctions between legal and economic systems, "it would amount to a revolution in civil law"[24]; and, reciprocally, considerable parts of the economy would collapse

---

22 Luhmann expounds on how instruments of structural couplings separate and link systems by referring to the distinction between *analog* and *digital* processing. Systems grow older in the same timeframe without having to measure it, and in this sense they age analogously. If they connect past and future events, they process their temporal contexts digitally. N. Luhmann, *Law as a Social System* (Oxford: Oxford University Press, 2004), 382.

23 N. Luhmann, *Law as a Social System* (Oxford: Oxford University Press, 2004), 400.

24 A direct communication between law and money can be internally observed as a form of corruption or bribery. N. Luhmann, *Law as a Social System* (Oxford: Oxford University Press, 2004), 381.

"if the law were totally enforced."[25] This means that the instruments of structural coupling have to integrate social systems by avoiding their total fusion. They could not only rely on functionally compatible intersystemic features but also measure intersystemic incompatibilities, reducing in this way the risk of crises, which could be particularly dangerous and incontrollable if suddenly extended to different systems.[26]

According to Luhmann, the most abstract instrument of structural coupling related at the same time to legal and political systems is constitution. It provides, at a higher and sometimes merely symbolic level, "political solutions for the problem of the self-reference of the legal system and legal solutions for the problem of the self-reference of the political system."[27] While for a legal system constitution is a supreme statute, a sort of basic law, for a political system it is an instrument of politics, in the sense of instrumental politics (which changes states of affairs) or only symbolic politics (which does not). The main point of reference, for this kind of intersystemic connection, is the adequacy of legal norms to the interests and ideals accepted and stabilized within a given society. Constitution has thus different meanings in legal and political systems. In other words, it can be treated as a sort of formal "hypertext," which can allow different interpretations in different social contexts. In general, the constitution constitutes the "state", and presupposes that the state could eventually emerge as the carrier of the structural coupling between political and legal systems.[28] The positivistic process of changing legal norms through legal norms finds in constitutions its highest point of reference which defines at the same time possibilities and limits of formal legal change.

At a macro-level, democracy may be also considered as a comprehensive instrument of structural coupling. It assures functional relations between political and legal systems through the external legal cultures of normal citizens. By offering access to this extremely articulated spectrum of legal cultures, democracy provides, in a differentiated society, a substantial source of variety for changing established normative contents and political decisions. The main point of reference for this intersystemic communication is the effectiveness of legal regulations. In order to implement this essential task, democracy avoids destroying possibilities for future decisions. In the long run, what is excluded now could be reconsidered

---

25 A "more effective administration of criminal justice would cause problems for prisons": N. Luhmann, *Law as a Social System* (Oxford: Oxford University Press, 2004), 478.

26 Cf. P. F. Kjaer, G. Teubner, and A. Febbrajo (eds), *The Financial Crisis in Constitutional Perspective: The Dark Side of Functional Differentiation* (Oxford: Hart Publishing, 2011).

27 N. Luhmann, *Law as a Social System* (Oxford: Oxford University Press, 2004), 410.

28 Consequently, the present fading out of the traditional functions of the state affects the modern constitutionalism as it is particularly visible in periods of transition. See A. Febbrajo and W. Sadurski (eds), *Central and Eastern Europe after Transition: Towards a New Socio-legal Semantics* (Farnham: Ashgate, 2010).

later in different situations. In this way, democracy legitimizes legal and political systems, maintaining a sort of variety pool for periodic legislative innovation.[29] Democracy is based on the measure of consensus, and new decisions can be accepted only because their consensus is based on democratic procedures.

Likewise, one may view the market as a macro-instrument of structural coupling. Market can be considered as an institutionalized bridge between legal and economic systems since, within the market, legal norms and their criteria of allocation are normally connected with economic criteria of rationality.[30] The market constantly selects decisions on the basis of processes based on typical criteria of purposive rationality, which exclude legally possible decisions incompatible with economic requirements. The concept of efficiency seems to be the main point of reference for intersystemic communication, since, through shifting price determination, the market should allow an optimal use of resources and a possible convergence of individual and general interests. Market is thus dependent on the proper functioning of legal and political systems, and is condemned to become dysfunctional when, for any reason, this intersystemic connection fails to work positively. Money produces money, but this self-referential circle is only a part of the reality of economic systems, which are able to develop intersystemic relations at global level between legal and political systems.

All these macro-instruments of structural coupling appear oriented to the common task of managing the risks that every law produces. At a functional level, they assure "temporal" stabilization (constitution), "social" variation (democracy), and "substantial" selection (market) of legal regulations. But which system is leading the game in the single cases? This could be determined by the procedures which, as supporting instruments of structural coupling, define the constitutionality of a bill, the results of an electoral campaign and the prices of certain goods. Through the uncertainty of their outcomes, these procedures multiply the possibilities for constitutions, democracy, and market to maintain communicative feedbacks and to perceive the changes intervened in other social systems. They produce, for instance, new forms of juridification of politics or of politicization of law without defining in advance which system will in the end prevail, and to what extent.

The relevance of the instruments of structural coupling is essential also at a micro-level. In general, psychic systems are affected by intersystemic communications channeled through instruments of structural couplings. As a matter of fact, every communication needs the active participation of consciousness. This implies a constant structural coupling between consciousness and communication

---

29 N. Luhmann, *Die Politik der Gesellschaft* (Frankfurt am Main: Suhrkamp, 2002), 96ff.

30 An anti-normativistic and *ante litteram* "intersystemic" definition of law based on a theoretical combination of normative and cognitive criteria of rationality in legal and economic systems was elaborated 50 years ago by Bruno Leoni. See B. Leoni, *Freedom and the Law* (Princeton, NJ: Van Nostrand Co., 1961).

according to which expectations and generalizations, as well as procedures and intersystemic communication, could redistribute different meanings at the level of the individuals. "Only when consciousness is involved ... can society be affected by its environment. Only in this way is it possible to develop a high level of complexity in the operatively closed systems of society, on the basis of communication." In short, at a micro-level "society depends on a structural coupling with systems of consciousness."[31]

A double-edged analysis at a macro- and micro-level underpins all the following chapters. They are concentrated on some of the main forms of structural coupling, which in the contemporary representations of the legal system contribute to a definition of its multilevel and intersystemic communication. In particular, they deal with: a) the open models of legal systems presupposed by influential self-representations of contemporary sociolegal studies; b) the strict intersystemic and psychological presuppositions of specific legal constructions such as contracts, which are connecting legal and economic systems; c) the increasing interrelations of legal systems with political systems and the media.

In the first part, starting from differing portraits of contemporary sociology of law formulated by two of its leading figures, A.-J. Arnaud and R. Cotterrell, the hypothesis suggested is that the "new" sociological concept of law which is emerging in sociolegal studies is increasingly oriented towards its environment and challenged by the problem of being structurally coupled with other social systems. In particular in Chapter 1 André-Jean Arnaud underlines that, in the last decades, sociolegal studies have been characterized by different critical analyses of internal legal cultures. From the 1970s attention was concentrated on a "denunciation" directed "to supersede the traditional conception of a law restricted to codes or judicial decision making." During the 1990s sociologists of law focused on "remodeling" the contents of legal norms, in line with the upsurge of various movements for the defense of "new" rights. In the present phase, sociolegal studies are expected to provide decision-makers with scientific results in order to orient public policymaking within the different realms of society.

In Chapter 2 Roger Cotterrell proposes a different typology of the phases of contemporary sociology of law. His general presupposition is that the discipline has been predominantly conditioned by the changing role of the state. In a first phase, when law and state were expected to exercise direct control over society, sociology of law was inspired by a sort of legal instrumentalism which treats "law and society as inseparably linked." In a second phase, the main point of reference of sociology of law was a transnational orientation based on a largely shared vision "of human dignity for all mankind." In the present situation, the attention of sociology of law has been attracted by globalized cultural contexts where contracts and commercial law are particularly open to economic influences.

---

31   N. Luhmann, *Law as a Social System* (Oxford: Oxford University Press, 2004), 384.

In Chapter 3 Alberto Febbrajo sets out to demonstrate that these reconstructions of contemporary sociology of law are, in spite of their different terminology, fundamentally convergent. They could be considered as a logical development of a critique of the traditional normative approach, on the basis of three fundamental types of empirical control of legal norms proposed by classic sociology of law (efficiency, adequacy and effectiveness). In order to find a solution for the difficult coexistence within the legal system of normative and cognitive strategies, which at the same time attempt both to command society and to learn from it, social systems theory is now combining closure and openness of the legal system by resorting to complex strategies of institutionalization of internal self-reflection and external communication at an intersystemic level.

In the second part of the volume, attention is concentrated on the intersystemic relationships between state regulations and economic system. Gorm Harste, in Chapter 4, suggests, from the perspective of a theory of self-referential communication, that in the process of European state formation the single states established internal forms of structural coupling (for instance between law, war, finance, etc.). In particular, the structural coupling of law with war led to a new description of just and unjust wars based on a connection of their codes of communication according to which neither war nor law could completely neglect each other. In this context, even a self-description of political systems correspondent to the single states has to be largely abandoned since their communications are inevitably trans-territorial and transnational.

In Chapter 5 Julien Broquet, in seeking to contribute to an adequate post-national concept of governance, underlines the territorial aspects which seem decisive in the evolving complexity of modern society and in the emergent framework of the post-sovereign states. He focuses on the strict connections between law, economy, and politics, and between law and the four freedoms of markets (finance, labor, commodities, and services). In this context he discusses, from the point of view of modern systems theory, how instruments of structural coupling could impact on a European governance based on a constant readjustment of intersystemic relations and on a territorial organization inherited from previous segmentary and stratified differentiations.

In Chapter 6 Niels Åkerstrøm Andersen presents an overview of some of the recent theoretical debates on contract law. Looking at contracts as they were widely used in society, he considers them as functional responses to a lack of "steering" control through intersystemic communication. On the one hand, contracts bracket the internal communication of organizations provided by specific functional codes and, on the other, link communication with external organizations. In this way, contracts play the role of instruments of structural coupling which demonstrate that neither individual subjects nor specific systems are the masters of contractual relations. Contracts establish a translation of widely differentiated interests and promises between the parties, and assure that the partners in the future will maintain the promises that they were willing to make in different systemic contexts.

John Paterson, in Chapter 7, observes that for the financial system any normative regulation suffers from cognitive deficit and normative uncertainty. While the legal system codes its interventions in terms of control and tries to establish effective regulations on this basis, the financial system codes its communication in terms of risk. This means that, if contracts are essential instruments of structural coupling, they, as was largely demonstrated during the credit crisis of 2008–10, establish contractual relationships between organizational systems, in particular between the legal system and the financial system. This "contractual fragmentation," however, does not exclude that some Utopian models of constitutionalized unity of contracts could still represent a normative ideal.

In Chapter 8 Victoria von Groddeck sustains that "values" seem to indicate a sort of internal communication system. The semantics of "values" provides therefore "invaluable structural coupling" between organization systems and their environment. The function of value communication involves two forms of structural coupling: the first between the single organization and its environment, and the second between organizational practices and their temporal context. In general, when organizations communicate about values, they suggest that there is no conflict between an outside and an inside, and that no part within the organization and no stakeholder group outside the organization would be disturbed by values such as quality or innovation.

In Chapter 9 Diane Laflamme, assuming the point of view of the world of internal meanings, observes that communication systems cannot operate if they are not structurally coupled to psychic systems. The basic meaningful/meaningless distinction, which is constituted by intentional acts of consciousness, simultaneously "interpenetrates" psychic and communication systems. It allows a distinction between different levels of observation concerning who is addressed in a social dimension, what is communicated in a substantial dimension, and when communication takes place in a temporal dimension. But communication is not always and in every respect linked to a common consciousness. Moralized communication is thus conceived in a skeptical way, as we cannot expect moral semantics to integrate society in its entirety.

The third part of the book is devoted to the analysis of some constitutional problems connected with intersystemic communications: How can law harmonize its different formal and social sources in a homogeneous set of norms? How is it possible to absorb the irritations generated by the media and to defend the unity of the legal system through instruments of structural coupling? In Chapter 10 Jan Winczorek, starting from the presupposition that, in music as in law, interpreters transform texts into socially relevant elements, underlines the risks of interpretations that are unpredictable or unrecognizable. In the realm of music, these risks are limited by the presence of a conductor (in the case of jazz, by "some thick rules of collective performance"), but in the realm of law the analogy presupposes a powerful state, which seems to have "disappeared." In this context, even "the coupling between law and politics through constitutions", seen as a sort of second-order level of observation, appears insufficient and has to be enlarged "utilising not just political and legal but also economic and technological means of regulating social relations."

In Chapter 11 Pierre Guibentif tackles the constitutional dimension of subjective rights and the psychological dimension of consciousness. If Luhmann considers psychic systems in a "more fragmentary and essayistic way" in comparison to social systems, this does not exclude their centrality in his architecture. The concept of consciousness appears important at intersystemic level for "the coevolution of psychic systems and communication" and for the distinction between social systems and environment. Among the different mechanisms of structural coupling required by these connections, Guibentif focuses his attention on the central concept of "meaning," which is considered as "a common medium for consciousness and communications," and on the subjective rights which are "at the borderline between the law and other functional systems."

In Chapter 12 Katayoun Baghai explores the right to privacy as another form of structural coupling. While privacy seems to remain outside the communication of legal systems, it reappears inside the legal system when law's communications, including what was excluded, uses "privacy" in autopoietic communication in order to demarcate society from individuals. Indeed, societal communication systems have constantly regulated forms of respect for individuals. Since the right to privacy reappears as an instrument of structural coupling, court opinions are analyzed as self-descriptions of the legal systems which, at least implicitly, operate the right to privacy according to specific criteria of inclusion.

In Chapter 13 Richard Nobles and David Schiff focus attention on the structural coupling between the system of law and the media which affects constitutional values. The media have assumed, particularly in criminal trials, the function of supplying cognitive elements to a normative background. Since society needs to communicate about abnormal matters, and to irritate itself with the extreme cases that can often be found in courts in order to discover what counts as normal, the media prevalently irritate the external communications of legal systems. In these cases, the story is about what went wrong, and the presupposition is that normality can be narrated, not as "true reality", but reducing complexities and mediating the "realities" that are being constructed and appear to represent society.

Starting from Luhmann's conception that constitutions are fundamental instruments of structural coupling between legal and political systems, in Chapter 14 Lasha Bregvadze analyzes the position of constitutions at the summit of the legal order and inserts their legitimization into a circular process. Constitutions, seen as a second level of observation, "constitute and are constituted" also outside the legal orders created by states. In particular, being at the same time objects and subjects of evolutionary processes, they are able to structure "internal components of social interactions." A wider application of this instrument of structural coupling extends the impact of law to cover a plurality of social systems and implies, in constitution-based normative orders, a sort of "demolition of classical narratives" and a postmodernist "deconstruction of social reality".

The contribution of Gunther Teubner, in Chapter 15, focuses on structural coupling to redefine legal pluralism in terms of "productive misreadings" of different social discourses which create new boundaries between subsystems and human beings. Communications are "positively distorted" in a multiplicity of processes which could be considered as instruments of structural coupling since their "inter-discoursivity" is created not only by the internal differentiation of legal subsystems (no longer univocally state-oriented) but also by the external connections of legal and nonlegal discourses. This new kind of legal pluralism "is characterized by specialized institutions that bind law to a multitude of functional subsystems and formal organizations," and reaches a coevolution based on the multiple membership of legal communications in different domains.

Summing up, the theses discussed in all these chapters suggest a reconsideration of the abstract hypotheses of the functionalism of distinctions and of the functionalism of links. In this context, the real fulfillment of the typical functions of legal systems is not dependent on the hierarchy of normative structures, but on several intersystemic overlappings, with normative and cognitive character, which can be concretely registered using the model of structural coupling. Social change depends not so much on the normal functioning of single social systems or on the hegemony of one system upon the others, but on a series of macro- and micro-structural interactions which produce new combinations of systemic rationalities. Starting from this presupposition, the present volume tries to offer an empirically oriented overview based on a series of examples of the intersystemic intertwinings required by the real functioning of legal systems. In particular, they signalize that instruments of structural coupling could also be applied to the analysis of psychic and cultural subsystems, which are normally left outside the borders of the official representation of legal systems.

PART I
Sociology of Law and the Intersystemic Openness of Legal Systems

Chapter 1
The Transplanetary Journey of a Legal Sociologist[1]

André-Jean Arnaud[2]

Speaking of a transplanetary journey of a legal sociologist could be a humorous—maybe eccentric—use of words, able to create several possible meanings. Indeed, transplanetary travel can be seen from various points of view.

As to the object of sociolegal research, this could suggest several planets through which the researcher has the possibility to travel: the gender planet, the human rights planet, the public policies planet, the governance planet, and so on. As to sociological theory, this could be the systemic planet or the communicational planet.

If we transfer to our field—sociolegal, or law and society, studies—the feeling which haunts the film *Planet of the Apes*, by Franklin J. Schaffner—we could imagine an interplanetary rocket leaving the Earth two decades ago. In this case what changes might a legal sociologist find on coming back to Earth?

I would like to draw the following thesis. We created the Oñati International Institute for Sociology of Law at the end of a world that no longer exists. This world was the planet of *denunciation*, where all the forces were involved in the effort to impose sociological approaches in the law faculties which were dominated by legal positivism. Legal sociologists denounced any law-making which did not take into account facts, reality, society. Meantime, radical changes had happened, the beginning of a globalized world. This would be the second visited planet: the planet of *re-modelization*—a 15-year re-modelization. In this "Runaway World," as Giddens calls it, we could ask if what is actually in question is not the deep epistemological base of legal sociology.

A third step would be constituted by discovering another planet where sociolegal studies would be aiming to produce experts in public policymaking. This would be a trip dedicated to thinking differently about the role of sociology of law for the future.

---

1   This chapter and the following reproduce the inaugural speeches held in Oñati in 2009 for the 20th Anniversary of the International Institute for the Sociology of Law (IISL).

2   My thanks to Prof. Roger Cotterrell who amicably agreed to revise and comment upon this chapter.

Denouncing

We can easily understand why the theoretical and methodological work of legal sociologists had their roots in the main European intellectual systems of reference: Max Weber together with Eugen Ehrlich and Theodor Geiger were the torches, respectively, of Italian and North European legal sociology; Emile Durkheim and Georges Gurvitch were the pillars of the French school of sociology; Marx and Marxist sociologists were dominant among legal sociologists of socialist countries, and the inspiration for a number of researchers in Western European countries. Beyond the respect and appreciation which we have for these great Fathers, we must recognize that sociolegal research has been oriented by their thought.[3]

Following in their paths, sociology of law aimed to supersede the traditional conception of law as restricted to codes or judicial decision-making. What were, at this time, the main subjects of sociolegal research? What methods were used to pursue fieldwork?[4] A complete picture would deserve a thorough project of research among the various Journals and books which were dedicated to legal sociology, sociology of law, law and society matters.

Among Renato Treves' work, we can find, above all, the creation of the journal *Sociologia del Diritto*. In the first issue, in 1974, Renato Treves underlined the importance of the dialectics between theory and practice in sociolegal research. The first dossier was dedicated to a debate on the nature of sociology of law.[5] The discussion involved many other authors.[6] For instance, who did not read with the greatest interest, in a 1983 issue of the *Journal of Law and Society*, a paper by Roger Cotterrell titled "The Sociological Concept of Law," followed, the next year, by his book *The Sociology of Law: An Introduction*?[7]

We must also quote the publication, successively in 1987 and 1989, of two major books by Boaventura de Sousa Santos: *Um discurso sobre as ciências* (A discourse on the sciences) and *Introdução a uma ciência pós-moderna* (An

---

3 Weber had a remarkable influence across the Atlantic. Parsons himself borrowed from various European sociologists, notably Weber, Pareto, and Durkheim. About Durkheim's reception by Anglo-American colleagues, see an important review essay by Roger Cotterrell, "The Durkheimian Tradition in the Sociology of Law," in the *Law and Society Review* 25/4 (1991), 923–45.

4 For an overview, cf. A.-J. Arnaud (ed.), *Dictionnaire encyclopédique de théorie et de sociologie du droit* (Paris: Librairie générale de droit et de jurisprudence, 1988).

5 The whole discussion was focused on what must be specifically a discipline dedicated to sociology of law. Among the protagonists, apart from Renato Treves, three major elders of our international community were invited to participate in this scientific exchange: Norberto Bobbio, Jean Carbonnier, and Adam Podgórecki.

6 Cf. my book *Où va la sociologie du droit?* (Where is sociology of law going?), published some years before the inauguration of this Institute.

7 See also the paper titled "I soggetti e la sociologia del diritto. Una nuova '*Methodenstreit*,'" published by Vincenzo Ferrari, two years later, in the *Italian International Review of Legal Philosophy*.

introduction to a post-modern science). We must remember that the author, 20 years before—more or less—was already doing fieldwork in the heart of the favelas in Rio de Janeiro, for his doctoral thesis. In the same year, 1989, the first year of our Institute, Hubert Rottleuthner was writing a paper on "The limits of Law: The Myth of a Regulatory Crisis," published in the *International Journal of the Sociology of Law*. In these pages, we read:

> Sociology of Law has returned to its evolutionist roots. Having established itself as an empirical discipline dealing with such concrete issues as judicial administration, access to law, legal needs and legal services, alternatives to law and knowledge and opinion about law, legal sociology has again become a field in which broad, comprehensive and evolutionary theories are heralded.

And he criticized both Gunther Teubner and Helmut Willke, who were developing Niklas Luhmann's thesis on regulatory crisis. This was such a basic question that Niklas Luhmann was invited to the IISL at the very beginning of our scientific activities. At the same time, the journal *Droit et Société* was publishing a special issue on Niklas Luhmann and German legal sociology.

The following year, 1990, in a collective book, scholars of the 35 national legal cultures represented in the Research Committee on the Sociology of Law had the opportunity to describe the specificity of sociolegal research and teaching in their country.[8] The result was a portrayal characterized by: (a) the impressive progress of sociolegal research, (b) the increasing role taken by legal sociologists in legal and judicial decision-making as well as in the control of the efficiency of norms, and (c) the connection between the progress of sociolegal research and the economic and political environment. Indeed, on the one hand, only wealthy countries are able to pay for such research; and on the other hand, there is a clear relationship between the development of such research and the progress of democracy.

In the same year, Felice J. Levine published her LSA Presidential Address in the first issue of the 1990 *Law and Society Review*—a long paper entitled "Goose Bumps and 'The Search for Signs of Intelligent Life' in Sociolegal Studies: After Twenty-five Years,"[9] In this paper, she suggested that sociolegal studies were best understood from a broad-based, multidisciplinary perspective "that includes, but does not privilege, legal scholarship."

In the light of the past, three areas of contemporary concern were mentioned: the centrality of law in social life and the expansion of its boundaries beyond state law—it is important "to understand Law with a little 'l' in everyday lives,"

---

8   V. Ferrari (ed.), *Developing Sociology of Law: A World-wide Documentary Inquiry* (Milan: Giuffrè, 1990).

9   The author—she was the President of the LSA between 1987 and 1989—was a specialist in research on attitudes to and perceptions of law and justice, the dynamics underlying compliance, and legal socialization.

she says—as well as the impact of policy, politics, and reform motives, and also the nature of science. According to her, these topics were presenting the greatest opportunities for growth and change in this specialized field.

As to the theoretical bases of the various methodologies, let me recall what Alberto Febbrajo was writing on this matter in 1990. He was pleading for "a stronger theoretical and conceptual base than the one originally adopted some twenty years ago."[10] But, generally, sociolegal researchers went on doing their work by applying sociological methodologies developed from Weber, Durkheim, and some others, to their own field. It is not surprising then that the main question, at that time, was precisely the following: Is it suitable to apply methods that have come from general sociology to the specific field of sociolegal studies?

With these examples, we do not pretend to be exhaustive. But, as Felice Levine observed, when talking about the mainstream studies undertaken by legal sociologists: "Everyone has his or her own list of favourite works in the field."[11] The too schematic cartography of sociolegal studies which I have drawn for the period in which the IISL was created, allows us to mention some main keywords which shape this first planet. The first keyword is *legal pluralism*, considered as the main consequence of the common determination among legal sociologists to reject the centrality of positive law as the only juridical way of regulation. As a consequence, a second keyword is *regulation*, a word restricted for a long time to

---

10 A. Febbrajo, "Sociology of Law or Sociologies of Law?" in V. Ferrari, op. cit., pp. 899ff. It would have been opportune to mention important earlier contributions as well, such as the fundamental paper by Philip Selznick on "The Sociology of Law," published in 1965 in *Sociology Today* edited by Robert K. Merton. Febbrajo wrote: "As for the basis in theory, it seems that we can search for [this] neither within the formalistic current nor within the natural law current, from which sociology of law has constantly kept its distance as an empirical science; nor, however, can we search for it within the behaviourist current"—here, we can think of Donald Black's position—"as it proves to be unsuitable as soon as we want to go beyond the confines of any one research project, to make links and draw conclusions that demystify ideologies. What we have left is the great current of functionalism which, as a theory and as a method, has enormous potential for linkage and demystification that has so far been exploited only in part." On the other hand, Per Stjernquist, in V. Ferrari, op. cit., pp. 915ff., pointed out that many researchers, applying critical perspectives, were evaluating legal and social development from ideological viewpoints. "My thesis," he wrote, "is that critical theories generally are based upon the author's subjective social evaluations. The theoretical analyses are, in such cases, not a generalization of practice but postulated ideals to be projected upon practice." And, he adds: "Let me extract some basic values from social macro-theories at present in vogue: *Classical Marxism* [...], The *Habermas* School [...], and *Teubner*: liberation of 'self-regulating and self-reproducing social organizations' from arbitrary governmental control."

11 She adds: "If a newcomer walks into my office, I usually say, 'If you want to learn something interesting [...] just take a look at my bookshelf.' And then, almost at random, I take down a sample of books." And she concludes: "Taken as a group, these studies [as examples] span the history of research in sociolegal studies, and, within any five-year period, I could easily have chosen many more, equally deserving examples."

the language of economists, which begins to enter other social sciences through the work of legal sociologists, who emphasize the existence of many types of regulation apart from the law, and the importance of studying them. Another keyword is *behavior*, since it becomes important, for sociolegal researchers, to recognize each person as a social actor, and every community as a place for socio-juridical regulation. Consequently, *culture* appears also as a main keyword. Last, but not least, in relation to the preceding keywords, another one is *decision-making*, because of the help which could be—or rather which ought to be—required from legal sociologists both before a legal or judicial decision is taken, and after, when the question is to control the real impact of these decisions.

This was the context in which we were living 20 years ago on this planet, a world which no longer exists. The Fathers of Sociology of Law created a discipline in a context where law was conceived and implemented far from complex situations, the treatment of which requires specific epistemological grounds which the common positivist epistemology was unable to offer. The "modern" legal rationality, as conceived from the seventeenth century, and with which we are still living, includes simplicity as a paradigm, which excludes the representation of the complexity of legal exchanges. What is defined as complex in this epoch is a set of phenomena which do not strictly pertain to Law, such as those Jean Carbonnier designated as "contre-droit" (a kind of soft law which opposes the Law), or the phenomena which exists "alongside the Law," or which constitute "presque droit" (what we could translate as "quasi-Law"). The same Jean Carbonnier said: "when I am teaching Law, I dress in my toga; when I teach sociology of law, I leave it aside."

Sociology of law has been developed specifically to break down this inability of the Law to deal with complexity. But the problem is that this first sociology of law was unable to analyze complexity thoroughly.

The Oñati Institute was conceived on this path. As from 1989, we gathered a group of scholars to build a thesaurus of sociolegal studies from which would be drawn the structure of the future library of the Institute.[12] We decided to register books and journals in seven sections, dedicated respectively to the following fields: General Perspectives on Law and Society, Production and Change of Legal Norms, Implementation of Law, Formal/Informal Conflict Resolution, Legal and Judicial Occupations, Public Policies and Rights.[13]

---

12   Terence Halliday, Boaventura de Sousa Santos, Valerio Pocar, Hans Harms, Vittorio Olgiati, Angelica Schade, and Wanda Capeller were present at the first meeting. Later on, several other colleagues joined the group. Among them, Phil Thomas, Steve Carr, Roger Geary, Bert van Roermund, Peter Alldridge, Vincenzo Ferrari, Rogelio Perez-Perdomo, and Fanny Tabak, that is to say colleagues belonging to a variety of legal cultures.

13   In particular, the structure of the library was so articulated: 1. *General Perspectives on Law and Society* 101. Sociology of Law; 102. Basic Concepts; 103. Theoretical approaches relevant for the Sociology of Law; 104. Disciplines related to Sociology of Law – 2. *Production and Change of Legal Norms* 201. State and Official

In the everyday work of the library, however, it appeared very quickly that a large proportion of the books had to be cataloged in the section "public policies," the only section able to encompass them because of their lack of a specific connection to another section. This was one more example—or proof—of the necessity to pass over into another phase of sociolegal studies.

Modeling[14]—Sociolegal Studies at the Turn of the Century: A Radical Change on a New Planet?

The special task of legal sociologists during this phase would be to attempt to restructure sociological approaches to Law by imagining a new sociology of law. This new world constitutes the second visited planet. After *denouncing*, *re-modeling*. Our legal sociologist landed on this second planet in the 1990s. He found there the problem of globalization.[15] This new preoccupation—even if the word "global" was not absent from earlier sociolegal concerns—testifies through its predominance to the new, strong impact of Anglo-American sociolegal studies on the restructuring or "remodeling" of the IISL. The change of Scientific

---

Lawmaking; 202. Emergence of Legal Norms – 3. *Implementation of Law* 301. Law Enforcement; 302. Effectiveness–Efficacy; 303. Crime and Social Deviance; 304. Social Control and Deviance – 4. *Formal/Informal Conflict Resolution* 401. Dispute Processing; 402. Dispute Institutions; 403. Auxiliary Institutions; 404. Access to Justice – 5. *Legal and Judicial Occupations* 500. General. History; 501. Legal Work; 502. Social Organization; 503. Education and Training; 504. Professional Regulation; 505. Politics and Ideology; 506. Occupational Economics – 6. *Public Policies* 601. Consumer-Producer Policy; 602. Crime Policy; 603. Economic Regulation; 604. Educational and Cultural Policy; 605. Environmental Policy; 606. Family Policy; 607. Health Policy; 608. International Relations Policy; 609. Labour Policy; 610. Population Policy; 611. Public Policies; 612. Science and Technology Policy; 613. Social Policy – 7. *Rights* 701. Debates on Rights; 702. Types of Rights; 703. Discrimination.

14 When speaking of "Modeling," we also refer to these theories of complexity which press on Herbert Simon's works. He has coined concepts such as "Modelization," to distance itself from the common language which would use "modeling." Several colleagues have shown the importance of modeling or schematizing an orderly chain of facts or phenomena, responding to some plan and ending in a definite result, a continuous suite of operations constituting the way to reach a result, like the process of decision-making.

15 In 1993 a Master Program of the IISL was entitled "Global Legal Interaction." Volkmar Gessner was the originator of this program in which he taught on "Cross-border Legal Interaction". There were other courses on specialized matters: "Globalism and the Localism Trend in Contemporary Law" (by Vincenzo Ferrari), "International Law: Theoretical Consequences of the Process of Globalization" (by Julio Faundez), "The Legal Profession in Global Legal Interaction" (by Vittorio Olgiati), "Cross-border Illegal Interaction" (by Wanda Capeller), and "Criminal Justice Reactions to Cross-border Illegal Interaction" (by Johannes Feest). In the following years, courses on *lex mercatoria*, Transnational Environmental Problems, and so on, were added.

Director[16] is a masterly way of introducing fresh visions through new networks. It has proved to be a success. During a period of 15 years, the Institute developed new themes and new approaches, corresponding to new preoccupations of legal sociologists throughout the world.

But, if we grant that *globalization* has become a keyword in sociolegal studies, can we speak of some "dominant streams" throughout the various legal cultures, and which ones?

Regarding the Topics

During this period, sociolegal studies developed a variety of topics such as Affirmative Action, Environmental Law, Gay and Lesbian Marriage, Globalization, Governance, Democratic Participation, Human Resource Management, Immigration, Economic Inequality, Internet Law, Nongovernmental Organizations, Neuroscience, Nuclear Power, Organ Transplants, Restorative and Transformative Justice, Risk, Risk Society, Securities Regulation, Terrorism, Technology (Legal Practices and New-), Transparency, Truth Commission, etc.[17]

But, whatever the topic, what is important to know in a globalized world is how to put together so many official and unofficial regulations, born not only in the framework of national or international Law, but also outside: above the Law, below the Law, alongside the Law, beyond the Law, even through the Law (as in the case of many transnational regulations).

In addition, many regulations are no longer perceived as implemented through Law. The development of public policies is a clear demonstration of this new situation. Sociology of law and sociolegal studies cannot continue to avoid dealing with these matters under the pretext that they do not strictly pertain to "law" or are not strictly "legal".

The same statement can be made about the use of the key concept of civil society. A vanguard of researchers in legal sociology had been working on what the basis of everyday life was in communities where official Law was not applied. However, the concept of civil society—implying the idea of participation and governance—was not considered as a basic concept for sociolegal research.

---

16   Initially, every year according to the statutes of the IISL, but now every two years.

17   Many of these topics have been integrated in the IISL Master's Programs and Workshops. Indeed, we find, alongside general matters, such as Comparative Legal Culture, Quantitative Methodology, Theory and Practice, and traditional themes (Gender, Mediation and Negotiation, Conflict, Dispute Resolution) some more specific ones: Transnational Criminal Justice, Globalization, Transitional Justice, Dissenting Opinions, Democracy, Territory and Sustainability.

Regarding the Approaches

On this second planet, one attaches less importance to any disciplinary opposition between general sociology and sociolegal studies than to working on a "field," such as defined, for instance, in 1994 by David M. Trubek, Yves Dezalay, Ruth Buchanan, and John R. Davis as: "the ensemble of institutions and practices through which law is produced, interpreted and incorporated into social decision-making."[18] To design a field is already to design a project.[19] Precisely, the word "project" refers to a specific epistemological standpoint. Positivist epistemology was focused on the "object," but if we use the idea of a project, we are reasoning in the framework of a constitutive epistemology.

Actually, legal epistemology was not the center of attention. In 1989 a paper on critical empiricism was published by David Trubek and John Esser in *Law & Social Inquiry*. In a comment on this paper, Boaventura de Sousa Santos pointed out, in the same issue, that "the critical sociology of law they are aiming at is perhaps more modern than postmodern."[20]

The critical legal movements born in the 1970s,[21] by taking for their target legal positivism without attacking the postulates of positivist epistemology, had no chance to escape the main stumbling block: the epistemological one. They should have begun by discarding some basic old oppositions: that of art and science, that of internal knowledge and external knowledge, that of the object and of the subject, that of observation and interpretation.

According to Reza Banakar and Max Travers, there still remained a few years ago a deep divide between law and society, despite half a century of efforts aiming to bring the two together.[22] From an epistemological point of view, this issue was

---

18 D. M. Trubek, Y. Dezalay, R. Buchanan, J. R. Davis, "Global Restructuring and the Law: Studies of the Internationalization of Legal Fields and the Creation of Transnational Areas," *Case Western Reserve Law Review* 44/2 (1994), 411. Previous definitions of "legal field" could be found, as from 1981, in A.-J. Arnaud, *Critique de la raison juridique*, vol. 1, *Où va la sociologie du droit?*, op. cit., p. 346 seq.; and P. Bourdieu, "La force du droit: Éléments pour une sociologie du champ juridique," in *Actes de la recherche en sciences sociales* 64 (1986), 3–19.

19 D. M. Trubek and J. Esser, "'Critical Empiricism' in American Legal Studies: Paradox, Program, or Pandora's Box?," *Law and Society Inquiry* 14/1 (1989), 1–52.

20 B. de S. Santos, "Room for Manoeuver: Paradox, Program, or Pandora's Box?" *Law & Social Inquiry* 4 (1989), 149–64. A reflection pursued and developed in *Toward a New Common Sense: Law, Science and Politics in the Paradigmatic Transition* (New York: Routledge, 1995).

21 A.-J. Arnaud, "Gouvernants sans frontières: Entre mondialisation et post-mondialisation," in *Critique de la raison juridique*, vol. 2, (Paris: LGDJ, 2003), 368.

22 R. Banakar and M. Travers (eds), *An Introduction to Law and Social Theory* (Oxford and Portland, OR: Hart, 2002).

presented at this time in a talk given at the University of Manitoba, Winnipeg,[23] as a problem related to the double nature, normative and social of legal epistemology.[24] The need was pointed out, in sociolegal studies, "to revisit the epistemological ambiguities which are at the basis of the distinction between 'legal science' and law considered as 'social science.'"[25] The idea would be to reach a legal epistemology which would make it possible to consider law as a socio-normative phenomenon. The aim would be to constitute legal epistemology as a science able to give an account of law as a set of socio-normative occurrences.[26]

As to the consequences of such a lack of epistemological thinking on law on this planet, I would like to point out one of the main results. For a long time, many legal sociologists—including myself—remained prisoners of the premises of the same epistemology which was underpinning the object of our criticisms.[27] To consider the practice of sociology of law as a scientific alternative in order to criticize positivist Law only succeeded in allowing the elaboration of a hybrid of legal science and positivist sociology. Such a collusion does not make it possible either to explain or to foresee crises in a fundamental and systematic way, or to find answers to them. This stage was a step toward an external knowledge of law, a step that I still consider useful and necessary at this time, but one that obscured the most important thing: the necessity of taking an initial position in favor of an epistemology able to reintroduce a teleological dimension in research and to replace the "object" with the "project."

Here lies the main keyword of this second planet: *complexity*.[28] As already mentioned, the approach which is specific to the positivist epistemology born from "modern" legal and political philosophy does not provide the means for understanding and managing a complex world full of crises arising from complex situations. Law is directly concerned because it is no longer possible to provide answers by applying top-down, simple, plain, unsophisticated norms to complex situations. It is necessary to appeal to theories of complexity, which lead to complex decision-making.

Now complex decision-making can be identified by some attributes. It exists only through a project, the project which this complex process will allow to

---

23   M. Saint-Hilaire, "Pour un développement de l'épistémologie juridique au Canada ... comme ailleurs," Forum juridique, University of Manitoba, Winnipeg, June 2, 2004: http://www.law.utoronto.ca/documents/zcalt04/SAINT-HILAIRE.doc.

24   The author refers to a debate between Michel Berthelot and Wanda Capeller, "Comment les sciences du social se pensent-elles?: À propos de *Épistémologie des sciences sociales*, J.-M. Berthelot (ed.), (Paris: PUF, 2001)," published in the *Journal Droit et Société* 53 (2003), 215–28.

25   Wanda Capeller, op. cit., 224–5.

26   Id., 225.

27   For instance, see the example mentioned in my book *Le Droit trahi par la sociologie: Une pratique de l'histoire*, (Paris: LGDJ, 1998), 77ff.

28   A.-J. Arnaud and V. Olgiati (eds), *On Complexity and Socio-legal Studies: Some European Examples* (Oñati: IISL, 1993).

complete. Here, many problems arise. Who is going to construct this project? Who will control the ability of this project to solve the initial problem? Will these tasks be left only to the usual state authorities? If there is no participation in decision-making (whatever form that participation might take), decision-making by state authorities will remain "top-down" in character and, inevitably, the complex decision-making process portrayed in the theory of complexity will be rejected.

Such a process can be summarized very briefly in three principles. First, the same actors cannot intervene at the stage of the construction of problems, of their formulation as plans for action, and of their implementation. Secondly, these three operations must be made with the aim of being "satisfactory" in relation to the project ("satisficing" according to the language used by Herbert A. Simon). Finally, interrelations must be maintained permanently between the different levels mentioned, which all contribute to give a permanently ongoing character to public action, allowing it to escape from the rigid "top-down" characteristics of decision-making that are so often criticized in sociolegal studies. This is "participation" in law decision-making.

In short, globalization necessarily leads to a management of complex phenomena; but management of complexity supposes new epistemological bases allowing a different understanding of sociolegal phenomena.

Moreover, such an approach and its implementation entail that this epistemological viewpoint, which is assumed as its basis, must be taken consciously into account. I am not sure that, on this second visited planet, there was a deep awareness of the epistemological break which had happened in comparison to how life was on the first planet. This is the reason why I want to set out what I believe I am seeing on the third visited planet ... but I wonder if it is not only a dream. After *denouncing* and *re-modeling: rethinking.*

Rethinking: A Future Planet for Sociolegal Research

And so, look at what appears now that our spaceman gets his first glimpse of the third planet.

Beyond the philosophical shift corresponding to the shift from modernity to postmodernity, beyond the learning about (and training in how to manage) pluralism and complexity, what is striking on this planet is the worldwide determination to deal with a true democratic participation in public life. The keyword would be *governance*, a process—or rather, a tool—which fits with the process of complex decision-making; a keyword, moreover, which infers the existence of a permanent dialectic between theory and practice. Here, we are at the very heart of sociology of law. No practice without theory, and no governance without practice. That is to say that training in sociolegal studies cannot avoid aiming at practice.

But also a keyword which implies rethinking a future for sociolegal research, since this practice is tied, *par essence*, essentially, to civil society. In this perspective, sociology of law appears as the specific training field for teaching and learning how to test and orient public policymaking in a satisfactory way.

At this point, it turns out that our spaceman feels at ease so he cannot refrain from intervening. For this reason, let me add a personal comment in the form of a possible contribution to the future development of sociolegal studies on this third planet. I would like to draw your attention to the importance which ought to be given to the introduction of a complementary scientific project: to introduce and develop in sociolegal studies what we could name "Policy Intelligence."

But perhaps you will ask: What is Policy Intelligence? What can Policy Intelligence be useful for? How does this Policy Intelligence work? In short, how to justify the introduction of such an innovation? These are some questions which I shall try to answer briefly.

First, what could "Policy Intelligence" be? Policy: everybody knows what it is. But "Intelligence"? *Intelligere* is: to understand, to discern (*inter*, between, and *legere*, to collect, to gather, to choose). In other words: to know how to collect information and know how to choose what is satisfactory in a given situation. "Policy Intelligence" could be defined as "the art of collecting information and knowing how to choose what is satisfactory in the elaboration and reorientation of policies," especially public policies.

Today it is very common to speak of "intelligence" in many specialized fields close to our own speciality which is sociolegal research, such as Economic Intelligence or Strategic Intelligence. The thesis which I would like to sketch is that policy intelligence corresponds specifically to what is expected by decision-makers—more especially public decision-makers—of researchers working in the sociolegal field.

Everyone knows what Economic Intelligence is. We can find for instance, on the Internet, an advertisement for an Economist Intelligence Unit, described as a company which provides "a constant flow of analysis and forecasts on more than 200 countries and six key industries," and is able to "help executives make informed business decisions through dependable intelligence delivered online, in print, in customized research as well as through conferences and peer interchange." Moreover, there is a long list of organizational sites related to Economic Intelligence, and a lot of books and papers dedicated to this matter.

This art—can we call it a discipline or science?—was developed to allow business groups and enterprises to respond to a crucial need: obtaining "good" information at "the" good moment to be able to make "the" good decision. It deals with the capacity of an organization to collect, to interpret and to apply crucial information to ensure the full success of a decision. In summary: to make it possible to reach more satisfactory decision-making solutions according to the initial project carried out by the organization which makes this decision.[29]

---

29 See, e.g., H. A. Simon, *Organizations* (New York: J. Wiley and Sons, 1958); "Theories of Decision-Making in Economics and Behavioral Science," *American Economic Review* 49/1 (1959), 253–83; *The Science of the Artificial* (Cambridge, MA: MIT

This is exactly what is expected from sociolegal researchers: that they present to decision-makers (public as well as private) scientific results obtained through research activities centered on collecting and interpreting information about what is expected from policies and how the implementation of policies is received. In order to realize this aim, why not make the principles of Economic Intelligence our principles too, and adapt them to the specificity of our work and field of research? This would be "Policy Intelligence."

Let me introduce, here, as an example, what is done by researchers belonging to the UNITWIN Network of my UNESCO chair "Human rights and violence: public policies and governance." We take into consideration the lack of effectiveness or efficiency in the implementation of one public policy. We analyze the reasons for such a failure. We contact the NGOs and the governmental organizations working on this topic. We do fieldwork with them. Finally, we try to elaborate a new policy. We propose this reorientation to the decision-maker.

So, like the researchers in Economic Intelligence, we are already engaged in gathering the set of human resources and the technological means used to contribute to the development of our field. Already, as has happened in the context of Economic Intelligence, we have gone beyond the stage of pure rationalization of the collection and accumulation of information. Already, as in the case of Economic Intelligence, we have taken into account alterations introduced by globalization; we have introduced the analysis of complexity into our methodology in relation to the production of the decision. Already, as with Economic Intelligence, we try to know what is done beyond our own familiar environment.

But even doing that work, we do not *consciously* use theoretical bases relevant to Policy Intelligence.[30] We must yet elaborate a real strategy concerning Policy Intelligence; we have to integrate our tools of research, awareness, monitoring, and management of knowledge, into processes that can make this information useful—that is to say, apply it in innovative ways. Economic and Strategic Intelligence suggests mastering information, protecting it, and using it in an "offensive" way. This is "innovation." It is worthwhile for Policy Intelligence to do the same.

This means not only that Policy Intelligence must be organized in a complete and integrated system of techniques and human competences. It also entails that all the partners in the project toward which our activity aims must be aware of the benefits for them, and be ready to accept it and commit themselves to this process of Policy Intelligence. Indeed, we have to convince the decision-makers, public as well as private, that they must be interested in this approach to Policy Intelligence, in the same way that the sharpest managers have understood that they have the

---

Press, 1969). Intelligence and complexity such as presented by this Nobel Prize–winner for Economics have been theoretically developed by the French economist Jean-Louis Le Moigne.

30 Cf., e.g., "Tracking Impact. Case Studies on the Research Policy Nexus," *International Social Science Journal* 179/3 (2004).

greatest interest in taking advantage of the contributions of those who are applying Economic or Strategic Intelligence approaches.

To foresee, to be able to anticipate and make a more satisfactory decision: We recall the famous expression "To know—To plan and foresee—To be able to," coined by Auguste Comte. It is true that times have changed, and complexity has made us change our approaches. But to foresee, to anticipate and to offer decision-makers elements for a satisfactory decision: This is doing *intelligent* work; this is working with *intelligence* about policymaking; this is implementing Policy Intelligence.

So, the future consists of sharing the specific resources and competences of each actor participating in the process of decision-making. This participation-through-sharing in common objectives allows not only for satisfaction to be attained as to the consequences of a decision, but also for knowledge, know-how, and methods to be continually tested. This cooperation is fundamental among actors who frequently still misunderstand each other. The implementation of coherent strategies of Policy Intelligence is absolutely necessary today. We no longer live in the time of the decision-maker who was supposed, like the boss described by Charlie Chaplin in *Modern Times*, to know all the information which would allow the best decision among all the possible decisions to be made. The process of *complex decision-making* has—or should have—definitely replaced the style of decision called *one best way*. We, legal sociologists, have to be the promoters of such Policy Intelligence. This is, at least, the dream-project on this third planet.

We have to insist, therefore, on the essential joint implication of internal and external competences (I translate: the requisite cooperation between scientific research based on and in participation with civil society on the one hand, and on the other hand, governmental and nongovernmental experimentation as well as decision-making power). The decision-maker needs specialists, experts, consultants, and cannot choose them only according to his wishes or inclinations; he is frequently unaware of work done by researchers to whom he is not sufficiently connected to take them into account.[31] These researchers are nevertheless among those who are the most capable of bringing the information to the attention of the decision-maker, including basic information from the grassroots sources and in cooperation with civil society, and to offer reorientations for public policies *freely*, without any personal interest.[32] They are best equipped to help the decision-maker

---

31 Here, it would be important to discuss the role taken by "think tanks," what they are, how they are appointed, how the terms of reference for their work are established, and how they function.

32 See, e.g., J. Butler, "Non-governmental Organisation Participation in the EU Law-making Process: The Example of Social Non-governmental Organisations at the Commission, Parliament and Council," *European Law Journal* 14/5 (2008), 558–82. The channels of participation mentioned by the author do not consider researchers' work; what is missing is precisely a global Policy Intelligence.

to ensure an effective balance between observation and interpretation in the light of methodologies scientifically tested and validated.

Some sociolegal researchers are already working in this spirit of Policy Intelligence, even though to date a general theory of Policy Intelligence has not been elaborated in this context.

When I really open my eyes, conscious that I have indeed landed on this third planet, and looking at the Oñati International Institute for the Sociology of Law, I should like to say, in contrast to Charlton Heston: "My God, that's great, they've done it!"

Chapter 2
The Growth of Legal Transnationalism[1]

Roger Cotterrell

Introductory Remarks

What is *legal transnationalism*? The term is taken here to cover two kinds of familiar phenomena. The first consists of emerging or newly expanded regulatory regimes with supranational scope or ambition: for example, international human rights, transnational regulation of the internet and of intellectual property, international criminal justice, international financial and trade law, international commercial arbitration and modern *lex mercatoria*, and WTO law. Increasingly, laws (and forms of regulation that some observers call law and some do not) reach across state boundaries – but often not in the manner of traditional international law linking states as subjects. Sometimes transnational law bypasses state authorities, or uses them as conduits for regulation created and interpreted primarily by agencies other than state authorities. Sometimes it is created 'unofficially' in professional practice or as collective self-regulation. Then, more 'official' law has to decide how to deal with it. Often transnational law is intended to affect individuals, organisations or groups directly. So 'transnational' refers to a reaching across nation-state borders. The second, no less important, aspect of legal transnationalism is the influence exerted directly on the regulatory policies and practices of nation states by economic, cultural and political pressures taking shape outside their borders, and to that extent beyond their control.

Legal transnationalism haunts sociology of law or sociolegal studies (the terms will be used interchangeably here) in a somewhat spectral way. It is something seen but not seen; real but not fully real as a presence; mysterious, hard to pin down and certainly hard to view clearly and as a whole. Much research is now being done on transnational regulatory processes, institutions and aspirations, but it is difficult to see how these research developments affect outlooks in sociology of law *in general*.[2] Like a ghost, transnationalism flits around sociolegal studies, revealing aspects of itself in research topics and findings, but rarely allowing a view of something larger that might be forming, or might need to form: perhaps a new general view of law, or a new conception of the sociolegal field to reflect the impact of transnationalism.

---

1 This is an adapted version of an article already published in *Journal of Law and Society* 36 (2009), 481–500.
2 For a valuable outline of relevant issues, see Gessner 1995.

This chapter does not focus on particular fields of transnational regulation. Its concern is with the cumulative effect of their development, and the social forces they represent, on the foundations on which modern sociology of law has been constructed. Do these foundations need excavating and relaying in the light of legal transnationalism? My argument is that they do. The theoretical implications of legal transnationalism unsettle the basis of 'law and society' research – indeed they challenge its most basic concepts. Specifically, the meaning of both 'law' and 'society' in the sociolegal field needs to be re-examined radically in the face of legal transnationalism. The result should be to transform the outlook of sociolegal studies in general.

Legal Pluralism as Conceptual Resource

Many lawyers now confront the complexities of transnational legal practice, and that involves negotiating a great diversity of regulatory regimes, influences and sources. Yet the legal theories that most lawyers presume (and most law students are taught) – if any need is felt for a broad view of the legal terrain – still convey images of distinct, unified legal systems, identifiable basic norms or rules of recognition, stable legal hierarchies and lines of legal authority, reliable tests of legal validity, and assumptions of general legal effectiveness. The dominant forms of legal philosophy that influence juristic theory have in the main not noticed the theoretical challenges of legal transnationalism,[3] although recent writing in international law and social theory has made important contributions.[4]

Western lawyers' typical modern view of law in general is not difficult to characterise. First, it makes *the state* and its agencies central (as creator, authoriser, interpreter, adjudicator and enforcer of law). Second, it sees law as *monistic*, not pluralistic, in form (with international law as an extension of the reach of nation-state legal authority through treaties and the recognition of shared customs). Third, it assumes law's *autonomy* in one or more of several senses: as a *normative order* distinct from others such as those of morality or custom; as an *object of study* distinct from the social as an object of study; or as a *science* distinct from empirical social science. Fourth, it almost always assumes settled *internal/external distinctions* that define the legal field, marking off the experience, reasoning or understanding of legal 'insiders' (usually lawyers) from outsiders. And fifth, it assumes that state law makes a practical difference; it has general *effects in society* of such significance that this law cannot safely be ignored in social practice.

Each of these views of law was challenged in profound ways by the pioneer theories of legal sociologists early in the twentieth century. And, significantly, the subversive beginnings of modern sociolegal critique – most influentially expressed

---

3   For a thoughtful recent attempt to transcend legal philosophy's typical views of the relations of law and state, see Melissaris 2009.

4   See the wide-ranging references and discussion in Nelken 2006.

in Eugen Ehrlich's work – occurred (just before the First World War) at perhaps the exact historical moment of greatest acceptance of the Westphalian nation-state system and its correlative view of state-centred legal systems (Ehrlich 2002). In the Westphalian conception, states were seen as 'more or less economically self-sufficient units' and 'as politically homogeneous ... without internal political differentiation' (Buchanan 2000: 701). But, from the beginning, sociology of law emphasised legal diversity; it questioned juristic ideas of legal unity and system, and of centralised legal authority. It developed a tradition of legal pluralist theory (see, e.g., Dalberg-Larson 2000) that treated as normal an unstable overlapping of different regulatory systems (including those of state law) in the same social arena, competing for or negotiating their authority in relation to each other, as well as their chances of regulatory effectiveness.

Social scientific legal pluralism is the main theoretical tradition that sociology of law possesses to conceptualise legal transnationalism. A legal pluralist outlook is needed to consider sociolegal phenomena that usually escape legal philosophers' gaze. These include:

1. culturally based conflicts of legal understandings and aspirations between population groups inside increasingly multicultural national political societies[5] (*intrastate legal pluralism*);
2. conflicting or inconsistent legal understandings within state agencies and between them in the same political society[6] (*state legal pluralism*);
3. a vast range of transnational legal understandings and aspirations at many regulatory 'levels' and taking account of many different kinds of regulatory forms (e.g. municipal or international, 'hard' or 'soft' law; external regulation or self-regulation) – what has been called 'global legal pluralism'[7] but might better be labelled *transnational legal pluralism* (Zumbansen 2009); and
4. intersections of authority between state legal systems that are inadequately captured in terms of juristic concepts of sovereignty and reflect differential power relations between states (*interstate legal pluralism*).

---

5   Within a huge literature see, e.g., Grillo et al. (eds), 2009; Rohe 2007; Shah 2005.

6   See Graver 1990; Dalberg-Larsen 2000: 103–14. For an interesting recent study of legal pluralism within a single state judiciary, see Tezcür 2009. What is to count as a *state* agency in some societies may be unclear, and with such an issue come further obscurities or conflicts as to where the loci of practical legal interpretation lie. See also Peterson and Zahle 1995.

7   See, e.g., Snyder 1999; Snyder 2002. The term is here used in Snyder's sense, embracing a wide range of regulation, the status of some of which as 'law' would be controversial or typically denied by juristic commentators. The term's meaning varies in the literature and is not always precise. See also Perez 2003; Berman 2007; Fischer-Lescano and Teubner 2004.

These intersections of authority may be expressed directly or indirectly in, for example, extradition practices, the practical extraterritorial effects of the laws of some nation states inside others, international taxation and foreign investment policies, and the transnational use of human rights rhetoric.[8]

Legal pluralist theory should not be seen (as it sometimes is) as part of a philosophical debate about the definition of law (what forms of regulation are to be recognised as law). It should be seen instead as supporting the radical claims that, as regards their practical authority, forms of social regulation form a *continuum*; that lines between the 'legal' and 'non-legal' depend on *perspective*; and that the legal character (however assessed) of regulation is often a matter of *degree* (Abbott et al. 2000) and (not necessarily resolvable) *debate*. Some sources of regulation may seem more 'official' than others, but what counts as official becomes a matter of controversy and varies with viewpoint, as sources of regulatory authority compete. A legal pluralist approach rejects typical legal positivist assumptions that the authority of regulation as legal can be determined from distinct and stable social sources. Instead, it signals that this authority is unsettled in many social fields, a *matter of conflict* to be resolved – perhaps only provisionally and temporarily for particular purposes in particular contexts – by negotiation, power or influence.

The emerging new pluralistic world of law, created by legal transnationalism, is one in which legal regimes with overlapping or unclear jurisdictions have indefinite relations with each other; and legal authority is relative and frequently disputed. The legal future is one of increasing displacement of traditional state-centred, positivist legal understandings (Cotterrell 2008a). And this future is not an aberration soon to be corrected, with normal juristic service resumed and stable lines of legal authority re-established.[9] Legal anthropologists have always assumed the normality of legal pluralism in non-Western contexts. But in Western contexts, too, it is becoming necessary to recognise that relative authority is to be determined in what Julia Black has called 'regulatory conversations' and by making accountability claims in diverse, intersecting 'legitimacy communities' (Black 2002; 2008). The authority of centralised state agencies, and traditional modes of interpreting and developing state law, will be a part of a very diverse spectrum of legal experience.

Law, State and Transnationalism

The test of legal sociology's success is not whether it influences legal practice. It is whether it can explain and interpret, in its own terms, the changing regulatory

---

8   For diverse illustrations of and arguments around such intersections of authority, see Fidler 1997; Holzmeyer 2009; Goldberger 2007; Levy and Sznaider 2006.

9   For strong claims about the permanent fragmentation of regulatory regimes, see Fischer-Lescano and Teubner 2004; and for critique, see Paulus 2004.

terrain. That involves not just producing illuminating empirical studies of particular legal phenomena but also plausibly characterising the broadest directions of sociolegal development. In a bewildering transnational regulatory landscape, legal sociology is called upon to provide intellectual leadership in a way that gives it huge responsibilities. Its destiny is to be not a marginal social scientific enterprise but one that is central to social inquiry: exploring the conditions for, and guiding the development of, regulation in a changing world. The most disturbing spectre haunting legal sociology is the possibility that, despite the great wealth of its empirical research, it will not adequately – or sufficiently quickly – renew itself theoretically in the face of legal transnationalism; and that certain orientations of the field, set early in its development and still colouring its dominant outlooks, will impede this renewal.

What orientations are these? They relate primarily to dominant views about the relation of *law and state*. The most frustrating part of the vast literature on globalisation and contemporary international relations may be the part that asks in entirely abstract terms whether the state is 'in retreat' (cf. Strange 1996) in the face of international and transnational pressures. Ultimately it is not helpful to speak generally about the 'demise' or 'collapse' of the nation state (Bauman 2002: 233) or about a 'shrinking' domain of state authority (Strange 1996: 82); nor to claim that 'the state is about over as an economic unit' (Kindleberger quoted in Kudrle 1999: 213) or, conversely, that this is 'more than ever a world of nation-states' (Wood 2003: 69), that the state is '*indispensable* and *irreplaceable*' for global business (Beck 2005: 158, emphasis in original) or that 'the market depends on modern sovereignty' (Buchanan and Pahuja 2004: 81). Such blanket claims are commonplace but states are very diverse in nature and their regulatory capacities and energies may vary dramatically depending on what regulatory functions are being considered. All this is a matter for empirical study.

However, some general hypotheses about states subject to transnational influences might be drawn from the literature, as long as these recognise differences between kinds of states and kinds of policies. Here are some suggestions:

i. States generally seek to *support key businesses* seen as essential to the national economy, often acting as a conduit for international capital and seeking to harness it to national goals; to that end they may deliberately create conditions that favour it.
ii. *Limited fiscal resources* may sometimes mean that key economic sectors are supported by the state as a priority at the expense of other legal and social services (e.g. criminal justice, welfare).
iii. Since 'big business' is increasingly international, its *total or partial relocation abroad* may be possible. Through threats to do this, its power to influence state policy and law may be enhanced.
iv. Some states have *more power than others* to aid their own key economic actors and can use this power (sometimes through political or legal pressures) against weaker states.

v. Much collective regulation operating among economic actors or social groups with strong transnational ties or allegiances is *not visible on the state's radar* and not enshrined or recognised in state law; it derives from many sources, including the actors or groups themselves.
vi. Insofar as states focus their law and policy on dealing with transnational pressures and opportunities at the expense of other areas of regulatory responsibility, *citizens may become disillusioned with the state's ability* to protect their interests, values, traditions and distinctive allegiances.
vii. The result can be a degree of *withdrawal of support from the state* by citizens and from law as a communal resource, and a more 'privatised' use of law, sometimes in claims against state agencies seen as 'alien' to their concerns. In such circumstances state agencies themselves can be demoralised as regards their public functions.
viii. States may seek to avoid such consequences by addressing *local 'cultural' demands* (relating, for example, to citizens' material interests, traditions, beliefs and values, or emotional allegiances), in the face of transnational pressures. But this kind of strategy risks a degree of isolation from transnational networks.

These possible scenarios are mentioned here schematically only to illustrate a more general idea: that to see the state as originating, interpreting and enforcing law, and as the sovereign political source of law's authority, is neither right nor wrong; legal transnationalism makes the state's relation to law complex, ambiguous and variable.[10] It disrupts ideas about law's intellectual unity and hierarchy of authority, confronting legal philosophy's models of legal system with an untidy, indeterminate legal pluralism. And it disrupts the idea that *a uniform relation to the state* adequately defines modern law's nature and functions in practical terms. Yet here it will be argued that that idea has informed much modern empirical legal sociology: its undermining poses challenges for sociology of law's self-understanding and identity as an intellectual field.

Legal Instrumentalism as Sociolegal Theory

In the mid-twentieth century, modern empirical sociolegal research began by treating law and state as inseparably linked, with law as the state's key regulatory instrument. This research gained its major funding, intellectual urgency and institutional legitimacy primarily from assumptions about the state's autonomous regulatory power, and from the idea that the symbiotic relationship of law and state was broadly settled. Zygmunt Bauman (2002: 3, 27) writes strikingly of sociology generally as having aimed to be the state's 'intelligence unit' and having

---

10 I have tried to show how this complexity is reflected (but also disguised) in certain powerful ideologies of law's functions. See Cotterrell 1995: ch. 12.

had a tendency to imagine society 'after the pattern of an administrative office'. It is certainly true that modern sociolegal studies began by assuming the state as the stable source and guarantee of law; thus making the nature of law in general unproblematic.

In the 1960s law and the social sciences competed in the United States in claiming expertise and funding to aid the state in addressing 'tumultuous issues of racial discrimination, poverty and crime' (Mather 2003: 275); a new empirical research field of 'law and society' was promoted for this purpose (Garth and Sterling 1998). In several European countries, at much the same time, sociology of law was institutionally supported to aid the evolution of the welfare state, or to inform the state about popular consciousness of legal matters and the contexts and consequences of state regulation (Ferrari ed. 1990; Treves and Glastra van Loon eds 1968). The result was that modern empirical sociology of law began with an at least implicit theory of law as primarily a technical instrument of the modern directive state; a view of law's functions that was so useful and entrenched that it could seem unnecessary to ask deeper questions about law's nature.

Certainly, sociolegal scholars were not restricted in their research by thinking of law in this way. They did not need to study law's effectiveness as an instrument of state policy; nor did they need to support its use as such an instrument. The focus could be, for example, on how the regulated (citizens, social groups, corporations and their advisers) could relate effectively to state-controlled regulation. Yet, overwhelmingly, *empirical sociology of law adopted a view of the state as sole author, enforcer and facilitator of law*, rather than a legal pluralist view raising deeper issues about law's nature, sources of authority, and regulatory power.

Yet, as noted above, early in the twentieth century, legal pluralist ideas had been a means of attacking the regulatory hubris of Westphalian states – demanding that law be thought of as something whose destiny might be separable from that of the state. Legal pluralist thought has continued to be an important strand in sociolegal theory but it has been overshadowed by monistic, state-focused views since the rapid development of empirical sociolegal research from the mid-twentieth century.

Such an orientation is not just linked to funding opportunities and aspirations towards practical usefulness. It also harmonises easily with vaguer ideas of 'legal instrumentalism'. Brian Tamanaha (2006: 1) sees an 'instrumental view of law – the idea that law is a means to an end' as one that is 'taken for granted in the United States, almost a part of the air we breathe'.[11] But this is far from being just

---

11   See also Summers 1982, describing a tradition of 'pragmatic instrumentalism' in American legal theory, which treats 'legal rules and other forms of law' as 'most essentially tools devised to serve practical ends' and focuses on 'the goals law may serve; law's implementive machinery; the kinds of means-ends relationships in the law; the variety of legal tasks that officials must fulfil to translate law into practice, the efficacy of law; and its limits' (p. 20). Sarat and Silbey 1988: 104–11, argue that the state-policy focus of sociolegal research reflects a selective view of American legal realist theory; a view that

an American phenomenon. Tamanaha claims that the American 'law and society' movement powerfully reflected and contributed to the spread of this instrumental view that treats law as a resource of power available to serve any interests that can harness it. Legal instrumentalism, in Tamanaha's view, ultimately threatens to displace from legal thought and practice all ideas of a 'common good' independent of special interests.

But the concept of legal instrumentalism is nebulous. What does it mean to say law is a means to an end? Is this just to say law is expected to be useful? If so, why would anyone want it not to be? Mid-twentieth-century empirical legal sociology, assuming a particular view of the state and its relation to law, gave the idea of legal instrumentalism a much sharper focus. Insofar as this research asked how to make law effective for chosen *governmental* aims or (harnessing its state-derived coercive power) to serve the aims of citizens, corporations or social groups, it could claim to show what *kind of instrument* law is and the conditions and effects of using it.

Much empirical sociolegal research up to the present has been influenced by this orientation, not necessarily in support of aims to which law is directed, but usually reacting to them, even (perhaps increasingly as social activism has been replaced by regulatory conservatism) declaring their futility or misguided nature – as 'hollow hopes' (Rosenberg 2008) or pernicious 'juridification' (Teubner 1987).[12] With such an agenda other kinds of questions are likely to be marginalised: for example, about ultimate values which law might serve; about law's relation to traditions (the past, the familiar, the secure) as opposed to projects (the future, the innovatory, the planned); or about law's relevance to emotional attachments and emotional rejections that are sometimes volatile, diffuse, seemingly irrational and hard to conceptualise.

Legal instrumentalism is surely the implicit legal theory of most empirical sociolegal research. Without it the vast research literature cannot be theoretically mapped in any coherent way. If there is a widely accepted theoretical 'other' of state-centred legal instrumentalism (i.e. a totally different way of thinking about law in general) in modern sociology of law, it has yet to be identified.[13] Hints of what it might be are found in studies of legal transnationalism, legal

---

firmly distinguishes technical policy implementation (through law) from the practice of politics.

12   See also, e.g., Galanter 2002, detailing popular 'too-much-law' critiques which developed in the United States from the 1970s, alongside the expanding institutionalisation of law and society research, and which eventually influenced legal and social science professionals.

13   Niklas Luhmann's autopoiesis theory would, for some scholars, be a worthy candidate. I see it primarily as indicating (controversially) how to do social analysis and what is to be expected from this enterprise. Certainly, it provides a radical alternative to traditional instrumentalist thinking in sociology of law. Yet ultimately, by its nature, autopoiesis theory refuses to explain theoretically how to *connect* law and the social, or to *locate* law's place in social networks of community (the enduring central projects of

pluralism, legal consciousness, or legal values, and of the 'private legal systems' of organisations and communities. But it might be said that in sociology of law as a whole *we do not know what law is*; that is, we do not have an accepted general theory of the nature of law considered apart from the state, though we know how something conventionally called law 'works' or does not 'work' in an immense range of settings.

How could law appear differently – not tied to the state? It would be much less definite than has often been assumed: a kind of regulatory spectrum, a normative network of 'interlegality' (Santos 2002: ch. 8), an inchoate 'global legal pluralism' in which state regulation plays a major part but in an overall pattern of regulatory relations that remains indeterminate. We need to make sense of this overall pattern in sociolegal theory – to map and conceptualise it to guide and integrate research – but without imagining that the pattern's shifting shape can be captured in any definitive way. Useful practical criteria of the legal will not simply lead back to the state or any other single source of authority or coercive power, yet will recognise that the legacy of the Westphalian state system still powerfully colours most legal experience. The 'law' side of 'law and society' is in flux.

Convergence Thinking and the Social

So too, however, is the 'society' side. The sense that sociolegal studies are somehow still trapped inside nation-state jurisdictions – separate political societies – has been addressed by scholars in various ways. Lynn Mather (2003) in a presidential address to the Law and Society Association in 2002 argued passionately that the LSA should adopt an increasingly international orientation. David Trubek, following her lead, advocated collaboration between organisations to build a 'global sociolegal network' (Trubek 2003: 302–3). As regards the research field itself, efforts have been made to lay foundations for a genuinely comparative sociology of law, deeply respectful of cultural differences but seeking to speak across them – breaking out of the research arena of distinct national societies.[14]

Links of sociology of law with comparative legal studies have been strengthened: comparative lawyers increasingly recognise that they cannot assume (as dominant functional perspectives often do) that a social or economic problem addressed by law in one society is likely to be much the same problem in others (see, e.g., Örücü and Nelken eds 2007). Studies of transnational regulation inevitably presume diverse regulated populations, some being those of national political societies, others not. The nature of the social that this regulation addresses is an issue. For example, the European Union has provided

---

legal sociology), though it gives sophisticated (if ultimately dogmatic) warnings (Luhmann 2004: ch. 10) as to how not to undertake such projects. See Cotterrell 2008b: ch. 9.

14   Nelken ed. 1997; Nelken and Feest eds 2002; and see the rich discussion of issues in Nelken 2006.

a superb laboratory for exploring not only aspects of transnational regulation but the sociological character of the 'Europe' that constitutes their social setting (e.g. Delanty 2003; Delanty and Rumford 2005). The social indicated by legal transnationalism no longer equates with political societies of nation states. It is better seen as numerous, diverse networks of social relations of community, some coterminous with the boundaries of national political societies, others stretching across those boundaries; some embracing only certain aspects of the life of national political societies – affecting certain groups within these; others remaining indefinite or fluctuating in reach, as with certain extraterritorial applications of law or extradition practices, the incidence or effectiveness of which may be affected by power relations between states. So, in the perspective of legal transnationalism, the social – the 'society' to which law relates – varies in character and can be, in some ways, unstable and indefinite.

Yet not everyone is convinced that a radical rethinking of the legal or the social is needed. A simple and familiar (but inadequate) response to the need for legal perspectives beyond the nation state is often merely to project existing understandings of 'law' and 'society' onto a larger canvas without changing them. An illustration of this is *convergence* thinking in both comparative legal studies and sociology of law. Much effort towards harmonisation of European private law is based on it. One important study notes a convergence of 'the municipal legal systems of states that are highly integrated into transnational practices' (Wiener 1999: 19). Some legal sociological writings glimpse an emerging uniform 'modern legal culture' (Friedman 1994), a legal *lingua franca*; even a 'global legal culture' (Friedman 2002). In the 1970s Harold Lasswell and Myres McDougal (1997: 143, 144) saw, expansively, a 'global community process' already in existence, a 'homogenization of all perspectives … in an industrial, science-based civilization' supporting a 'perception of global interdependence and community' and moving towards 'an increasingly shared vision' of human dignity for all mankind. The grandest convergence claim of all, Francis Fukuyama's announcement of the imminent 'end of history' with the triumph of liberal democracy, was made in the very year the International Institute for the Sociology of Law was founded (Fukuyama 1989).

Convergence talk sometimes expresses a hope for hard-won democratic transnational consensus, but it is often the (perhaps unconscious) projection of national interests or parochial perceptions on a global canvas. Lasswell (1977: 181, 184), treating a universal value of human dignity as capable of morally uniting the world, saw himself as 'in step with ideal values of the American tradition', as expressed in the US Declaration of Independence. In convergence theories there is always a danger of assuming that the way some societies see things must be the way others do or, inevitably, will do; that the way 'we' understand values (for example, the rule of law, freedom, democracy, dignity) is how 'they' do, too – the familiar language translator's problem of 'false friends', but here transposed into sociolegal thought.

In both comparative legal studies and sociology of law, convergence approaches presume that both 'law' and 'society' can be preserved as familiar unities; that what Mather (2003: 270) called 'a universal, one-size-fits-all approach' can operate. Following this approach, harmonised law can be seen as extending familiar forms of law to a larger jurisdiction, or to a set of jurisdictions that, to the extent that legal convergence has been achieved, can be treated as a unity. The idea of a 'modern legal culture' also designates a unity: a uniform 'modern' way of experiencing and relating to law. It suggests that there is still a single unified social (even if not restricted to a particular nation state) to which law relates. Describing this as a culture and assuming the uniformity of the culture allows the universality of the social (the idea of society as a bounded social totality) to be maintained for sociolegal thought.[15]

But 'culture' is actually a great diversity of networks of social relations based on contrasting types of bonds: those of convergent projects, shared beliefs or values, affective allegiances, and traditions.[16] These social bonds do not necessarily overlap to produce clear cultural boundaries or unities; neither do their legal supports. Once this is recognised, the idea that cultures identify distinct social totalities, or spatial blocks like those of territorially defined political societies, becomes problematic. Instead, the social has to be seen as made up of innumerable networks of social relations. Law and law-like regulation address these networks. Many of them remain confined in nation-state borders, but many do not.

Certainly, it often looks as though convergence is occurring. But what appears as convergence is the extension of *some* (often economic) networks of social relations (and their regulatory needs) across nation-state borders. But if some are extended in this way, others are not; they are more localised; and those that are extended are not necessarily extended in the same way, with the same reach. Social networks (unified by, for example, economic interests, common beliefs or values, emotional allegiances, or common history, language or traditions) are very diverse; their patterns, which transnational legal pluralism increasingly regulates, cannot be adequately characterised as simple convergences of national political societies.

What theoretical resources are available to make sense of the social environments which this pluralism assumes? Most useful may be the kinds of social theory that focus on relatively abstract but closely defined forms of social relations, or on social categories not territorially specified in any restrictive way. Georg Simmel's (1971) basic social forms (e.g. 'exchange', 'conflict', 'sociability', 'domination') and his general social types, such as 'the stranger' or 'the metropolis', are examples of the *kinds* of concepts that may be useful. Also

---

15   Thus, Gessner (1995: 90–91, 93) sees a 'developing global legal culture' and links this with the idea of 'world society' as a complex system, which is said to provide a 'global frame of reference' for sociology of law.

16   Cotterrell 2006: ch. 6. On the empirical complexity of 'culture' as a focus of comparative sociolegal research, see Nelken 2006.

conceptually suggestive are Georges Gurvitch's subtle analyses of 'sociality' (Gurvitch 1947; Bosserman 1968: chs 5 and 6). I have advocated elsewhere a way of examining the social (for the purposes of legal theory) as made up of a strictly limited number of contrasting (Weberian) pure types of social relations of community combined in innumerable networks of varying size and scope. This approach suggests a way to consider law's regulated populations as social networks not necessarily coextensive with or bounded by political societies. And it can treat law's practical jurisdictions as not necessarily limited by the borders of nation states.[17]

Interest Analysis and the Social

Worries about legal instrumentalism and about convergence thinking have been expressed with unusual passion by some writers and have attracted much attention. But, to take two striking examples, neither Brian Tamanaha (2006) on legal instrumentalism nor Pierre Legrand (2006; 1996) on convergence theory has been able to put forward alternatives in any precise or wholly persuasive way. What they have done, instead, is to register a deep sense that something is wrong – morally wrong – with law. Because of the uncertain focus it is easy to be dismissive; perhaps in each case the arguments somehow do not hit their mark – what is being attacked is not an easy target to define. But what is certainly important in these critiques is the sense of *moral outrage*, the idea that law has lost its way; that it may be too focused on technicality, on facilitating means without examining the worth of ultimate ends; too concerned with economic rather than wider cultural concerns, or with aiding private or sectarian interests rather than some larger general social good.

A less clamorous disquiet comes across in other, different writing. The legal philosopher Scott Veitch has argued that liberal law stifles a genuine liberalism that would seek to identify and respect incommensurable *ultimate values* and to address conflicts between them. Instead, law has reduced liberalism to 'rule-based individualism' and 'interest politics' (Veitch 1999: 7, 184, 204, 207). The implication is that Max Weber's view of modern law as the means of compromise of conflicting interests (Weber 1978: 874–5) is not enough: there is more for law to do, but it is not doing it. And, according to Tamanaha, legal instrumentalism has indeed largely reduced law to serving and managing individual and group interests.

Perhaps this kind of reduction is also the general tendency of convergence theory. The most prominent such theory in legal philosophy is Roscoe Pound's (1942) sociological jurisprudence which reduces most legal issues to a balancing

---

17   Cotterrell 2008b: ch. 2 outlines the approach. Applications of it are found in Cotterrell 2006, chs 6, 7 and 9, and Cotterrell 2008b, part 4. Cotterrell 2008a relates it specifically to legal transnationalism.

of interests. Pound's view of society is an image of vast diversity reduced, through law, to a systematic, well-coordinated unity, in which potentially conflicting interests can be made to coexist as harmoniously as possible in a single, comprehensive legal and social scheme. Presenting human experience in the form of interests – essentially as claims, demands or desires of individuals (Pound 1942: 68) even where these have very important social or public dimensions – creates a sense of uniform manageable packages of '*self-regarding wants*'[18] which law can sort and compare. Pound's theory is a reminder that almost any human concerns can be expressed as interests and so processed into functionally uniform units of legal concern. Such an approach might make convergence seem even inevitable – a matter of good technical management (social engineering) through law – if only the correct balancing formulae can be adequately refined, and the interests systematically formulated.[19]

I think that similar assumptions underpin many harmonisation efforts in comparative law. These efforts seem most successful in areas of law governing instrumental social relations of community – mainly contract and commercial law. Here what is to be achieved is what Pound called 'such an adjustment of relations and ordering of conduct as will make ... the means of satisfying human claims to *have things* and *do things*, go round as far as possible with the least friction and waste' (Pound 1942: 65, emphasis added). The process may seem efficient and obviously beneficial when law is invoked to help satisfy what can be easily understood as self-regarding wants; seemingly universal types of individual claims and projects. This is often the case where aims are linked to what is seen as economic benefit, growth or progress.

Harmonisation projects are less assured when legal issues broaden out to embrace Veitch's incommensurable values; when ultimate aims become matters of dispute or misunderstanding; or when what need to be taken into account are ambiguous, diffuse and complex desires, feelings, allegiances, insecurities and commitments, often related to collective goods. If these are definable as interests, their scope and weight may nevertheless be hard to measure, or translate into terms that allow precise legal balancing or comparison. In a world of transnational influences and pressures people seek general affirmation and recognition of their distinct fundamental values and beliefs (religious or secular). They see no reason

---

18   See Swanton 1980; Reeve and Ware 1983. Neal (1964: 75) treats interests as referring to 'desires for special advantage for the self or for the groups with which one is identified'. These can be contrasted with (ultimate) values indicating abstract or universal conceptions of the good, held to for their own sake. Cf. Weber 1978: 24–5.

19   There is certainly a close link between such an interest-focused approach and legal instrumentalism. If the latter sees law as merely an instrument of specific actors pursuing particular aims, the former sees law's task as being to satisfy those actors' aims as far as possible. But Pound insisted that general legal values, reflecting a larger 'common good' drawn from legal experience, should govern the balancing of interests, and he did not consistently affirm a purely instrumental view of law: Cotterrell 2003: ch. 6.

why law should not contribute to this; not necessarily expressing the beliefs and values directly in legal precepts but actively defending a place for them as part of culture. The diversity of ultimate values and beliefs matters; convergence thinking may seem to belittle this.

At the same time convergence thinking often does not address affective allegiances such as special emotional attachments to nation or community. People may want not only technically useful law but also law that they can see as 'truly theirs': law expressing what they see as the distinctive character of their nation or community – even if this is *felt* rather than understood, and cannot be equated with specific traditions, collective goals, beliefs or values. The element of emotion that sometimes informs law is too easily ignored. At the same time a need is often also felt for law to respond to tradition in a broad sense – that is, for it to focus not only on facilitating change and assisting chosen projects (what Santos calls 'rights to options') but also on protecting valued *local environments* ('rights to roots') (Santos 2002: 177) – natural and cultural. Hence demands are made for law to protect, for example, customary practices, languages, historical memories, landscapes and wilderness, established neighbourhoods, architectural treasures, and national traditions – what might be called the settled fabrics of everyday life.

While law serves networks of primarily economic instrumental relations, many of which now extend beyond the boundaries of nation states, there are also innumerable social networks linked by bonds of *tradition*, *affect*, and *beliefs or values*, in the senses indicated above. Multiculturalism confronts law with special challenges to take account of the diversity of these networks inside political societies, but the legal challenges of tradition, affect, beliefs and ultimate values should certainly not be seen as limited to the concerns of cultural minorities. The challenge for legal regulation is to recognise fully (and even-handedly) the different types of communal bonds that unite and differentiate people. Perhaps the distinctiveness of each of these types becomes more obvious insofar as they become *transnationally* focused; not integrated features of a political society but diverse in their range of reference within and beyond nation-state boundaries. The task is to recognise legally the richness of the social, rather than reduce it to regulatory 'packages' that are convenient for purposes of legal harmonisation and for instrumental state-centred views of law.

Conclusion: Theory in Flux

Is it possible to envisage new conceptions to replace the old views of law and society that underpinned sociology of law when its focus was securely on nation states and their relatively self-contained legal systems? It would defeat the purpose of the argument here to suggest that sociolegal theory should aim to produce some definitive concept of contemporary law or of the social regulated by law. Useful theory will recognise that *everything is in flux*; not imagine a new settled sociolegal world replacing the old Westphalian one.

Some scholars, with some justification, think there is too much sociolegal theory anyway but this chapter's argument is that theory is needed as long as it is of the right kind. Theory needs to accomplish a difficult trick. It must envisage the sociolegal field *as a whole*, so as to give the whole sociolegal research enterprise a sense of direction and a means of confronting the outdated general views of law and its social contexts that dominate legal philosophy. As regards widespread juristic assumptions about law, it needs to show, directly and forcefully, that, even on their own terms (for example, in emphasising law's systematic character and unity, and its stable hierarchies) they are seriously in error.

Yet theory needs somehow to envisage the entirety of the sociolegal field in ways that always stress legal and social *variation*. That is, the labels 'law' (which must be rethought now as a regulatory continuum) and 'society' (which must be re-envisaged as the social not limited to politically organised society) should be treated as indicating variable *clusters* of elements, not united intellectually or politically, yet forming identifiable patterns. So sociolegal theory, in the face of legal transnationalism, needs to emphasise and address sociolegal *change*, its *processes* and underlying *forces*; such theory will have to go beyond mapping a new sociolegal terrain.

This chapter has also tried to suggest some diffuse but highly influential orientations in social and legal thought that tend to impede this. They have been discussed here in terms of the three concepts of *legal instrumentalism*, *interest analysis* and *convergence thinking* – a kind of 'Bermuda triangle' of assumptions about law and society into which imaginative thought about the nature and scope of the legal and the social tends to disappear.

Clearly, much valuable theoretical literature is available to build on. If some of it does envisage broad convergence scenarios, it does so in ways that attempt to make explicit their conditions. For example, John Rawls' (1999) 'law of peoples' thesis postulates a liberal democratic convergence to be achieved through law, but with a tolerance of less liberal regimes that respect basic human rights principles. Yet Rawls' outlook has been criticised as a modified Westphalian view that does not recognise the extent of politically significant cultural divisions within states (Buchanan 2000). And it emphasises 'peace by satisfaction' as opposed to 'peace by power' (Rawls 1999: 46–8); perhaps an ideal rationalisation rather than a 'realist' observation of world conditions.

By contrast, Michael Hardt's and Antonio Negri's idea of 'Empire' is of a vast overarching network of global order, an unequal and fractured world of powerful, if decentred, transnational control, never free of conflict, even if they see also a transnational realm of resistance to this forming (Hardt and Negri 2000; 2005). Carl Schmitt's still-influential work on international law can stand here for a different, ultimately more conservative scenario rooted in familiar state forms – the extension of traditional national sovereign power to dominate an international arena, and the reality of ongoing (at best repressed) interstate conflict. Schmitt's emerging *nomos* of the earth envisages the control (by force or consent) of the world by an all-powerful hegemonic power centre or by several transnational power blocs confronting each other in uneasy balance (Schmitt 2003: 354–5).

Such expansive theories, and others offering comparably large vistas, provide vivid scenarios but they are not specifically theories of legal transnationalism because the diversity of regulation, as such, and of regulatory environments, is not usually the centre of attention in them. They usefully imply, however, two broadly contrasting visions of development: one in which *voluntas* (authority based in coercive power) dominates, through the creation of a monopoly or competing monopolies of transnational force; and another in which a transnational web of legal principle (*ratio*) gradually takes shape through a process of influence, reconciliation or compromise between regulatory regimes. If the second of these two visions of development may seem the more attractive, an interplay of both is surely inevitable (*voluntas* and *ratio* being inseparable aspects of law) and it may be suggested that neither will produce a settled system of transnational regulation for the foreseeable future.

Sociology of law also has much valuable, empirically-rich 'middle-range' theory addressing particular legal aspects and instruments of globalisation, and the transnational shaping of legal demands and aspirations. Building on these resources, new perspectives will develop.[20] It is important that they should not ignore the question of whether law, confronted by a vast range of technical demands, can find what Durkheim (1987: 150) called its moral 'soul'. What this can be taken to refer to here is its multi-facetted *moral meaningfulness* to its regulated populations; a responsiveness and sensitivity to the lived experience of these populations in their diverse social networks of community; a capacity to express their aspirations – whether focused on economic concerns, on shared beliefs or ultimate values, on emotional allegiances or resistances, or on the security of shared traditions and common environments. Moral meaningfulness demands regulation that can support *all* the diverse bases of community.

Spectres of transnationalism may be friendly ghosts. They may help to locate empirical legal sociology's inbuilt instrumentalism in a larger perspective; undermine its over-hasty assumptions about convergence, reinvigorate its legal pluralist traditions and extend its moral ambitions for law and its sense of law's social importance. They may help to dislodge the increasingly anachronistic modern urge to remake the world, rather than to learn to live respectfully within it. Sociology of law, from its very beginnings, aimed at being useful. However subversive it set out to be, it directed its subversion at building more socially satisfying regulatory structures, guided by empirical study of the circumstances of time and place. Because it still embodies this constructive subversion in its intellectual traditions, it remains vitally important as a research enterprise.

---

20 See, e.g., sources cited in Nelken 2006. Cutler 2003: ch. 3 provides a useful survey – primarily from an international law and international relations perspective – of theoretical resources to address law's role in the global political economy.

But the intellectual challenges posed by legal transnationalism serve the valuable function of undermining relationships that could become too comfortable for the sociolegal enterprise and neutralise its critical power; that is to say, too close connections with the policy imperatives of states, and with established juristic and legal professional outlooks. Legal transnationalism should set sociology of law free in the new, still largely uncharted areas beyond the familiar old landmarks of 'law' and 'society'. Legal sociology has to decide for itself how to envisage law today as a social phenomenon, and what law's full range of responsibilities to its regulated populations in a changing world can and should be. It has to take the lead in envisaging the legal structures and ambitions appropriate for the transnational future.

References

Abbott, K. W., R. O. Keohane, A. Moravcsik, A.-M. Slaughter and D. Snidal, 'The Concept of Legalization', *International Organization* 54 (2000), 401–19.

Bauman, Z., *Society under Siege* (Cambridge, MA: Polity, 2002).

Beck, U., *Power in the Global Age: A New Global Political Economy*, trans. K. Cross (Cambridge, MA: Polity, 2005).

Berman, P. S., 'Global Legal Pluralism', *Southern California Law Review* 80 (2007), 1155–237.

Black, J., 'Regulatory Conversations', *Journal of Law and Society* 29 (2002), 163–96.

____, 'Constructing and Contesting Legitimacy and Accountability in Polycentric Regulatory Regimes', *Regulation & Governance* 2 (2008), 137–64.

Bosserman, P., *Dialectical Sociology: An Analysis of the Sociology of Georges Gurvitch* (Boston: Porter Sargent, 1968).

Buchanan, A., 'Rawls's Law of Peoples: Rules for a Vanished Westphalian World', *Ethics* 110 (2000), 697–721.

Buchanan, R. and S. Pahuja, 'Legal Imperialism: Empire's Invisible Hand?', in P. A. Passavant and J. Dean (eds), *Empire's New Clothes: Reading Hardt and Negri* (London: Routledge, 2004), 73–93.

Cotterrell, R., *Law's Community: Legal Theory in Sociological Perspective* (Oxford: Clarendon Press, 1995).

____, *The Politics of Jurisprudence: A Critical Introduction to Legal Philosophy*, 2nd edn (Oxford: Oxford University Press, 2003).

____, *Law, Culture and Society: Legal Ideas in the Mirror of Social Theory* (Aldershot: Ashgate, 2006).

____, 'Transnational Communities and the Concept of Law', *Ratio Juris* 21 (2008a), 1–18.

____, *Living Law: Studies in Legal and Social Theory* (Farnham: Ashgate, 2008b).

Cutler, A. C., *Private Power and Global Authority: Transnational Merchant Law in the Global Political Economy* (New York: Cambridge University Press, 2003).

Dalberg-Larsen, J., *The Unity of Law: An Illusion? On Legal Pluralism in Theory and Practice* (Glienicke, Berlin: Galda + Wilch Verlag, 2000).

Delanty, G., 'Conceptions of Europe: A Review of Recent Trends', *European Journal of Social Theory* 6 (2003), 471–88.

Delanty, G. and C. Rumford, *Rethinking Europe: Social Theory and the Implications of Europeanization* (London: Routledge, 2005).

Durkheim, É., *La Science sociale et l'action*, 2nd edn (Paris: Presses universitaires de France, 1987).

Ehrlich, E., *Fundamental Principles of the Sociology of Law*, trans. W. L. Moll (New Brunswick, NJ: Transaction, 2002).

Ferrari, V. (ed.), *Developing Sociology of Law: A World-wide Documentary Enquiry* (Milan: Giuffrè, 1990).

Fidler, D. P., 'Libertad v. Liberalism: An Analysis of the Helms-Burton Act from within Liberal International Relations Theory', *Indiana Journal of Global Legal Studies* 4 (1997), 297–354.

Fischer-Lescano, A. and G. Teubner, 'Regime Collisions: The Vain Search for Legal Unity in the Fragmentation of Global Law', trans. M. Everson, *Michigan Journal of International Law* 25 (2004), 999–1073.

Friedman, L. M., 'Is there a Modern Legal Culture?', *Ratio Juris* 7 (1994), 117–31.

____, 'One World: Notes on the Emerging Legal Order', in M. Likosky (ed.), *Transnational Legal Processes: Globalisation and Power Disparities* (London: Butterworths, 2002), 23–40.

Fukuyama, F, 'The End of History?', *The National Interest* 16/Summer (1989), 3–18.

Galanter, M., 'The Turn Against Law: The Recoil Against Expanding Accountability', *Texas Law Review* 81 (2002), 285–304.

Garth, B. and J. Sterling, 'From Legal Realism to Law and Society: Reshaping Law for the Last Stages of the Social Activist State', *Law & Society Review* 32 (1998), 409–71.

Gessner, V., 'Global Approaches in the Sociology of Law: Problems and Challenges', *Journal of Law and Society* 22 (1995), 85–96.

Goldberger, R., 'It's Just Not Cricket: Is the Principle of Reciprocity being Honored in the U.S.–U.K. Extradition Treaty?', *Cardozo Law Review* 29 (2007), 819–52.

Graver, H. P., 'Administrative Decision-Making and the Concept of Law', in A. Görlitz and R. Voight (eds), *Postinterventionistisches Recht* (Pfaffenweiler: Centaurus Verlagsgesellschaft, 1990), 177–94.

Grillo, R., R. Ballard, A. Ferrari, A. Hoekema, M. Maussen and P. Shah (eds), *Legal Practice and Cultural Diversity* (Farnham: Ashgate, 2009).

Gurvitch, G., *Sociology of Law* (London: Routledge, 1947).

Hardt, M. and A. Negri, *Empire* (Cambridge, MA: Harvard University Press, 2000).

____, *Multitude: War and Democracy in the Age of Empire* (London: Hamish Hamilton, 2005).

Holzmeyer, C., 'Human Rights in an Era of Neoliberal Globalization: The Alien Tort Claims Act and Grassroots Mobilization in *Doe v. Unocal*', *Law & Society Review* 43 (2009), 271–304.

Kudrle R. T., 'Market Globalization and the Future Policies of the Industrial States', in A. Prakash and J. A. Hart (eds), *Globalization and Governance* (London: Routledge, 1999), 213–37.

Lassswell, H. D., 'The World Revolution of Our Time', in D. Marvick (ed.), *Harold D. Lasswell on Political Sociology* (Chicago: University of Chicago Press, 1977), 177–220.

Lasswell, H. D. and M. S. McDougal, *Jurisprudence for a Free Society: Studies in Law, Science and Policy*, student edn (The Hague: Kluwer / New Haven: New Haven Press, 1997).

Legrand, P., 'European Legal Systems are not Converging', *International and Comparative Law Quarterly* 45 (1996), 52–81.

____, 'Antivonbar', *Journal of Comparative Law* 1 (2006), 13–40.

Levy, A. and N. Sznaider, 'Sovereignty Transformed: A Sociology of Human Rights', *British Journal of Sociology* 57 (2006), 657–76.

Luhmann, N., *Law as a Social System*, trans. Klaus Ziegert (Oxford: Oxford University Press, 2004).

Mather, L., 'Reflections on the Reach of Law (and Society) Post 9/11: An American Superhero?' *Law & Society Review* 37 (2003), 263–81.

Melissaris, E., *Ubiquitous Law: Legal Theory and the Space for Legal Pluralism* (Farnham: Ashgate, 2009).

Neal, M. A., 'Methodology for the Examination of the Function of Values and Interests in the Process of Social Change', *Sociological Analysis* 25 (1964), 75–90.

Nelken, D., 'Signalling Conformity: Changing Norms in Japan and China', *Michigan Journal of International Law* 27 (2006), 933–72.

____ (ed.), *Comparing Legal Cultures* (Aldershot: Dartmouth, 1997).

Nelken, D. and J. Feest (eds), *Adapting Legal Cultures* (Oxford: Hart, 2002).

Örücü, E. and D. Nelken (eds), *Comparative Law: A Handbook* (Oxford: Hart, 2007).

Paulus, A. L., 'Commentary: The Legitimacy of International Law and the Role of the State', *Michigan Journal of International Law* 25 (2004), 1047–58.

Perez, O., 'Normative Creativity and Global Legal Pluralism: Reflections on the Democratic Critique of Transnational Law', *Indiana Journal of Global Legal Studies* 10 (2003), 25–64.

Petersen, H. and H. Zahle (eds), *Legal Polycentricity: Consequences of Pluralism in Law* (Aldershot: Dartmouth, 1995).

Pound, R., *Social Control through Law* (New Haven: Yale University Press, 1942).

Rawls, J., *The Law of Peoples* (Cambridge, MA: Harvard University Press, 1999).

Reeve, A. and A. Ware, 'Interests in Political Theory', *British Journal of Political Science* 13 (1983), 379–400.

Rohe, M., *Muslim Minorities and the Law in Europe: Chances and Challenges* (New Delhi: Global Media Publications, 2007).

Rosenberg, G. N., *The Hollow Hope: Can Courts Bring About Social Change?*, 2nd edn,(Chicago: University of Chicago Press, 2008).

Santos, B. de S., *Toward a New Legal Common Sense: Law, Globalization, and Emancipation* (London: Butterworth, 2002).

Sarat, A. and S. Silbey, 'The Pull of the Policy Audience', *Law and Policy* 10 (1988), 97–166.
Schmitt, C., *The Nomos of the Earth in the International Law of the Jus Publicum Europaeum*, trans. G. L. Ulmen (New York: Telos Press, 2003).
Shah, P., *Legal Pluralism in Conflict: Coping with Cultural Diversity in Law* (London: GlassHouse, 2005).
Simmel, G., *On Individuality and Social Forms: Selected Writings* (Chicago: University of Chicago Press, 1971).
Snyder, F. G., 'Governing Economic Globalization: Global Legal Pluralism and European Law', *European Law Journal* 5 (1999), 334–74.
___, 'Governing Globalisation', in M. Likosky (ed.), *Transnational Legal Processes: Globalisation and Power Disparities*, (London: Butterworths, 2002), 65–97.
Strange, S., *The Retreat of the State: The Diffusion of Power in the World Economy* (Cambridge: Cambridge University Press, 1996).
Summers, R. S., *Instrumentalism and American Legal Theory* (Ithaca: Cornell University Press, 1982).
Swanton, C., 'The Concept of Interests', *Political Theory* 8 (1980), 83–101.
Tamanaha, B. Z., *Law as a Means to an End: Threat to the Rule of Law* (New York: Cambridge University Press, 2006).
Teubner, G., 'Juridification: Concepts, Aspects, Limits, Solutions', in G. Teubner (ed.), *Juridification of Social Spheres: A Comparative Analysis in the Areas of Labor, Corporate, Antitrust and Social Welfare Law* (Berlin: Walter de Gruyter, 1987), 3–48.
Tezcür, G. M., 'Judicial Activism in Perilous Times: The Turkish Case', *Law & Society Review*, 43 (2009), 305–36.
Treves, R. and J. F. Glastra van Loon (eds), *Norms and Actions: National Reports on Sociology of Law* (The Hague: M. Nijhoff, 1968).
Trubek, D. M., 'Cracking the "Red, White and Blue" Ceiling: Toward a New International Role for the Law and Society Association', *Law & Society Review* 37 (2003), 295–303.
Veitch, S., *Moral Conflict and Legal Reasoning* (Oxford: Hart, 1999).
Weber, M., *Economy and Society: An Outline of Interpretive Sociology*, trans. E. Fischoff, et al. (Berkeley: University of California Press, 1978).
Wiener, J., *Globalization and the Harmonization of Law* (London: Pinter, 1999).
Wood, E. M., 'A Manifesto for Global Capitalism?', in G. Balakrishnan (ed.), *Debating Empire* (London: Verso, 2003), 61–82.
Zumbansen, P., '"New Governance" in European Corporate Law Regulation as Transnational Legal Pluralism', *European Law Journal* 15 (2009), 246–76.

Chapter 3
A Comment

Alberto Febbrajo

Introductory Remarks

The reflections of André-Jean Arnaud and Roger Cotterrell on contemporary sociolegal studies, in spite of their different perspectives, suggest two substantially complementary representations of the discipline which could be considered as two sides of the same coin. Arnaud, by focusing attention primarily on the functional impact of legal regulations, describes a sociology of law which is concentrated on the limits of the internal culture of legal decision-makers; Cotterrell, by focusing attention on the structural aspects of legal regulations, describes a sociology of law that is overwhelmingly challenged by the twilight of the centralized power of the state.

In particular, Arnaud presents the development of sociology of law in the last decades as a succession of different kinds of criticisms against the traditional normative vision of legal regulations. These criticisms have been respectively oriented at: a) "denouncing" the rigidity of a purely dogmatic legal culture which legal sociologists could temper through empirical data; b) "remodelling" the structure of legal decisions through a deeper social sensibility; 3) "rethinking" the current models of hierarchical governance through a realistic evaluation of the many interests which are emerging in various sectors of society.

Cotterrell, on the other hand, presents a sociology of law that, in the same period, was compelled to redefine the role of the state because of the tide of transnationalisms which seems to submerge national legal orders. According to the different social situations, contemporary sociolegal scholars have thus attempted: a) to use "an instrumental view of law" based on the presupposition that the state is the "sole author, enforcer and facilitator" of legal norms; b) to support an increasing integration and adjustment of values and practices at international level; and, finally, c) to analyze the interactions between legal and social regulation which are moving "beyond national boundaries."

In short, Arnaud and Cotterrell describe a sociology of law concentrated on the one hand on the pragmatic limits of the reproduction of legal regulations without sufficient empirical insights, and on the other on the structural crisis of the role of the state which is no longer seen as the overarching symbol of the unity of legal orders. These two representations, inspired by a prevalently pragmatic-oriented (Arnaud) and a prevalently state-oriented (Cotterrell) perspective, appear to be influenced by complementary notions of the tasks of the discipline. Indeed, Arnaud and Cotterrell respectively follow different but convergent strategies: to dismiss conceptual tools basically tailored for defending the normative horizon of traditional legal culture, and to assume a wider perspective not confined within the borders of single nation states. In so doing they ascertain, at least implicitly, how contemporary sociologists of law define the most important social factors of the fundamental problems of the genesis, harmonization, and implementation of law.

Table 3.1 Two models of contemporary sociology of law

Arnaud	Cotterrell	Sociolegal problem
(pragmatic-oriented strategies)	(state-oriented strategies)	
Denouncing	Legal instrumentalism	Genesis of legal rules
Remodelling	Legal adjustment	Social harmonization of legal orders
Rethinking	Legal transnationalism	Implementation of global law

The representations of Arnaud and Cotterrell raise a fundamental question: What kind of relations can establish sociolegal studies with a normative approach to the study of law? As a matter of fact, the relationships of sociology of law with the world of jurists reveal a cyclical alternation of moments of opposition and collaboration. As in literary works, where the protagonists of the stories, after appearing separated, are later drawn together, in the history of sociolegal studies the initial methodological opposition to normativism was often combined with various strategies of collaboration on the basis of a mixed use of normative and empirical instruments.

I will now attempt to demonstrate that the just-stressed characteristics of contemporary sociology of law are strictly connected, on the one side with elements that are already present in classic sociology of law and, on the other, with recent proposals developed by social systems theory. It is fair here to recognize that Cotterrell would not pursue his diagnosis of the problems of sociology of law into accepting a systems theory perspective. In his other writings he has developed a theoretical approach that firmly rejects Luhmann's systems theory of law and its associated concept of structural coupling.[1] Sharing some of his critiques, the social systems theory here presented will be not considered as a sort of sociological dogmatics. This will allow us to recognize not only its basic continuity with classic models of sociology of law, but also its ability

---

1 See, for example, R. Cotterrell, *Living Law: Studies in Legal and Social Theory* (Farnham, UK: Ashgate, 2008) ch 9 ("The Representation of Law's Autonomy in Autopoiesis Theory").

to be adapted to recent developments in sociolegal studies and in the internal perspectives of legal professionals.[2]

Classic Approaches to Sociolegal Studies

Sociology of law has always criticized a top-down vision of the legal structure, and has proposed instead a bottom-up approach based on the analysis of sociological factors of legal evolution. The cultural roots of this process were heterogeneous. In Germany, the sociological science of law, since its beginnings, was combined with diffused sociological sensibilities represented by the juridical movements of "sociological jurisprudence" and of the "jurisprudence of interests."

In this context, sociologically oriented jurists decidedly contributed to the newborn discipline by redefining the normative presuppositions of internal legal culture and by submitting state regulations to different kinds of empirical control.[3] The result was the emergence, within sociolegal studies, of different sociologically oriented "institutionalisms," developed as society-based alternatives to the normativistic architecture of legal orders. We could here distinguish three basic forms of sociological institutionalism (pluralistic, relativistic, and behavioristic), respectively inspired by the fundamnental problems of the genesis, harmonization, and implementation of law. A few examples will help to illustrate this point.

Eugen Ehrlich, whose first field of interest was Roman law, in his major sociolegal work outlines a historically and sociologically inspired theory of the "genesis" of law.[4] After having drastically reduced the importance of a centralistic state and thus abandoned the formal concept of "unity" of the legal order, he focuses on the key concept of "living law." This concept seems to be strictly connected with an evolutionary approach. Society is presented as the producer of spontaneous regulations within autonomous associations, which gradually select, through trial-and-error processes, the norms best equipped to survive

---

2   For a distinction of possible interpretations of social systems theory, cf. A. Febbrajo, "The Autopoietic Approach and Its Form," in G. Teubner and A. Febbrajo (eds), *State, Law and Economy as Autopoietic Systems* (Milan: Giuffrè, 1992), 19–33.

3   Not by chance in the legal culture prevalent at the end of the nineteenth century, the introduction of sociological methods was firstly claimed by the less dogmatic-oriented areas of the legal sciences. This explains the large contribution of jurists with a historical and comparative background to the classic sociology of law. For an overview on the origin of the discipline, see A. Febbrajo, *Sociologia del diritto* (Bologna: Il Mulino, 2009).

4   E. Ehrlich, *Fundamental Principles of the Sociology of Law* (New York: Russell & Russell, 1962). Cf. also A. Febbrajo, "Introduzione" to the Italian translation of the former work: E. Ehrlich, *I fondamenti della sociologia del diritto* (Milan: Giuffrè, 1976).

in the specific social contexts.⁵ It is here important to stress that the concept of living law, which is implicitly linked to the concept of *efficiency*, is relevant from a legal *and* from an economic point of view. In other words, living law is oriented to a legal protection of social interests in the different associations only if this is compatible with an economic balance of results and efforts. Living law is historically able to generate spontaneous legal orders that are more adapted to maintain acceptable levels of efficiency than a state law, which is often reduced to a sort of paper law. Therefore the concept of living law on the one hand corresponds to the organization of autonomous social associations which are far more important than state legislation for the everyday life of single actors; on the other it is considered as the result of the creative interpretations of legal professionals who are directly exposed to the influence of social factors. This means that local criteria of rationality are affecting not only social associations but also judges' criteria of decision, which appear in this context as a form of free *Juristenrecht*.

A second approach elaborated by classic sociologists of law is linked to the sociological concept of functional *adequacy*. In the work of Weber,⁶ the functions of legal institutions are based on forms of rationality typical for different cultural contexts. Adopting a wide comparative approach, which includes non-Western forms of civilization, Weber examines the problem of the social harmonization of legal regulations, paying particular attention to their cultural embeddedness. Legal regulations appear functional to different cultural perspectives, for instance to economic variables and to value-oriented forms of political legitimization. Even a formalistic methodology strictly oriented to the concept of "legality" can be thus considered a form of rationality which, in certain social situations, is functionally adequate to both, the specific interests of legal professionals, and the specific expectations of formal certainty diffused among social actors.⁷

In classic sociology of law the most radical revision of the normativistic approach *à la* Kelsen is proposed by legal realism in its Scandinavian and American versions. According to the manifesto of Scandinavian realism, exposed with extraordinary coherence by Theodor Geiger,⁸ this movement was radically

---

5   Here lies the main source of the "hidden" sociological theory of Ehrlich, which is often ignored or underestimated even in recent reconstructions. Cf. M. Hertogh (ed.), *Living Law: Reconsidering Eugen Ehrlich* (Oxford: Hart Publishing, 2009).

6   Cf. M. Weber, *Max Weber on Law in Economy and Society*, ed. M. Rheinstein (Cambridge, MA: Cambridge University Press, 1966).

7   Cf. A. Febbrajo, "Kapitalismus, moderner Staat und rational-formales Recht," in M. Rehbinder, K.-P. Tieck (eds), *Max Weber als Rechtssoziologe* (Berlin: Duncker & Humblot, 1987), 55–78.

8   See T. Geiger, *Vorstudien zu einer Soziologie des Rechts* (Neuwied: Luchterhand, 1964); A partial Engl. trans. in Geiger, *On Social Order and Mass Society* (Chicago: University of Chicago Press, 1969). Geiger includes in his definition of the concept of effectiveness the empirical regularities of the behaviors of social actors and of the institutionalized sanctions against deviant behaviors.

directed at substituting the "formal" monism of a normativistic reconstruction of the legal order, exclusively based on the "validity" of state-produced norms, with an "empirical" monism, exclusively based on the *effectiveness* of factual regularities of human behaviors. Against the a-critical tendency to accept as real what a legal norm dictates (only a valid norm is a norm), legal realism tried to verify, through statistical situation/behavior connections, the level of the effective correspondence of norms to real behaviors (only an effective norm is a norm). Developing this approach, Geiger adopts a fact-oriented strategy for controlling legal regulations. This implies that the empirical distinction between effectiveness and ineffectiveness of single norms becomes a gradual one.[9] Given the almost unavoidable presence of deviant behaviors in spite of the diffusion of reciprocal processes of "mimesis" which assure general stability and uniformity, sociologists of law must thus face the empirical question: what degree of implementation of single legal norms is statistically recognizable in given social situations?

The sociolegal approaches outlined here suggest different types of empirical observation of legal norms, respectively oriented towards: the control of efficiency, based on the resources required by their genesis within autonomous social associations in terms of balance of costs and utility (Ehrlich); the control of adequacy, based on the mutual compatibility of legal and non legal cultures in terms of the harmonization required by typical models of rationality (Weber); the control of effectiveness, based on the correspondence between norm and behavior of social actors in terms of the level of statistical implementation of legal regulation (Geiger).

These classic contributions have the merit of explicitly including in the realm of sociolegal studies important themes, such as the social costs of legal interventions, which could reveal the inefficiency of state law, the cultural variability of human criteria of rationality, which could signalize the inadequate legitimization of legal institutions, and the role of deviant behaviors, which could underline the reasons of large areas of ineffectiveness of legal norms.

From the list of the models of sociology of law proposed by classic authors and recently developed by Arnaud and Cotterrell emerges an important element of continuity: both classic and contemporary sociology of law clearly reject a hierarchical vision of the legal order and attempt to substitute the traditional pillars of the normative conception of legal order with empirically based forms of legal control.

---

9   The inevitable graduality of the effectiveness of legal norms is opposed to the yes/no alternative typical for the normative concept of validity. From a sociolegal perspective, the target of a complete, 100-per-cent effectiveness is not only impossible to reach, but could generate negative consequences. An example is the so-called "white strike," i.e. a strike which, by introducing rigorous application of all relevant legal norms, produces the equivalent of a normal strike, namely the complete paralysis of a certain activity.

Table 3.2 Classic approaches to sociology of law

	Source of regulation	Main point of reference	Model of institutionalism	Type of control	Formal aspect of legal order	Sociolegal problem
historic (Ehrlich)	custom	autonomous associations	pluralistic	efficiency	unity	genesis
functional (Weber)	rationality	cultural orientations	relativistic	adequacy	legality	harmonization
realistic (Geiger)	mimesis	statistic regularities	behavioristic	effectiveness	validity	implementation

Obviously, unlike classic sociology of law, contemporary sociology of law has to face culturally and socially different situations. They are characterized, as suggested by Arnaud and Cotterrell, by a stronger perception of a differentiated impact of new social tensions on legal regulations and by the reduced role of the state in the construction of legal orders. Consequently the emerging questions are concerned: no longer with the absence of an official recognition of historically consolidated pluralisms, as proposed by Ehrlich, but with the increasing presence, at a relational level, of an imported pluralism devoid of local roots; no longer with the coexistence of convergent forms of institutional legitimization, as analyzed by Weber, but with the diffusion at a substantial level of an increasing legal fragmentation; no longer with the overwhelming importance of consistent regulations of social behaviors, as described by Geiger, but with the emergence, at a spatial level, of heterogeneous supranational regulations connected with the eclipse of the state and accompanied by the emergence of uncontrollable forms of globalization.

Table 3.3 Problems of classic and contemporary sociology of law

Dimension	Classic perspectives	Contemporary perspectives
Relational	Internal pluralism	Imported multiculturalism
Substantial	Institutional legitimization	Legal fragmentation
Spatial	Consistent regulation	Uncontrollable globalization

These parallels underline that the concept of law has now to be based, more explicitly than in the past, on a combination of moments of cognitive openness and of normative closure toward the social environment. But how is it possible to integrate the various sociological criticisms developed by classic and contemporary sociology of law into a comprehensive theoretical framework?

A Complex Model of Legal Regulation

The explanatory ambitions of social systems theory suggest a new semantics to sociolegal studies, which substitutes, in the role of sentinels of law, the formal concepts of unity, legality, and validity of the legal order with the more complex concept of autopoiesis. Literally interpreted autopoiesis indicates that legal systems reproduce themselves from within. This seems to correspond to the way of thinking of traditional legal culture, which declares that only a valid norm can produce a valid norm. Nevertheless, autopoiesis does not limit itself to reproposing with different terminology the well-known process of self-production of norms within legal systems. It also implies that the self-production of norms is not necessarily regulated by a state placed at the top of a pyramid, but simply by a chain of self-reflexive decisions which are mutually learning and correcting themselves. In this way the empirical controls of efficiency, adequacy, and effectiveness, elaborated by classic sociology of law, could be absorbed by the autopoietic process and translated into its different moments: "selection" of spontaneous efficient regulations; "variation" of inadequate and not sufficiently legitimized legal orders; "stabilization" of statistical regularities of behavior.

Being explicitly characterized by the use of reflexive mechanisms of "regulation of regulation" and by multiple processes of "self-observation",[10] the highly sophisticated autopoietic approach gives rise to a self-correcting feedback between legal inputs and social outputs. Law is thus considered by Luhmann an "immunization system" of society which reduces the probability of new "infections" seen as the unfavorable consequences of legal interventions.[11] Consequently, autopoiesis is regarded as an attempt to free legal language from old conceptual antinomies [12] and to overcome them through a circular "observation of observation" of the same process.[13]

A complex framework able to provide such a mutual reinforcement within legal systems is the scheme of the hypercycle as it was developed by Teubner.[14] The main elements of the autopoietic process are in different ways connected with the traditional components of the legal system (judiciary, administration, legislation, doctrine). The development of the legal system is thus presented as the result of a combination of normative and cognitive strategies of control because these various levels of self-observation enrich the strategies of institutional regulation and strengthen their possibilities to react to external irritations.

Using the previously adopted terminology we can say that the judiciary is primarily directed towards a control of *effectiveness* in order to stabilize normative structures on the basis of communications interpreted recurring to the dual code legal/illegal; the administration is primarily directed towards a control of *efficiency* in order to selectively apply the contents of normative structures; the legislation is primarily directed towards a control of *adequacy*

---

10   Luhmann distinguishes between self-observation and self-description. Self-observation is merely the recursive coordination of individual operations with structures and operations of the system. Self-description is the presentation of the whole system by a single part of the described system. Cf. Luhmann, *Law as a Social System* (Oxford: Oxford University Press, 2004), 424.

11   Cf. Luhmann, *Law as a Social System* (Oxford: Oxford University Press, 2004), 171.

12   An essential list of these antinomies in W. Friedman, *Legal Theory* (London: Steven & Sons, 1967).

13   A. Febbrajo, "From Hierarchical to Circular Models in the Sociology of Law: Some Introductory Remarks," in *European Yearbook in the Sociology of Law* (Milan: Giuffrè, 1988), 3–21.

14   G. Teubner, *Law as an Autopoietic System* (London: Blackwell, 1997).

in order to change legal norms which need to be innovated according to criteria of coevolution. In addition, the doctrine is directed to a sort of meta-control of *coherence* which covers the entire legal system in order to confirm its own identity absorbing possible incongruities.

A systemic definition of the traditional concept of "justice" provides another way to combine the different empirical controls elaborated by sociology of law. Indeed, a sociological analysis of this concept has to take into consideration that legal decisions produced on the basis of a sense of justice typical for legal professionals or institutions (internal legal cultures), and as such oriented to the homogeneity of the decisional criteria, could generate outcomes empirically unacceptable for the social actors oriented to external legal cultures.[15] We may thus speak, instead of a control of justice, of a control of injustice. According to this kind of control, every decision appears "unjust" which, even if formally acceptable for legal decision-makers, negatively affects the normal functioning of other systems from the point of view of the social actors involved. In a functional perspective, the control of injustice is thus directed not only against the limits of a formal control, but also towards the definition of a flexible continuum of intersystemic (in)compatibilities.[16]

The crisis of credibility of the unity of the legal system and the increasing awareness of the limits of the formal concepts of validity and legality, justify the passage of sociolegal studies from a hierarchical to an empirical and circular model of law. Among legal professionals, as suggested by Arnaud and Cotterrell, a diffuse loss of confidence in the ability of the legal system to control itself through the state, was accompanied by an increasing sensibility for the factual consequences of legal decisions.[17]

But in what terms and under what conditions is a revision of the "normative" nature of law really sustainable? To what extent can a normative system correct

---

15 D. Nelken and J. Feest (eds), *Adapting Legal Cultures* (Oxford: Hart Publishing, 2001).

16 A few examples: From a legal perspective, not to pay taxes is generally perceived as incompatible with a concept of justice. However, the total payment of the prescribed amount of taxes could be perceived, from the point of view of the economy of the single family, as unjust if not balanced by an adequate amount of public services. Abortions could be accepted as compatible with the functioning of the public health perspective but not from the point of view of a family system, and social assistants could assure in these cases a sort of structural coupling in order to combine both points of view at an interdiscursive level. Cf. A. Febbrajo, "Per una ridefinizione sistemica del concetto di giustizia," in *Giusto, vero, ragionevole* (Naples: ScriptaWeb, 2011), 49–68.

17 On the dilemma of whether internal legal culture should follow logical presupposition or empirical consequences, see N. Luhmann, *Rechtssystem und Rechtsdogmatik* (Stuttgart: Kohlhammer, 1974). In this context it is possible to point out the general relevance of the problem also from the perspective of the educational process. It also requires from a teacher a combination of normative and cognitive strategies in order to prevent possible rebellions of the "educated" persons.

norms on a cognitive basis without losing its own specificity? A contemporary answer to these questions appears insufficiently defined by a "strict" autopoietic approach. The translation of the formal legislature/ judiciary dichotomy, on which the traditional legal culture was constructed, into empirically oriented and more flexible typologies (teleological/conditional, cognitive/normative), provides a grey zone which contemporary sociologists and theorists of law cannot ignore. In order to exploit this area, they must seek to substitute dual alternatives and rigid deductive methods with a continuum of possible solutions. Not by chance in many Western legal systems legal professionals appear influenced by a widely diffused "common law mentality" characterized by dialogical, instead of hierarchical, relationships between courts. Normative structures are admitting constant changes and self-corrections under the influence of external, although not necessarily higher, authorities. This emerging legal network, based on the horizontal exchanges of communication at a transnational level, is independent from centralized authorities, and seeks, as a collective actor, to produce a new kind of "living law" which legitimizes supranational forms of "material" constitutions especially in the area concerning fundamental rights.[18]

In this context law is represented both as the cognitive observer and the normative performer of its own regulations. A similar duality is relevant not exclusively for sociological, in particular sociolegal, studies. The intriguing and somewhat paradoxical process of self-observation is at the center of many literary representations. In one of Pirandello's novels, a man, walking along a street, stares by chance at his image reflected on a mirror. At first glance, the image seems to be that of someone else, but when he realizes that it is really his own, he feels that it is impossible for him to look at his image any longer and continue to live. The image seems to obey his orders, to move or to be immobile at his command; yet it is not alive in the strict sense of the word.[19] Individual systems, according to Pirandello's argument, cannot live and observe themselves at the same time, but their self-observations must interrupt their spontaneous vital reactions. For a legal system this means that a process of assiduous self-observation can suspend its ability to influence other autopoietic systems, and significantly reduce its regulative power. The autopoietic circuit runs the risk of no longer being virtuous, and law can

---

18 N. Luhmann, *Grundrechte als Institution: Ein Beitrag zur politischen Soziologie* (Berlin: Duncker & Humblot, 1965).

19 "When I stood before a mirror, a kind of arrest took place inside me; all spontaneity vanished, my every movement seemed artificial, an imitation. I couldn't watch myself live." L. Pirandello, *One, No One and One Hundred Thousand* (New York: Marsilio, 1992), 13. Following an analogous scheme, Sartre observes that a social actor could feel himself restrained in his freedom when he is observed and treated by others merely as an object of observation. Cf. J.-P. Sartre, *Being and Nothingness* (New York: Citadel Press, 2001).

lose, with consequent identity crises, its traditional functions producing increasing social risks instead of greater certainty.[20]

From the point of view of the social systems theory, a possible answer to these problems is internal differentiation. While parts of the system are deciding, others may observe the decision makers, and others may observe, normatively or cognitively, the observers. This articulated perspective is a possible solution but raises further problems. It admits, for example during a trial, different perceptions of time for actors and for observers. In addition, the institutionalization of different mechanisms of action or of self-reflexive control requires the introduction of instruments of intersystemic connections which could be concretely incompatible with the functioning of some systems, or of parts of them.

In short, if an increasing differentiation of the borders of single systems can reconstruct the various intersystemic channels of communication which theoretically assure their coevolution, only an "un-reified" and empirically adjusted autopoietic approach can avoid both an excess of formalism, based on the illusionary assumptions that the normative models of society are real, and an excess of confidence in a cognitive approach, which could overemphasize the adaptability of legal orders to social regulations.

Conclusions

A new concept of law is thus emerging in sociolegal studies. It seems to reach a higher level of structural complexity and a more articulated combination of normative and cognitive moments of self-observation and self-correction extending in this way the possible interaction of the legal system with its own environment. In this cultural situation both sociologists of law and jurists have to take into consideration that, independently of the iron "ego" of law represented by legal dogmatics, legal systems could be more conciliatory, extroverted and cognitively "human." In other words, legal orders seem destined to become less normative—that is, able to alternate cognitive and normative strategies. Law has to "think"[21]—that is, to interpret its own environment moving from a learning perspective. Law has thus to become increasingly intelligent assuming a wider spectrum of reactions toward other social systems because of the weakness of the formal concepts of validity and legality, and of the absence of a powerful state.

---

20   A. Febbrajo, "The Failure of Regulatory Institutions: A Conceptual Framework", in P.F. Kjaer, G. Teubner, and A. Febbrajo (eds), *The Financial Crisis in Constitutional Perspective: The Dark Side of Functional Differentiation* (Oxford and Portland, OR: Hart, 2011), 269–302.

21   G. Teubner, "How the Law Thinks," *Law and Society Review* 23 (1989), 727–57; *Global Law without a State* (Dartmouth: Ashgate, 1997).

This new image of law seems to share elements already underlined by Arnaud and Cotterrell and by other contemporary legal sociologists: the *flexible droit* (Carbonnier), the responsive law (Nonet and Selznick), the law as instrument of social engineering (Podgorecki). For this reason, contemporary sociology of law, still inspired by the traditional criticisms against a normativistic approach, and no longer restricted within the borders of the nation state, tries, especially after the definitive *adieu* to the traditional concept of sovereignty and the emergence of social systems theory, to insert the concept of law into a broader intersystemic framework.

The further definition of this concept of law requires more cognitive flexibility and a new kind of collaboration between legal and sociological cultures. Indeed, in order to assure the possibility to combine, in a legal system, normatively selected empirical openness and empirically selected normative closure, a constant communication between internal and external communication is essential. This complex process of "communication of communications" leads to a model of law which presents both a wider ability to interact, with an extended societal horizon, and a greater awareness of its limits, in the global intersystemic connections of a society of societies.[22] But an increasingly cognitive law could also become "less law".

This could explain the growing importance acquired by the intersystemic instrument of communication called "structural coupling." Such an instrument, representing a conceptual bridge between law and other social systems, could succeed in analyzing, in direct contact with other systems, the various levels of closure and openness that a legal system explicitly or implicitly establishes with its environment. Furthermore, instruments of structural coupling allow us to criticize the typical self-representation of the legal system based on rigid dual codes and conditional programs, and to analyze external compatibilities and intersystemic sources of regulative conflicts.

In this context a new kind of legal pluralism emerges. It was depicted by classic sociologists of law as a defense against a too powerful state, and now becomes inspired by the recognition of a decline of the traditional role of the state, and by the limits of a monolithic vision of law. This new legal pluralism maintains unexploited possibilities to fruitfully interpret the present functions of the legal system[23] since the opportunities to clarify the still-cloudy connections between legal and social communications through instruments of structural coupling are far from being exhausted.

---

22   N. Luhmann, *Die Gesellschaft der Gesellschaft* (Frankfurt am Main: Suhrkamp, 1997).

23   These functions, after the crisis of regulative models, can be defined restrictively, that is in a residual way (to decide what is otherwise undecidable), or in a self-referential way (to create conflicts that would not have occurred, in the absence of legal decisions). Cf. R. Nobles, D. Schiff, "Introduction", in Luhmann, *Law as a Social System* (London: Routledge & Kegan Paul, 1985), 8.

References

Cotterrell, R., *Living Law: Studies in Legal and Social Theory* (Farnham, UK: Ashgate, 2008).
Ehrlich, E., *Fundamental Principles of the Sociology of Law* (New York: Russell & Russell, 1962).
Febbrajo, A., "Kapitalismus, moderner Staat und rational-formales Recht," in M. Rehbinder, and K.-P. Tieck (eds), *Max Weber als Rechtssoziologe* (Berlin: Duncker & Humblot, 1987), 55–78.
____, "From Hierarchical to Circular Models in the Sociology of Law: Some Introductory Remarks," in *European Yearbook in the Sociology of Law* (Milan: Giuffrè, 1988), 3–21.
____, "The Autopoietic Approach and Its Form," in G. Teubner and A. Febbrajo (eds), *State, Law and Economy as Autopoietic Systems* (Milan: Giuffrè, 1992), 19–33.
____, *Sociologia del diritto* (Bologna: Il Mulino, 2009).
____, "Per una ridefinizione sistemica del concetto di giustizia," in *Giusto, vero, ragionevole* (Naples: ScriptaWeb, 2011), 49–68.
____, "The Failure of Regulatory Institutions: A Conceptual Framework." in P. F. Kjaer, G. Teubner, and A. Febbrajo (eds), *The Financial Crisis in Constitutional Perspective: The Dark Side of Functional Differentiation* (Oxford and Portland, OR: Hart, 2011), 269–302.
Febbrajo, A., and W. Sadurski (eds), *Central and Eastern Europe after Transition: Towards a New Socio-legal Semantics* (Farnham: Ashgate, 2010).
Friedman, W., *Legal Theory* (London: Steven & Sons, 1967).
Gehlen, A., *Man: His Nature and Place in the World* (New York: Columbia University Press, 1988).
Geiger, T., *Vorstudien zu einer Soziologie des Rechts* (Neuwied: Luchterhand,1964).
____, *On Social Order and Mass Society* (Chicago: University of Chicago Press, 1969).
Habermas, J., *Between Facts and Norms* (Cambridge. MA: The MIT Press, 1996).
Hertogh, M. (ed.), *Living Law: Reconsidering Eugen Ehrlich* (Oxford: Hart, 2009).
Leoni, B., *Freedom and the Law* (Princeton, NJ: Van Nostrand Co., 1961).
Luhmann, N., *Grundrechte als Institution: Ein Beitrag zur politischen Soziologie* (Berlin: Duncker & Humblot, 1965).
____, "Normen in soziologischer Perspektive," *Soziale Welt* 20 (1969), 28–48.
____, *Rechtssystem und Rechtsdogmatik* (Stuttgart: Kohlhammer, 1974).
____, *Legitimation durch Verfahren* (Frankfurt am Main: Suhrkamp, 1983).
____, *A Sociological Theory of Law* (London: Routledge & Kegan Paul, 1985).
____, *Die Politik der Gesellschaft* (Frankfurt am Main: Suhrkamp, 2002).
____, *Law as a Social System* (Oxford: Oxford University Press, 2004).
____, *Die Gesellschaft der Gesellschaft* (Frankfurt am Main: Suhrkamp, 1997).

Nelken, D. and J. Feest (eds), *Adapting Legal Cultures* (Oxford: Hart Publishing, 2001).

Nobles, R. and Schiff, D., "Introduction," in Luhmann, *Law as a Social System* (London: Routledge & *Kegan Paul, 1985).*

Pirandello, L., One, No One and One Hundred Thousand (New York: Marsilio, 1992).

Romano, S., L'ordinamento giuridico (Florence: Sansoni, 1977).

Sacco, R., "Legal Formants: A Dynamic Approach to Comparative Law," *The American Journal of Comparative Law* (1991), 1–34, 343–402.

Sartre, J.-P., *Being and Nothingness* (New York: Citadel Press, 2001).

Teubner, G., *Law as an Autopoietic System* (London: Blackwell, 1993).

____, "How the Law Thinks," *Law and Society Review* 23 (1989), 727–57.

____, "Self-subversive Justice: Contingency or Transcendence Formula of Law?" *Modern Law Review* 72 (2009), 1–23.

____, *Global Law without a State* (Dartmouth: Ashgate, 1997).

Weber, M., *Max Weber on Law in Economy and Society*, ed. M. Rheinstein (Cambridge, MA: Cambridge University Press, 1966).

PART II
Social Communication and Legal Regulation

Chapter 4
The Big, Large and Huge Case of State-building: Studying Structural Coupling at the Macro Level

Gorm Harste

Introduction

After the linguistic turn in social philosophy and social analysis, it has been common to elaborate all kinds of skills in semantic and discourse analyses. Society is observed as a form of communication and with Niklas Luhmann it is even seen as a system of communication. Whatever one might think of that linguistic or communicative turn, the observation of communication undoubtedly points towards a decisive character of social phenomena and what happens among people no matter what.

The aim of this chapter is not to describe once more how to establish such a communication theory. Even for sociologists in small research communities, it is now common to put a major emphasis on, for example, Niklas Luhmann's theory of social communication systems in order to describe developments in communication theory or even in social, political or legal theory (Harste 2009a, 2009b; Hagen 2005).

A rather important problem attached to this communicative turn is that it is difficult or even impossible to aggregate small semantic descriptions into macro-phenomena. We might work with distinctions and forms of utterances, phrases, sentences or gestures, with monuments, texts and contexts. But even if we can gather whole series of texts and archives of, for instance, organisational self-descriptions, we are still far from an analysis of, say, the evolution of law, economics and politics from the high medieval era to the French Revolution. How could we describe and test claims such as Samuel Huntington's 'Clash between Civilizations', or claims about the differences between Eastern and Western European states, when we have an infinite number of phrases from which we can draw an infinite number of distinctions?

My thesis is that systems analysis creates possibilities to solve such problems. Luhmann distinguishes between a linguistic turn and a communicative turn in legal theory. Communicative interpretation of sense and non-sense cannot be reduced to textual interpretation (Luhmann 1993: 340–42). Systems are observed as second-order observations that in the course of history might emerge at such a level of differentiation that systems can describe themselves. If our aim is to consider large macro-processes, we should look for second-order descriptions. When are they established, which form do they have, where are they established, what differentiates them from other kinds of second-order descriptions, whom do they involve and how are they stabilised? Furthermore, it is possible to clarify the exact form using systems analysis. In the following overview, the aim will be to clarify that to work with systems analysis is to work with the grounding of theory. Although Luhmann's systems theory is a 'Grand Theory', it is also a *grounded theory* that is transformed when used.

This chapter will begin by mentioning some methodological devices to be used for investigations of state-building before it discusses in the first section (I), the case of state-building as a composed organisation of differentiated functional systems (II–V). Finally, the chapter will draw a few conclusions about the validity of such research (VI).

I. A Methodology of Communication: Linking Micro and Macro

In the 'Danish School' of systems analysis, Niels Aakerstrøm Andersen has established a whole range of analyses that have demonstrated their usefulness in a great number of empirical investigations at middle- and small-range levels (Andersen 1999, English trans.). They are also useful in order to describe macro-phenomena. The range includes the analyses of semantics, distinctions, forms, codes, functions, system/environment, differentiation, and structural couplings. This chapter will add evolution analysis and temporal analysis.

Let me go directly to the point. In order to describe macro-phenomena, the form of second order is interesting. Here my macro-case is to study such wide, large, huge and big phenomena as European state-building without losing the empirical touch of archives and particular semantic developments that occur in particular situations among certain persons. We might bear Norbert Elias's wonderful analysis in *Über den Prozeß der Zivilisation* (1976 [1939]) in mind when considering a functional analysis touching upon evolutionary processes and establishing links among configurations and chains (*Verflechtungsketten*) between micro and macro levels. But Elias's analysis did not aim at describing semantics, although his empirical material to a large degree consisted of old books about manners. My point is that the form of coding links the small-level range of semantics and distinctions *and* the macro level of system/environment or structural coupling. Semantic transformations take place everywhere – coding, too – but not all codes happen to stabilise themselves and emerge as such established codes as, for instance, those which rule between the legal and the illegal, or between war and peace. Luhmann calls these forms, which happen to be the 'directing differences' (*Leitdifferenzen*), second coding (*Zweitcodierung*). When established codes emerge, they code themselves on a second-order level – that is, they duplicate their form into themselves and immunise themselves against external contingencies. Law treats law and treats unlawful behaviour in the form of a legal communication between the legal and the illegal, a form that law itself treats as a lawful code (Berman 1983; Luhmann 1975: 34ff., 1972, 1981b, 1989, 1993a; King and Thornhill 2003: 57, 107–113).

In order to find the right archives among the kilometres of historical records, it is decisive to keep our observations simple. Codes are everywhere. But sometimes they codify themselves, and we could look for codes about codes. Whenever codes begin to re-enter into themselves, something might happen, especially if these forms of re-entry succeed in establishing themselves and monopolising a specialised function differentiated from other functions, which in turn have to specialise their form in order not to enter into the otherwise monopolised first form.

Now, at this still quite methodological and theoretical level, it might be useful to take a somewhat remote stance towards both theoretical insights and empirical debates. When we use systems theory, or whatever other theory we might use, we most often enter into a more or less already well-described field of studies with schools, authors, key works, teaching books, reviews, conferences, organisations and practices. In this research field, a great number of historians and a somewhat smaller number of historical sociologists earn their living and have contributed numerous insights.

Let me just mention one, Charles Tilly, who has tried to solve the macro puzzle in his booklet *Big Structures, Large Processes, Huge Comparisons* (1984). His point is that grand theories of historical evolution are not the same as broad and weak conceptions about, for instance, unbalanced differentiation and integration, social order and disorder, society and individuals. Since his analysis is nonetheless from a somewhat 'pre-communicative turn' era, he focuses on how it is possible to 'include work on a small scale' and to locate 'times, places, and people within those two processes' 'of the development of capitalism and the formation of powerful, connected national states' (Tilly 1984: 15). This problem still remains one of processes and structures. As an agency–structure problem, it is seemingly not far from methodologies offered by Bourdieu and Foucault. Likewise, Luhmann replaces agency by semantics while structural differentiation still seems to have emerged at the macro level. However, structural differentiation is conceived in terms of codified forms of differentiation between communication systems. Furthermore, semantics and communication is not simply distinguishable as a distinction between the particular and the general. As in linguistic utterances, communicative operations are always both. The problem is to localise and select operations linking small-scale studies with the grand narrative.

Historians also work with texts – that is, with communication analysis. Conceptual history distinguishes between two or three schools which are the historians' answer to the communicative turn in social theory. Reinhart Koselleck's enormous project of conceptual history developed parallel to Luhmann's in Bielefeld, but it had already begun with Otto Brunner and the historical aftermath to Max Weber's early conceptual analysis (Weber 1904/1980:

207–9; Mitteis 1940/1972; Kantorowicz 1957; Brunner, Conze and Koselleck 1975–1991). Other historians work in research fields such as history of state institutions, military history, legal or financial history, and so on. Thus we can easily see that analysis of state-building is an overwhelming task. The material, the discussions, archives and data might become far too complex if we cannot identify the selections we are looking for. Whatever macro field research touches upon, such an overwhelming task might become disappointing or frightening and seem hopeless.

In historical sociology, this overload does not seem so scary, either when it comes to systems theory or when historical research is touched upon. Nor is it a problem in specialised fields of study, such as, for instance, military history. The point is that historical sociology, historical research and military history also look for such decisive turning points in history when new forms of codes are established. But in most cases, historians do not have a comprehensive theory about what they are looking for. To some extent, theories might be used in legal history or economic history, and sometimes, more rudimentarily, in organisational history or military history. In all these cases, we can observe important and still-growing debates about not only classical phenomena such as political or industrial revolutions, but also, for example, Tocqueville's 'administrative revolution' and any number of other revolutions: legal, organisational, financial, disciplinary, military, educational and scientific. When we look into these debates using systems theory, we can observe how historical and evolutionary research is most often centred around what I will call the irreversible 'take-off' in a certain form of second-order codification, whether administrative, financial, military, legal and so forth.[1] My thesis is that systems theory can establish such selection processes of research and make it much easier to find the take-offs in (r)evolutions. Talcott Parsons analysed some of these so-called revolutions, but he did so without the clear codes of emerging communication systems.

Furthermore, it should be added that because of the second-order observation of whatever is to be observed, a system theoretical reconstruction of state-building does not fall into the quite common trap of reductionism. A great deal of, especially, Anglo-Saxon historical sociology reduces state-building to the interlinked rationalisation of military development and the development of its finances, though sometimes with an eye on the political legitimacy of those processes (Kennedy 1988, Tilly 1992, Downing 1992, Ertman 1997). But other functional and organisational systems develop and rationalise as well, and we can already observe theoretical observations among these lines in the self-descriptions of, for instance, Jean Bodin (1576), Charles Montesquieu (1748) and Frederick the Great (1752), not to speak of the systems theory in Henri d'Holbach's *Système social* (1773).

---

1   The pragmatic term 'take-off' simply indicates the reflexivity of a distinction after] before. This reflexivity establishes a reflexion process (cf. Luhmann 1984: 601, ch. 11).

Günther Teubner has tried to describe a kind of evolutionary range in three steps from reflection through self-organisation to autopoiesis (Teubner 1987, 1989: 25–80). His concerns are about the so-called emergent properties, namely emergent properties of self-description, self-observation and self-reference, or what legal theory has called 'secondary rules' after the famous study by H.L.A. Hart. The take-off in such processes occurs whenever a mechanism of affiliation ('Anschlussmechanismus') is established from weak and loose operations to a stronger affiliation with a secured selection. In these studies, Teubner aims to avoid too many diffuse concepts of self-X (where -X might be replaced by -description, -observation, -constitution, -organisation, -reflection, -creation, etc.). Those concepts could describe different evolutionary stages using the scheme variation, selection and stabilisation.

When looking back in history, it is not difficult to observe how evolution of self-referential social systems was established. Furthermore, evolution grounded on historical descriptions of state-building can be refined from three into six stages (Harste 1998: 191–201): first, the reflection level, which concerns the establishment of a *basic self-reference* in variations; second, *reflexive self-reference* as the co-emergence of variations coded in similar binary forms; third, *self-organisation* (when the codes select themselves in a form of re-entry, as when an organisation organises itself); fourth, when *autopoiesis* is established because self-organisation creates the elements it uses in the operation of itself as whenever states transform agriculture and city population in order to get higher taxes; fifth, whenever *self-observation* in social communication is discernible as part of the autopoietic self-reproduction, and sixth and last, when *self-descriptions* are used as explicit parts of such autopoietic self-reproduction.

Now, such a process is of course *improbable* just as it is improbable that it will follow an irreversible not to say linear evolution (Spruyt 1994, Richet 1973, Harste 2012). The successful history of states is in fact quite improbable; empires, city networks, weak and failed states may emerge and have emerged. Nevertheless, in the course of history, states took power over the mapping of history. States empowered themselves beyond anything else. Power emerged even as a self-referential concept used to form power organisation , and the concept of power is one of those many pre-scientific concepts that had to establish a conceptualisation of itself as *plenitudo potestatis* in order to retain power (Quillet 1972, Faber et al. 1982, Harste 2010b). Not in English, but in French, German and the Scandinavian languages, the self-reference is obvious when we say 'Macht macht Macht' or, as the French chancellor d'Aguesseau eloquently expressed it, 'le pouvoir peut établir le pouvoir de pouvoir' ('power empowers power'). Power is basically a verb and not a substantive.

If such an evolutionary emergence of system take-off is correct, my point is that we should try to focus on the third level of self-organisation, that is, when codes re-enter themselves as codes about codes. This is the take-off in the emergence of systems. States blocked in the re-entry of codes eventually disappeared (Burgundy because of a missing military revolution, Poland because of a missing organisational revolution, *ancien régime* France because of a missing financial revolution). It is difficult to verify if these second-order (r)evolutions are irreversible; to some functional systems, such as war and research, arguments in favour of irreversibility are quite strong while in others such as legal systems, they are less well supported by empirical and theoretical evidence.

We will also be able to observe self-descriptions even in the first stages. However, it is most unlikely if such self-descriptions are differentiated and subdivided into a certain function and handled by a certain organisation; they can only be traced back as forms of ex-post-narrated rationalisations of history; they do not find a substance or a unity in their origin as referred to in Carl Schmitt's idea of 'land-taking'. The origin of codes takes place as the establishment of a difference (Luhmann 1989c: 11–64).[2] For instance, the Old Testament as well as the Koran are concerned not only with theological self-descriptions about what transcendent faith is in a world of contingency, but also with legal rules, conduct of war, family rules, descriptions of economy or agriculture.[3] The Bible, written during the heyday of the quite well-established and to some level institutionally differentiated Roman Empire, could much more easily draw its famous distinctions about how to 'give to Caesar what belongs to Caesar' and outline transcendent religious self-descriptions as second-order distinctions.[4] Other ancient self-descriptions with some discernible subdivided form do exist both in art and in the art of war, as for example, Sun Tzu, Xenophon, Thucydides, Aeneas, Asclepiodotus, Onasander, Frontinus, Vegetius, Caesar (van Creveld 2000). Most often, however, they mix military strategy with politics and teaching.

This chapter will describe the evolution of the legal functional system, the organisational system, the system of war, and the financial system, followed by some possible conclusions and questions. This can be described with the technical devices of distinction analysis, code analysis, medium/form analysis, systems analysis and differentiation analysis as displayed heuristically in Figures 4.1 and

---

2   We might doubt whether a late self-description of war such as Clausewitz's *Vom Kriege* (1832/1952) is research or (reflexive) organisation; on the other hand, Plato's writings were certainly quite academic. Still, at the end of the sixteenth century there were no strong differentiations between defending positions in the medium of communication in (German) churches, in (London's) theatres, in (French) courts and in parliaments.

3   Henri Pirenne's *Charlemagne et Mahomet*, describing the post-Roman re-establishment, north and south of the rump Byzantine–Roman empire, offers some ideas about semantic conditions for religious self-descriptions that had to operate all forms of societal communication (cf. Luhmann 1987c: 230ff.).

4   The Roman Empire probably did not achieve a level of full functional differentiation, a level which not even the organisational system of permanent coding could achieve. I will describe this with reference to Luhmann later on. As a concept of legal forms of expectations, the term 'institutionalisation' might be adequate to describe the form achieved in the Roman Empire (Luhmann 1993: 356).

4.2 below.[5] It could lead to proposals for classifications of strong states, weak states, failed states and collapsed states useful to empirical analyses of contemporary state developments whether in Europe or in less-developed regions.

The methodology is to observe the stabilisation in coded semantics that has taken place with the duplicated codes in the form of re-entries. This stabilisation indicates three levels of coding in, for example, the form of legal coding that will be explained in section I below (Luhmann 1993: 174–87, ch. 4, II) and Figure 4.1. The opposite to what is observed as legal is illegal and not, for instance, brain neurones, waves in the oceans, or linguistic verbs, though all such phenomena take place in the external world (*Umwelt*). When we communicate about the form of the code that has established an asymmetric distinction between legal and illegal we do not differentiate the form from waves in the South Atlantic – though we may, as Grotius, describe a law of seas, and we may make laws for people with brain diseases. But we do differentiate between legality and, for example, illegal preventive war or corrupted bank credits. Hence we have to delimit the logical horizon of the form used in functional differentiated communication. This delimitation is indicated with the third sketch in Figure 4.1.

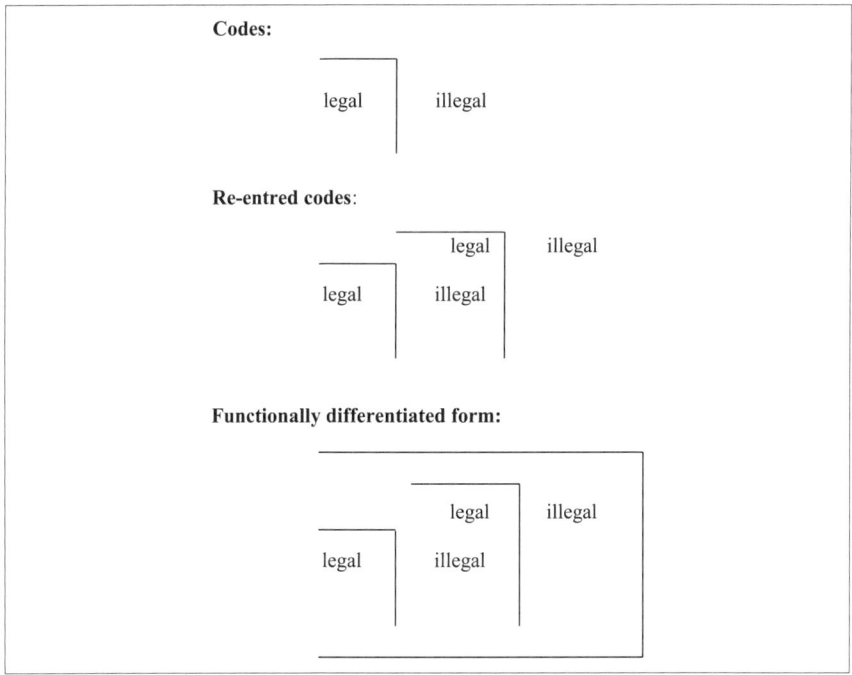

Figure 4.1 Codes, re-entries, and forms functionally differentiated

---

5   Inspired by Baecker (2005) and Husserl, I use a simplified form analysis postulating that all (textual) distinctions operate inside a contextual horizon of possibilities.

In Figure 4.2, I will indicate the different forms of re-entered codes that I use to construct the historical macro object, historical state-formation. States are observed as organisation systems that are structurally coupled to differentiated functional systems. Other functional systems could be indicated too, but those of legal communication, war communication, and financial communication will suffice here. These figures could probably be drawn more aptly, but their function is only to be used as heuristic devices for text reading and text interpretation. They shall make it easier to establish an overview in the construction of the macro object.

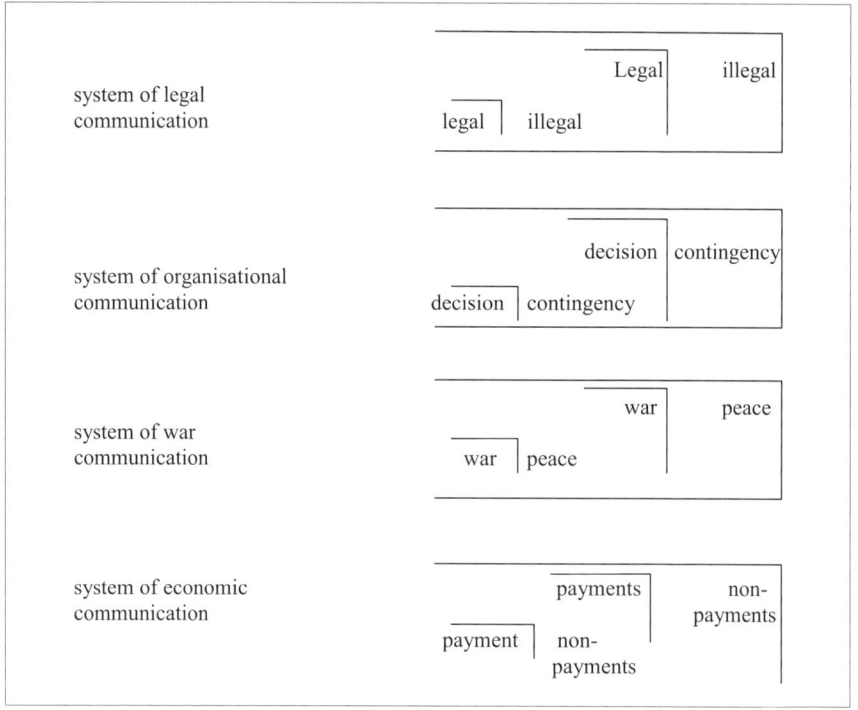

Figure 4.2 A methodological construction of the state as an organisation system structurally coupled to functional differentiated systems with forms of re-entered codes

II. The Legal (R)evolution

Legal evolution is, of course, filled with texts, and Teubner can undoubtedly find evidence for an overall evolutionary re-description in legal history. Nevertheless, we shall remember Gadamer's dictum that history is not available as an object for a hypothetical-deductive Popper–Hempel model. Of course, this warning could be stated in relation to all social phenomena.

Since the legal system is one of the constitutive four or five functional systems used in state development, I will shortly comment on the form of evolution that has taken place in the legal system. Harold Berman has written a convincing masterpiece, *Law and Revolution*, about what he calls the legal revolution that took place between roughly 1050 and 1250. The penetrating take-off marks the new 'legal system' which is the result of Gregory VII's dictate of 1075; in the religious system, it takes place as a monopolisation of what it really means to be included in, and excluded from, the Christian interaction community. In system theoretical terms, which do not seem inappropriate to Berman's description, the communication of the distinction inclusion exclusion includes itself (Luhmann 1995, 2000b: 230–36). It establishes a hierarchy with the pope as the bishop's bishop. Excommunication is monopolised. This continuing political and organisational specialisation of self-reference in the religious system conditions the possibility that Roman law begins to be re-described as a *corpus juris*, a coherent system (Stein 1999: 38–70; Quillet 1972).

Bologna University began teaching law in 1086, and lawyers were trained to communicate about canonical law used by the church. The codes of legal/illegal have been used ever since on law itself, and since then laws could be banned as illegal or legal. This led to a period of written laws, such as the Constitutions of Melfi, the Magna Carta, the Edict of Mainz, and Land's laws in Scandinavia. However, a number of codes and specialisations in the function of law were still to follow (Berman 1983: 115ff., 409ff.; Fenger 2001: 59–60).

Berman's second volume of *Law and Revolution* (2004) concerns legal developments in Germany and England during the sixteenth century. The point is that Protestantism monopolised law, but the Protestant kings had the upper hand. Nevertheless, Berman did not analyse the more decisive French developments where standardising processes had begun; these processes probably specialised law more independently from absolutist rule, if not right away in the sixteenth century then at least beginning with those organisational specialisations that took place when commissioned offices under the king (Henri IV and especially Sully) were separated and specialised in organisation around 1600 in what Bernard Barbiche calls 'une revolution administrative' (Barbiche 1987: 286). In *Méthode de l'histoire* (1566/1951), Jean Bodin in fact clearly describes separated power (Bodin 1566/1951: 289), and in 1576 in *Les six livres de la république* begins to use a form of 'system' theory to replace the former *corpus* conceptualisation (Bodin 1583/1961: 662, 1056).

After a long period of political, military and organisational pressure during the seventeenth century, when the military state used and abused legal reforms as it pleased, the complexities of legal taxation and legal administration made lawyers' codifications of law turn inwards into far more self-referential specialisations of law, and so-called positive law was developed, with the philosophical Chancellor of France d'Aguesseau as the main codifier. This process resulted in the Code

Napoléon and the Prussian General Land Law, which are the outstanding modern law reforms (Stein 1999: 111–15).

My point here is that we can follow the development of self-referential processes in texts and courts and clearly demonstrate how legal powers emerged and became separated to the point of a clear functional differentiation which Charles Montesquieu describes for the first time in legal sociology.[6] Thus, one thing is to find a constitutive form of law about law. Another task in grounding a theory of law and state-building is to find the functional separation and differentiation of a legal system codifying what is accounted as law. I have found the first form, as a kind of second-order observation of law, in Chancellor d'Aguesseau's speeches, writings and activities from 1706 to 1738, which – as Bourdieu has remarked somewhat briefly – display an enormous variety of semantic evolution a little before Montesquieu's today much more famous masterpiece (Bourdieu 1989: 539–48, Engl. 1998: 377–82; Harste 2001a: 41–70, 2003c: 109–135; d'Aguesseau 1819; cf. Phytilis 1977). Bourdieu's concepts of a *vision* about the *illusio* of law enacted by legal scholars certainly do not observe how d'Aguesseau's philosophical second-order undertakings reformed the distinctions between morals and law in *Méditations métaphysiques* (1722/1819/2005) and *Essai d'une institution au droit public* (1727/1819). Bourdieu only describes the interests legal elites had in order to universalise their noble semantics. Typical to the difference between Bourdieu and Luhmann: Luhmann does not stay on the staircase outside but enters the courtyards (or the museums, in the case of the sociology of art) and wonders how people get worried, impassioned or irritated by their observations (Harste 2010a). However, Luhmann did not enter those analyses of the neglected Chancellor of France either, though he did refer to his teacher, Jean Domat, and to Linguet and Pothiers (Luhmann 1993: 341, 410, 460). Of course, one direct change was that inherited property was subjected to positive law standards that transcended privileges; hence heritage law was the first reform to be enacted, in 1732, among those of d'Aguesseau's reforms that eventually led to the famous Code Civil in 1804. Contracts could not establish equalities among equals before such transitions. D'Aguesseau's legal and moral semantics came closer to Kant's than any other Enlightenment philosopher.

With Kant we have not only a formula of functional differentiation in *Die Metaphysik der Sitten* (The Metaphysics of Morals; 1798), in which it is expressed how separated powers beyond a 'syllogism' do not 'usurp' each other, but we also find a systems theory of self-organisation in his *Kritik der Urteilskraft* (Critique of Judgement; 1790, §§65–7). Elsewhere I have re-described Kant's theory of European integration as compatible with a theory of convergence through functional system differentiation (Harste 2009c). In Kant's reconstruction, legal

---

    6 Cf. Behrens 1985, Olivier-Martin 1997, Cosandey and Descimon 2002. Such descriptions offer a much more departmentalised and functionally differentiated point of view than what we find in Foucault's analyses. Bourdieu's brilliant analysis (in 1989) rather points to the scandalous over-integration of codes of function that should be kept separated.

reforms had to be copied from state to state. The legal state was not the sovereign state of France or Denmark, but the state of a self-referential functional form transgressing borders. Those who copied and established similar organisations of law were embedded in organisation systems.

III. The Organisational (R)evolution

In his article 'Distinctions directrices' (1986/1987), Luhmann describes the form of such a duplication as we have seen in law. Semantic distinctions appear everywhere, but they are fairly often loaded with a preferred value that offers some kind of asymmetric binarity.[7] The somewhat difficult and, some may say, even obscure point is that the code can de-block itself if its form is differentiated from its programme and re-enter the description of this form/material into its own description of itself because the material programme is left out and only the form remains contained. However, the idea is also simple as we can see when we study the evolution of law about law, or when we observe the payment of payments, research about research conditions, mass-mediated communication about mass media, or war against forms of war, and so on.

In his book *Ecological Communication*, Luhmann describes the more sophisticated aspect of this point in an astonishing way. He briefly mentions the linkage between micro-semantics and macro-evolution which he displays more fully in 'Staat und Staatsräson im Übergang ...' (1989b). The point is to describe how the organisational condition for the political functional system emerged. It was established with the semantic transformation about what it means to be in office. Luhmann made an accurate description of the structurally uncoupled state of offices in dynastic states where positions were appointed, at a time when the form of employment and its adjoined programmes were still hardly invented (budgets, office buildings, permanent commissions, delimitation of tasks, etc.):

> The holding of state offices cannot be legitimized by being held once and for all, for example, by a dynastic family. Holding such offices is contingent, a process of selecting persons and programs and is under continual examination. Political election and the formation of governments serve to bring the code and program into agreement for a certain amount of time, i.e. to hand over the government to those who personally and professionally seem to offer the guarantee of carrying out the preferred political programs. This presupposes a structural uncoupling

---

7   Reinhart Koselleck also studies this asymmetric duality between counter-concepts in his gigantic project *Geschichtliche Grundbegriffe*, and it is discussed in a number of his other books as well as in other contributions by the school of conceptual history. To systems theory and social theory this endeavour is, of course, interesting but unsatisfying since it does not lead on to further aggregations describing structural differentiation (Luhmann 1980: 14–15).

of code and program, i.e. the possibility of opening access to other programs. The political complexity that is attained in this way can best be understood if, for the purpose of historical comparison, the theory of 'reasons of state' (*Staatsräson, raison d'État*) is considered. By the year 1600 the idea of 'state government' was already detectable. But the organisation of the state and the holding of offices (especially the holding of the leading offices by a prince) were not clearly distinguished in the concept of the state. Therefore 'reasons of state' were directed at a methodology of holding-on-to-the-government, while the necessity of 'reasons of state' was justified by the necessity of government itself. In other words, the concepts of domination and state were not yet separated, so that one could still say: '*L'État c'est moi*'. The code function of the leading offices – the fact that their occupation by one person excluded that by another – was not yet differentiated from the program function, i.e. not distinguished from the question of by whom and according to which programs is the government to be executed properly. (Luhmann 1986: 171–2; Engl. 1989a: 86–7)

Alexis Tocqueville was the first to describe what he called an 'administrative revolution' that apparently took place when organisational offices became distinct from the tasks, the individuals in office, and the situated commands to which they were subjected (Mousnier 1971, 1974, 1980). This is what Luhmann describes in the citation; and although he – after a short chapter in *Zweckbegriff und Systemrationalität* (1968/1973: 87–104) – never described an organisational history in the elaborate way (tracing paths back to early modernity) established in his major works on functional systems, he described again and again the form established by the estate society when it described itself in an even more hierarchically monopolised way (Luhmann 1989b, 1990, 1997: 678–743, 2000a: 189–227, 319–71).[8]

Again, it is essential to find the codification of an organisation that is able to describe and codify its own organisation (Dohrn and Böckenförde 1975, Harste 2003a): how and when are second-order organisational codes used to further organise first-order organisational codes with the same standardised form as the second-order codes? Although we can find a great semantic variation on this theme in the theological debates on delegation in the high medieval quarrels between decentralists and centralists (the so-called nominalists and realists – cf. Quillet 1972, Salisbury 1153/1993), the take-off theoretically begins with Jean Bodin's legal sociology (or *science politique*) in the enormous *Les six livres de la république* from 1576 (especially Book III, chapter 7; Harste 2001).[9] But, above

---

8   Bourdieu also offers a description (2004).

9   Note that both Foucault and Bourdieu have investigated the same theme (Foucault 1978/2004, Bourdieu 2004). However, to put it succinctly, the difference between Luhmann's and their analyses is that they do not handle the temporal dimension in the meaning of office-building as Luhmann does. Bourdieu sticks to a Simmel-like form analysis of heterodoxy and orthodoxy when focusing on how innovations lead to involution

all, historians agree that Colbert's construction of the central administration is the turning point. The central organisation of regional organisation becomes codified when we bear in mind the self-observation of the central perspective from Versailles (Colbert 1661–83/1873, Trenard 1975, Tocqueville 1856/1988: 98–110, 299–312, King 1948/1972, Richet 1973, Mousnier 1974, 1980, Smedley-Weil 1995, Mukerji 1997, Harste 2003a).

In organisational sociology there is a lot of talk about the so-called span of control; a span clearly codified at the time. Central administration is a self-organisational system from that time, a lesson quickly learned all over Europe from Stockholm to Naples. It is not functional since it includes members as commissioned officers with strongly codified duties. It is as hierarchical as the estate society, and has been so ever since bureaucracies could be described according to hierarchised models of the self-inclusion among the included members. Luhmann keeps returning to the question of semantics of membership of the corps of people in service or office, and his descriptions of coded semantics can be found in the emergent organisational literature in early modernity (Luhmann 1989: 101–19, von Pommern 1575/1996, Wilhelm 1722/1997).

Some may wonder why Luhmann distinguishes organisational systems from interaction systems and functional systems. There are mainly two reasons. First, the three forms of systems have various degrees of inclusion/exclusion of individuals; interaction systems operate with inclusive semantics, organisational systems with membership of persons, and functional systems with exclusion. Second and above all, organisation systems got most of their semantics from a stratified society: decisions, hierarchies, membership, control, delegation. Thus, the theory of organisation systems is grounded in early modern history. While the temporal code of interaction systems was one of presence/absence, in the organisational system it is one of synchronicity/simultaneity. The organisational diagram and its central perspective coordinates not only space but synchronises at the same time as it enables different functional systems to operate structurally coupled within a form of simultaneity though with uncoupled temporal bindings. This uncoupling can be observed as a risk.

Foucault described the history of many semantic forms; the difference between Foucauldian and Luhmannian analysis is that Luhmann differentiates the emergence of functional systems much more than Foucault – and this differentiation re-enters into the forms available to the organisational system. While Foucault describes steering and control in a *governmental* continuation of organised war, Luhmann describes a *departmental* differentiation. In Foucault's observations, war is a strategic principle organised militarily (Foucault 1975: 170, 1997: 41). To systems theory, war should be observed as a functional system that is not identical with military organisation systems.

---

in the course of evolution. The famous so-called Louis XIV dictum makes better sense if the plural form 'l'État c'est nous' is used, meaning 'we' and/or 'I and my office'.

IV. The (R)evolution in Warfare: War Codifies War

Still, we may wonder how anything like an evolutionary process becomes possible. Why should stages rather than some non-linear devolution emerge? One – philosophical – answer might come from the philosophy of history: because we describe historical processes observed from our own time, our self-description is the self-implication of evolutionary processes (Luhmann 1981a: 31), Quite as if we stood at the top of a gigantic tree and – in spite of all its complexities and branches – were able to describe the main path we had taken to climb the tree.

Historical sociology describes another departure: evolution 'necessarily' follows a number of irreversible innovations when we observe why organisational revolutions had to take place. The point is that the organisational revolution followed a military revolution (Mousnier 1980: 7–10; Downing 1992). Military innovations have led to evolution, as they are inescapable (Harste 2003b). Thus we can describe a functional system of war following tactical codes of destruction capacities and strategic codes of peace and war. The code of security⌐danger is replaced by risk⌐danger, first, because it becomes a risk if a military organisational system is not sufficiently developed to cope with the dangerous contingencies of warfare and second, because there is a risk that war destroys control and planning and entails extreme steering problems.

Hence, basic to an adequate systems theory about war (and there are many obsolete first-order systems theories about warfare) we have to draw a distinction between war as functional system and warfare according to military organisation systems. This distinction explains why Carl von Clausewitz had to operate with a distinction between absolute war and real war. In real war, warfare is structurally coupled to conditions of other functional systems by logistic means such as finance, political support, organisational delimitations, law, and so on. It is only through these structural couplings that 'war is the continuation of politics but mixed into other means' (Clausewitz 1832/1952). Protracted wars of attrition transform first-order warfare into a second-order war about which material conflict concerns whom, and for how long, and thus push the gravitational centre of wars into questions of credit, public opinion and organisational cohesion (Clausewitz 1832/1952: 875).

At the time of the Crusades, a number of semantic developments filled the debates about holy war and wars fought for the sake of God's peace. The Christian and Islamic codes of war and peace were transformed and constituted in the period from about 1000 to 1250. Again, at the beginning of the twenty-first century, codes of war, peace, and sacred justifications stretching back to the Crusades are repeatedly discussed (Rosén 2009). Nonetheless, until the end of the sixteenth century, war was codified by the 'upper hand' of religion, and by law and politics. Councils formulated what counted as legitimised war (*jus ad bellum*) and although wars, tactics and strategy have been codified since the Greek introduction of the first hoplite revolution in warfare, other political and religious semantics still had a say about what counted as military honour and as peace and justice in wars.

A much more inescapable evolution began with the military revolutions that accelerated from the end of the fifteenth century – that is, after the invention of the printing press, the canons, and the fortification ideas. In 1955 the Irish historian Michael Roberts formulated the concept of a military revolution that took place from 1560 to 1660. Debates have demonstrated that much earlier and later developments could also be described as types of innovation in the form of 'necessities' to all involved parts whether in conflicts over territories, as a medium of state self-descriptions, or over sea access (Rogers 1995, Knox and Murray 2001). However, with the Thirty Years' War (1618–48), war turned into a form that codified itself. Warfare became self-referential. No other power than the power of war could take power over whatever could be meant by war. Accordingly, all other codes had to reform themselves in order to find their own forms and codes, whether in law, religion, or politics. The code peace'war transformed its asymmetry into a code war/peace: war favoured itself and could no longer be governed or steered. Thus, we may speak about a revolution in warfare. Since wars could be organised, war paved the way for the organisational build-up outside the realm of the church. Hence, as Kant observed, by the 'cunning of history' (Hegel's concept), war became conditioned by the complexities of organisation, especially legal tax organisation. The military revolution not only had implications for the organisational self-organisation outside the reach of warfare, but also for a revolution in the legal self-reference and a revolution in the financial system.[10] The functional system of war conditioned its own structural couplings described by means of a new organisational system that described itself as 'the state' (Luhmann 1989a: 88; 1993: 172)

Luhmann hardly ever wrote more than a few hints about war and the directed distinction (*Leitdifferenz*) of peace'war. However, it is possible to write a kind of book about 'Society's War' ('der Krieg der Gesellschaft'; Harste 2003b, 2009d, 2013). The most difficult part of such a macro endeavour is not to find the self-descriptions. Tactic and strategic self-descriptions are manifold from Sun Tzu through Clausewitz to the so-called asymmetric warfare. It is more demanding to draw a clear analytical line between the functional system of war and the military organisational system. The latter concerns, for instance, Napoleon's army, the Red Army, the Wehrmacht, or the NATO coalition in Afghanistan. The functional system of war is a codified form of communication that keeps changing codes in order to

---

10 Quantitatively oriented studies often focus on number of troops and establish tables about men under arms in comparison between states from, say, 1500 to 1800 in order to demonstrate the increases (Tilly 1992: 79; Porter 1994: 67; Downing 1992: 67). The same could be said about increases in administrations. Luhmann's temporal point about permanency adds the dimension of stability (cf. Tallett 1992: 7): 30,000 men permanently under arms are many more than the same number under arms for two days. Furthermore, the third dimension of logistics available to those men should be taken into account, whether arms, food, garrisons, uniforms or office-buildings, libraries, postal services, etc. Therefore: number x permanence x logistics = an explosive revolution in costs, strength, and power.

establish contingencies in a still more refined system of double contingencies. Because of the systematic production of contingencies, warfare is always a sudden surprise and always surprisingly more expensive than aggressors have planned or imagined. Warfare finances are almost always explosive and impossible to control politically (Kindleberger 1986) and are much higher than military budgets. Their temporal bindings involve far-reaching welfare expenditures. Thus war systems are indeed risky systems. However, the risk is not only in future unpleasant experiences; rather, the risk is that we have the systems we have, and we observe with the systems we have. The risk is the military–industrial complex as it evolves at the present time. The risk is the decisions we make now, in the present time, whether we decide, or we decide not to decide (Luhmann 1993b: 129ff.). Wars are expensive, they increase the demand for money here and now, and they demand more than what is available.

V. Financial (R)evolution: 'Money, money, money' – Called Credit

This has led to what has been called a financial revolution. Money costs money. To get quick and easy money in the short term, you have to accept long-term costs; that is, an amount of money, say X, does simply not only cost an amount of money equal to X, say Y, but costs additional money, namely interest. Thus interests tell a story about future contingencies and risks. However, destiny was God's domain, and the church could find sayings in the Bible forbidding interest and condemning it as usury. Therefore, interest had to be codified in the strangest ways. It was forbidden to charge interest to people nearby, but people from other religions or from far away could charge interest, and thus international financing was important even when religious Christian power was still decisive (Fontaine 2008).

There were two problems about financing. One was, and still is, to find a code of payments that is not too material, which is Georg Simmel's final point in his last chapter of *Philosophie des Geldes* (1909/1981). Money is not only in the form of a certain material, say soap, cigarettes, beer, or gold and silver; nor is it only a social form of exchange between subjects. It should be noticed that money is also a form of temporal binding (Luhmann 1987). Money is a codified form that reduces the complexity in all those three dimensions (material, social and temporal).

Thus, interest and finance are, above all, forms of temporal bindings; the seventeenth century had problems finding the right form of that binding – problems that were highly congruent with the problem of finding a sufficiently abstract form as discussed by Luhmann in the long citation above (Rey 2002, Grénier 1996). Hence, silver and gold still had to stabilise payments as material references to money as a symbolically generalised medium of exchange until the successive breakdowns in 1919, 1933, 1944 and 1971 (Kindleberger 1984, Germain 1997, Eichengreen 2007). But they stabilised more than an increasing economy could accept. It is utterly absurd that money available to market transactions should depend on South African gold mine production. Material references are not sufficient in a future where the economic potential keeps increasing at the speed we have seen since the end of the 1950s. Similarly, before about 1550 there was not enough gold and silver (or Swedish copper) to let markets function without complex contracts of exchange. Contractualised creditworthiness was a symbolic form of faith, trust and confidence. Contracts are a reduction of complexities in the three dimensions of complex matter, complex social relations, and complexities in a contingent future. Credit is to make contracts about such contracts. Thus they entail a second-order analysis, for example, about what is accounted for as future reimbursements. Therefore, markets and especially financial markets and credit markets cannot function without structural couplings to the legal system. However, because of the permanency of the state organisation the state became creditor 'of last resort'.

The second problem concerned the financial problem of states in war. Kingdoms and states have always urgently needed finance in order to handle a military logistic that, in major wars, always became much more expensive than any economic planning and any bankers could imagine. This was the background for the financial revolution in the Dutch and English credit systems. As Dirk Baecker has demonstrated in his book *Womit Banken Handeln?* (1991), finance is a way of trading short-term payments into long-term loans. Thus, banks trade with time and money – that is, with trust and risk. Credit questions creditworthiness and accountability, and displays a form of moral trust between people who depend on each other. Elena Esposito has exposed the systems theory of credit systems as systems communicating about the contingencies of trust and time in an even more elaborate analysis (Esposito 2010).

The history of the form of creditworthiness is also the history of a form that turned more and more abstract, from people *internally* linked by the same religious *credo* to people sufficiently far from each other to allow for explicit codes of what such creditworthiness should cost. French nobles could not explicitly communicate about such creditworthiness, and in order to remain as tax-free estate, they had to lend the state money. In an *internal* credit system they, as an estate, were lenders, borrowers, buyers, and estate holders. In such a state, budgets were not explicit. In the French state, the credit of the estate was as eternal as the words 'state', 'status' and 'raison d'état' implies. The state of the state was tacit knowledge held in arcane secrecy (Dessert 1984, Bosher 1970, Stolleis 1990, Luhmann 1989b). This was true of budgets, too.

Banks trade in narrative anticipation of future possibilities. In a detailed study, Michael Hutter has demonstrated how money, as a coded form of communication, is lent with deposits as security for a loan. The classic history is somewhat complex. It is not only goldsmiths who lend more long-term money to people than they have as short-term deposits in gold (Hutter 1993, 1999). Credit systems were well known during the trade fairs and in city-state relations, not to mention the Medicis in the fifteenth and the Fuggers in the sixteenth centuries. But they had still not shown their effect as functional systems; they were still based on interaction systems and organisational systems. Anyway, after the cities of commercial entrepreneurs, first the Bank of Amsterdam (that followed ideas from Venice and Genova) and then the Bank of England, still a private bank in 1694, offered vast deposits as central banks that lent money to military states in desperate need of finance and with the guarantee that parliament could secure future taxes and later also land enclosures including positions in colonies that could serve as payments for finance. This established an explicitly and *externally* coded credit system.

Paradoxically, the more Catholic states were more reluctant to communicate about interest and credit, thus their codified discipline of creditworthiness was less standardised and more indirect than what we observe in northern Protestant- and especially Calvinist-oriented states. As an unintended consequence, the Spanish and French states suffered from higher interest than the Dutch and English states. Before Napoleon, the rapidly increasing finances of war were apparently much more costly in Spain and France than in the United Provinces and England which through the Rothchilds' networks developed credit systems even further (Kennedy 1989, Brewer 1990, Dickson 1967, Bonney 1995). Thus, the selective research process for systems theory is to find descriptions of credit crises in cases of prolonged wars. There were fierce debates after each increasingly expensive war, especially from the end of the seventeenth century. After the First World War an extensive literature intensified the debates – the most famous probably being John Maynard Keynes' analyses. The Iraq and Afghanistan wars and the overstretching of American power and finances have seen the return of these debates (Eichengreen 2007; Stiglitz and Bilmes 2008: 125—6; Krugman 2009). Trading in the so-called derivatives or futures is a risky affair that developed as a consequence of the flood of dollars on international markets and the lowered rent after the deficit financing of the Iraq and Afghanistan wars (Esposito 2010).

VI. Improbable Well-organised States and Fragile States

The European idealised state has emerged as an improbable organisational system structurally coupled to an open, if not infinite number, of more or less worldwide functional systems cross-cutting territorial borders. To each of these functional systems a wide range of programmes is organised. Functional systems concern not only finance, war and law, but also politics, religion, research, education, art, mass media, care, health care, and sociologically less discussed medium/form problems operated by systems communication such as transport, garbage, agriculture, or even sport and love/family reproduction. Thus, Max Weber's classic definition of the state as some form that has monopolised the authoritative use of physical violence inside a territory with a given population does not suffice to be used as criteria, even if Bourdieu's notion of 'symbolic violence' is added. For a state theory all the functional systems and their organisational operation by programmes should be described, especially as to what concerns their structural couplings. Structural couplings stabilise operations; communication about them are to be expected, while they are contingent in weak, fragile, and failed states and non-existent in collapsed states. For instance, the coupling of law into the other functional systems is expected to have an elaborate set of expectancies programmed in the form of education. What counts as entrance criteria and passed examinations in education systems is expected to be operated as if they could be communicated in codes of law. Thousands of such codes are operated in well-formed states, though even in those states the differentiation of codes is far better formed, structurally coupled, identifiable, semantically clear, and distinctive, in the centres than in the peripheries in remote mountains, islands and small villages. At such far-away places interaction systems are still important, and organisation systems operate over-integrated functional systems with overlapping programmes. New laws, reforms, instructions, information, and regulations available through Internet messages easily overload the organisational capacities. There is a lack of organisationally specified functional differentiation. In fragile states this organisational deficit is the case in the centres as well. Modern states cannot run their functions without organisations that have to be financed, staffed, equipped, specialised, differentiated, and authoritatively respected. Accordingly, it is possible to sketch a system theoretical scheme of well-formed states, weak and fragile states, failed states, and collapsed states.

It is a paradox that states able to organise an extensive functional differentiation on the one hand are extremely stable – because contingencies in one functional system structurally uncouple these irritations from what could irritate other functional systems. On the other hand, such states also operate extremely interdependent functions: a breakdown in one functional system, say credit systems, transport, or garbage treatment, irritates all other functional systems simultaneously. However, functional systems are only synchronised with themselves, with time lags and with expectancies that flexibilities occur – 'since the other functional systems are not organised operatively as well as we use to do in our operations'. Functional equivalents are expected to be operated smoothly. In well-organised states nearly everything functions, yet in some states most things can also be arranged by interaction or organisation systems or in other functional systems. In states – or peripheries – with lesser organisation of functional differentiation, a few things function but nearly everything can be arranged. In weak and fragile states everything is vulnerable, few things function, and few things can be arranged. Since the end of the Cold War debates about fragile, weak, and failed states are preponderant. But a systems theory about such states is still lacking. Here, I can only indicate a few frames.

> A fragile state is significantly susceptible to crisis in one or more of its subsystems. It is a state that is particularly vulnerable to internal and external contingencies and domestic and international conflicts. In a fragile state, organisational arrangements will easily preserve the conditions of crisis: in economic terms, this could be with codes about, for instance, property rights that reinforce stagnation or low growth rates, or embody extreme inequality (in wealth, in access to land, in access to the means to make a living); care systems

codes may embody extreme inequality or lack of access altogether to health or education; political codes, may entrench exclusionary coalitions in power (in ethnic, religious, or perhaps regional terms). In fragile states, legal codes are vulnerable to challenges by rival institutional systems be they derived from traditional authorities, devised by communities under conditions of stress or based on privileges (in terms of security, possessions or welfare), or be they derived from warlords, or other non-state power brokers. The opposite of a 'fragile state' is a 'well-ordered state' – one where systems or codes appear able to withstand internal and external contingencies, whereas structural couplungs have forms which allow for reforms.

Organisational systems (institutions) shall handle terms and codes of economy, care, law politics and even war (Harste 2012). Hence the problem of fragility, weakness, failure and collapse could be re-described by a systems theory of states. A fuller scheme of criteria is indicated in Figure 4.2. Coherent well-ordered states can be observed as through and through structurally coupled to functionally differentiated systems. When we observe strong ordered states, the separation of powers seems to be less clear. We can furthermore observe that weak and fragile states only organise structural couplings with a few functional systems and the programmes are not well organised and often not at all in the peripheries. In failed states only a few programmes are organised in the centre and among the functional systems, the war system (civil wars) is structurally coupled to a relative strong military organisation system with centrally organised programmes.

To use Luhmann's systems theory is to observe with concepts and counter-concepts. We tend to categorise with counter-concepts as states/failed states. Hence, we can try to observe what we do not observe with this distinction. We do not observe empires. Empires, as huge organisation systems are comparable to states; in fact they are probably not only bigger, but also have a much longer history – examples include the Persian Empire, the Roman Empire, the Chinese Empire, the Tsarist Empire, the Soviet Empire and, more recently, the Russian Empire; the United States has developed as an empire and Canada and Australia could probably be described as empires. Brazil, India and Pakistan, too, could probably be better described as empires than as states. Austria-Hungary was an empire that separated itself from the Holy Roman Empire of the German Nation, replaced it, and was finally only dissolved as late as after the First World War when the Paris treaties also toppled both the newly erected German Empire and, especially, the Ottoman Empire. Colonial empires have almost all passed away. Most often only a few less populated islands remain under the umbrella of empires. When empires fell under the pressure of the much more cohesive European territorial states, an extensive amount of so-called failed states emerged at their peripheries. Thus, we are probably led to a new distinction – that of empires/failed states. This distinction happens to describe a blind spot in most historical sociology of states, the present one included.

Table 4.1 A system theoretical typology of states (with different degrees of structurally coupled programmes coded in organisational and functional communication systems)

Systems and programmes	Coherent well-ordered states	Strong ordered states	Weak and fragile states	Failed states	Collapsed states
Central administrative organisation system • centre • regions • periphery • central statistics • population registration	+	+	±	±	÷
Financial system • central bank • stable currency • international credit liaisons • bank system • tax system • homogenised taxation rules • system of budgeting and revision • monetised economy	+	+	±	÷	÷
Legal system • separated powers • central court • local legal courts • juridically trained judges, lawyers • faculties of law • principles of law (rule of law) • written law • system of laws • constitution	+	±	±	÷	÷
Military system • department of defence • system for appointment of officers • education of officers • garrisons, • staff/line • separated staff functions • military research academies • conscription	+	+	+	±	÷

Table 4.1 continued

Systems and programmes	Coherent well-ordered states	Strong ordered states	Weak and fragile states	Failed states	Collapsed states
Infrastructural system • connecting transport lines centre/periphery • connections between peripheries • water transport • unhindered land transport	+	+	±	÷	÷
Educational system • universities • teachers colleges • schools • obligatory school • alphabetisation • open, universal access	+	±	±	÷	÷
Mass-media system • broadcasting stations (TV, radio) • countrywide papers • access to foreign papers and media • local media • freedom of speech	+	±	±	±	÷
Political system • central political elite • parliament • free trusted exchange in opposition/government rivalry • parliamentarism • regional councils • local councils • parties • free elections	+	±	+	±	÷
Religious system • organised 'churches' etc. • specialised 'priests' • religious loyalty • religious tolerance	+	+	+	±	±

Table 4.1 continued

Systems and programmes	Coherent well-ordered states	Strong ordered states	Weak and fragile states	Failed states	Collapsed states
International system • participation in peace congresses, treaties, UN, etc. • participation in regional confederations, associations • foreign embassies • embassies abroad • commitments to international conventions and courts	+	+	+		

Conclusions: To Find and to Falsify

How is it possible not to get lost, not to lose the thread, in the stories of history and not lose judgement in favour of reductionism and prejudices (*Deutsche Sonderweg* or Whiggish history)? Discussing state formation and social evolution from Antiquity to the twenty-first century is to enter extremely complex stories. How can history and evolution be told in a simple way and at the same time elicit curiosity and excitement and unblock reductionism?

In order to make a systems theory of grand formations such as European state-building, it has been necessary to proceed with an abductive form of grounded work – that is, to ground the grand master theory in detailed research. Some of the texts observed are famous and easily available, some are more difficult to find but often not that difficult to identify. furthermore, texts containing important semantic inventions and codes, well known to later observers, must have been there at that spot in that situation among those authors – and then they are there too. The most interesting task is, of course, to reformulate what can be found in such texts, which are also usually somewhat overloaded with other operations, semantics and codes. It has been necessary to reformulate a few aspects of Luhmann's systems theory and sometimes – as in the case of the establishment of a theory of war and peace – to add completely new foundations to it. This is, of course, also a test case for systems theory. If Luhmann's theory cannot be used to establish a theory of war, military systems and peace, it has a major problem as a grand theory of society. However, this systems theory of 'Der Krieg der Gesellschaft' seems to have been able to handle quite a number of operations, tactics, and strategies over hundreds or even thousands of years.

Once again, it is possible to narrate a master story about macro developments, huge comparisons, and large processes with a detailed emphasis on the transformation of codes about codes. We do not have to open all banks' debit books, nor find all letters among all civil servants, or read all laws and all trials. We have to select certain codes, find the decisive texts, find exact criteria about why decisive transformations should occur at this exact spot at a certain moment. It is not possible to select such findings without a grand, though grounded, theory about the emergent differentiation and structural coupling of functional systems and organisational systems. Establishing the archives of self-descriptions for each form of system evolution (organisational, legal, financial, warfare, political, etc.) is, then, also to pinpoint those textual selections where the codes + and the codes of codes can be found (Luhmann 2002: 71; Baecker 2005). The extremely complex classification and displacement problem known from Foucault's writings is also complex at the semantic level in systems analysis, but not when concerning the codes and the second-order codes. Rather than studying Foucault (with Foucault as a replaced study of history), we can concentrate on history with systems analysis and at the theoretical level focus on only a few codes.

In his studies about European universities, Rudolf Stichweh (1991) has demonstrated the usefulness of systems theory in his study of scientific and educational revolutions. This is part of a system theoretical re-description of the European state system. States are organisational systems describing themselves as if political systems could refer to the government of states simply because decisions are central to the communication of organisation systems if and only if those organisation systems decide to communicate about messages such as central decisions.

However, those organisation systems have to deal with differentiated functional systems separated in law, war, science, education, and economy. Bureaucracies and governmental steering and control might point towards one form of narrative about European state-building as if forms of government (democracy, aristocracy, monarchy or despotism) were sufficient to interpret the complexities of state organisations and their structural couplings to functional systems. However, this form of governmental interpretation has been obsolete since the sixteenth century.

Another falsifying test therefore takes place when we compare, for instance, Luhmann's differentiation theory of systems theory with Foucault's and Bourdieu's genealogies of *governmentality* and *étatisation*, respectively. In concordance with Luhmann, we might rather speak of *departmentality* (Dorwart 1953). Functional systems are not easy to govern and steer. However, it applies to both Foucault and Carl Schmitt that, 'politics is the continuation of war but with other means' (Foucault 1975: 170, 1997: 41; Schmitt 1932/1963: 107). A Luhmannian theory of war and politics would rather differentiate and reformulate the steering problem in the famous Clausewitz dictum of war as the continuation of politics but in another medium differentiated from politics.

To summarise and conclude the present chapter: systems theory tells a story about state-building and societal evolution which describes the formation of a number of functional systems – by cross-cutting how states have organised territories. Neither organisational systems nor states are territorial by necessity. But they happened to establish organisational systems that for some centuries were not trans-territorial networks (of interaction systems), but were submitted to hierarchies with capitals or other organisational power centres to centralise and decentralise. Hence, systems theory can re-describe a number of paradoxes belonging to historical concepts such as regulation, sovereignty, identities of nation-states, territorial states, not to mention ideas of identities between state, society, people, nation, economy and security (Luhmann 2000a: 319–71; Albert and Hilkermeier 2003).

References

d'Aguesseau, H.-F., *Œuvres complètes du chancelier d'Aguesseau*, 16 vols (Paris: Fantin, 1819).
Albert, M. and L. Hilkermeier (eds), *Observing International Relation* (London: Routledge, 2003).
Andersen, N.A., *Diskursive analysestrategier* (Copenhagen: Nyt fra samfundsvidenskaberne, 1999) (Engl. trans.??).
Baecker, D., *Womit Handeln Banken?* (Frankfurt am Main: Suhrkamp, 1991).
____, *Form und Formen der Kommunikation* (Frankfurt am Main: Suhrkamp, 2005) .
Barbiche, B., 'Une révolution administrative', in A. Stegman (ed.), *Pouvoir et institution en Europe au XVIème siècle* (Paris: Vrin, 1987).
Behrens, C.B.A., *Society, Government and the Enlightenment* (London: Thames and Hudson, 1985).
Berman, H., *Law and Revolution* (Cambridge, MA.: Harvard University Press, 1983).
____, *Law and Revolution, II* (Cambridge, MA.: Harvard University Press, 2004).
Bodin, J., *Les six livres de la république* (Aalen: Scientia, 1576/1583/1961).
    Methodus ad facile historiarum (French 1951) La Méthode de l'histoire (Paris: PUF 1566/1955).
Bonney, R. (ed.), *Economic Systems and State Finance* (Oxford: Clarendon Press, 1995).
Bosher, J.F., *French Finances, 1770–1795* (Cambridge: Cambridge University Press, 1970).
Bourdieu, P., *La noblesse d'État* (Paris: Les éditions du minuit, 1989).
____, 'Esprits d'État: Genèse et structure du champ bureaucratique', in *Raisons pratiques* (Paris: Seuil, 1994).
____, 'From the King's House to the Reason of State: A Model of the Genesis of the Bureaucratic Field', *Constellations* 11/1 (2004), 16–35.
Brewer, J., *The Sinews of Power: War, Money and the English State, 1688–1783* (Cambridge, MA.: Harvard University Press, 1990).

Brunner, O., W. Conze and R. Kosseleck (eds), *Geschichtliche Grundbegriffe*, 7 vols (Stuttgart: Klett-Cotta, 1972–1992).
von Clausewitz, C., *Vom Kriege* (Bonn: Dümmler, 1832/1952).
Colbert, J.-B. and P. Clement (eds), *Lettres, instructions et mémoires de Colbert*, 7 vols (Paris: Imprimerie nationale, 1661–83/1873).
Colbert, J.-B., 'Mémoire pour messieurs les maitres des requêtes commissaires départis dans les provinces', in L. Trenard (ed.), *Les Mémoires des intendants pour l'instruction du Duc de Bourgogne* (1698) (Paris: Bibliothèque nationale, 1664/1975).
Cosandey, F. and R. Descimon, *L'Absolutisme en France* (Paris: Seuil, 2002).
Creveld, M. van, *The Art of War* (London: Cassel, 2000).
Dessert, D., *Argent, pouvoir et société au Grand Siècle* (Paris: Fayard, 1984).
Dickson, P.G.M., *The Financial Revolution in England, 1688–1756* (London: Macmillan, 1967).
Dohrn-Rossum, G. van and E.-W. Böckenförde, 'Organ, Organismus, Organisation, politische Körper', in O. Brunner W. Conze and R. Koselleck (eds), *Geschichtliche Grundbegriffe*, vol. 4 (Stuttgart: Klett-Cotta, 1978), 519–622.
Dorwart, R.A., *The Administrative Reforms of Frederick William I of Prussia* (Cambridge, MA.: Harvard University Press, 1953).
Downing, B., *The Military Revolution and Political Change* (Princeton, NJ ; Oxford: Princeton University Press, 1992).
Eichengreen, B., *Global Imbalances and the Lessons of Bretton Woods* (Cambridge, MA: MIT Press, 2007).
Elias, N., *Über den Prozess der Zivilisation*, 2 vols (Frankfurt am Main: Suhrkamp, 1939/1976).
Elton, G.R., *The Tudor Revolution in Government* (Cambridge: Cambridge University Press, 1953).
Ertman, T., *Birth of the Leviathan* (Cambridge: Cambridge University Press, 1997).
Esposito, E., *Die Zukunft der Futures: Die Zeit des Geldes in Finanzwelt und Gesellschaft* (Heidelberg: Carl-Auer, 2010).
Faber, K.-G. et al., 'Macht, Gewalt', in O. Brunner, W. Conze and R. Koselleck (eds), *Geschichtliche Grundbegriffe*, vol. 3 (Stuttgart: Klett-Cotta, 1982).
Fenger, O., *Lov og Ret i Europas historie* (Aarhus: Aarhus Universitetsforlag, 2001).
Fontaine, L., *L'Économie morale: Pauvrété, credit et confiance dans l'Europe préindustrielle* (Paris: Gallimard, 2008).
Foucault, M., *Surveillir et punir* (Paris: Gallimard, 1975).
____, *Il faut défendre la société* (Paris: Gallimard, 1997).
____, *Securité, territoire, population* (Paris: Gallimard, 2004).
Friedrich der Große, *Das politische Testament von 1752* (Stuttgart: Reclam, 1987).
Grenier, J.-Y., *L'Économie d'Ancien Régime: Un monde de l'échange et de l'incertitude* (Paris: A. Michel, 1996).

Hagen, R., 'Niklas Luhmann', in H. Andersen and L.B. Kaspersen (eds), *Klassisk og moderne samfundsteori* (Copenhagen: H. Reitzels, 2005).

Harste, G., 'Statsdannelse som emergens af enhed?' in A. Berg-Sørensen and M. Greve (eds), *Staten, det er: stat og politik: historisk, politologisk, og sociologisk* (Roskilde: Roskilde Universitetsforlag, 1998).

____, 'Early Reflexive Modernity', in M. Carleheden and M. Jacobsen (eds), *The Transformation of Modernity* (Aldershot: Ashgate, 2001a).

____, 'Jean Bodin om suverænitet, stat og centraldministration – enhed eller kompleksitet?', *Distinktion* 2 (2001b), 35–51.

____, 'The Emergence of Autopoietic Organisation', in T. Bakken and T. Hernes (eds), *Autopoietic Organization Theory* (Oslo: Abstrakt, 2003a).

____, 'Society's war', in M. Albert and L. Hilkermeier (eds), *Observing International Relations* (London: Routledge, 2003b).

____, 'La Décision', in H. Højlund and M. Knudsen (eds), *Organiseret kommunikation – systemteoretiske analyser* (Copenhagen: Samfundslitteratur, 2003c).

____, 'Fra statsræson til magtdelt retsstat', *Politica* 40/4 (2008), 425–41.

____, 'Niklas Luhmanns kommunikationsteori', in J. Helder et al. (eds), *Kommunikationsteori* (Copenhagen: Hans Reitzels Forlag, 2009a).

____, 'Politisk systemteori', in L.B. Kaspersen and J. Loftager (eds), *Klassisk og moderne politisk teori* (Copenhagen: Hans Reitzels Forlag, 2009b).

____, 'Kant's Theory of European Integration', *Jahrbuch für Recht und Ethik/ Annual Review of Law and Ethics* 17 (2009c), 53–84.

____, 'Linking Political Systems and War Systems: Systemic Risks, Paradoxes and Blind Spots', *Forum of Public Policy* June (2009d).

____, 'Kampen om Retsstaten. Bourdieu og Luhmann om oplysningstiden magtdeling', *Praktiske Grunde* 1–2 (2010a), 33–56.

____, 'Magtens autopoiesis', in L. Hilt, K. Venneslan and B.V. Mortensen (eds), *Luhmann og Magt* (Copenhagen: Forlaget Unge Pædagoger, 2010b).

____, 'The Improbable State', in P. Haldén and R. Agnell (eds.), *A New Agenda for State-building* (London: Routledge, 2012),

____, *Fra Korstog til Korstog. Krigens og Fredens Sociologi fra det 11. til det 21. århundrede – et perspektiv på selvreferentielle systemer* (Aarhus: Aarhus University Press, 2013).

Hutter, M., 'The Emergence of Bank Notes in 17th Century England', *Sociologica Internationalis* 31 (1993), 23–39.

____, 'Wie der Überfluß flüssig wurde: Zur Geschichte und zur Zukunft der knappen Ressourcen', *Soziale Systeme* 5/1 (1999), 41–54.

Johnson, H., *Frederick the Great and His Officials* (New Haven: Yale University Press, 1975).

Kantorowicz, E., *The King's Two Bodies* (Princeton, NJ: Princeton University Press, 1957).

Kennedy, P., *The Rise and Fall of Great Powers* (New York: Random, 1989).

Kindleberger, C., *A Financial History of Western Europe* (London: Allen and Unwin, 1984).
King, J., *Science and Rationalism in the Government of Louis XIV* (New York: Octagon Press, 1972).
King, M., and C. Thornhill, *Niklas Luhmann's Theory of Politics and Law* (London: Palgrave, 2003).
Knox, M.G., and W. Murray (eds), *The Dynamics of Military Revolution, 1300–2050* (Cambridge: Cambridge University Press, 2001).
Koselleck, R., W. Conze, G. Haverkate and D. Koppel (eds), 'Staat und Souveränität', in O. Brunner et al. (eds), *Geschichtliche Grundbegriffe*. vol. 6 (Stuttgart: Klett-Cotta, 1990), 1–155.
Krugman, P., *Return of Depression Economics* (London: Penguin, 2009).
Luhmann, N., *Zweckbegriff und Systemrationalität* (Frankfurt am Main: Suhrkamp, 1968/1973).
____, *Rechtssoziologie*, 2 vols (Hamburg: Rowohlt, 1972).
____, *Macht* (Stuttgart: Enke, 1975/1988).
____, 'Gesellschaftsstruktur und semantische Tradition', in N. Luhmann, *Gesellschaftsstruktur und Semantik*, vol. 1 (Frankfurt am Main: Suhrkamp, 1980).
____, 'Selbstreferenz und Teleologie in gesellschaftstheoretischer Perspektive', in N. Luhmann, *Gesellschaftsstruktur und Semantik*, vol. 2 (Frankfurt am Main: Suhrkamp, 1981a).
____, *Ausdifferenzierung des Rechts* (Frankfurt am Main: Suhrkamp, 1981b).
____, *Soziale Systeme* (Frankfurt am Main: Suhrkamp, 1984).
____, *Ökologische Kommunikation* (Opladen: Westdeutscher Verlag, 1986).
____, 'Distinctions directrices. Über Codierung von Semantikken und Systemen', in *Soziologische Aufklärung*, vol. 4 (Opladen: Westdeutscher Verlag, 1986/1987).
____, 'Lässt unsere Gesellschaft Kommunikation mit Gott zu', in *Soziologische Aufklärung*, vol. 4 (Opladen: Westdeutscher Verlag, 1987).
____, 'Staat und Staatsräson im Übergang von traditionaler Herrschaft zu moderner Politik', in *Gesellschaftsstruktur und Semantik*, vol. 3 (Frankfurt am Main: Suhrkamp, 1989b).
____, 'Im Anfang war kein Unrecht', in *Gesellschaftsstruktur und Semantik*, vol. 3 (Frankfurt am Main: Suhrkamp, 1989c).
____, 'The State of the Political System', in *Essays on Self-reference* (New York: Columbia University Press, 1990).
____, Das Recht der Gesellschaft (Frankfurt am Main: Suhrkamp, 1993a).
____, Beobachtungen der Moderne (Opladen: Westdeutscher Verlag, 1993b).
_____, 'Inklusion und Exklusion', in *Soziologische Aufklärung*, vol. 6 (Opladen: Westdeutscher Verlag, 1995).
____, *Die Gesellschaft der Gesellschaft*, 2 vols (Frankfurt am Main: Suhrkamp, 1997).
____, *Die Politik der Gesellschaft* (Frankfurt am Main: Suhrkamp, 2000a).

____, *Organisation und Entscheidung* (Opladen: Westdeutscher Verlag, 2000b).
____, *Die Religion der Gesellschaft* (Frankfurt am Main: Suhrkamp, 2000c).
____, *Einführung in der Systemtheorie* (Heidelberg: Carl-Auer-Systeme Verlag, 2002).
Mitteis, H., *Der Staat des hohen Mittelalters* (Darmstadt: Wissenschaftliche Buchgesellschaft, 1974).
Mousnier, R., *La Vénalité des offices sous Henri IV et Louis XIII* (Paris: PUF, 1971).
____, *Les Institutions de la France sous la monarchie absolue*, 2 vols (Paris: PUF, 1980).
Mukerji, C., *Territorial Ambitions and the Gardens of Versailles* (Cambridge, MA.: Cambridge University Press, 1997).
Olivier-Martin, F., *L'Absolutisme français & Les Parlements contre l'absolutisme traditionnel au XVIIIe siècle* (Paris: LGDJ, 1997).
Parker, G., *The Military Revolution* (Cambridge, MA.: Cambridge University Press, 1996).
Phytilis, J., *Justice administrative et justice déléguée au XVIIIe siècle* (Paris: PUF, 1977).
Pommern, J.F. von, 'Die Hofordnung Johann Friedrichs von Pommern', in B. Roeck (ed.), *Deutsche Geschichte in Quellen*, vol 4 (Stuttgart: Reclam, 1996).
Porter, B., *War and the Rise of the State* (New York: The Free Press, 1994).
Quillet, J., *Les clefs du pouvoir au moyen âge* (Paris: Flammarion, 1972).
Rey, J.-M., *Le Temps du crédit* (Paris: Desclée de brouver, 2002).
Richet, D., *La France moderne: L'esprit des institutions* (Paris: Flammarion, 1973).
Rogers, C. (ed.), *The Military Revolution Debate* (Boulder: Westview Press, 1995).
Rosén, F., 'Third-generation Civil–military Relations', *Security Dialogue* 40/6 (2009), 597–616.
Salisbury, J., 'Policraticus', in C. Nederman and K. Langdon (eds), *Medieval Political Theory* (London: Routledge, 1993).
Schmitt, C., *Der Begriff des Politischen* (Berlin: Duncker & Humblot, 1963).
Simmel, G., *Philosophie des Geldes* (Frankfurt am Main: Suhrkamp, 1981).
Smedley-Weill, A., *Les Intendants de Louis XIV* (Paris: Fayard, 1995).
Spruyt, H., *The Sovereign State and Its Competitors* (Princeton: Princeton University Press, 1994).
Stein, P., *Roman Law in European History* (Cambridge: Cambridge University Press, 1999).
Stichweh, R., *Der frühmoderne Staat und die europäische Universität* (Frankfurt am Main: Suhrkamp, 1991).
Stiglitz, J.E., and L.J. Bilmes, *The Three Trillion Dollar War* (New York: Norton, 2008).
Stolleis, M., *Staat und Staatsräson in der frühen Neuzeit* (Frankfurt am Main: Suhrkamp, 1990).

Tallett, F., *War and Society in Early-modern Europe, 1495–1715* (London: Routledge, 1992).
Teubner, G., 'Hyperzyklus in Recht und Organisation', in H. Haferkamp and M. Schmid (eds), *Sinn, Kommunikation und soziale Differenzierung: Beiträge zu Luhmanns Theorie sozialer Systeme* (Frankfurt am Main: Suhrkamp, 1987).
____, *Recht als autopoietisches System* (Frankfurt am Main: Suhrkamp, 1989).
Tilly, C., *Big Structures, Large Processes, Huge Comparisons* (New York: Sage, 1984).
____, *Coercion, Capital and European States* (Oxford: Blackwell, 1992).
Tocqueville, A., *L'Ancien régime et la Révolution* (Paris: Gallimard, 1967).
Weber, M., 'Die 'Objektivität' sozialwissenschaftlicher und sozialpolitischer Erkenntnis', in *Wissenschaftslehret* (Tübingen: Mohr, 1980).
Wilhelm, F., 'Instruktion und Reglement König Friedrich Wilhelms I. für das 'Generaldirektorium' 1722', in H. Neuhaus (ed.), *Deutsche Geschichte in Quellen und Darstellung, Band 5: 1648–1789* (Stuttgart: Reclam, 1997).
Willke, H., *Systemtheorie III: Steurungstheorie* (Stuttgart: Lucius & Lucius, 2001).

Chapter 5
Reflexive Governance in the European Union? An Example of Structural Coupling

Julien Broquet

Introduction

When applied to society, the polysemous term of governance can be roughly summarized by two main ideas: on the one hand, a growing interaction between different levels of decision-making, and on the other the enlargement of the panel of logics implied in attempts to steer society. This version of governance has been widely developed in relation to the European project and its evolutions. In particular, the specific coevolution and articulation of different levels of political decision-making in the European Union (EU) have catalyzed the use and development of this notion resulting in a plethora of academic research on the subject in terms of "network" or "multi-level governance."

We intend here to underline that this approach on governance deals with specific mutations of politics within the European context and with the societal echo of these mutations. We particularly argue that this approach can take great advantage of the so-called Modern Systems Theory (MST) as a consistent theoretical framework. Despite a first contact in some way problematic, numerous academic works argue on behalf of this rapprochement (for a review, see notably Brans and Rossbach 1997). Whereas we take here governance of society as strictly related to a political impulse, if not to the political system's perception of social reality, this chapter comes most importantly within the scope of reflections on the relation of the political system to its societal environment. Modern systemic works on governance then focus on the way steering may rely on structural couplings and on a form of societal reflexivity through which miscellaneous structural couplings earn themselves an inter-coupling connective value. These theoretical aspects will be developed in the first part.

Regarding the EU, one can witness a twofold ongoing process: the re-territorialization of social systems—previously referred to as "uneven Europeanization" (Jachtenfuchs 1997)—and the re-composition of various territorialized structural couplings between those systems. As territorialized processes, both rely on the political system and result in a peculiar "institutional design." In the theoretical context mentioned above, the issue of European economic governance firstly relates to the interpenetration of economic and political systems in Europe, to the re-territorialization of processes of coupling, and to specific organizations materializing these processes, which we propose to study in the second part. By doing so, we may have at our disposal some grounds to further discuss the reflexivity of governance processes in Europe.

Defining Reflexive Governance

We will first try to tackle the fuzzy notion of governance from the theoretical point of view allowed by MST. In the first section, we will observe how governance confronts MST in an ambivalent way. In a second section, we will go further on systemic differentiation and intersystemic relations, claiming for a three-way differentiation approach. Finally, the theoretical issue of reflexivity will be studied in order to underline how the object of European governance may benefit from an MST perspective.

Modern Systems Theory and Governance: Coordination of Coordination versus Irreducible Polycontexturality of Modern Society?

Despite common premises about modernity, a first rapprochement between governance and MST may turn out to be problematic unless we narrow the notion of governance. As a starting point, we may thus underline that this term covers a broad range of meanings, which in a very preliminary approach can be classified according to the scope and object of governance. One can then identify a common feature: Whether it applies to a micro, a meso, or a macro level, whether to a firm, an administrative department or to world trade, governance has to do with a waning of hierarchy. Top-down approaches may have shown less and less efficiency at regulating whatever field is concerned, resulting in a search for alternative modes of regulation.

In an MST perspective our interest firstly goes to a hypothetical governance of society, resulting from Luhmann's description of modern society as a global system, namely the totality of communications which from now on can be interconnected all over the globe (Albert 1999: 253). On governance of society, we may first turn to Mayntz (2003), who delivers a useful summary of the evolution of the idea of governance from a political point of view. This author identifies several extensions of the so-called "governance paradigm" as regards society, relating to a softening of the hierarchical approach and a widening of the scope, from local to European and global governance. Three main meanings of "societal" governance are thus evoked, respectively, "a new mode of governing that is distinct from the hierarchical control model, a more cooperative mode," "the different modes of coordinating individual actions, or basic forms of social order," and a "third meaning of governance [which] now includes the two more narrow understandings of the term as sub-types" (Mayntz 2003: 27–8). Mayntz insists on the broadest one, in order to release the analysis from the very idea of political structures of control (34–5). On the one hand, the focus on coordination rather than on constraint implies a very uncertain reception of the governance incentives by the different social targets. On the other hand, governance involves a wide variety of structures, and in particular involves nonpolitical structures. In other words, as governance theory should be able to tackle its object as political, and as a result of globalization and Europeanization, this shall be done without referring to a specific structure of political control.

This version of governance has indeed to do with various processes concurring to the reconsideration of the place of the state within modern society. Mayntz's crucial statement of "a growing disjunction between increasingly unbounded and far-flung economic and communication networks, on the one hand, and bounded political systems on the other" (Mayntz 2003: 36) is thus shared with numerous other authors. Brock's "debordering of the State" (2004), Zürn's "societal uneven denationalization" (2000), or Sand's "polycontextuality" of modern society (2004) all point at processes through which economic, scientific, legal, mass-medial, etc., communications increasingly cross territorial boundaries.

This "dissolution of the territorial congruence of state, economy and society" (Brock 2004: 89) is echoed in Luhmann's analysis as an increasing disjunction between territorial and functional boundaries (Luhmann 1982). More generally speaking, Luhmann's modern society echoes the context of governance when this author takes modern society as a *unitas multiplex*, the unity of the plurality of its subsystems. Since to him modern society is polycontextural, namely it implies as many social "realities" as functional systems, each system emerging and effectuating its autopoiesis through a specific medium and a specific positive/ negative code defines its own society and *excludes any other code* (Luhmann 1992). Modern society, then, shows a deficit of rationality, while social rationality takes place within each of these subsystems; social order is conceived as the contingent result of multiple functional rationalities and systems' interactions. In Luhmann's words: "Society itself has delegated all the problems and therefore does not possess any agencies that could, as a superfunction of perception, perceive all the functions. [...] [T]here is, in the strict sense of the word, no self-steering of society at the level of the entire system" (Luhmann 1997b: 49–50). Instead, social subsystems evolve within a peculiar context of mutual autonomy/ interdependency.

Whereas disjunction and debordering put the ability of the state to ensure the regulation of society in doubt (see Zürn 2000), we still take governance of society as a political process insofar as it has a view to regulate and coordinate social forces by the means of political decisions. We will thus?? comprehend?? governance as the different modes of coordination within society with a view to regulating society; following Jessop's works (2003) we may be more interested in "meta-governance" than in governance itself, the variety of coordination mechanisms being superseded by the attempt to coordinate these mechanisms. As a consequence, Mayntz's conclusion regarding the lack of a structure of political control remains more than crucial, for without a structure of control it still raises the question of a global structure of coordination. We have induced that MST is a fruitful theoretical apparatus to tackle governance issues, and yet it implies a radical skepticism towards political coordination of autonomous systems.

One can thus summarize the problem between governance and Luhmann's version of MST as follows: In Luhmann's view, social order as the result of a decentralized process of coevolution of social systems is nothing but highly contingent; society is unable to steer itself, and furthermore every steering attempt will collide with the unavoidable polycontexturality of modern society.[1] The difficulty in the rapprochement thus has to do with the radical aspect of Luhmann's position:

- Social spheres (here, systems) are indeed autonomous, but in Luhmann's sense this simply means that they *cannot* be steered since it is not possible by any means to override a system's informational and operational closure;
- Society is indeed the locus for various rationales at work, but these are mutually exclusive and *cannot be combined*: in particular, polycontexturality cannot be accessed through a functional subsystem, but may only be reproduced through the bias of its own code (Luhmann 1992). In other words, the autopoietic exclusiveness (*tertium non datur*) of the binary code banishes polycontexturality *per se* from every functional system.
- Society is certainly center-less, but in Luhmann's view this mostly implies that it is by no means to be understood as unitary, which is perhaps his strongest—and most debated—contribution to a theory of society, as to him there is no such thing as a commonly united *Lebenswelt*, and a communication event will take on different meanings within different social systems. As a result of this multitude of realities and values, society *cannot* be steered.

Yet, we believe that these postulates may overshadow other aspects in Luhmann's own work that may be of great interest to our subject here. Mentioning internal MST debates may be useful here.

Governance at the Stake of a Three-way Differentiation

We will now argue that alongside functional differentiation, territorial and organizational differentiations shall be duly taken into account in order give a proper image of the complexity of intersystemic coevolution. A governance perspective will provide us with a well-delimited angle of attack for such a broad question.

---

1   The interesting point is precisely that Luhmann mainly argues about the limits of steering which are directly implied by the very concept of autopoiesis. Given the informational and operational closure of social systems, all steering is an internal operation of the system, and consequently can be conceived of only as self-steering (Luhmann 1997b).

While steering issues may seem to be reducible to the claim that an autopoietic system is strictly closed, intersystemic relations have to be thought of in terms of mutual irritation. Luhmann's concept of structural coupling then relates to the perception by the system of the irritations originating from its environment to "the specific way the system presupposes states or specific changes within its environment, *and relies on them*" (Luhmann 1993: 86, my translation, my emphasis). Despite Luhmann's well-known argument that no guarantee exits as to the consistency of various functional subsystems' development (Luhmann 1997b: 76), this author conceives of intersystemic relations as fundamental regarding autopoiesis itself and societal evolution, even claiming that what lies in the system's environment can be more important than what is inside (Luhmann 1995: 212). In order to go further on structural coupling and governance issues, a few remarks on Luhmann's conceptual apparatus may be useful to justify a theoretical approach in terms of a three-way differentiation.

Firstly, one should note how Luhmann characterizes organizations as autopoietic social systems and, as such, self-referential, reproducing communication on the basis of their communications and constituted on the basis of a difference from their environment. This position has important consequences as regards the existing developmental link between organizations and functional systems: The emergence of functional systems comes with specific organizational systems. The former, as ungraspable rationales of communication reproduction, "do not constitute unities capable of action" (Teubner 1993: 131, my translation); organizations are thus crucial, for only organizations can communicate (Albert and Hilkermeier 2004), be addressed with communication, and be influenced via decisions. On the other hand, organizational communication can only acquire societal relevance through a functional echo (Albert and Hilkermeier 2004: 192). In other words, not only are organizations and functional systems not mutually exclusive, they are also complementary, and "neither the possibilities of the development of the societal system and its functional differentiation nor the possibilities of a technical rationalization of organizations can be fully exhausted if both system types are fused into one" (Luhmann 1990: 90).

Organizations and functional systems being both autonomous systems, their interrelations are to be thought of in terms of mutual perturbation *and* interdependency. The crucial point regarding organization and coupling may reside in the organizational use of functional mediums. Organizations are *multilingual* (Teubner 1996) in the sense that they can use several functional mediums: the organizational medium, decision, is always coded into a functional medium in order to gain societal relevance. A firm as an economic organization will not limit itself to economic communications: It has to conform to legal procedures, it may have to orient its decisions regarding political issues, it may dispose of a communication department to cope with mass media, and so forth. This multilingual characteristic puts organizational systems at a central place for intersystemic linking, as "they constrain [functional systems] to handle in parallel the specific information they produce from the same events" (Teubner 1996: 160). Organizations favor intersystemic structural coupling, and various self-steering processes within society may thus interact through organizational systems. Most importantly, one can argue that steering as a contingent attempt to affect the environment is made through and toward organizational systems alongside structural couplings. In particular, polycontexturality may be accessible only through organizations and coupling, and may never be accessed directly by an all-encompassing structure.[2]

Secondly, we may clarify the issue of territoriality in a world societal system. Whereas functional analysis is largely accepted as a basis for MST, the very idea of world society as an autopoietic system has been criticized even within this school of thought (see Kerwer 2004, Rossbach 2004). For us, from an autopoietist perspective, Luhmann's skepticism about self-steering of society is to be duly taken into account. However, while in Luhmann's view self-steering is clearly not a societal attribute, society, if taken as a system, should show specific systemic processes. Yet, self-descriptions and self-observations are limited to a functional level (see Luhmann 1995: 430–32). One could thus argue that society may be considered recursive since it reproduces its elements by means of its elements, while its reflexivity may be put to doubt while the societal system cannot "re-entry" itself the difference from which it is constituted. This point turns out to be crucial in our context: Society as a world system being questioned, Luhmann's exclusive focus on worldwide phenomenon may be reasserted.

Similar criticism can be made as regards the political system. On the one hand, Luhmann takes the political system to be global, and territorially segmented as a means to achieve consensus-formation (Luhmann 1982: 240). On the other, the political system is self-described through the semantics of statehood (Luhmann 1990), territorial boundaries are considered obsolete in relation to functional differentiation as the primary form of differentiation (Luhmann 1982), and international relations cannot fulfill the political function insofar as they mainly imply organizations (see Kerwer 2004: 203–4, quoting Luhmann). One can identify here a blind spot as regards the very autopoiesis of the political system and its world/state duality.[3] Due to increasing transnational irritations within its societal environment, and similarly to world society, the world political system may be torn between several self-descriptions, relative to several territorialities. Globalization, regionalization, and persistence of the state combine to bring about a complex imbrication of multiple self-descriptions within the global political system.

---

2 Therefore, in this view Jessop's claim for governance as "a revaluation of different modes of co-ordination not just in terms of their economic efficiency or their effectiveness in collective goal attainment but also in terms of their associated values" (Jessop, 2003: 104) could only be understood as an organizational, or inter-organizational process.

3 See, in particular, Albert's valuable suggestion according to which the complexification of an international political system and regionalization processes argue for the possibility that the political system is not yet a world system per se (Albert 1999).

Moreover, despite territoriality being a political artifact, other social systems are territorialized as a result of their coupling with a political system which has based its very autopoiesis on a territorial differentiation. Through coupling, territorialization may thus become essential to its own autopoietic reproduction (see Luhmann 1982: 241). Territoriality as a political construct has gained societal resonance because of specific structural couplings between the state-oriented political system and other functional systems of society. Territorial differentiation has been validated at a societal level whenever this specific territorial distinction has been used by other social systems. In this sense we believe that territory has a specific "societal relevance" or "connective capacity for social relationships" (Luhmann's terms; see Luhmann 1995: 392–3), which from a steering perspective is valuable as a vector for intersystemic coevolution. Most importantly, and still due to an essential coupling with the political system, organizations on which functional systems have to rely are historically territorialized, and as a consequence the latter are territorialized as well. As Esmark puts it, "the internal differentiation of the system of politics takes place through organization-building and [...] territorial segmentation always takes the form of territorial organization" (Esmark 2004: 136).

One can here identify a dual movement by which the political system differentiates itself through organizations, while the functional subsystems of society territorialize themselves through these very organizations.[4] This process was nicely depicted by Willke as the "tragedy of the state," where the state has to increasingly "rely heavily on the professional judgment of the very subsystems that supposedly were to be guided" (Willke 1986: 465). Such a departmentalized state (Harste 2000; see n. 4) has accessed polycontexturality through the development of various organizations, which by their very emergence as autonomous systems, and *a fortiori* as autonomous systems related to other functional subsystems of society, escaped from its influence.

Finally, we must return to the relationship between societal steering, governance, and politics. We will argue here that the political system may have a special affinity with societal steering. Within our still-Luhmannian perspective this certainly does not mean that politics performs operations of societal steering, but rather that the political system develops a specific self-description oriented towards societal steering. Self-steering and steering within society are indeed available to every functional subsystem, but the political system has "intervention claims" (Teubner 1993: 113) oriented towards society's integration (Brans and Rossbach 1997: 426–7). It may then develop a specific relationship with its environment, which could be understood as a *necessary illusion for the self-description of politics as an action system*, with a view to perform its function towards the societal system. Although this is not steering *per se*, in Luhmann's

---

4 See G. Harste, "Separating the Powers: Departmentality, Governmentality, Étatisation. Luhmann, Foucault and Bourdieu on the Differentiation of the French State." *Aarhus Universitet, 22–23 March 2000*, unpublished.

constructivist perspective the effects on society of this specific self-description of the political system and internal apprehension of its environment are of first importance (see, in particular, Luhmann 1997b: 47).

As to such an internally differentiated political system, the preceding remarks lead us to a specific transnational self-description oriented toward societal steering which we can refer to as governance. While Esmark argues that the state, through territorial segmentation, has made a certain form of control possible through territorialized organizations and territorialized couplings (Esmark 2004: 138–9), the context of governance, witnessing debordering and disjunction, amplifies a three-way differentiation. This context seems to further a departmentalization logic, a multiplication of organizations by which the wider political use of power implies its *dilution* (Harste 2000; see n. 4), and thus raises the question of the evolution of the political system of society regarding its very function of producing collective binding decisions. Whereas governance as political self-description results in societal effects through organizational design and structural coupling, what is at stake is the reflexivity of the processes it involves. For governance, the issue is still the risk of seeing these processes become inconsistent.

Defining Governance as Reflexive

We may conclude this first part with a section devoted to the "goal" of governance, returning, for that purpose, to steering. Even if one softens Luhmann's radicalism on autonomy and steering, societal steering can no longer mean (political) control. Instead, societal steering firstly aims at lessening negative aspects of differentiation(s), debordering, disjunction, and so forth, in modern society (see Albert 1999). At this point in time, following other authors of MST, steering tends more to the emergence of a social order than to an attempt of control: It relies on the self-regulation of the different components in society, and aims at coordinating these self-regulations. In a broad sense, societal steering and, by extension, governance aim at a form of *reflexivity of the social order*. The result is that this reflexivity issue is one more bridge between MST and governance approaches.

In order to first tackle this question in a not-too-modern-systemic-way, we can turn to Voß and Kemp (2006) and their meticulous attempt to define reflexive governance in their introduction to *Reflexive Governance for Sustainable Development*.[5] The point being the potential reflexivity of processes of governance, the authors identify here two crucial aspects: A "first-order reflexivity" has to do with the way governance may deal with its own implications, namely with self-induced problems of modernity (Voß and Kemp 2006:6); a "second-order reflexivity" refers to the cognitive aspect of such matters – how dealing with self-induced problems may affect the way these problems are tackled. This second

---

5   Whereas this attempt focuses on the concept of sustainability, the authors state very clearly that reflexive governance, and the way they tackle this notion, goes well beyond this peculiar aspect.

aspect may signalize the most crucial issues related to reflexive governance, insofar as:

> second-order governance consists of a procedural approach towards reflecting the interdependencies, understanding aggregate effects of specialized concepts and strategies, and engaging in the modulation of ongoing societal developments by establishing links and organizing problem-oriented communication and interaction among distributed steering activities. (Voß and Kemp 2006: 7)

Thus, second-order governance aims at enabling reflexivity through the different aspects of a multipolar governance. While it relies on feedback from numerous self-regulating social spheres, and on the ability to identify the interactions between these spheres and to contribute to their coordination, one should note that such a view undoubtedly supposes a political will for regulation and societal integration, and, most importantly, a coordinator. If governance supposes in this sense that one acknowledges the limits of unilateral action by a regulator (see notably Jessop's (2003) requisite irony), it still presupposes a regulator.

Turning now to a systemic view on governance, this has been the source of a rich MST literature already.[6] Within these approaches the authors may not have focused on a regulator, but on the reflexivity of regulation processes and their ability to cross systems boundaries. In other terms, one can single out as the central feature of an MST view of governance a form of societal reflexivity *where miscellaneous structural couplings earn themselves an inter-coupling connective value*. A few words on Teubner's reflexive law (1983, 1993) may help us to clarify this peculiar idea of reflexivity. According to this author, reflexive law has an integrative function, mainly served by a self-limitation of law which favors the reflexivity of various social components, their self-regulation and co-evolution: "Law realizes its own reflexive orientation insofar as it provides the structural premises for reflexive processes in other social subsystems" (Teubner 1983: 275). In other words, acknowledging social systems' autonomy often implies a self-limiting conception of steering: What is at stake is the self-regulation of the targets, an idea which is undoubtedly encompassed in the very notion of governance. There are only self-steering processes, which may however be influenced by governance structures. Whether or not autonomous couplings will give rise to the emergence of a higher level of determination is still a debated issue.[7] Luhmann himself takes double-contingency, the confrontation of self-referential systems, as the source of the emergence of determinacy from uncertainty, precisely residing in a connective

---

6   One can cite different analysis in terms of "reflexive law" (Teubner 1983, 1993, 1996), "meta-governance" (Jessop 2003), and "de-centralized context steering" (Willke 1992).

7   See, for instance, Teubner's "ecological recursivity" (Teubner 1996: 160), Willke's "reflexive rationality" (Willke 1992: 374), or Albert's "'second-order' functional subsystems of world society" (Albert 1999: 258).

value reinforced from every selection made by the interacting of the systems (Luhmann 1995: 116). Within a strict autopoietist perspective, this connective value may in fact be Luhmann's truncated version of a *Lebenswelt*.

As a conclusion, we may argue that a modern systemic analysis must keep in mind the polycontexturality of modern society and the subsequent limits of steering Luhmann has exposed. We believe that governance precisely implies to rely on the idea that polycontexturality can only be accessed through organizations and coupling, and more precisely through multiple interacting organizations: Governance would then express how governing a polycontextural society implies a polycontextural way of governing. Within this view, societal steering is thought of as social systems' coevolution in the shadow of a political impulse: Societal coevolution and potential reflexivity are jointly the result of political self-description, political intervention's claims, and self-steering of social systems mutually irritated through structural coupling processes.

Reflexive Governance in the EU

Despite Luhmann's view being deeply rooted in a European perspective, and despite the great potentialities of MST as regards European studies, Luhmann has shown at the very least little interest in the European Union as a regional process. As we mentioned, Luhmann takes society as global, with the consequence that "the autopoietic system of this society can be described without any reference to regional particularities" (Luhmann 1997a: 72). Yet, once the problematic issue of the exclusively worldwide character of society has been raised, it leaves the door open to a modern systemic observation of Europe as a huge laboratory of modernity. The diachronic character and the heterogeneity of numerous functional processes, the re-composition of complex, territorialized structural coupling and organizations, the processes of functional self-descriptions and their link with these organizations are all issues which one can identify as crucial as regards European processes. European studies and MST have encountered one another before, and we will rely on numerous valuable works here.[8]

European Studies and Modern Systems Theory—The Governance of Europeanization?

The key issue being the multiplicity and heterogeneity of European processes, one can identify the first problem of a world societal focus of MST as the theoretical status of the European Union (EU). The EU is neither society, nor a functional system, an interaction nor organization; it is not a social system *per se*, but expresses a peculiar interference between functional differentiation, territorial differentiation,

---

8   See, in particular: Albert 2002; Jachtenfuchs 1997, 2001; Sand 1998a, 1998b; and, more recently, Kjaer 2010.

and organizational differentiation. The multiplicity and heterogeneity of European processes traduces the way it is crossed by functional rationales, multiple political self-descriptions, and relies on specific organizations and structural coupling processes (Sand 1998a, 1998b). Within a dual MST/governance perspective, Jachtenfuchs (1997) has defined the EU as a dynamic multi-level system, a form of political system where governance is oriented towards collectively binding decisions. As we call for a more frankly polycontextural approach, we may be closer to Albert or Sand's view. Albert considers the EU as an agglomeration of dynamic multilevel systems (Albert 2002: 305), whereas Sand has focused on differentiated processes and organizational differentiation (see Sand 1998a). As regards our own approach, this insistence on organizations allows a multiple focus, namely on:

- a political impulse which favors a specific institutional design, major societal transformations being guided by international negotiations and treaties;[9]
- various functional processes which operate a filtering of this political impulse while relying on the emergence and self-reinforcement of specific organizations;
- the highly contingent coordination and coupling of a multiplicity of organizational logics.

We may here comment on Offe's statement that governance grasps "on the one hand, institutions (a "structure of rules"), and on the other hand, a process (that of steering), which is taking place in the framework of these institutions" and oscillates between these aspects (Offe 2009: 550). Our MST perspective precisely leads us to focus on institutions (organizations), on steering attempts (alongside other functional processes), and maybe most importantly on the coevolution processes between those institutions. In the preceding sections, we have insisted on territoriality, organization, coupling, and *their crucial interference*; this approach appears particularly promising as regards the EU. Despite a political bias, Jachtenfuchs is to be given due credit for his early works, which have provided strong bases to grasp the complexity of European functional processes as an "uneven Europeanization of social systems" (Jachtenfuchs 1997). Europeanization precisely echoes here the way social systems re-territorialize at the level of the EU, the key issue being processes of structural coupling which may be needed given the heterogeneity of these processes (see Albert 2002).

We may exemplify this, and in order not to impinge too much on later sections, the legal system seems an appropriate point of departure. We can turn here to Weiler and his well-known "transformation of Europe" (2005) to clarify our view:

---

9 At this point, it is clear how focusing on a three-way differentiation leads us to distance ourselves from Luhmann, who clearly states how little international relations matter to him (Luhmann 1997a; see also Kerwer 2004).

This author relies on a legal/political analysis which carries a great interest in underlining the autonomy of legal processes, the underlying political impulse, and the interdependencies between different functional rationales. Despite the fact that Weiler does not adhere to modern systems theory, he states that the political impulse to Europeanization has been followed by self-referential political and legal developments, namely a political decline (of the Community), and a legal constitutionalization of Europe. What is striking in Weiler's works is, then, his description of the Europeanization of the legal system through self-referential processes, in particular the development of constitutional legal doctrines within a federal European legal structure, gradually widening the Community's very competences. To that extent, the European Court of Justice as the Europeanized legal organization is of utmost importance, as was expressed by Stein:

> Tucked away in the fairyland Duchy of Luxemburg and blessed, until recently, with the benign neglect by the powers that be and the mass media, the Court of Justice of the European Communities has fashioned a constitutional framework for a federal-type structure in Europe. (Stein 1981, quoted by Joerges and Everson 2004: 164).

The importance of this organization has been widely supported by the self-reinforcement of the legal rationale, here a doctrinal logic which crossed national boundaries, and mostly crossed national and the Community's courts (Weiler 2005: 32–3; Joerges and Everson 2004: 164) and which undoubtedly echoes Luhmann's statement of an increased dissonance between territorial and functional boundaries.

Although we do not take the EU as a political system, in the theoretical view that we have developed the duality of a political system is of particular interest, as political impulses in the societal environment result in unattended outcomes with which the political has to deal. As a matter of fact, political Europeanization assumes an ambiguous character: Whereas the territoriality of Europeanizing functional systems is a result of structural coupling processes with the political system, the latter may witness the most tedious process for its own Europeanization. When looking at Luhmann's description of the political system, the crucial point may be the lack of state semantics at a European level. Moreover, as regards the political system's internal differentiation in terms of politics, administration and the public, (see Luhmann 1990), it cannot be missed that, as a result of a faulty supranational logic, *administration* (namely governments and the European Commission) has to a large extent been internationalized, while *politics* (the Parliaments) is still torn apart between a European parliament with limited powers and isolated national parliaments, and whereas the public (electorate) is still widely national (for example, Weiler 2005:8 4) or Europeanized in a very specific way, namely through euroskepticism. To that extent, political inclusion as a crucial feature of the political system remains for a large part a national process.

This is where European governance comes back into the debate: We have evoked Luhmann's dual definition of the political system, whose ambiguity may echo the political system's uneasiness whenever several territorialities are at stake. As mentioned, governance as a political theory, and as such a political self-description, has emerged in order to tackle functionally, organizationally, and territorially differentiated interacting processes. In Jachtenfuchs' words, again, European governance, and in particular network or multilevel governance:

> is not only an analytical concept but also a political ideology, a kind of micro-constitutionalism of the European Union, because it starts from the assumption developed in modern systems theory (Luhmann 1995) that society is constituted by a number of sub-systems which largely function according to their own autonomous logic. For efficiency as well as for normative reasons, the autonomy of these sub-systems should be respected. Hierarchical governance in such a setting is not a very promising endeavor. If one adds territorial subsystems to this perspective, one has an exact image of the European Union. (Jachtenfuchs 2001: 254–5)

In other words, governance and European governance may be understood as the political system's acknowledgment of its societal environment's autonomy, and the re-entry of this very idea within political self-description, in view of a more efficient "steering."

The European version of governance is specifically multilevel; namely, it develops a functionally differentiated aspect (Sand 1998b) which relates to the political system's perception of a societal environment, and a territorially differentiated aspect among member-states, Community, and lower levels of political decision. As such, the transnational characteristic of European governance may result in a competition with other political self-descriptions such as state semantics. The European materialization of the political system thus seems to prefigure a form of functional federalism where functional interdependencies replace hierarchy through sectoral governments and an exploded institutional order (see Boyer and Dehove 2001, Jachtenfuchs 1997, Sand 1998b). European governance is thus torn apart between functional logics relying on independent institutions (e.g. the European Court of Justice, the European Central Bank): on independent agencies of regulation, or on committees. Now, as regards their couplings, these institutions' relationships are thought of in terms of heterarchy, open coordination, multilateral surveillance, and so forth: governance aims at easing the interrelations between autonomous organizations and at favoring the emergence of a reflexive transnational, trans-organizational logic.

As a conclusion to this prefatory section, we may thus come back to (European) reflexivity, which European governance as a political perception of (European) society aims at favoring. What is at stake is thus the signifying value of an "empty signifier" (Offe 2009), namely European governance itself as a trans-systemic connective value, a "common" perception of a peculiar mode of governing. In Kohler-Koch's words:

> the permissive attitude of governments and the responsiveness of societal actors rests on a shared, if diffuse, understanding that a mix of complementary elements—functional representation, technocratic regulation, institutionalized deliberation—will increase the legitimacy of European governance. Each of these elements has been part of EC governance from the very beginning. (Kohler-Koch 1999: 18)

Whereas in Europe the dilution of power may expose the political system to a "tragedy of governance," the sheet anchor can only reside in the political system's ability to produce connective value and to actually favor reflexivity. In other words, we will argue here that a "European reflexivity," by definition a territorialized process, has to do with a political way of handling reflexivity. Whereas Luhmann insists on the political systems being *pares inter pares*, political reflexivity remains crucial to him, in particular when he states that the political system cannot just internally reproduce societal functional differentiation, for "politics would just mirror the division of society into economics, law, science and other functional subsystems, and hence reproduce controversial issues rather than decide them" (as exposed by Brans and Rossbach 1997: 427). In other words, the risk exists for the political system of a complete dilution of its medium in a functionally differentiated apprehension of reality.

A Few Prospects from Economic Governance

Theoretical milestones are now in place for a first assessment of reflexivity in the economic governance in the EU. From our theoretical viewpoint as exposed in the preceding sections, economic governance should be apprehended as a peculiar aspect of governance, namely one referring to the relationships between the political system and the economic system. For a first general definition of economic governance, a quote from Gamble may be useful:

> Governance denotes the steering capacities of a political system, the ways in which governing is carried out, without making any assumption as to which institutions or agents do the steering. For any social order like the economy, governance needs to be understood at two levels. First, there are the basic laws, rules, standards, and principles which provide the constitutional framework for governing. [...] Second, there are the techniques, tools, practices, and ethos of governing. (Gamble 2000: 110)

Despite the fact that the author is not tied to MST, several crucial issues regarding our own approach are gathered here, which we shall clarify before we start our assessment of European economic governance. Firstly, having defined governance as a political self-description with societal effects, and underlined that some form of political "control" could possibly result from a territorial matching of various organizations (Esmark 2004: 139), our first concern is the organizational materialization of the two functional systems in Europe, and the structural coupling processes between them. Secondly, and most importantly, this view also implies that the political and economic systems are not the only ones which should be looked at when studying economic governance. Gamble evokes a framework within which the so-called steering takes place, and which is also a part of what he calls economic governance. He thus refers to law and to a constitutional framework, stating that an economy relies on rules furnished by an "economic constitution" which:

> denotes the rules and norms which constitute an economic order, but also the modes, the institutions, and the procedures of governance, which determine the division of powers, the representation of interests, the locus of decision-making, the limits within which power is exercised, the boundary between the public and the private, and the objectives of policy. (Gamble 2000: 212)

The scope of this chapter will not allow us to go much further on economic constitutions, but this undoubtedly brings us back to the legal system and its role in political and economic systems' interpenetration. Concerning recent European history, the "economic constitution" undoubtedly echoes how a political/economic relationship backed by law has been crucial to the political project in Europe, or as Laurent and Le Cacheux put it, how "The European economic constitution embedded in the Treaty of Rome was the original constitution of the original constitution of the European community" (2007: 16). This reappearance of the legal system in the theory of political/economic interpenetration brings us back to polycontexturality and its *dual* aspect: On the one hand, functional systems as contextures cannot be brought together, but on the other hand the very autonomy of these systems rests on functional differentiation itself, which presupposes that other societal functions are taken care of. In a nutshell, radical autonomy comes with strong interdependency. Most importantly, polycontexturality still implies that, if mutual observation of two systems means two coevolving "monocontextural processes," their interpenetration can and will always involve an abundance of other social systems: Modern society as polycontexturality implies numerous, impenetrable, but permanently irritating social realities.

In Gamble's as in Mayntz's or Jessop's conceptions, governance is described as the use of a panel of coordination modes in a view of societal reflexivity. Economic governance would then consist of an attempt to coordinate different coordination modes as regards economic/political interpenetration. In our view, economic governance consists in a political will to steer the economic system as an acknowledged autonomous one (Jachtenfuchs 2001), which results in a specific institutional design and in attempts to favor reflexivity within this institutional design. Economic governance has to deal with territory, functions, and organizations, and with a trans-territorial, trans-organizational and trans-functional reflexivity. We propose here to tackle this somewhat overwhelming issue in a deliberately simplistic way, namely through an introductory typology of different modes of coordination within the previously introduced perspective of a three-way differentiated emerging Europe. Obviously, the theoretical status of numerous and various entities involved in governance may still be difficult to determine for such an ongoing process. However, such "coordination modes" materialize first through relationships between specific territorialized organizations, and in particular through territorialized structural couplings. This should be our entry point, and once this first step is taken the reflexivity of the processes involved in European economic governance can be discussed and hopefully assessed in a preliminary way. We will thus look first at the market as economic self-description, second, at independent agencies as potential macro-organizations, third at rules and fourth at open methods of coordination as structural coupling processes.

Market It is well known that governance's first alternative to hierarchy may be a reliance upon markets. In our precise case, one can undoubtedly assume that the political will to build Europe has heavily relied on the deployment of a single market in a functionalist view marked by anticipated spill-overs. With the Single Act in 1986 came a great step for the Europeanization of the economic system, and it has been argued that the implementation of a first economic constitution started in 1957 with the definition of a rule of free circulation of goods and the first evocation of a unified market (Laurent and Le Cacheux 2007: 17).

In Luhmann's view, the market is not a system in itself—namely, it is not limited to an organizational system or an aggregation of organizations dealing with persons or roles; nor is it a subsystem of economics per se (see Luhmann 2001: 47). Instead, the market constitutes an "internal environment" to the economic system and a self-referential circle: By concurring in the mutual perception of consumers and producers, this self-referential mirror allows operational self-reference, for what one does partly depends on what the other does (Luhmann 2001). While this conception of the market is related to a global economic system, our view on territoriality leads us to consider the single market as a territorialized self-description for a Europeanizing economic system.

The crucial point here is that markets are territorialized as a result of their dependence on rules and institutions emanating from political and legal systems. As Jachtenfuchs puts it, "the political goal of creating a European market requires a substantial degree of regulatory activity. In this view, markets are not self-constituting and self-stabilizing, but require constant regulation in order to constitute and maintain them" (Jachtenfuchs 2001: 252–3; see also Fligstein and Mérand 2002). To that extent, the Europeanization of the economic system via a single market still results from a political impulse, a "political-legal project" (Fligstein and Mérand), although it concurs with a self-referential process of the economic system. For Fligstein and Mérand, by leading firms to focus on a European market, the single market has indeed participated in the diffusion of a common view between economic actors in Europe, a "conception of control," "a worldview that allows actors to interpret the actions of others and a reflection of how the market is structured."

We may evoke here competition policy and the semantics of competition/ competitiveness which accompanied the internal market. Because of a polysemous characteristic, competition has an ability to encompass multiple political goals, and this semanticsmay have emerged not as a goal in itself, but as a political means: Competitiveness can be understood as states' competitiveness, firms' competitiveness, and as states' competitiveness through its firms, as it can imply interstate competition. In Wise's terms:

> Policy statements now stress efficiency, consumer welfare and competitiveness. The mission statement of DG Competition sets out a number of possible goals, including in the same sentence both the welfare of consumers and the competitiveness of the European economy. [...] [T]he Commission's 2004 annual report on competition policy, while mentioning the general notion of improving efficiency, highlights the Lisbon agenda to promote European competitiveness, being careful to note that "competition policy is not an end in itself, but one essential tool to achieve efficient market outcomes". (Wise 2005: 15)

Rosamond provides us with a great insight on this point: The economic European identity may be as important as the political one, insofar as it may lead to an attribution of meaning to the very idea of "Europe": "'Europe' cannot be competitive until such time as sufficient economic actors believe in 'Europe' as a plausible economic space. [...] 'Europe' will/cannot exist in any meaningful sense unless it is actively imagined" (Rosamond 2002: 161). Following the market's theoretical aspects, its fulfillment in Europe, the trans-systemic logics and semantics it has implied, one can observe that the European Single Act has been based on the use and perpetuation of functional interdependencies. To this extent, it may be described if not as reflexive, as a polycontextural project in the dual way we have understood this term.

Independent agencies Another well-known attribute of governance is the delegation of power to independent agencies, as a solution to the commitment problem and moral hazard in multilevel entities. While Luhmann defines economics on the basis of its money medium, and from our brief look at economic construction of meaning, from a MST point of view the single market may not be the first achievement in terms of a Europeanization of economics. The single currency is in this regard a major step, providing this system with a territorialized incarnation of its medium. The euro supports transnational economic communications and to that extent contributes to the making of an internal environment for a Europeanized economic system. More generally speaking, as regards the Europeanization of this system and as regards the consequences in terms of economic governance, the shock of the single currency is tremendous. Money is indeed no longer related to a sovereign state (or, here, to sovereign states), but within a monetarist perspective it comes primarily with an economic functional rationale. To that extent the single currency seems to bear a monocontextural approach, through which economic/

political differentiation is furthered. However, we should be cautious on this point, and a better way to present this may be that the single currency results from a political impulse, has been led through a dialogue with central economic actors, but resulted first in a technical compromise (see Snyder 1999, Verdun 1999). Most of all, this project has been set up through an agency freed from political pressures.

As to this respect, the EMU seems to have relied on a technical view of governance, taking its grounds from the growing interdependencies between member-states, notably as a result of the single market. The EMU has been perceived as a means to overcome the tensions issuing from a multilevel political governance through supranational institutions, for example as a way to avoid monetary crises or exchange crisis between several member-states (see Cameron 1998). One could thus see a furthering of economic/political differentiation in the statuses of the economic organization which accompanies the European currency, namely a European Central Banking System (ECBS) overhung by a very independent European Central Bank (ECB).

The ECB participates in the diffusion of the money medium and the reproduction of payments in a territorialized way and on the scale of Europe. Its independence is dual; namely, it applies both to means and goals: On the one hand the ECB defines its own objective(s)—a single goal in terms of inflation—and is not accountable to another entity that could change its statuses; on the other hand it also defines the means that are to be used to reach these goals (see Fitoussi 2002). This statutory independence is furthered by the disjunction we have evoked many times: Having to face not one but several public opinions and governments, the euro-system is widely freed from political pressures, and more generally speaking it is sheltered from social pressures which remain diffuse thanks to a widely state-centered political system (Artus and Wyplosz 2002: 29). From a more practical point of view, when the EMU *de jure* deprives states of various instruments, the ECB is even more *de facto* strengthened and able to capture competences that are not planned by the treaties, as Créel et al. (2007) have described regarding the euro-area change policy.

The organizational materialization of the EMU consequently strictly separates political and technical aspects. In particular, the ECB gets its legitimacy from its technical status, with a unique technical objective of inflation as opposed to employment as a political objective (see Jabko 2001, Williams 2005). At first glance the ECBS thus seems to be built as a negation of coupling, and does not seem to rely on a semantics with intersystemic connective value, but rather on a monocontextural/strictly economical one: "sound money and sound finance" (Hodson and Maher 2001: 721). Whereas this may result from a specific historical context (Snyder 1999), it can also be interpreted as a constitutionalization of the economic systems' autonomy possibly resulting from a three-way differentiation, while a transnational structure *de facto* increases the temptation to have recourse to expertise (see Verdun 1999). Political governance shows here a self-limiting aspect, when based on technical knowledge and social systems autonomy.

However, one may object that through the governors of national banks, or in Luhmannian terms through roles designed in relation to national organizations, the ECB functioning *may* be irritated by multiple territorialities (see Fitoussi 2002, Artus and Wyplosz 2002). Furthermore, the ECB may also be irritated through its objective(s) whose uniqueness may in practice be placed in doubt: Whereas ECB communication sticks to the unique inflation target, the institution may have turned more pragmatic when facing harsh economic situations (Artus and Wyplosz 2002: 119). Thus, borrowing Williams' conclusion, one may assert that the ECB may be considered monomaniac as to its unique objective and its independence, and schizophrenic when following unspoken objectives or secretly urging for legitimacy through a cautious relationship with other European institutions (e.g. the European Parliament; see Jabko 2001).

Rules As pointed out by Williams (2005), independent agencies imply providing crucial coordination mechanisms,[10] which is especially true in a transnational framework where territorial differentiation combines with functional differentiation and results in complexified consequences of separated powers. The formal independence of the ECB is backed up by the Stability and Growth Pact (SGP). The latter can be understood as a structural coupling process, and for several reasons. Indeed, it has different political and economic incentives: On the one hand, it contains fiscal policies from the member-states within the scope of strict rules to keep it from constraining the single monetary policy; it ensures the solvency of states so that the payment system is guaranteed, as well as the payment's continuity and thus the economic self-reproduction. On the other hand, it has a political goal to ensure that member-states will not use their membership to follow lax policies and allow the community bear the burden. The pact is political insofar as it stems from political decisions, but it aims first at the economic goal of preserving price stability and monetary policy. The first incentive for strict fiscal rules resides in the assumption that fiscal and monetary policies are interrelated, and in the will to avoid negative spillovers between multiple fiscal policies and a unique monetary policy. From a more general point of view, without a unitary political macro-organization the regulation of power is jeopardized, every decision being subject to tedious negotiations, divergent interpretations, or simply uncertain enforcement. A rule, as strict as it might be, may allow the reduction of those risks, and as such the pact institutionalizes the negation of political decision in order to protect the euro (see Fitoussi 2002: 43).

The major issue with the pact is thus rules-related: Are they well defined, transparent, simple enough, flexible, adequate relative to final goal, enforceable, consistent, underpinned by structural reforms?[11] We cannot go into detail here

---

10   "One major danger of the agency approach is that, however responsibly an agency fulfills its specified remit, related but unspecified concerns may fail to be addressed" (Williams 2005: 83).

11   See Kopits and Symansky 1998.

on the weaknesses and strengths of the pact. On the one hand, strict rules are supposed to compel member-states to fiscal discipline through simple, clear, and common objectives backed up by strong sanctions. On the other, the pact has been criticized mainly for the existing gap between its objectives (national solvency) and its rules (the deficit target being overestimated in relation to the debt target), the historical contingency of the digital targets, its uniformity vis-à-vis various national economies, its lack of incentive in a favorable economic situation (a pro-cyclic bias), and for problematic, potentially partisan enforcement, member-states being both judge and judged.

When looking at the difficulties in defining and reforming the SGP, one can observe how its consistency problem has to do precisely with its political–economic nature and its coping with a three-way differentiation. When it comes to reform, poor economic performances underline the rigidity of the pact, whereas modifying the objectives puts the pact's fragile credibility at risk. The definition and redefinition of the pact are about political compromise, and are symbolic for commitment to European rules. As Snyder states on convergence criteria:

> They express valid concerns regarding risks in respect of price stability, economic convergence, and putatively shared values of economic culture and, I would add, legal culture. They seek to reconcile conflicting interests, in particular by integrating the demands of the Bundesbank and Germany. They "serve as a try barrier or a screening device under incomplete information", . They signal preferences or even induce the revelation of preferences. Finally, they indicate the past and present "stability culture" of different countries. (Snyder 1999: 447)

To that extent, the pact has to cope with functional and territorial differentiation, and the latter is patent when it comes to the enforcement of the rules—that is, the soft-coordination aspect of the SGP implied by stability programs and multilateral surveillance.

"Open" coordination The discussion thus brings us back to intergovernmental deliberation. Having quickly discussed specific European organizations (e.g. the ESCB) and strictly institutionalized structural coupling (e.g. the SGP rules), we may continue by looking at more diffuse modes of governance—that is, at the so-called Open Method of Coordination (OMC). The OMC has been institutionalized through the Lisbon strategy as a means to turn Europe into the most competitive economy in the world. It relies, however, on numerous and various coordination processes, which have been mobilized before.[12] In Amtenbrick and de Haan's terms:

> The open method of co-ordination does not stand for a single mode of governance. [...] Rather, it describes a dynamic policy process in which a wide

---

12 For instance, see Hodson and Maher 2001: 720 as regards employment.

range of elements can be identified, such as the recognition of diversity, the broad participation in policy making, the coordination of multi-level government, use of information, benchmarking, peer review and peer pressure, the lack of any particular rule or single policy objective, as well as structured but unsanctioned guidance by the Commission and the Council. (Amtenbrick and De Haan 2003: 1079)

To that extent, the OMC echoes Jessop's meta-governance, a form of multilevel governance with a view to reflexivity: it is designed to take charge of negative spillover from sectored policies in a decentralized way and institutionalizes the coordination of various forms of coordination "in the shadow of post-national statehood" (Jessop 2006: 152). The OMC may thus constitute a change as regards three aspects, namely subsidiarity, flexibility, and legitimacy (Hodson and Maher 2001: 727). The OMC's flexibility relies on soft law and a non-constitutional characteristic (Szyszczak 2006: 490); it echoes territorial differentiation by institutionalizing subsidiarity, a form of autonomy for national administrations (Hodson and Maher 2001: 740); as for its legitimacy, a more specific example may be useful.

The most interesting application of open coordination within European governance is undoubtedly the Eurogroup, a body presenting the same characteristics of economic/political structural coupling as the SGP does,[13] whereas its theoretical status is more complex to define because of its informal nature. The debate motivated by the informal characteristics of the body and its functioning is indeed of greatest interest. A first view, as carried by Puetter (2004), states that this very informality enables the Eurogroup to play a specific role in European economic governance. According to him, this peculiar form allows the emergence of learning processes and of a common conception among member states:

> Owing to the thin legal basis of the Eurogroup's work, the evolution of the group's working method and its agenda takes place through informal agreements and the routinization of practices and procedures inside the group. [...] A further stimulus to frank discussions is the strict confidentiality of the debates. Ministers can voice criticism and think aloud about policy options. In particular, the debates on budgetary policy and the dialogue with the ECB would be impossible within a more open setting. There are no formal conclusions or minutes of the discussions. Press briefings by the Eurogroup president do not necessarily reflect the structure of the actual meeting, let alone the discussion behaviour of individual participants. (Puetter 2004: 858)

---

13 As an example: "In the words of Dominique Strauss-Kahn (1997), then French Finance Minister, its purpose was both political (to avoid the ECB being regarded as 'responsible for growth, employment, or even unemployment') and economic ('to match increased monetary interdependence by closer economic and budgetary co-operation')." (Pisani-Ferry 2006: 828).

This view contrasts with tenants of a strengthened Eurogroup, which would have to face the ECB in a more balanced institutional framework. Jacquet and Pisani-Ferry thus argue for more precisely defined responsibility, working methods, external visibility, and power of decision (2000: 26), referring in particular to the euro-area growth and the exchange rate surveillance as potential responsibilities for the Eurogroup. In other words, whereas the existence of the Eurogroup was consensual (Puetter 2004: 856; Pisani-Ferry 2006: 826), its potential form echoed two different visions of European governance (Pisani-Ferry 2006). We may note here that an economic government led by the Eurogroup remains contingent to the evolution of the political system in Europe. Within the scope of this article, Puetter's view may thus be the one to focus on now, considering transnational and trans-institutional deliberation as crucial in the Eurogroup as a specific coupling process dealing with territorial, functional, and organizational differentiations.

The main issue, then, is legitimacy as long as the Eurogroup's political membership still relies on the technical expertise of members who will continue to deliberate in an opaque way. Yet, according to Puetter, this very informality precisely allows for more open discussion and subsequently for more effective political deliberation (Puetter 2004: 860). Its major asset would then be the ability to produce shared economic ideas in a framework freed from strict intergovernmental constraints, which, according to Puetter, has proved fruitful as regards a common view on the SGP and the EMU. Major objections can be made here. The first regards deliberation itself, which appears to be limited because of the ECB's statutory independence and because the "free" discussion rests upon an economic framework that is already defined by the treaties. Moreover, as Hodson puts it, there is no guarantee that the deliberation will lead to a consensus, or that this consensus will indeed be enforced, insofar as this may depend on local authorities which may not have participated in the deliberation (Hodson 2004: 238). Secondly, we can turn to Schelkle and his pragmatic interrogation:

> Why is it that the Eurogroup—still held in high regard by the Commission, the European Central Bank, and supporters of stronger EU economic governance—has proven fairly useless as a preventive guardian of the Pact? A political economist thus wonders why the particular policy consensus formed in the Eurogroup is not self-enforcing. It casts doubt on the technocratic belief in consensus formation among policy makers, no matter what consensus. (Schelkle 2007: 277)

Following Kjaer, the OMC implies a "voluntary internalization of preferences and norms [...] amongst relevant actors in the member-states" (2010: 100). We may conclude this section by further exploring this issue.

A Few Insights From the Current Crisis

Actually, an overview of current economic issues in Europe may cast light on the issue of the emergence of contingent couplings. We have described both a technical compromise whose definition was delegated to epistemic communities (e.g. the ECB; Verdun 1999), and the political constraint on such compromises (e.g. the SGP). Polycontexturality implies polycontextural compromises: Notwithstanding the importance of interstate compromises, we wish to insist here on mutual irritation pushing toward "a reciprocal contribution to the selective constitution of elements" (Luhmann 1995: 215). Such compromises are forms of coupling dealing with a three-way differentiation, and can be considered more societal than political. European organizations (e.g. the ECB), and territorialized structural couplings (e.g. the SGP) may thus express the very contingency of such intersystemic coevolution. The current crisis may help us exemplify this.

First, if we observe the 2008 banking crisis, the way it struck and has been managed in Europe does reveal the multilevel characteristic of European governance, the multiplicity of couplings involved, and the necessity to rely on these couplings and organizations to develop an adequate response. Coordination was necessary given that governments or central banks could not face such a systemic crisis alone: Whereas the affluence of dubious assets may even have jeopardized central banks' independence (see Gros and Micossi 2008a), commercial banks were too big to be rescued by a sole government. The response has been to feel the way gradually, by implying multiple organizations. During the spring of 2008 the ECB injected assets into the interbank market to prevent credit shortage, which turned out to be insufficient to cope with the interbank coordination failure and lack of mutual confidence. Subsequently, governments have engaged in individual responses (e.g. guaranteeing private deposits) which denoted state-centered approaches, a delusional perception of commercial banks as national entities, and even more, a functionally oriented view of the crisis.[14] On October 4, 2008, a first interstate coordinated attempt failed within the so-called G4 (Germany, United Kingdom, France, and Italy). Eight days later, with Gordon Brown in attendance to propose a generalization of his own rescue plan, the Eurogroup finally agreed on common measures of state insurance of interbank loans and the recapitalization of commercial banks suffering bad conditions.

More recently, in March 2010, concerns emerged about the Greek debt being a threat to the single currency and about the subsequent confidence crisis which spread to other EU countries. EU governments agreed on a conditional rescue plan, the first in the history of the euro-area. The plan relied first on euro-area member-states' assets and for about one-third on IMF assets, and was finally

---

14 Gros and Micossi thus note how "the attention of our confused European leaders has also turned to other matters that may soothe disgruntled taxpayers but cannot help restore orderly market conditions—such as limitations on executive pay and risk-taking by financial intermediaries and mark?-to-market accounting rules" (2008b: 2).

implemented as a €110 billion package in May, whereas an additional rescue package of €750 billion in loans was agreed on by the euro-area member-states to be made temporarily available for other possible candidates. The genesis of this plan undoubtedly pushed EU leaders to face the contradictions at the heart of the EMU structure. Quite interestingly, as an additional measure and following the Commission's view, governments agreed on strengthening the SGP, drawing conclusions as to its deficiencies.Furthermore, an agreement was concluded on a sovereign debt default mechanism to allow member-states to default when their debts became unsustainable.

A quick view of some scholars' comments are useful here. Gros and Mayer (2010) have discussed the appropriateness of making the temporary bail-out plan permanent and called for a European Monetary Fund which could cope with the failure of member-states without endangering the whole euro-area. It has been pointed out that reinforcing the SGP has been the result of a misinterpretation of the crisis: There would be an increase in national debt as a result of unsustainable debt accumulation in the private sector, and of the latter's rescue by governments (Gros and Mayer 2010, De Grauwe 2010a). Most importantly, Paul de Grauwe (2010a) qualified the sovereign debt default mechanism as a "mechanism of self-destruction of the eurozone." Judging by these criticisms, the compromise may seem to denote a political contingency which fails to address the polycontextural issue here, as well as a misleading political functionally oriented view.

We may conclude by following Offe, who distinguishes the institutions and the process of governance (Offe 2009), and by underlining again the paradoxical nature of a governance as a political self-description which tends towards *depoliticization*:

> Participants in the discourse on governance tend to adopt the perspectives of negotiating organizational elites without taking into account the significance of conflicts of interests and values that take place in the public outside the negotiation room. (Offe 2009: 558)

Concerning institutions, the necessity to coordinate policies in the EMU to cope with interstate dependencies has given rise to a certainly depoliticized rule-based framework for fiscal policy (Fitoussi 2002), backed up by an open coordination mechanism for economic policy. The sub-optimality of Europe as regards the traditional criteria of Optimum Currency Areas (e.g. labor mobility, price/wage flexibility, a fiscal transfer mechanism, a shared business cycle) makes this necessity even more important. Yet, we have underlined the political contingency of the Pact, and this "rules-based framework for fiscal policy" has proved to be insufficient (e.g. Gianviti et al. 2010). As regards the institutionalized OMC and the Eurogroup, Szyszczak's interrogation remains unanswered as to whether the governance form that lies behind the OMC tends to *aggregate* preferences and organize their interactions, or, as Joerges, Puetter, or Hodson and Maher call for, leads to a *modification* of these preferences, to common views and common perception of policy issues (Szyszczak 2006: 489).

As for the process(es) of governance, the contingency and the tentative aspect of coordination in the above-described framework are striking. During the banking crisis, the first responses were decentralized and monocontextual; the coordinated response came later. As for the debt crisis, measures have been controversial and criticized for their contingency and short-sightedness. As De Grauwe (2010a) puts it:

> Under pressure from the German government, which is only concerned about its own reputation, the other eurozone governments seem to have accepted to do what sovereign governments should never do, i.e. to announce that they may debase their own debt. The sovereign debt default mechanism, if implemented, will lead the eurozone governments to downgrade their own sovereign debt. There is no surer path to self-destruction.

One can thus underline how power reappears in the depoliticized framework we have described. This very compromise is thus marked by the emergence of a German lead which by transferring its own priorities to the European level will "constrain others" freedom of manoeuvre" (Grant 2010). The variety within the EU can be perceived as a means to enlarge and improve the decision-making process by multiplying the options covered and selecting the good ones, but this variety also implies disequilibrium and contradictory reactions as regards heterogeneous economies and different national interests. The reflexivity of the political system being doubtful at a European level, the EMU has to cope with (at least partially) nationally formed worldviews, which imply (at least partially) nationally formed divergent macro-economic divergences.[15] Whereas Luhmann pays little attention to interstate relations, as regards European economic governance such issues appear of tremendous importance when looking at intersystemic couplings in Europe, *a fortiori* in a constructivist perspective such as MST's.

Conclusion

It has been argued in this chapter that within a MST view, reflexive governance first echoes the specific political conception of a self-limiting political intervention in a societal environment thought of as partly self-regulating (Jachtenfuchs 2001: 254), translated through self-steering programs aimed at facilitating intersystemic coupling.

Whereas "the condition for political control, even though in a limited sense, is a matching territorial organization in the different functional subsystems of world society" (Esmark 2004: 139), Europeanization as the re-territorialization of various social systems in Europe shows a problematic unevenness which might be coped

---

15 As an example, see De Grauwe on nationally formed "animal spirit" (2010b).

with through reflexive, multilevel governance processes. The evolution of the EU is then thought of as an ensemble of processes impulsed by the political system, but still acentric and polycontextural, emanating from an intergovernmental process and notably materializing in the treaties (Sand 1998a: 101–3). As regards the reflexivity of these processes, it appears that polycontexturality as *mutual irritation* between self-referentially constituted realities and as a form of coevolution of social systems, may be opposed to the much expected reflexivity potentially induced by political decisions.

When looking at European economic governance, polycontexturality's dual nature is striking. At first sight, economic governance in Europe seems to be constructed as a negation of coupling, notably as regards the EMU and its institutional design. However, a closer look reveals that the SGP's strict rules show a large amount of flexibility when it comes to their enforcement,[16] while the definition and evolution of these rules is contingent for political reasons. Moreover, the formal fully fledged independence of the ECB is established through a complex equilibrium with its environment: This independence, although statutory, relies on a rhetoric which must constantly justify the uniqueness and the technicality of the ECB's mission. Polycontexturality implies here that the economic system and its organization are constantly irritated by their environment, and the strict sectorization of EMU governance is thus put into doubt.

By focusing on a three-way differentiation, we have implied that polycontexturality was particularly marked by organizational differentiation, for multilingual systems, organizations—and *a fortiori* multiple organizations— allow access to a semblance of polycontexturality. The European context of governance is then characterized by an internal differentiation of the political system through an increased differentiation of the organizational level of society, resulting in increasingly diluted power. Reflexivity is perceived as a means to coordinate these organizations, and even more precisely to coordinate the various ways these organizations may coordinate. Within the European context, this is vectored through the OMC, whose reflexivity may, however, remain doubtful. The OMC seems to sidestep a persistent political problem and strong territorial issues, while legitimacy still rests on national bases and coordination processes depend on soft constraint and national transmission channels.

We can finally return to Luhmann regarding two issues. First, despite the fact that Luhmann acknowledges national specificities, he pays little attention to them (Luhmann 1997a), particularly in terms of historically constructed views. However, the debate as to whether or not the Eurogroup should gain a more formal status is the by-product of a two-sided view on European governance (see Pisani-Ferry 2006), and of divergent nationally constructed views on economic governance which are of great importance with regard to an historically contingent organizational design. Secondly, following Boyer and Dehove (2001) one may wonder if a fully fledged economic government in Europe could ever be satisfactory, given that we

---

16   E.g. when Germany and France overstepped the SGP constraint in 2003.

are no longer heading for a regulatory coordination, but for an executive one. In other words, governance issues in Europe may be more about political reflexivity itself than about a supposed politically impulsed societal reflexivity. As to this political issue, Luhmann's work leads us to question the reflexive governance as follows: How could an organization or a network of organizations, however suited to polycontexturality, agree to the accomplishment of a political function without politics? The current uneasiness of the political system in Europe seems to give this question a particular topicality.

References

Albert, M., "Observing World Politics: Luhmann's System Theory of Society and International Relations," *Millennium: Journal of International Studies* 28/2 (1999), 239–65.

―――, "On Governance, Democracy and European Systems: On Systems Theory and European Integration," *Review of International Studies* 28/2 (2002), 293–309.

Albert, M., and L. Hilkermeier, "Organizations in/and World Society: A Theoretical Prolegomenon," in M. Albert et al. (eds.), *Observing International Relations: Niklas Luhmann and World Politics* (London and New York: Routledge, 2004), 177–95.

Amtenbrick, F., and J. De Haan, "Economic Governance in the European Union: Fiscal Policy Discipline versus Flexibility," *Common Market Law Review* 40/5 (2003), 1075–106.

Artus P., and C. Wyplosz, *La Banque centrale européenne: Rapport du Conseil d'analyse économique* (Paris: La Documentation française, 2002).

Boyer, R., and M. Dehove, "Du 'gouvernement économique' au gouvernement tout court. Vers un fédéralisme à l'européenne," *Critique internationale* 11 (2001), 179–95.

Brans, M., and S. Rossbach, "The Autopoiesis of Administrative Systems: Niklas Luhmann on Public Administration and Public Policy," *Public Administration* 75/3 (1997), 417–39.

Brock, L., "World Society from the Bottom Up," in M. Albert et al. (eds.), *Observing International Relations: Niklas Luhmann and World Politics* (London and New York: Routledge, 2004), 86–102.

Cameron, D. R., "Creating Supranational Authority in Monetary and Exchange-rate Policy: The Sources and Effects of EMU," in W. Sandholtz et al. (eds.), *European Integration and Supranational Governance* (Oxford: Oxford University Press, 1998), 188–216.

Creel, J., E. Laurent, and J. Le Cacheux, "La politique de change de la zone euro ou le hold-up tranquille de la BCE," *Revue de l'OFCE* 100 (2007), 7–30.

De Grauwe, P., "A Mechanism of Self-destruction of the Eurozone," in Centre for European Policy Studies, *CEPS Commentary* (2010a). Available online at http://www.ceps.eu/ceps/download/3894 [accessed 24 November 2010].

____, "What Kind of Governance for the Eurozone?," in Centre for European Policy Studies, *CEPS Commentary* (2010b). Available online at www.ceps.eu/ceps/download/3747 [accessed 24 November 2010].

Esmark, A., "Systems and Sovereignty: A Systems Theoretical Look at the Transformation of Sovereignty," in M. Albert et al. (eds.), *Observing International Relations: Niklas Luhmann and World Politics* (London and New York: Routledge, 2004), 121–41.

Fitoussi, J.-P., *La Règle et le choix: De la souveraineté économique en Europe* (Paris: Éditions du Seuil, 2002).

Fligstein, N., and F. Mérand, "Globalization or Europeanization? Evidence on the European Economy since 1980," *Acta Sociologica* 45/1 (2002), 7–22.

Gamble, A., "Economic governance," in J. Pierre (ed.), *Debating Governance* (Oxford: Oxford University Press, 2000), 110–37.

Grant, C., "The Price of German Leadership," *Financial Times*, n. 16 (2010). Available online at http://www.ft.com/cms/s/0/1755538a-f1ba-11df-bb5a-00144feab49a.html#axzz16NWOR91p [accessed 24 November 2010].

Gros, D., and T. Mayer, "How to Deal with Sovereign Default in Europe: Create the European Monetary Fund Now!" (2010), in *CEPS Commentary*. Available online at http://www.ceps.eu/ceps/download/2912 [accessed 24 November 2010].

Gros, D., and S. Micossi, "The Beginning of the End Game" (2008a), in *CEPS Commentary*. Available online at http://www.ceps.eu/ceps/download/1536 [accessed 24 November 2010].

Gros, D., and S. Micossi, "The Cost of "Non-Europe"?" (2008b), in *CEPS Commentary*. Available online at http://www.ceps.eu/ceps/download/1552 [accessed 24 November 2010].

Hodson, D., "Macroeconomic Co-ordination in the Euro-area: The Scope and Limits of the Open Method," *Journal of European Public Policy* 11/2 (2004), 231–48.

Hodson, D., and I. Maher, "The Open Method as a New Mode of Governance: The Case of Soft Economic Policy Co-ordination," *Journal of Common Market Studies* 39/4 (2001), 719–46.

Jabko, N., "Expertise et politique à l'âge de l'euro : la banque centrale européenne sur le terrain de la démocratie," *Revue française de science politique* 51/6 (2001), 903–31.

Jachtenfuchs, M., *Democracy and Governance in the European Union* (1997). Available online at http://eiop.or.at/eiop/pdf/1997-002.pdf [accessed 24 November 2010].

____, "The Governance Approach to European Integration," *Journal of Common Market Studies* 39/2 (2001), 245–64.

Jacquet, P., and J. Pisani-Ferry, "La coordination des politiques économiques dans la zone euro: bilan et proposition," in Conseil d'analyse économique (ed.), *Questions européennes* (Paris: La Documentation française, 2000), 11–40.

Jessop, B., "Governance and Meta-governance: On Reflexivity, Requisite Variety and Requisite Irony," in H. P. Bang (ed.), *Governance as Social and Political Communication* (Manchester: Manchester University Press, 2003), 101–16.

____, "State- and Regulation-Theoretical Perspectives on the European Union and the Failure of the Lisbon Agenda," *Competition and Change* 10/2 (2006), 141–61.

Joerges, C., and M. Everson, "Law, Economics and Politics in the Constitutionalization of Europe," in E. O. Eriksen et al. (eds.), *Developing a Constitution for Europe* (London; New York: Routledge, 2004), 162–79.

Kerwer, D., "Governance in a World Society," in M. Albert et al. (eds.), *Observing International Relations: Niklas Luhmann and World Politics* (London and New York: Routledge, 2004), 196–207.

Kjaer, P., *Between Governing and Governance: On the Emergence, Function and Form of Europe's Post-national Constellation* (Oxford and Portland: Hart, 2010).

Kohler-Koch, B., "The Evolution and Transformation of European Governance," in B. Kohler-Koch et al. (eds.), *The Transformation of Governance in the European Union* (London and New York: Routledge, 1999), 14–35.

Kopits, G., and S. Symansky, 1998. *Fiscal Policy Rules,* IMF Occasional Paper 162 (Washington D.C.: International Monetary Fund).

Laurent, E., and J. Le Cacheux, *What (Economic) Constitution Does the EU Need?* (2007). Available online at http://www.ofce.sciences-po.fr/pdf/dtravail/WP2007-04.pdf [accessed 24 November 2010].

Luhmann, N., "Territorial Borders as System Boundaries," in R. Strassoldo et al. (eds.), *Cooperation and Conflict in Border Areas* (Milan: Franco Angeli, 1982), 235–44.

____, *Political Theory in the Welfare State* (Berlin and New York: De Gruyter, 1990).

____, "The Coding of the Legal System," in G. Teubner et al. (eds.), *State, Law, Economy as Autopoietic Systems* (Milan: Giuffrè, 1992), 145–85.

____, "Clôture et couplage," in A.-J. Arnaud et al. (eds.), *Niklas Luhmann observateur du droit* (Paris: Librairie générale de droit et de jurisprudence, 1993), 73–95.

____, *Social Systems* (Stanford: Stanford University Press, 1995).

____, "Globalization or World Society: How to Conceive of Modern Society?," *International Review of Sociology* 7/1 (1997a), 67–80.

____, "Limits of Steering," *Theory, Culture and Society* 14/1 (1997b), 41–57.

____, "L'économie de la société comme système autopoietique," *Sciences de la société* 52 (2001), 23–59.

Mayntz, R., "New Challenges to Governance Theory," in H. P. Bang (ed.), *Governance as Political Communication* (Manchester: Manchester University Press, 2003), 27–39.

Offe, C., "Governance: An 'Empty Signifier'?," *Constellations* 16/4 (2009), 550–62.

Pisani-Ferry, J., "Only One Bed for Two Dreams: A Critical Retrospective on the Debate over the Economic Governance of the Euro-area," *Journal of Common Market Studies* 44/4 (2006), 823–44.

Puetter, U., "Governing Informally: The Role of the Eurogroup in EMU and the Stability and Growth Pact," *Journal of European Public Policy* 11/5 (2004), 854–870.

Rosamond, B., "Imagining the European Economy: 'Competitiveness' and the Social Construction of 'Europe' as an Economic Space," *New Political Economy* 7/2 (2002), 157–77.

Rossbach, S., "'Corpus mysticum': Niklas Luhmann's Evocation of World Society," in M. Albert et al. (eds.), *Observing International Relations: Niklas Luhmann and World Politics* (London and New York: Routledge, 2004), 44–56.

Sand, I-J., "Understanding the EU/EEA as Systems of Functionally Different Processes: Economic, Political, Legal, Administrative and Cultural," in P. Fitzpatrick et al. (eds.), *Europe's Other: European Law between Modernity and Postmodernity* (Aldershot: Ashgate, 1998a), 93–109.

____, "Understanding the New Forms of Governance: Mutually Interdependent, Reflexive, Destabilised and Competing Institutions," *European Law Journal* 4/3 (1998b), 271–93.

____, "Polycontextuality as an Alternative to Constitutionalism," in C. Joerges et al. (eds.), *Transnational Governance and Constitutionalism* (Oxford and Portland: Hart, 2004), 41–65.

Schelkle, W., "Book Review: *The Eurogroup. How a Secretive Circle of Finance Ministers Shape European Economic Governance*. By U. Puetter. Manchester and New York: Manchester University Press, 2006," *European Law Journal* 13/2 (2007), 276–7.

Snyder, F., "EMU Revisited: Are We Making a Constitution? What Constitution Are We Making?" in P. Craig et al., *The Evolution of EU Law* (Oxford: Oxford University Press, 1999), 417–77.

Szyszczak, E., "Experimental Governance: The Open Method of Coordination," *European Law Journal*, 12/4 (2006), 486–502.

Teubner, G., "Substantive and Reflexive Elements in Modern Law," *Law and Society Review* 17/2 (1983), 239–85.

____, "La régulation de la société par le droit réflexif," in G. Teubner (ed.), *Le Droit, un système autopoietique* (Paris: Presses universitaires de France, 1993), 101–57.

____, "Régulation et pluralité juridique: comment la politique prélève la plusvalue normative de la circulation de l'argent," in G. Teubner (ed.), *Droit et réflexivité* (Paris: Librairie générale de droit et de jurisprudence, 1996), 149–70.

Verdun, A., "The Role of the Delors Committee in the Creation of EMU: An Epistemic Community?," *Journal of European Public Policy* 6/2 (1999), 308–28.

Voß, J.-P., and R. Kemp, "Introduction: Sustainability and Reflexive Governance," in J.-P. Voß et al. (eds.), *Reflexive Governance for Sustainable Development* (Cheltenham; Northampton, MA: Edward Elgar, 2006).

Weiler, J.H.H., "The Transformation of Europe," in J. H. H. Weiler (ed.), *The Constitution of Europe: "Do the clothes have an emperor?" and Other Essays on European Integration*, 5th edn. (Cambridge: Cambridge University Press, 2005), 10–101.

Williams, G., "Monomaniacs or Schizophrenics? Responsible Governance and the EU's Independent Agencies," *Political Studies* 53/1 (2005), 82–99.

Willke, H., "The Tragedy of the State. Prolegomena to a Theory of the State in Polycentric Society," *Archiv für Rechts- und Sozialphilosophie* 72/4 (1986), 455–67.

____, "Societal Guidance through Law?," in G. Teubner et al. (eds.), *State, Law, Economy as Autopoietic Systems* (Milan: Giuffrè, 1992), 353–87.

Wise, M., *Competition Law and Policy in the European Union* (2005). Available online at http://www.oecd.org/dataoecd/7/41/35908641.pdf [accessed 24 November 2010].

Zürn, M., "Multilevel Governance: on the State and Democracy in Europe," in M. Albert et al. (eds.), *Civilizing World Politics: Society and Community beyond the State* (Lanham: Rowman and Littlefield, 2000), 149–68.

Chapter 6

Contract as a Form of Intersystemic Communication

Niels Åkerstrøm Andersen

Contracts as Communication

In his renowned article "Des tours de Babel," Derrida writes:

> The debt does not commit living subjects but the names at the edge of the language or, more rigorously, the trait that contracts the relation of the aforementioned living subject to his name, insofar as the latter stays at the edge of the language. And this trait would be that of the *to-be-translated* from one language to the other, from this edge to the other of the proper name. (Derrida 2007: 208)

Derrida goes on to state that this translation contract "would be the contract itself, the absolute contract, the contract for all the contracts, that which allows any contract to be what it is" (Derrida 2007: 209).

Professor of law Gunther Teubner has found inspiration in these lines for the understanding of modern contracting. For Teubner the importance of contracting is not so much the mutual obligation of persons, but the linking of a multitude of world systems of communication:

> Global society consists of a plurality of contracting worlds which display the double meaning of this expression. Various social systems are contracting, shrinking, specializing toward only one orientation, one function, one code externalizing everything simultaneously. The regulation of their interrelations is not governed by hierarchical coordination but by heterarchical contracting. Contracting that is supposed to play its multifaceted role today must do so under the new condition of fragmentation of global society into a plurality of specialized discourses. (Teubner 2000: 403)

What Teubner does with a little help from Derrida is to push contract theory from the level of inter-personality to the level of inter-discursivity. Contracts allow not only for people but more importantly for languages to meet. Contracts are always contracts between languages, but the contract does not facilitate the transport of content between those languages, or communication between them. In contracts, languages meet only as tangential circles in one fleeting single point. Thus contracts should not simply be perceived as communication, but as the linking of heterogeneous communications which cannot communicate with one another.

Teubner focuses on the possible legal consequences of this move from inter-personality to inter-discursivity, including the possibilities for defining discursive rights. I would like instead to develop a broader communications theoretical point to make this move while maintaining a Luhmannian systems theory approach,

The reason to do so is empirical. I believe that we are faced with new communicative complexity, which compels us to look for a new theoretical language for the observation of processes and roles regarding contracting and the communicative afterlife of contracts. A significant number of studies show that new types of conflicts around contracts have emerged and that many of these conflicts intensify as a result of detailed contracting undermining trust relations (Neu 1991; Andersen 2000; Seal and Vincent-Jones 1997).

When a public municipality outsources home care to a private company, for example, the contract should be read not only as an economic and legal commitment. The contract also has to make political sense as the implementation of a particular policy and political decision. Moreover, the contract has to make sense within the care communication responsible for translating the contractual definition of services into care practice. But economists and lawyers negotiating and writing the contract are seldom aware of this. They write the contract to meet legal and economic objectives, which is complex enough in itself. Several examples from the outsourcing of home care show that contracts by no means always allow for a care-based reading. When care performances become specified in detail so that each home care operation is defined both in terms of content and duration, it means that the care communication is precluded from providing the contract with a meaningful afterlife, and home care workers are no longer caregivers but simply service workers. With exact definitions of the amount of minutes allotted to help with tooth brushing, shaving, hair washing, etc., there is literally "not much to talk about" in terms of care. Care becomes simplified into service (Højlund 2009; la Cour and Højlund 2003). And this again limits politics to decisions among service packages rather than discussion about what makes a worthy old age. Accordingly, in modern contracting, contracts become relevant events to a variety of communicative systems, and this increases the necessity of a communication theoretical perspective on contract.

Of course, a communication approach has not been totally absent. Communication was always an aspect of legal contract theory as discussions of the relation between the original text and its interpretations by contractors. But it was precisely only an aspect of a larger legal and economic whole. This chapter will try to outline a communications theory of contract, which takes as its points of departure Niklas Luhmann's theory of social systems of communication, Derrida's ideas on translation contracts, and Gunther Teubner's extensive work on the subject, which highlights contracts as inter-discursive coupling.

The chapter will begin by addressing legal theory and its discussion of the communications aspect of contracting. Then it will move toward a systems theoretical alternative to explore what systems theory has to offer regarding the complexity of contract communication. My guiding idea is based on Teubner's thesis about contract as inter-discursivity. Finally it will be argued that the new multiplicity of contract has significant impact on organizational systems forcing them in the direction of heterophony.

The Discourse of Discourse in Legal Discourse about Contracts

In what follows it will be observed how legal contract theory develops concepts regarding contracts as communication. This section will not review every discussion in this field but simply highlight three perspectives. The first perspective is Macneil's theory of relational contracts. Ian R. Macneil opens up the question of the impact of communication on contract formation. He also poses a question about complexity management in contracts. His goal is to include society in contract development as an extra-contractual element. The second perspective is Stewart Macaulay who, in addition to having an eye for the question of communication, opens up a kind of perspectivism with regard to the understanding of the specific life and interpretation of contracts. The third perspective is the discussion of reflexive elements in contracts. This perspective is highly heterogeneous and includes people like Hugh Collins, Peter Vincent-Jones and Peter Campbell.

Ian R. Macneil and the Concept of Promise

Ian R. Macneil's two most significant works are the article "The many futures of contracts" and the book *The New Social Contract*, from 1974 and 1980 respectively (see also Macneil 1985, 1987, 1988, 2003). Both create a firm connection between questions of contract and questions of communication.

Contract is defined as a legally sanctioned promise. A promise is fundamentally a particular form of communication: "Present communication of a commitment to future engagement in a specific reciprocal measured exchange" (Macneil 1974: 715). Contracts, he argues, represent a "projection of exchange into the future" (Macneil 1974: 712–13). Thus, promises become a question of a presentification of the future. This is what all promise communication is about: for the communication parties to install the future in the present as the premise of acting in the present.

A promise, writes Macneil, "is an affirmation of the power of the human will to affect the future. It affirms that an individual can affect the future now" (Macneil 1980: 6–7). It is precisely this temporal function of the contract that becomes constitutive of the social character of the promise. A promise both limits and individualizes freedom. It individualizes it by installing the participants of the promise communication as individuals with freedom of action to limit their freedom. It limits it by reducing the individuals' future dispositions:

Thus, the first two elements of promise in its contractual context are the will of two or more individuals with beliefs in the power of one to affect the future – subject to the linkage of the social matrix essential to exchange. A third element of promise is the doing of something now to limit the choices otherwise available to the promisor in the future. This is part of the notion of commitment encompassed in the Restatement definition. For example, a person entering an agreement to sell a house may no longer choose to sell it elsewhere without suffering the consequences of breaching his promise. These may be as intangible as a loss of reputation or as concrete as a judgment awarding damages (Macneil 1980: 6–7)

Promises, however, represent incomplete communication: certain limits apply to the presentification of the future as the premise for individual present and future action:

First of all, promises are condemned to being fragmentary: "Promises-e.3 are inherently fragmentary [...] Thus, promises can never encompass more than a fragment of the total situation" (Macneil 1980: 8). Attention is always limited since one cannot focus on everything. This also applies to promises, which become fragmentary as a result.

Secondly, sent communication is not the same as received communication: "a promise made and a promise heard are two different things," writes Macneil (1974: 728). Thus, he adopts a first-order cybernetic perspective on contract. He implies that communication consists of A coding and sending a message, which B receives and decodes, and this coding and decoding do not necessarily coincide. In fact, he points out that they can never coincide, which has dramatic implications for the possibility of promise. He writes: "Every promise is always two promises, the sender's and the receiver's" (Macneil 1980: 9). This means giving up the unity of the promise: "When differences between saying and hearing occur, [...] there is no way in which the future of the promise can be viewed as identical in all respects to the present world of reality because in the present there are *two* promises, declarer's and hearer's, and with them *two* contradictory futures, and both cannot be brought into a single present as present" (Macneil 1974: 728–9).

The problem is how promises can become possible when promises seem impossible. Macneil's answer is twofold. First, promise-based exchange presupposes non-promise-based exchange. The order of promise is defined as dependent on an order, which is not constituted by promise. Second, Macneil tells us that there are a number of alternatives to the promise as exchange projector, such as tradition, status, habits, and hierarchical commands. Then he adds that these alternative exchange projectors often exist alongside promises (Macneil 1980: 6–8). And finally he argues, "promises have always been accompanied by burdens of impurities of incompleteness of content, and communication, objectivity, implication, custom, usage, and above all, 'ongoingness' and its accompanying clouds of imprecision and future uncertainty" (Macneil 1974: 731). And he adds, "promise, even at its transactional narrowest, is always shadowed by non-promissory accompaniments" (Macneil 1974: 731). This adds up to a peculiar figure, which makes the possibility of promise dependent on non-promises: "Once promises are viewed as less than absolute, other exchange-projectors must inevitably come into play" (Macneil 1980: 9).

Having established this figure of argumentation, the distinction between promise-based and non-promise-based exchange is replaced by a distinction between discrete contracts and relational contracts.

Discrete contracts are defined as transactional relations, which are impersonal and without duration. Discrete contracts represent pure promises, pure transactions characterized by the fact that, apart from the exchange, no relations exist between the parties. Hence they are also called transactional contracts (Macneil 1974: 721–6).

Relational contracts, on the other hand, are defined as personal and permanent (Macneil 1974: 721). Relational contracts establish relational relations, which comprise whole persons, deep communication, and non-economic personal fulfillment (Macneil 1974: 723).

This makes it possible to construct a continuum of contracts with the transactional and the relational respectively as the two poles. Contracts can be more or less relational and transactional, more or less personal, more or less deep. However, Macneil's assertion is that any contract, however discrete, involves relations and hence must be relational (Macneil 1980: 10)! Discrete contracts are not relational relations, which occur in the relational. Society is fundamentally constituted relationally. Discrete transactional contracts are not. Thus, discrete contracts come to represent a form of occurrence of the nonsocial in the social on the terms of the social.

Macaulay and the Perspective-dependence of Contract

Like Macneil, Stewart Macaulay takes a communications-theoretical approach to contract law, but he adds a form of perspectivism, which expands the question of the possibility of fixing the promise.

This discussion will begin, however, by presenting the communications approach in its closest proximity to that of Macneil. In his article "The real and the paper deal: Empirical pictures of relationships, complexity and the urge for transparent simple rules," Macaulay looks at contracts from a communications perspective. It is, however, a communications perspective very different from Macneil's. To Macaulay, it is not simply a question of sending and receiving a message about a promise. Rather, it is a question of the contract as some kind of nexus between a flow of communication participants:

> Those who negotiate the deal often are not the people who draft the written document recording it. Still others must perform the contract. This opens the possibility that, for example, a firm's lawyers may have different assumptions and expectations than its purchasing agents, sales people and engineers. Strategy may be involved too. If I want a clause that says if event X takes place, then

consequence Y will follow, you may demand something in exchange that I do not want to give you. When I anticipate this, it may be better to avoid raising the issue in negotiations and hope that the matter can be resolved if event X ever takes place [...] In short, there are many reasons why the paper deal will fail to capture the real deal. As a matter of fact, there is a "text between the lines". (Macaulay 2003: 54–5)

What Macaulay means by "real deal" is: "both those actual expectations that exist in and out of a written contract and the generalised expectation that a trading partner will behave reasonably in solving problems as they arise" (Macaulay 2003: 54, note 6). Here, Macaulay opens his study of contract law up toward the discussion of the formation of expectations in contract communication, both in the development of the contract as well as in the contract's many communicative afterlives.

This has consequences for the understanding of contracts:

> Contracts are always more than the contract document. We have long known the many reasons for this: Words do not have a fixed meaning that every speaker of the language will translate the same way. We create the meaning of written language by bringing to the words some measure of context, background assumptions, our experiences, and, too often, our bias, ignorance and stupidities [...] Also, it is very hard to bring the future to the present and provide that X will happen if event Y takes place. Our ability to predict the future is limited, and even careful business people often leave gaps in written contracts. The world changes and surprises us: Wars break out in places where we do not expect them; or our contract may have dealt with a war but left open what happens when the direct effect of a major terrorist attack makes performance much more costly; OPEC drives up energy costs unexpectedly; new technologies, often involving computers, change things so that an older contract no longer makes sense. Even when we can foresee that it is possible that something might happen, there are limits on the time that we can or should spend on trying to provide for all contingencies in our contracts. (Macaulay 2003: 53–5)

Unlike Macneil, Macaulay is highly aware of the fact that contract communication is not simply communication between different individuals with different intents. It is also communication between different perspectives on the world, represented in Macaulay by professions. Macaulay is exceedingly aware of the internal differentiation of companies into particular functions and appertaining professions. This interest and focus date back to the early 1960s. As early as 1963, Macaulay illustrates in a number of interviews that different people think about very different things when referring to a contract. He also implies that people's thoughts are tied to their different roles in the company: the salesperson, financial workers, purchasing agent, and lawyer (Macaulay 1963a: 13–40). Businesspeople prefer to believe a man's word even when a transaction involves serious risks. Lawyers in turn often speak with regret about this attitude. Macaulay refers to a quote from an interview with a lawyer: "Often businessmen do not feel that they have 'a contract'—rather they have an order. They speak about 'canceling the order' rather than about 'breaching our contract'" (Macaulay 1963b: 61). He also quotes a businessman: "You can settle any dispute if you keep the lawyers and accountants out of it. They do not understand the give-and-take needed in business" (Macaulay 1963b: 61). Macaulay concludes by saying that detailed contract planning and legal sanctions play a crucial role in some exchanges. However, in many business exchanges these play only a minor role. Conclusion: "To understand the function of contract, the whole system of conducting exchanges must be explored fully" (Macaulay 1963b: 67).

In the 1980s, Macaulay expands on his analysis. He shows, for example, how written contracts in companies are given very different weight by different people. Businesspeople and sales personnel prefer a word for a word. They "are more concerned with emphasizing contract compliance than with planning what happens if problems arise such as unforeseen expenses or non-delivery, in the same way that they also do not ensure that their contracts are legally binding" (Macaulay 1987: 91; Macaulay 1963b: 60). Lawyers, attorneys, and budget managers are more focused on the writing of contracts—budget managers because the contract is seen as a management tool in relation to the various processes in a large organization.

Macaulay points out that contracts are not an integrating factor. Contracts cannot join together different professional perspectives because it would require a collective discussion of the contractual norms, which would increase the risk of conflict even before negotiations have really begun (Macaulay 1987: 99; Macaulay 2004: 792). Instead, businesspeople partake in an economic community in which it is assumed that relinquishments tend to be returned in the form of advantages. The economic community consists of social relations across formal channels and entails ample opportunity for sanctions. It is a social network, which functions as a system of communication. People tell on each other and that creates sanctions in the form of threats to someone's reputation (Macaulay 1985: 468).

Collins, Vincent-Jones and Campbell and Reflexive Contracting

Over the past decade, we have seen the emergence of a discussion of welfare law which builds upon the ideas of Macneil and Macaulay, often with a normative view to incorporate the insight produced by Macneil and Macaulay into contract development and contract law. One of the key concepts seems to be reflexivity. Hugh Collins, David Campbell, and Peter Vincent-Jones have been the most prominent voices in this discussion. The chief work in this discussion is probably Hugh Collins' book from 1999 with the provocative title *Regulating Contracts*, which is provocative because it signals an abolition of the distinction between public law and contract law. Another very important book is Peter Vincent-Jones' *The New Public Contracting* from 2006.

However, the central issue seems to be how to incorporate justice into contract law, including ensuring that contracts reflect more than the mere interest of the contractual parties (Collins 1993). Campbell writes: "What is needed to develop, at the heart of the law of contract, is a social self-consciousness of the necessary conditions of contractual justice" (Campbell 2000a: 490). This has to do with communication because it articulates a challenge in legal communication to be sensitive to extralegal considerations.

Hugh Collins defines the question in the following way:

> The general view seems to be that the law of contract does not embody as one of its aims the achievement of a particular pattern of distributive justice [...] The legal test for the formation of a binding contract merely establishes fair procedures by which individuals may reach their agreements; they do not ensure that the outcomes of the bargains conform to some fair distributive pattern of wealth in society. The law of contract purports to rest upon a platform of neutrality with respect to distributive outcome. (Collins 1992: 49)

In his book *Regulating Contract*, Collins suggests that both contract law and individual contracts should contain reflexive mechanisms. Private law must reinvent itself to become sensitive to a variety of different systems (Collins 1999: 65–9; Campbell 2000a: 496).

Willie Seal and Peter Vincent-Jones also argue that outsourcing and public–private collaborations may benefit from incorporating reflexive elements into their contracts. Seal even refers to "reflexive contracting" and public–private partnerships as couplings of closed systems (Seal 2000: 15; Seal 1996). Peter Vincent-Jones speaks about the enormous expenses associated with the lack of reflexive mechanisms in contractual relations across the public–private boundary (Vincent-Jones 1998: 371, 374). Vincent-Jones and Harries write that contracts can emphasize constructive collaboration (Vincent-Jones and Harries 1996: 191; Vincent-Jones and Harries 1995). In a subsequent article, Vincent-Jones argues that regulatory regimes can be assessed in relation to measures of reflexivity and responsivity (Vincent-Jones 1999: 314). Responsivity might be achieved to the extent that different interests meet in the contractualization process. A contract can be viewed as a mechanism linking ordering agent, executing agent, and consumer in a way that leads to more or less responsive regulation of quasi-markets. It is easier for responsive regulation to be achieved when the regulatory regimes are themselves reflexive (Vincent-Jones 1999: 310, 322; Vincent-Jones 2000: 317–351). Vincent-Jones's latest book tries to make a full diagnosis on the contractualization of the public sector. And again he insists on the extralegal qualities of contracting:

> Responsiveness [...] cannot be reduced to law or regulation. Responsiveness is ultimately a product of specific governance arrangements [...] Responsive or reflexive law may help secure the preconditions and determine the parameters

of the operation of responsive governance. Responsive governance is founded at least to some degree on responsive law. However, responsive governance is dependent on organizational, economic, administrative and political arrangements that have their own existence and influence outside the ambit of law and legal norms. (Vincent-Jones 2006: 102)

Conclusion

As we have discussed, the relation between contract and communication has been a topic of discussion since the 1960s. Legal theory has not been blind to communication issues. The discussion has opened up gradually.

The first such opening is the recognition of communication as an aspect of contract formation. Macneil argues that all contract formation involves a problem with respect to successful communication of promises between contractual parties. This problem can never be entirely overcome because each of the communication parties has their own personal context for understanding. However, the problem can be lessened through relational relations between communication parties, relations that define shared norms, and a mutually dialogical attitude.

The second opening consists in a form of perspectivism, primarily maintained by Macaulay. This perspectivism is constituted by observations of the fact that the appropriateness of the contract is fundamentally perceived differently from different positions in the company. However, it is a rather weak perspectivism. Macaulay sees that contracts are viewed differently from different perspectives but he does not see what determines these perspectives. He merely indicates these in statements such as "the sales person believes," "the lawyer on the other hand finds," etc.

The third opening consists in bringing reflexive elements into the contracts and in making contract law reflexive of nonlegal considerations. This is a recognition of the necessity of incorporating Macaulay's perspectivism into the concept of contract itself. However, the discussion about reflection remains rather abstract and tends in many instances toward community orientation along the same lines as Macneil. Reflexive mechanisms are defined as procedural participant involvement based on the notion of legal support of dialogue between interested parties. The concept of reflection remains an empty category without unequivocal content. There are frequent acknowledgments of different systems of communication but ultimately these become reduced to players in the capacity of *bonus pater familias*. Despite the recognition of many systems, the contract is still consistently seen as precisely legal. At the same time, nonlegal systems are merely indicated as nonlegal. Their individual logics are never described and are not included in the discussion. The existence and importance of nonlegal and noneconomic systems are recognized as such but remain an indefinite mass of incomprehensible communication. The discussion acknowledges the existence of a great number of systems but fails to give a detailed account of them by employing the concept of procedure to disregard their specific characteristics.

On the whole, we see a number of openings into contract theory; however, these openings are neither radical nor do they lead to sufficient implications to offer up a new theory on contract as communication. We are left with at least three problems:

1. *An internal contract problem:* legal contract theory observes an increasing gap between the preconditions of the formal contract and conditions pertaining to contract formations in society.
2. *An internal theoretical problem:* three approaches are employed in order to overcome the gap between the preconditions of the formal contract and the conditions of society: relationing, perspectivism, and proceduralization. However, the development of contract theory is impeded by the fact that it takes place within the distinction between action and language. From Macneil via Macaulay to Collins, there is an inherent presupposition that action is different from language. Entering a contract agreement is an action. Reading a contract is linguistic. These two entities are separated so that contract formation itself is not seen as language or communication.
3. *A problem external to the contract:* moreover, the discussion persistently takes place within the distinction between law and everything else on the basis of the premise that there is in principle something outside the law. Nevertheless, the law continues to function as the neutral ground within which the discussions take place. And that basically means that the complexity of society is represented only in legal terms. There is no possibility for transcending the systems and developing an eye for the way the law is closed around itself. The law becomes naturalized as the ultimate place "from which." This also becomes apparent in the discussion's implicit perception of the contractual parties. There is always the presupposition of subjects outside the contract with the status of *bonus pater familias*, which means that even subject positions become naturalized in relation to contracts.

We might be able to find the solution to these three problems in the systems theory of Niklas Luhmann who defines communication as the fundamental event of the social. This is what I will pursue in the following.

The Form of Contract

Inspired by Niklas Luhmann, I propose to view contract as a form of communication representing the unity of the difference of obligation and freedom. Form is here defined as an operation of a distinction governing expectations about further communication (Andersen 2003b). The form of contract can be formalized as shown in Figure 6.1:

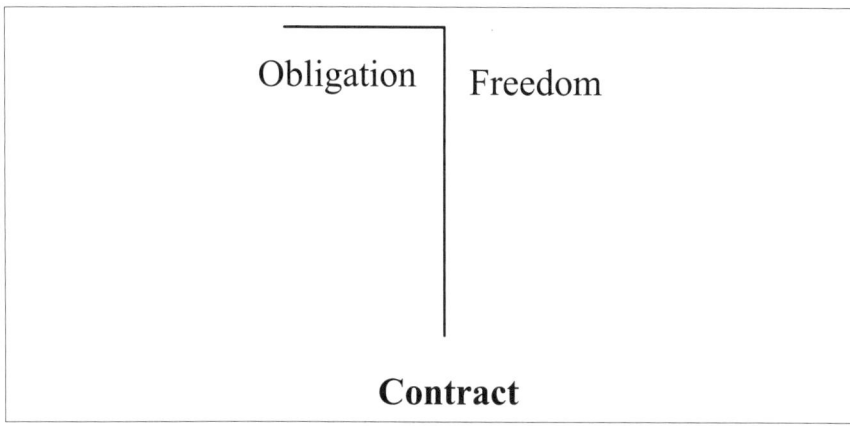

Figure 6.1 The form of contract

Luhmann proposes this view of contract as the unity of obligation and freedom (Luhmann 1981: 249). A contract ties the freedom of communication parties so that there is no obligation outside the freedom of the parties to limit their own freedom. On the other hand, however, freedom cannot exist without social realization of freedom, that is, through the linking of the freedom of communication parties in the form of obligation. Ownership, for example, can be realized only by entering into a relationship of obligation with someone else who then realizes his freedom.

Contractual operations do indeed communicate about obligations but always presuppose the freedom of the contractual parties as the outside of the contract. Freedom is not indicated or spoken about in the communication, but is presupposed as a necessary basis for the formulation of reciprocally binding obligations. In the words of Durkheim: "The only undertaking worthy of the name [contract] are those that are desired by individuals, whose sole origin is this free act of the will. Conversely, any obligation that has not been agreed by both sides is not in any way contractual" (Durkheim 1984: 158).

The traditional representation of contract (which is also present in Macneil and Macaulay) is as an agreement about exchange between individual wills. Teubner, on the other hand, argues that modern contracts can hardly be viewed as such. He writes: "Contract today can only be an interrelation between discourses" (Teubner 2000: 403). Contracts have to be viewed as an obligation between systems of communication rather than between individuals.

In order to function as contract, a contract needs an afterlife in which it is transformed by the related systems of communication. What constructs the contract as contract is primarily the communication that results from the contract. It is the reception, the interpretation, and generally the afterlife of the contract which makes a contract a contract. The afterlife of the contract consists in the fact that systems of communication continually establish internal order in relation to their own interpretation of the contract.

However, if that is the case, it would mean that it is not possible for a contract to have only one meaning. First of all, the meaning behind the contract obligations has to be continuously recreated and, secondly, this meaning is established in different ways depending on the specific logic of the meaning-creating system of communication. That installs a basic paradox within the form of contract, which Derrida formulates like this: "You are not responsible when you talk in the other's language" (Derrida 1988: 124)

Derrida writes:

> You can only enter into a contract […] if you do so in your own tongue. You're only responsible, in other words, for what you say in your own mother tongue. If, however, you say it only in your own tongue, then you're still not committed, because you must also say it in the other's language. An agreement or obligation of whatever sort – a promise, a marriage, a sacred alliance – can only take place, I would say, in translation, that is, only if it is simultaneously uttered in both my tongue and the other's. If it takes place in only one tongue, whether it be mine or the other's, there is no contract possible […] In order for the contract or the alliance to take place, in order for the "yes, yes" to take place on both sides, it must occur in two languages at once […] Thus, the agreement, the contract in general, has to imply the difference of languages rather than transparent translatability, a Babelian situation which is at the same time lessened and left intact. If one can translate purely and simply, there is no agreement. And if one can't translate at all, there is no agreement either. In order for there to be an agreement, there has to be a Babelian situation, so that what I would call the translation contract – in the transcendental sense of this term, let's say – is the contract itself. Every contract must be a translation contract. There is no contract possible – no social contract possible – without a translation contract, bringing with it the paradox I have just mentioned. (Derrida 1988: 125)

In terms of systems theory, this means that a contract is always a contract between different systems of communication that remain operatively closed to one another. As operatively closed systems, they bring meaning to the contract in each their own way. However, the way in which one system articulates the contract as something meaningful has to also make sense to the other systems. It has to be recognizable as obligation.

The paradox, in other words, is that a contract has to necessarily be both singular and multiple at the same time. The contract between systems of communication has to simultaneously be a joined contract and an individual contract. Contracts are only able to maintain their unity by also being a plurality. Figure 6.2 may serve to describe this:

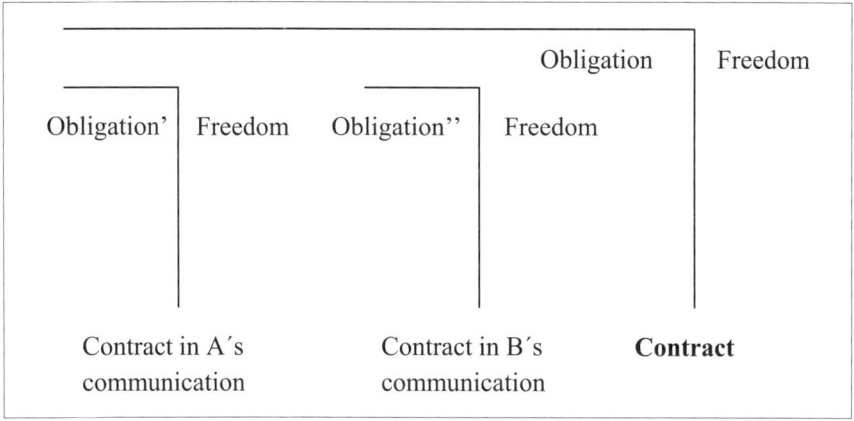

Figure 6.2 The multiplicity of contract

This means that a contract is not an independent system of communication but rather a coupling between different systems of communication. A contract has to presuppose the freedom of the systems of communication as the outside of obligation, but obligation cannot mean the same to different systems of communication, since every system has its own boundary of meaning and has therefore to define obligation within its communication in its own way. At the same time, however, obligation has to also have shared meaning, because without shared meaning there can be no connection. Teubner sums it up like this: "The unity of contract today is fractured in the endless play of discourses. It sounds paradoxical, but one contract is in reality broken into a multiplicity of contracts" (Teubner 2000: 403).

What creates the contractuality of the contract are the individual and mutually closed systems of communication who define the contract as an active communicative event in their respective systems: "As promise, the translation is already an event and the decisive signature of a contract" (Derrida 2007: 213).

Couplings are always only couplings in relation to mutually closed systems. Structural couplings between systems of communication presuppose systems differentiation. However, this difference between coupling and differentiation has to be a part of the very form of the coupling. As coupling, the contract is not something that exists in the space between systems. As coupling, the contract has to be inside each system from where it both joins and separates the systems (Luhmann 1992b: 1433). Contracts create mutual irritation through obligation. Contracts irritate the individual system of communication into a commitment to an internal translation of obligation and to letting it grow and create structures in the internal communication. Freedom, on the other hand, is not merely individual will. Freedom as the outside of irritation defines a necessary indifference to the translation of obligation in the other implicated systems. Contracts connect systems of communication by simultaneously committing the individual system to translating the contract and by allowing for freedom in translating. Without the freedom of the other in translating the contract, there can be no contractual obligation on the other's side. Figure 6.3 formalizes the specific form of coupling of the contract::

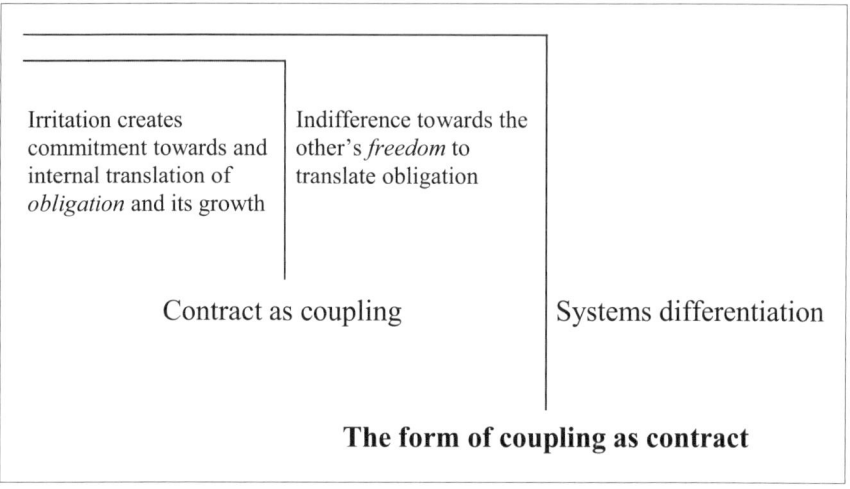

Figure 6.3 The contract as structural coupling

Thus, in this version, contract presupposes not only freedom of action as the other side of obligation but also freedom to translate obligation (Andersen 2008a).

Contract and Functional Differentiation

If contracts represent couplings between social systems, the next question becomes how society is differentiated into different systems of communication.

According to Luhmann, today's society is primarily functionally differentiated. Society is divided into function systems of communication, which are each closed around their own self-defined function, their own medium of communication, and their own code. Thus, economy, politics, law, love, religion, art, and education represent different communicative function systems.

The following expands on a single example of functional communication in order to clarify the logic fully.

The legal system of communication: the law comprises a particular medium and a particular binary code. The symbolically generalized medium of the law is "to apply" as in the expression "applicable law." The medium is symbolically recognized in the form of laws, clauses, legal decisions, and regulations. The code is right/wrong, and it is naturally seen as better to be right than to be wrong. Thus, as a symbolically generalized medium the law divides the world into right and wrong. Together, the code's two sides provide a complete description of the world. Right is always right in relation to wrong, and the distinction is not based in anything outside itself. Thus, the very establishment of the legal code means the exclusion of morality from the law. In legal communication, right is right and has nothing to do with justice. That also means that legal communication is paradoxically based, which becomes clear when the law inquires into its own code. Is the distinction right/wrong itself right or wrong? The binary code of law creates the certainty that, if a person is right, he is sure to have the law on his side. Uncertainty about the law exists only as something which can in principle be resolved with reference to decisions created within the legal system itself (Luhmann 1989: 64). Functionally, the legal system of communication is closed around the function of providing against conflicts and establishing stable expectations, which may survive specific disappointments. This function is expressed in the fact that the basic value of the legal system is the desire for social order. The fact that legal communication is directed at conflicts does not mean that law solves conflicts. On the other hand, when the law observes conflicts, the legal communication transforms them into legal problems about right and wrong. This is all that law understands. This is all that it is able to consider. The function of handling conflicts, therefore, is a question of defining rules that enable the law to transfer conflicts into the law and define them as legal. That excludes the conflict's original "substance." Assigning rights to persons is one of the law's most important tools for enabling the transformation of conflicts into legal problems. For example, without legal ownership of one's house, a neighbor dispute cannot be taken to court, and if it is taken to court, everything is excluded but the relevant facts for the determination of right and wrong, and legal communication might even employ the distinction right/wrong in considering what counts as legal, e.g. which facts are legal facts (Luhmann 1992b). The law simplifies conflicts and specifies precisely what is included in the conflict and disregards the rest if the rest cannot be formulated in legal terms. For example, personal motives and interests are irrelevant in conflicts about purchases if these cannot be discussed in legal terms as preconditions.

Table 6.1 is an attempt to sum up the most important modern function systems:

Table 6.1 Society's function systems

Function system	Medium	Code (+/-)	Function
The political system	Power	Govern/governed	Facilitates collectively binding decisions
The system of science	Knowledge	True/false	Seek new knowledge
The economic system	Money	Have/not have	Scarcity management
The educational system	The child	Better/worse educationally	CV sorting
The system of mass media	Information	Information/ non-information	Produce irritation
The legal system	Law	Right/wrong	Take measure against conflict formation
Moral communication	None	Respect/disrespect	Increase conflicts
The art system	The work of art	Art/not art	Observation of the world
The health care system	Treatment	Healthy/ill	Prevent death
The care system	Care	Help/no help	Inclusion
Intimate communication	Love	Loved/not loved	Address the outmost personal
The system of religion	Faith	Immanence/transcendence	Rule out contingency

Table 6.2 Poly-contextuality presented as a matrix of observation

	Law observed	Love	Economy	Mass media	Education
Law as observer		Love can be observed as a disruptive element and occasionally as a specific legal fact: a motive	Economy can be observed as legal fact in relation to the assessment of motives and permeates the notion of subject	Mass media are observed as public control but also as a risk for the derailment of legal communication and of the possibility of a fair verdict	Education can be observed in the capacity of legal recognition of formal qualifications
Love	Love can observe the law as its ultimate opposite		Economy can be observed as the boundary of anticipation	Mass media can be observed as a space in which one may declare one's love in front of others	Education can be observed as a specific forming of love
Economy	Economy can observe law as supplies of transaction forms and punishment as the price for particular behavior	Love can be observed as an article that can be bought		Mass media are observable as a space in which one can follow the development of the markets	Education is observable as priced competencies and thus be transformed into a scarce resource
Mass media	The law can be observed as a particular journalistic genre	Love is observable as a particular journalistic genre	Economy is observable as a particular journalistic genre		Education can be observed as a particular journalistic genre
Education	The law is observable as a necessary but problematic evaluation unit for learning	Love can be observed as the precondition of engaged learning	Economy can be observed as an obstacle to learning	Mass media can be observed as a specific social educational medium	

In this way, today's society is differentiated into a range of function systems each with their own symbolically generalized medium and their own binary code or logic. That makes communication between function systems impossible. They are not placed in a hierarchical structure and there is no center that can represent society as a whole. The function systems each have their own values, and these values, or codes, represent the blind spots of the systems, which allow them to throw themselves into the future with highly limited resonance capacity.

On the other hand, the function systems are able to observe each other from within their individual horizon of meaning, but the different horizons of meaning cannot be joined to form a whole. There simply is no one place of privilege from which it can be determined whether law is better than help or money better than love. They are immune to each other's logic of argumentation. The functions are operatively closed, but in turn cognitively open through observation. I have tried to illustrate the way in which they observe each other in Table 6.2 above (Andersen 2008a). I have not included all function systems, but hope that the five I have chosen will suffice to enable the reader to continue the line of thinking. As the table shows, the code in which communication takes place determines the theme that is constructed. The reason that I leave a blank field in the place where a particularly coded communication observes itself is not that it cannot be filled in but that it entails a comprehensive isolated question about self-reference and paradox which I have chosen to leave out. In brief, this question concerns the fact that the law, for example, when observing the law faces the paradoxical question about whether the code right/wrong is itself right or wrong.

We may now describe the relationship between contract and society like this: Society is on one hand functionally differentiated into a range of systems of communication, each communicating in their own medium and code and hence operatively closed to each other. On the other hand, they are able to observe each other, and these reciprocal observations can be strengthened by the systems couplings. Contract represents such a coupling. There are other kinds of couplings, primarily organizations, but also themes produced by the mass media. Thus, the relationship between contract and society can be illustrated as shown in Figure 6.4:

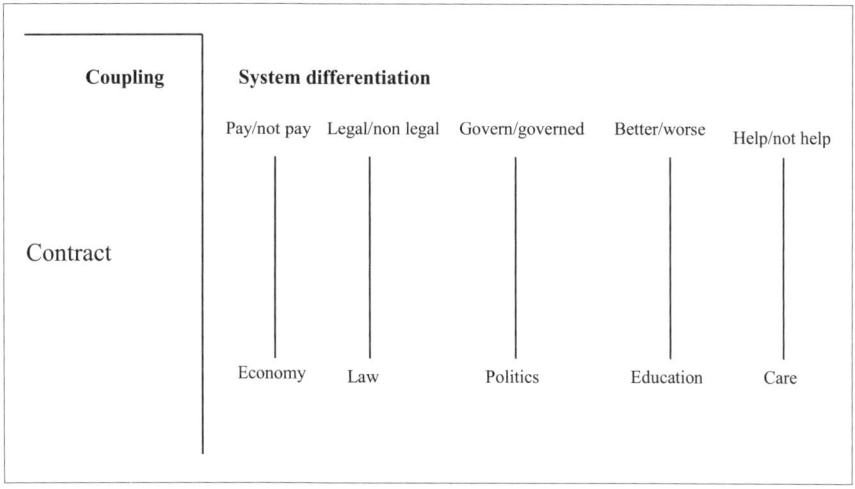

Figure 6.4 Contract vs. functional differentiation

If contracts can indeed function as couplings between different function systems, it means that the individual communicative function systems can create contracts in their own communication as a meaningful element. Basically, it is a question of how contracts are observable from inherently different communicative codes. The multiplicity of obligation in the different contract-reading systems is not a simple question of precision or weighting. A contract is constructed radically differently in the framework of different systems' observations of it (Teubner 2000).

However, in a historical perspective contracts are *not* created to join all types of function systems. If we begin by looking at traditional contracts, those contracts that Macneil refers to as transactional or discrete, they are characterized by a relatively simple content and short timeframe. These contracts are only observable as legal promise and economic exchange respectively, and from a legal point of view exchange is always the exchange of promises. From an evolutionary perspective, the classic contract is designed primarily to create a coupling between law and economy and as such functions as the precondition of company differentiation (Luhmann 2004: 395–6; Luhmann 1992a: 1435–6). For that reason, it is primarily within jurisprudence and economic science that a more sophisticated semantic in relation to contracts has evolved, whereas the concept of contract plays only a marginal role in political science and sociology. As a coupling between law and economy, the contract must be readable and translatable in a unique legal and economic way. The legal system communicates through the code right/wrong. From this perspective, a contract represents a promise and as such it enables the law to consider a conflict over an agreement and assess who is right and who is wrong. Legal communication is closed around the function of providing against conflict development and the writing of a formal contract is perceived in this light. The economic system communicates through the code to pay/not pay, and from this perspective the contract represents not a promise but an exchange program which conditions payments. Entering a contractual agreement means to arrive at the right price in a continual oscillation between the passive form of the code, to have/not have, and its active form, to pay/not pay. It is better to have than not to have, but to pay distributes both solvency and insolvency, and to buy something prevents someone else from buying that same thing. While law and economy can both assign their own meaning to the contract, they can also assign meaning to each other's interpretations of the contract. Thus, the law may understand exchange as the exchange of promise and economy may understand a promise as a transaction cost.

Until recently, the contract's capacity to link law and economy was sufficient, but the growing complexity and speed of society has placed further demands on the contract as structural coupling (Andersen 2008b). In the 1970s more contracts began to reserve a space of autonomy for the contractor to solve the contracted aim in the best possible way. Since the 1990s more and more contracts also leave an open space for subsequent specification of the performance demands in the contract. Sometimes we see very open partnership agreements whose only promise basically is to make future promises within an indicated shared horizon of expectations of the future and future possibilities of collaboration (Andersen 2008a). From a legal point of view Campbell and Harris formulate it like this:

> The form of long-term contracts as documents will tend to be open-ended and to display a rejection of the goal of presentation in favour of explicit flexibility. [...] in addition to the explicit sophistication of these documents, there will be a co-operative recourse to extra-legal strategies to resolve problems which cannot be handled under the documents.

This also requires, they say, that the parties to the contract will "adopt a co-operative rather than narrowly maximizing, opportunistic attitude to their own and others' performance" (Campbell and Harris 1993: 174).

The movement puts demands on contracts to become structural couplings not only with respect to law and economy but to all the communication systems involved in giving the contract an afterlife in their internal communicative production. And in the public sector we can observe growing use of contracting out that puts demands on contracts to be productive for and observable by the political system as instruments of implementation. In most outsourcings, at least four different function systems are involved in giving meaning to a contract in order to provide the contract with a communicative afterlife and hence function as an actual contract: the economic system, the legal system, the political system, and one (or more) welfare-related system. These four systems can never observe the contract in the same way. The contract becomes constructed in four radically different ways (Teubner 1998, 2000). In outsourcing, the political system of communication has to be able also to assign meaning to the contract in order for the contract to be given a political afterlife, for example in the form of a political decision to hold the mayor responsible for failing to oversee the contract. The political system communicates through the code govern/governed and can observe contracts as a way to realize and implement policies. When entering into an agreement with a private company about childcare or train services, the question is whether or not one obtains control through the contract. From a political perspective, the contract represents not a promise, nor an exchange, but primarily a form of governance where the goal is to maximize governance. That also means that a specific outsourcing project always has the option to choose an alternative form of governance. In political terms, the contract is one governance technology among others (Andersen 2008a).

Finally, outsourcing is essentially about welfare and services provided by one or more function systems. If the specific outsourcing project concerns hospital management, it becomes critical for the health care system to be able to assign meaning to the outsourcing as a health program. If the outsourcing concerns a specific social treatment facility, the contract has to be able to be read on the basis of the code of the social care system, help/no help, in which communication is always a question of transforming indefinite needs for help into definite needs for help through diagnosing that leads to treatment and intervention. Thus perceived, a contract represents a treatment program that provides certain possibilities for intervention on the basis of a specific diagnosis. If a contract is agreed upon between ISS Junior Service (Danish company running daycare institutions) and a municipality concerning three daycare institutions, the contract has to also be meaningful as a program for the pedagogical services. I could extend the list of examples, but the point should be clear: an outsourcing contract represents a coupling between different systems and can *only* work as such if the different systems are able to simultaneously construct an internal definition of a given contract and to remain selectively indifferent to the different contractual constructions of other systems. The construction of contract in different function system is shown in Table 6.3 below:

Table 6.3 Contractual constructions in function systems

System of communication	Code	Contractual construction
The legal system	Right/wrong	Promise
The economic system	Pay/not pay	Exchange
The political system	Govern/governed	Instrument for implementation
A service-related system (e.g. the care system or the health system)	+/- Performativity	Service program

Final Remarks on Contract Management

Where does this leave contract management? Most management of contracts within organizations is professionalized in the language of law and economy. In order for the organization to cope with the complexity of modern contracting, it needs to reproduce this complexity within the organization. But this is not without significant consequences for the nature of the organization. My argument is that when contracts become multiplied units, expected to link a wide range of functional perspectives, the same complexity comes to affect the involved organizations. The response to the multiplicity of contract is for an organization to become heterophonic. The organization basically needs to link up to many more function systems when managing contracts.

But what an organization is depends on the language of the observer. When the organization observes itself, it is always linked up with a function system whose code it uses for communication. And every new link to a function system produces new self-descriptions of the organizational system, since the languages of law, politics, care, and health provide different possibilities for organizational self-descriptions. This is illustrated in Table 6.4:

Table 6.4 Organizational constructions in function systems

System of communication	Code	Organizational construction
The legal system	Right/wrong	The organization is viewed as a formal structure and is usually perceived as a hierarchic framework of decisions and competences. The reference to the law allows for ascription of responsibility both internally and externally
The economic system	Pay/not pay	The organization is a form of exchange entailing a reduction in transaction costs which determines the capacity for action both internally and externally
The political system	Govern/governed	The organization is a sovereign domain of decisions, with a "politics" of decision-making
The education system	Better/worse educationally	The organization is perceived as a project and a resource. Pedagogy allows for the ascription of the individual to a (learning) position

So the organization becomes a kind of a *boundary object*. As an "object" it is stable enough to be recognizable across the borders of differently codified communications and sufficiently plastic that it can be ascribed different meanings in each of these communications (Star and Greisemer 1989: 393).

Organizational reference does not reduce the qualitative differences between codes. Rather, it allows for oscillation during interactions. "Organization" is communicatively used to enable code shifts within the communicative space, without (necessarily) excluding communication participants. "Organization" seems to create shared referential space but it does not try to bring the autopoietic differences under control *and* this is what makes continued communication possible. Obviously, this creates enormous pressure on the ascription of meaning or rather, on the establishment of the premises for understanding. When the output of the interaction is meant to relate to concrete future interactions, which premises are to be given authority, and how are they to be stabilized in the oscillating communication?

This challenges the organization's management of contracts. Perceived as a singular unit, the organizational system simply collapses as it becomes differentiated into sub- and alternative systems and at such speed that "organization" comes to represent flexibility and randomness. This defines what I term the heterophonic organization (Andersen 2003a; Andersen and Born 2007). The heterophonic organization is an organization which needs to oscillate between a range of codes and language, but has no position from which the totality of the organization can be represented. Or rather, it has many positions, each with their own definition of the whole. We are left with an organization that cannot represent itself from within its own boundaries, continually displacing itself according to the temporal dimension of change.

References

Andersen, N.Å. 2000. Public market – political firms. *Acta Sociologica* 43(1), 43–61.
Andersen, N.Å. 2003a. Polyphonic organisations, in *Autopoietic Organization Theory,* edited by T. Hernes and T. Bakken. Oslo and Copenhagen: Liber & Abstract, Copenhagen Business School Press, 151–82.
Andersen, N.Å. 2003b. *Discursive Analytical Strategies: Understanding Foucault, Koselleck, Laclau, Luhmann*. Bristol: Policy Press.
Andersen, N.Å. 2003c.The undecidability of decision, in *Autopoietic Organization Theory,* edited by T. Hernes and T. Bakken. Oslo: Liber & Abstract, Copenhagen Business School Press, 235–58.
Andersen, N.Å. 2008a. *Partnerships: Machines of Possibility*. Bristol: Policy Press.
Andersen, N.Å. 2008b. The world as will and adaptation: the inter-discursive coupling of citizens contracts, in *Critical Discourse Studies* 5(1), 75–89.

Andersen, N.Å. and Born, A. 2007. Heterophony and the postponed organisation: organizing autopoietic systems. *Tamara Journal for Critical Organizational Inquiry*, 6(2), 176–86.

Campbell, D. 2000a. Reflexivity and welfarism in the modern law contract. *Oxford Journal of Legal Studies* 20(3), 477–98.

Campbell, D. and Harris, D. 1993. Flexibility in long-term contractual relationships: the role of co-operation. *Journal of Law and Society* 20(2), 166–91.

Collins, H. 1992. Distributive justice through contracts, in *Current Legal Problems*, edited by R.W. Rideout and B.A. Hepple, vol. 45, part 2, Oxford: Oxford University Press.

Collins, H. 1993. The transformation thesis and aspiration of contractual responsibility, in *Perspectives of Critical Contract Law*, edited by T. Williamson. Aldershot: Dartmouth.

Collins, H. 1999. *Regulating Contracts*, Oxford: Oxford University Press.

Cour, A. la and Højlund, H. 2003. Care, standardization & flexibility, in *Autopoietic Organization Theory*, edited by T. Hernes and T. Bakken. Oslo and Copenhagen: Liber & Abstract, Copenhagen Business School Press,

Derrida, J. 1988. *The Ear of the Other*. London: University of Nebraska Press.

Derrida, J. 2007. Des tours de Babel, in *Psyche: Inventions of the Other*, edited by J. Derrida. *Volume 1*. Stanford California: Stanford University Press, 191–225.

Durkheim, É. 1984. *Division of Labour in Society*. London: Macmillan.

Højlund, H. 2009. Hybrid Inclusion: The New Consumerism of Danish Welfare Services, in *Journal of European Social Policy* 19(5), 421–31.

Luhmann, N. 1981. Communication about law in interactions systems, in *Advances in Social Theory and Methodology: Toward and integration of micro- and macro-sociologies*, edited by K. Knorr-Cetina and A.V. Cicourel. London: Routledge & Kegan.

Luhmann, N. 1989. *Ecological Communication*. Chicago: The University of Chicago Press.

Luhmann, N. 1992a. Operational closure and structural coupling. *Cardozo Law Review* 13(5), 1419–41.

Luhmann, N. 1992b. The coding of the legal system, in *State, Law, and Economy as Autopoietic Systems*, edited by G. Teubner and A. Febbrajo. Milan: Giuffrè.

Luhmann, N. 1993a. Die Paradoxie des Entscheidens. *Verwaltungs–Archiv. Zeitschrift für Verwaltungslehre, Verwaltungsrecht und Verwaltungspolitik* 84(3), 287–99.

Luhmann, N. 2000c. *Organization und Entscheidung*. Wiesbaden: Westdeutscher Verlag.

Luhmann, N. 2004. *Law as a Social System*. Oxford: Oxford University Press.

Macaulay, S. 1963a. The use and non-use of contracts in the manufacturing industry. *The Practical Lawyer* 9(7), 13–40.

Macaulay, S. 1963b. Non-contractual relations in business: a preliminary study. *American Sociological Review* 28(1), 55–67.

Macaulay, S. 1985. An empirical view of contract. *Wisconsin Law Review*, 465–82.

Macaulay, S. 1987. Et empirisk syn på kontrakter, in *Virksomheden mellem økonomi og jura – om retsøkonomi og styring*, edited by B.M. Blegvad and F. Collin. Copenhagen: Samfundslitteratur.

Macaulay, S. 2003. The real and the paper deal: empirical pictures of relationships, Complexity and the urge for transparent simple rules, in *Implicit Dimensions of Contract*, edited by D. Campbell et al. Oxford: Hart Publishing.

Macaulay, S. 2004. Freedom from contract: solutions in search of a problem. *Wisconsin Law Review*, 777–820.

Macneil, I.R. 1974. The many futures of contracts. *Southern California Law Review* 47, 696–816.

Macneil, I.R. 1980. *The New Social Contract*. London: Yale University Press.

Macneil, I.R. 1985. Reflection on relational contract. *Zeitschrift für die gesamte Staatswissenschaft*, 541–6.

Macneil, I.R. 1987. Barriers to the idea of relational contracts, in *The Complex Long-term Contract*, edited by F. Nicklisch. Heidelberg: C.F. Müller Juristischer Verlag.

Macneil, I.R. 1988. Contractland invaded again: a comment on doctrinal writing and Shell's ethical standards. *Northwestern University Law Review* 82(4), 1195–97.

Macneil, I.R. 2003. Reflection on relational contract theory after a neoclassical seminar, in *Implicit Dimensions of Contract*, edited by D. Campbell et al. Oxford: Hart Publishing, 207–217.

Neu, D. 1991. Trust, contracting and the prospectus process. *Accounting, Organizations and Society*, 16(3), 243–56.

Seal, W. 1996. Security design, incomplete contracts and relational contracting: implication for accounting and auditing. *British Accounting Review* 28, 23–44.

Seal, W. 2000. Performance indicators, regulation and management: towards responsive local governance. Working paper. Oslo: Norwegian School of Management, 11–14 May.

Seal, W. and Vincent-Jones, P. 1997. Accounting and trust in the enabling of long-term relations. *Accounting, Auditing & Accountability Journal* 10(3), 406–31.

Star, S.L. and Greisemer, J.R. 1989. Institutional ecology, "translations" and boundary objects: amateurs and professionals in Berkeley's Museum of Vertebrate Zoology, 1907–39. *Social Studies of Science* 19, 387–420.

Teubner, G. 1998. After privatization? The many autonomies of private law. *Currant Legal Problems*, 51, 393–424.

Teubner, G. 2000. Contracting worlds: the many autonomies of private law. *Social & Legal Studies* 9(3), 399–417.

Vincent-Jones, P. 1998. Responsive law in public services provision: A future for the local contracting state. *The Modern Law Review* 61(3), 362–81.

Vincent-Jones, P. 1999. The regulation of contractualisation in quasi-markets for public services. *Public Law*, 303–26.

Vincent-Jones, P. 2000. Contractual governance: Institutional and organizational analysis. *Oxford Journal of Legal Studies*, Oxford: Oxford University Press, 20(3), 317–51.
Vincent-Jones, P. 2006. *The New Public Contracting*, Oxford: Oxford University Press.
Vincent-Jones, P. and Harries, A.A. 1995. Partnership and co-operation in "contracting out" local authority refuse collection services: a case study, in *Public and Private Sector Partnerships in the Global Context*, edited by L. Muntanhero et al. Sheffield: PAVIC Publications.
Vincent-Jones, P. and Harries, A.A. 1996. Conflict and co-operation in local authority quasi-markets: The hybrid organisation of internal contracting under CCT. *Local Government Studies* 22(4), 187–209.

Chapter 7
Functional Differentiation, Financial Instruments and Regulatory Challenges[1]

John Paterson

Introduction

The ongoing financial crisis has raised troubling questions both for economists and for regulators. The former have had to explain why they apparently did not see the crisis coming[2] while the latter, on both sides of the Atlantic, have had to explain why they were unable to prevent it from happening (Department of the Treasury 2009; Turner 2009). There has been no shortage of suggested answers to these questions from a wide range of experts, observers, and commentators (Acharya and Richardson 2009).

In the midst of this maelstrom of activity, of accusation and recrimination as well as of diagnosis and prescription, the aims of this chapter are relatively modest. There is no claim to have an answer either to the question of why the problem was not foreseen or to the question of why it could not be prevented. Rather this chapter offers simply a different – and specifically a systems theory – perspective on one aspect of the crisis as a means of gauging the nature and scale of the challenges facing those now charged with responding. It begins with the observation that wherever one looks in the literature surrounding the crisis one encounters the phenomenon of the derivative financial instrument. If there are competing views on what precisely went wrong, there is at least consensus that these instruments were deeply implicated. This consensus is all the more significant given that a

---

1 An earlier version of this chapter was presented at the Applied Systems Theory conference held in Dubrovnik, Croatia, 14–18 September 2009. I am very grateful to the participants for helpful comments both during and after the conference. Any errors are, of course, my responsibility.

2 Most famously, in the UK economists were asked by the Queen to explain this oversight, eliciting a letter dated 22 July 2009 from the British Academy signed by Professors Tim Besley and Peter Hennessy. This identified the problem as 'principally a failure of the collective imagination' of economists 'to understand the risks to the system as a whole'. A further group of economists, led by Professor Geoffrey Hodgson, also wrote to the Queen. In a letter dated 10 August 2009, they developed the message of the earlier correspondence by pointing to a 'deficiency in the training or culture of economists' that favours 'mathematical technique over real-world substance' thus preventing an adequate view of the 'vital whole'.

key role for these instruments was supposed to be precisely the management of risk. How could it be, then, that something designed to solve a problem appears precisely to have contributed materially to it, if not actually caused it? On the face of it, this is an example of a situation where the deployment of a particular financial tool has not only failed to produce the planned and projected outcome, but has in fact given rise – or at least contributed – to exactly the opposite result. The fact that the regulators are also in the firing line is also significant. The approach to banking regulation has explicitly been said to be risk-based both at the international level (Basel Committee on Banking Supervision 2004) and at the domestic level in the most advanced financial markets (Financial Services Authority 2006). How could it be, then, that a regulatory approach that was supposed to be sensitive to risk appears both to have failed to notice the emergence of risks on an unprecedented scale and to have been powerless to intervene when those risks crystallised? On the face of it, this is an example of a situation where the deployment of a particular regulatory tool has not only failed to produce the planned and projected outcome, but has in fact allowed exactly the opposite result.

Confronted with these seeming failures of quite extraordinary proportions, it is not difficult to see why the received wisdom within economic and regulatory theory has come under close scrutiny and indeed been profoundly questioned. Systems theory, on the other hand, perhaps especially in its autopoietic guise, has never been taken aback by failure (Teubner 1992) and has always questioned the control assumptions that underpin the Enlightenment project (Luhmann 1997). Might it be the case, accordingly, that a systems theory perspective on the instruments at the heart of the crisis could shed new light on what happened?

It must immediately be acknowledged that there could be scepticism about this idea. Insofar as systems theory is perceived to have an inherently pessimistic worldview, would it add anything of value to the debate or would it simply and inevitably find failure before going on to counsel against the fantasy of exerting regulatory control over the economy (Rottleuthner 1989)?

An empirical approach to systems theory certainly engages the sociolegal researcher in profound questions about the nature of the process of research and about the relationship between theoretical concepts and empirical data in the field of law and regulation. Nor are the answers to those questions uncontroversial. Insofar as the theory forces the researcher to confront the implications of the normative closure and cognitive openness of not only the systems that he or she is studying, but also of the systems that he or she is deploying in the course of that study, autopoiesis can appear to place as insurmountable an obstacle in the way of the normal process of research as it appears to place in the way of regulatory interventions (Teubner 1985). Nevertheless, embracing that challenge rather than turning away from it can open up new opportunities for research and can produce results that are perhaps more modest and less likely to lead to disappointment. Specifically, it can offer a new map of the landscape – not one that claims to be 'right', but rather one that aims to be more adequately complex by being open to the range of systems in play in the empirical domain and one that is content to be judged, as maps are, on its usefulness as a representation of that landscape (Paterson and Teubner 1998). It is in that spirit that the analysis developed in this chapter proceeds and that the conclusions drawn are offered.

The basic question that is addressed in this chapter is accordingly: What does a systems theory perspective tell us about the nature of financially engineered derivative instruments and about the problems that consequently confront policy makers and regulators as they seek to respond to the role played by such instruments in the global financial crisis? After two scene-setting sections, which respectively review the nature and purpose of derivative financial instruments and consider their position in the financial crisis, the chapter develops, in section 4, a diagrammatic methodology to analyse one empirical situation from a systems perspective – specifically, the use of a credit default swap to hedge the credit risk associated with the purchase of a corporate bond. The results emerging from this approach give rise to a variety of possible interpretations, each of which is considered in turn. The interim conclusion drawn is that finance is best understood as an internally differentiated subsystem of the economy. Before the implications of this conclusion can be considered fully, the chapter acknowledges the observation that important decisions about the deployment of financial contracts are taken within corporate organisations. Section 5 accordingly considers those organisations from a systems perspective. In particular, it examines, once again adopting a diagrammatic methodology, the way in which the corporate interest (which lies at the heart of the legal obligations a company board must fulfil) must be understood from that point of view. Section 6 of this chapter unites the findings from the preceding analyses (at the levels both of the system and of the organisation) in the context of the corporate bond/credit default swap example to demonstrate how decisions about financial instruments within the organisation that are coherent in terms of its autopoiesis can produce perverse effects outside, not least because of the status of finance as an internally differentiated subsystem of the economy. The implications of these findings for policy makers and regulators are considered in section 7 before final conclusions are drawn.

The Nature and Purpose of Derivative Financial Instruments

It is necessary first of all to be clear about what a derivative financial instrument is. In essence, it is a contract which depends for its value upon an underlying 'more elementary' commodity or loan transaction (Kolb 1996: viii, McDonald 2009: 2). Thus, while the underlying transaction is often popularly referred to as being an element of the 'real economy', the derivative instrument is a creature of 'financial markets'.[3] Indeed, even before the financial crisis, there were suggestions that finance had become 'decoupled' from the real economy (Menkhoff and Tolksdorf 2001).

---

   3   See, for example, the definition of the 'real economy' provided by the *Financial Times*: 'The part of the economy that is concerned with actually producing goods and

Derivative instruments serve two basic purposes: to hedge risk; and to produce a profit. The party using the instrument wants to hedge risk; the party providing the instrument wants to make a profit. As a simplified example, assume that an oil company produces a certain amount of oil every month which it sells on the spot market. Assuming fixed costs, there is a particular spot price above which the company makes a profit and below which it makes a loss. All else equal, it would be entirely at the mercy of the vicissitudes of the market as to whether it made a profit or a loss or broke even. The company can, however, make use of a variety of derivative instruments with a view to 'locking in' the price that it receives for a block of production at a level that represents an acceptable rate of return on investment (factoring in, of course, the cost of the risk-hedging strategy itself).

The company could, for example, use *futures* (contracts to buy or sell a set amount of oil at a date in the future). The net effect of this approach is that losses on physical trades caused by a falling spot market will be offset by profits from balancing futures trades. In other words, such contracts allow 'a firm the freedom to pursue its line of business without having to worry about forecasting prices in the future' (Errera and Brown 1999: 86; Kolb 1996: 21; McDonald 2009: 168; Chance 2004: 270).

The oil company could also use *options* (essentially, contracts to buy or sell the right to buy or sell futures contracts by a specified date on payment of a premium). This approach has the advantage that it allows the producer to benefit from a rising market while still protecting it from a fall. The degree of risk borne by the provider will, of course, be reflected in the premium payable and in the duration of the contract (Sas 1992: 50–59; Kolb 1996: 73; McDonald 2009: 29; Chance 2004: 20).

Finally, the company could use *swaps*. In contrast to futures and options which are traded on exchanges and thus involve costs (not least the need to be able to post margin on a daily basis) and restrictions (standardised contracts, the presence of the exchange as counterparty to both buyer and seller, and regulatory oversight), swaps are traded over the counter (OTC). In other words, they are entered into either directly between the provider and the buyer, usually with the intermediation of a swaps broker or perhaps involving a swaps dealer who not only brokers the transaction but also takes a position in it. Swaps also operate to lock in a price but they are available for significantly longer periods than would be the case with an exchange-traded contract, involve much lower management costs, require only periodic premium payments and, crucially, are not regulated (Clubley 1998: 93; Kolb 1996: 123; McDonald 2009: 219; Chance 2004: 424).

---

services, as opposed to the part of the economy that is concerned with buying and selling on the financial markets.' At http://lexicon.ft.com [accessed 15 December 2009].

The same contracts as are used by sellers of commodities can also, of course, be used by buyers who are worried about price risk caused by market movements in the opposite direction from those which concern sellers.[4]

This simple example demonstrates the risk management function that derivative instruments can perform. It also demonstrates how they operate as a generator of profits for those who provide them, in the form of the premium payable. The fact that the use of a derivative contract involves in essence a bet on the movement of a market also reveals how these instruments can be used by speculators who have no stake in the underlying 'more elementary' transactions but who see them as a further investment opportunity that can offer the prospect of significant profits. Finally, then, this example also gives a hint as to the risks that are nevertheless inherent in the use of derivative instruments. Unless they are used appropriately and conservatively, even those whose aim is to hedge risk could expose themselves to significant losses. Those who offer such contracts must equally have a very sophisticated view of the extent of the risk they are taking on, how accurately the premium required prices that risk and how they would be affected by a market that performs contrary to their expectations. Finally, those who view them speculatively must have a very sophisticated understanding of the market and be in a position to weather potentially very significant losses (Culp and Miller 1999).

Derivatives in the Financial Crisis

The world of derivative instruments is, however, by no means exhausted by the simple examples briefly reviewed in the foregoing section. The task of financial engineers is to produce more sophisticated instruments which may use complex combinations of other derivatives with a view, on the one hand, to hedging more complex risk profiles and, on the other, offering new means to generate profits for providers – and indeed speculators. Insofar as these instruments are by definition bespoke they are not traded on exchanges, but rather are over-the-counter or OTC contracts and are thus beyond the purview of any regulator. While at first sight the absence of regulatory oversight for the most complex derivatives can appear surprising, if not indeed perverse and foolhardy, the expectation is that only those with the requisite degree of financial sophistication and financial resources will be involved with such instruments and that they will accordingly be able to look after themselves.

The financial crisis has prompted a reconsideration of this received wisdom. The complex instruments involved were constructed by financial engineers,

---

4   For a recent indication of the concerns that commodities buyers have about the possible impact of regulatory reforms on the cost of using financial instruments for hedging price risk, see Jeremy Grant, 'Derivatives: Airlines fight threat of increasing hedging costs', *Financial Times*, 16 November 2009.

were traded off exchange, and were thus not subject to regulatory oversight. The parties involved were indeed actors of considerable financial sophistication. They were, however, apparently unable to look after themselves and, more than that, their failures produced adverse effects that were felt much more widely, including by ordinary individuals of limited resources who had taken the most conservative approach to financial risk. Warren Buffett famously suggested that 'derivatives are financial weapons of mass destruction, carrying dangers that, while now latent, are potentially lethal' (Berkshire Hathaway 2002: 15). It is this fact that has prompted policy makers in recent months to reconsider the hands-off approach to the regulation of the most complex financial instruments (Department of the Treasury 2009; Turner 2009). The political and popular enthusiasm for this sort of intervention is undeniable, but it is a question whether it is a realistic proposition to attempt to regulate transactions which even the most sophisticated economists admit to not understanding.[5] Beyond the risk of regulatory failure in the sense that the intervention does not achieve the desired end, there is the risk that the intervention may produce unintended consequences. Always undesirable, unintended consequences in the realm of financial instruments would appear to raise very particular fears. At a more basic level, can policy makers be sure of what it is that they would want to achieve by intervening in this esoteric market? Insofar as the market itself claims to serve both risk-hedging and (taxable) profit-generating functions, it will be a brave policy maker who is able to determine where the balance should lie and what sort of intervention is appropriate to achieve it.

A measure of the difficulty policy makers will face in this regard may be gained by looking at one of the simpler financial instruments that has become a focus of attention since the onset of the global financial crisis: the credit default swap, or CDS.[6] In order to understand what a CDS is, assume the following: a company B wants to raise capital for its enterprise (say, developing a new technology) and thus issues a bond. Bank A buys the bond, thus becoming a creditor of B and exposing itself to the credit risk that B will default on the payments promised under the bond. In order to hedge that risk, A buys a credit default swap from investment bank C. In return for a premium, C promises to pay A in the event that B defaults (McDonald 2009: 373–8). Insofar as the concept of insurance is familiar to all, this looks like a very straightforward situation and one that would not excite much controversy. It can be illustrated with the following diagram:

---

5   Former Federal Reserve Chairman, Alan Greenspan, admitted in an interview for CNBC's documentary 'House of Cards' (12 February 2009) that 'he did not understand the details of the more complex securities on the market.' For details, see http://www.cnbc.com/id/28984151 [accessed 15 December 2009].

6   The collapse of Lehman Brothers caused such widespread damage not least because the investment bank was the counterparty to a significant number of CDSs.

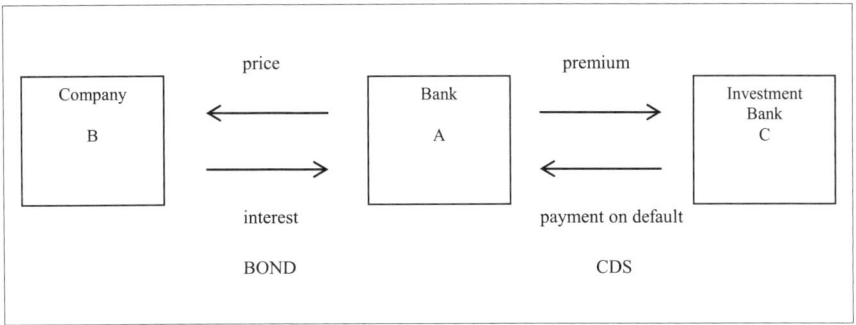

Figure 7.1 The relationship between a corporate bond and a credit default swap

This looks, then, like a perfect hedge arrangement that is well balanced and well adapted to the needs of the various parties. And yet such arrangements turned out to be a significant element in the unfolding of the global financial crisis. The very attractiveness of the CDS meant that by the end of 2007 the gross nominal value of the market was $60 trillion. Even if only the net value of outstanding positions is considered, the market still totalled somewhat under $4 trillion at the same point in time (Turner 2009: para. 2.5(iii)). For comparison, the US's GDP in 2007 was $14 trillion.[7] The scale of the global market in CDSs is, therefore, very large and the consequences of any failure on that market potentially very serious, but what would a policy maker have to object to with regard to the basic purpose of a CDS? Where would he or she identify a leverage point to allow regulatory intervention? Insofar as this looks like a rather neutral and innocent set of transactions, the best that could perhaps be offered on the basis of this admittedly superficial examination would be the proposal that the market for CDSs should be moved from the OTC realm to an exchange where at least there would be greater visibility. The difficulty is, of course, that the whole virtue of a swap transaction is that it can be tailored to the precise needs of the buyer. The very fact that CDS buyers confront a diverse and complex range of risks means that between a quarter and a half of all CDSs are entirely unsuited to the sort of standardisation that characterise exchange-based instruments. Turner notes, for example, that 50% to 75% of CDSs are standardised contracts, that is, 'referencing a standard index'. Accordingly, 'a large volume of bespoke contracts will continue to be traded in an OTC fashion', even if there was a move to take others on to an exchange (Turner 2009: para. 2.5(iii).

---

7 OECD statistics, at http://stats.oecd.org/Index.aspx [accessed 15 December 2009].

A Systems Theory Perspective on Corporate Bonds and Credit Default Swaps

It is at this point that a systems theory perspective can be brought to bear. There are obviously two distinct contracts in play in the above situation: one between B and A (the bond-issuing company and the bond-buying bank) and one between C and A (the CDS-selling investment bank and the CDS-buying bank). There is no contractual relationship between B (the company) and C (the investment bank). What do these contracts look like if they are modelled from a systems perspective?

Within systems theory, the unity of the contract is fragmented. Instead of a simple focus on the instrument itself, there is an appreciation of its multiple existences within a variety of discourses, economic, productive, and legal, where it is involved in a variety of transformations, economic, productive and legal (Teubner 2000 and 2007: 52). Despite these multiple existences, however, the contract is also seen as a means by which structural coupling – the 'twofold membership of events' in different systems (Luhmann 1987: 342) – can occur (Teubner 2007: 54). This does not mean that the autopoiesis of the systems involved is compromised. There is no transfer of information between systems in the way assumed by linear-causal models (Paterson and Teubner 1998: 457). There is instead only the internal construction of the contract by each of the systems in play (Luhmann 1995: 41). All that the presence of the contract adds (though in systems terms this may be a great deal) is the requirement for the systems involved to conduct their self-transformations simultaneously, if only momentarily (Teubner 2007: 52, 58). Adopting this perspective, the corporate bond contract can be illustrated diagrammatically as follows:

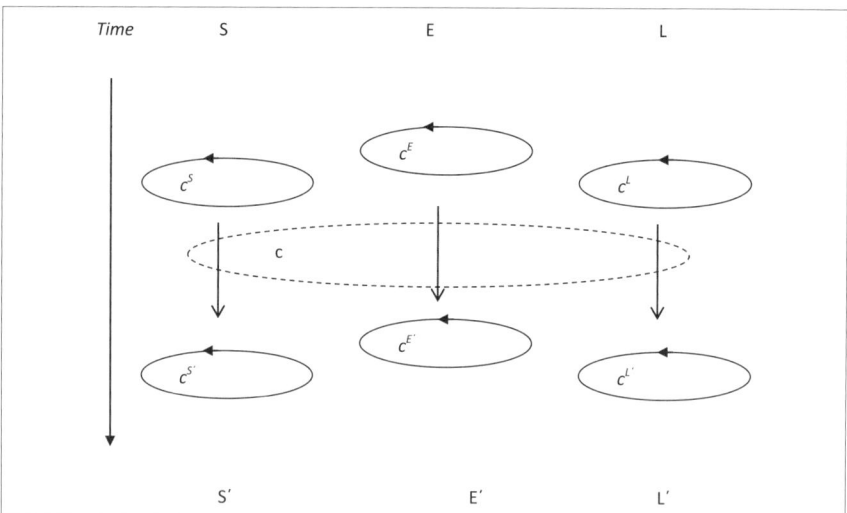

Figure 7.2 Systems theory representation of a corporate bond contract

In this diagram, it can be seen that the systems in play are economics (E), law (L) and a productive system. This productive system could be any from among those identified by Luhmann (science, medicine, etc.) (1995: 55, 374 and 381), but for the purposes of this example science (S) will be used. The presence of the contract (c) is represented by a broken line to signify the structural coupling, but, crucially, the contract also appears as a construct of each of the systems (c^E), (c^L) and (c^S). The systems are shown through one simultaneous transformation along the temporal dimension.

The question is then: How is the contract (the corporate bond) constructed by each of the systems through that transformation? The following answers may be offered:

S→S' The contract is a means of raising capital to develop a new technology
E→E' The contract is a means of continuing productive activity to generate future payments
L→L' The contract is a means of stabilising normative expectations within the context of the specific activity covered by the agreement

While this opens the way to a somewhat richer analysis of the contract than would otherwise have been the case, it is not yet obvious what systems theory might reveal that is new in an effort to gain a significant insight into the operation of financial markets. It is suggested, however, that the insight emerges only when this systems perspective on a corporate bond contract is compared with that on a credit default swap contract. Modelling the CDS in the same way, the following diagram emerges:

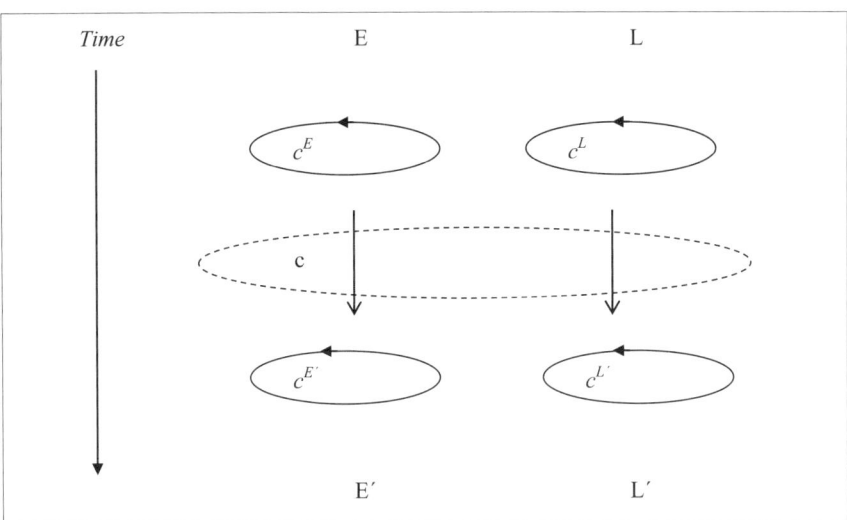

Figure 7.3 Systems theory representation of a credit default swap contract – version 1

Once again the question is: how is the contract (the CDS) constructed by each of the systems through one simultaneous transformation along the temporal dimension? The following answers may be offered:

E→E′   The contract is a means of reducing credit risk by guaranteeing payment in the event of default by the bond issuer
E→E′   The contract is a means of continuing productive activity to generate future payments
L→L′   The contract is a means of stabilising normative expectations within the context of the specific activity covered by the agreement

A number of observations may immediately be made:

1. The legal construction of the CDS contract is exactly the same as for the bond.
2. A productive system (in this example, science) is *not* in play in this contract.
3. There are two economic constructions of the CDS contract: one that is essentially the same as the construction for the bond; another that is quite different.

These observations can be considered further in turn. Firstly, it is clear that the legal system is essentially indifferent to the content of the contracts in this corporate bond/CDS example. The contract from a legal perspective is simply a means of stabilising the normative expectations of the parties, but the precise activity (unless it transgresses contract law to become a void or voidable contract) is unimportant. Secondly, the shift from the 'more elementary' setting of the real economy to the more esoteric world of financial markets is signalled in systems terms by the absence of a productive system. While this contract, the CDS, only exists because there is an underlying loan transaction, it does not itself include any such transaction. It is thus possible to postulate that a derivative contract may be defined in systems theory terms by the absence of its engagement of a productive system. Finally, but perhaps most importantly, it is necessary to deal with the fact that there are two economic constructions of the contract. One of these is derived from the way in which the CDS is understood by the protection seller (and indeed the speculator). The other is derived from the way in which it is understood by the protection buyer.

This last point gives rise to a further question: how is the presence of two distinct economic constructions of the contract to be accounted for in systems theory terms? There would appear to be three possibilities:

1. There is a separate system of finance, distinct from the system of the economy.
2. Different organisational systems are able to make simultaneous use of different economic steering programmes.
3. Finance is an internally differentiated subsystem of the economy.

It appears easiest to discount the first possibility. Looking at the code that is used in 'real' economic transactions and at the code used in financial market transactions, it is evident that it is the same in each case: payment/non-payment. Insofar as only one code is in play, there is only one system. The second possibility looks more promising. Luhmann (1997) makes the point that, while the system's code is invariable, different steering programmes are possible. Accepting that possibility does not, however, rule out the third possibility and might even depend upon it. Considering Luhmann's account of the process of internal differentiation, the third possibility looks, if anything, the most promising. Luhmann states that '[i]nternal differentiation connects onto the boundaries of the already-differentiated system and treats the bounded domain as a special environment in which further systems can be formed'. Indeed, this basic fact has a number of important consequences: firstly, the internal environment is characterised by a particularly highly developed approach to the reduction of complexity, meaning that any process of internal differentiation can proceed on the basis that 'certain capacities for regulation' are presupposed; this in turn provides a platform for '[n]ew, more improbable system formation'; thirdly, as improbable as any new system formation might be, it can only survive insofar as it 'can mobilize processes of deviation-amplification (positive feedback) to [its] own advantage and keep [itself] from being levelled out again'; finally, Luhmann stresses the extent to which the dependence of internal differentiation upon the system boundary serves to reinforce that boundary (Luhmann 1995: 189–90).

Taking each of these points from Luhmann in turn and considering them in the light of the suggestion that finance is an internally differentiated system of the economy, the following picture can be offered. Firstly, the fact that the system of the economy has already reduced complexity by means of the code payment/non-payment provides any process of new system formation within that system with a greatly simplified account of the environment on which to operate.[8] Secondly, the improbability of the emergence of the subsystem of finance is characterised by the extent to which an immense number of financial transactions is supported by a relatively small number of economic transactions – recall in this regard the scale of the CDS market discussed above. Thirdly, despite this improbability, finance is able to sustain itself and prevent its dissolution by successfully mobilizing positive feedback to its own advantage: in particular, it offers simultaneously enhancements in terms both of payments and of risk-minimisation. In other words, finance offers opportunities that are attractive from whichever angle they are viewed, which calls to mind Turner's observation of the extent to which the belief grew prior to the financial crisis that structured credit effectively reduced risk while simultaneously creating value (2009: 13–14). Finally, the fact that finance depends for its existence upon the system boundary established by the economy means that that boundary is itself reinforced. The extent to which practically every other aspect of every

---

8   The comments of economists asked to explain their failure to foresee the onset of the crisis reported at note 1 above take on a renewed significance in this context.

other system, communicative or living, has progressively been commoditised offers compelling evidence of the success of finance in strengthening the boundary between the economy and its environment. Among examples of the inventiveness of finance in seeking new ways to create value, life settlement-backed securities or 'death bonds' must rank particularly highly (Goldstein 2007).[9]

Taking this picture seriously allows a more accurate diagram of the CDS contract from a systems perspective to be drawn.

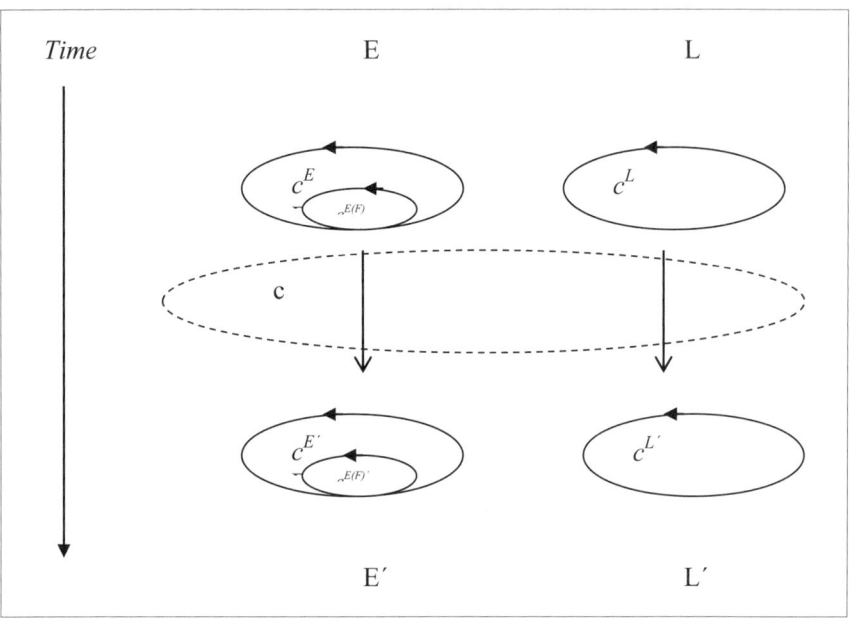

Figure 7.4 Systems theory representation of a credit default swap contract – version 2

The fact that the CDS is a pure financial contract means that it has a constructed existence both within the financial subsystem and within that part of the economic system which is otherwise the bounded environment of the finance subsystem. This dual economic construction allows the utilisation of the same contract for two separate economic difference-minimising steering programmes, one directed at the amplification of payments, the other at the management of risk. The improbability of that dual existence is testament to the success of the financial subsystem in establishing and maintaining its self-reproduction as an internally differentiated subsystem of the economy. Nor is that success difficult to understand when one

---

9   I am grateful to Katayoun Baghai for drawing my attention to this example.

considers the irresistibility of a subsystem which can simultaneously amplify payments (even exponentially) and enhance the management of risk (even to a point where the claim is that the risk has effectively been removed).

With this picture in mind, what does it mean in systems terms to speak of a 'decoupling' of the 'financial markets' from the 'real economy'? Clearly, something quite different is on offer. For a start, the word 'decoupling' might have to be reconsidered. Inasmuch as the self-reproduction of the financial subsystem is dependent on the self-reproduction of the economy, there is actually a very close relationship between the two. Insofar, however, as the financial subsystem is able to produce its own internal constructions of (in the present example) contracts that may be (and indeed almost by definition must be) quite distinct from those of the system of the economy beyond the internal boundary of finance, then it can be seen that the nature of the 'decoupling' of the two is that of *differential internal constructions of reality*.

The analysis conducted so far, then, offers an alternative perspective on one of the financial instruments involved in the crisis and in so doing provides support for the proposition that finance is an internally differentiated subsystem within the economy. The ideas have admittedly only been relatively briefly worked out, but insofar as the aim has been to determine whether systems theory can provide a distinctive and productive view of the financial crisis, the chapter is more concerned with mapping out the path that would need to be followed by a more extensive study than with developing a detailed picture of the whole landscape along the way. In this same spirit, the next section of the chapter does not pause to deepen the analysis by considering other (and inevitably more complex) financial instruments but rather moves on to consider what further dimensions of the crisis might be amenable to a systems theory analysis. In this regard, it commences from the observation that the decisions with respect to the contracts under consideration here are taken within commercial organisations. What, then, can systems theory reveal about the nature of such organisations that might add to the developing picture of the context of the crisis? Might one speculate, for example, that the complications revealed by the fragmentation of the contract among the functional systems might in some sense be mitigated in the context of the organisation?

A Systems Theory Perspective on Corporate Organisations

A systems theory perspective on corporate organisations has been provided by Gunther Teubner (1994) in the context of his analysis of the company interest. The definition of the company interest in any jurisdiction defines the scope of its company law – in other words, in whose interests must the company be run? This question has been debated for decades (Berle 1931; Dodd 1932) and still defies a ready answer. Most recently the subject in the UK of the lengthy and detailed Company Law Review (1999: ch. 5.1; 2000a: ch. 3.9; 2000b: ch. 3; 2001: ch. 3), the duty of directors has ultimately been defined in Companies Act 2006, section 172 as being to promote the success of the company for the benefit of shareholders while having regard to a range of other matters including: the likely consequences of any decision in the long term; the interests of the company's employees; the need to foster the company's business relationships with suppliers, customers and others; and the impact of the company's operations on the community and the environment.

The company interest that emerges from this statutory definition thus appears to involve a balancing of the interests of those with a financial stake in the organisation, on the one hand, and a range of others with a more or less close connection to the organisation, on the other. This approach to the company interest (which obviously does not involve the mechanical application of an algorithm, but rather involves the exercise of discretion by the board) was described by the Company Law Review as representing an example of the Enlightened Shareholder Value approach (1999: paras 5.1.12, 5.1.17–23). This is the idea that there is no necessary zero-sum game between the interests of shareholders and those of other stakeholders in the company, but rather that decisions taken which enhance the position of shareholders can simultaneously enhance the position of other stakeholders as well.

To express this in Teubner's terminology, the establishment of the company interest thus involves separating 'the main task of the enterprise ("function") from its contributions to other social sectors ('performance'), before recombining them as the corporate interest' (1994: 42). In systems theory terms, the *function* is the relationship of the organisation to the economy and society, namely 'securing ... as high a yield as possible to guarantee the satisfaction of future needs in society' (1994: 44). Similarly, its *performance* is the relationship of the organisation to its environment, constituted by its employees and shareholders as well as by its suppliers and creditors, and so on (1994: 44). The recombination of these dimensions is achieved by the organisation's *reflection*, that is, its relationship to itself or its autopoiesis. For Teubner, it is through the process of reflection that an ongoing balance is struck between the organisation's function and performance (1994: 44). This relationship between the three dimensions can be illustrated in the following diagram:

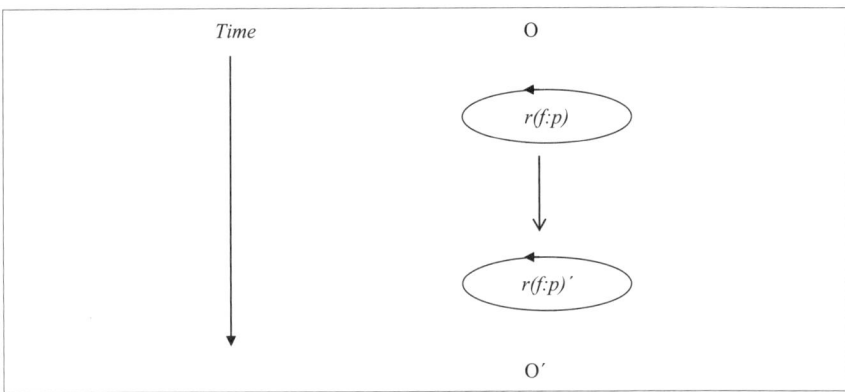

Figure 7.5 Systems theory perspective on the company interest

The corporate interest thus emerges dynamically from moment to moment as the product of the operation of the organisation's (O) autopoiesis (or reflection (r)) on the relationship between its function (f) and performance (p). This autopoietic reading of the organisation has significant implications for law – and indeed for economics. Traditional notions of the company's natural residual claimants must be abandoned along with the control presuppositions of regulators. The recognition of the key role played by the organisation's reflection implies that debates about its insiders and outsiders become redundant. Shareholders, customers, employees are all reduced to constructed artefacts of the system's self-reproduction. Similarly, the debate about whether it is appropriate to impose functions on organisations in a market economy takes on a new appearance. The most that could be hoped for from interventions with such aims is that they might produce irritations that might move the organisation somewhat in the desired direction – always presupposing that there would be consensus on what the function should be, to say nothing about sufficient agreement on the necessary legal and regulatory tools. And so it is with performance. Law and regulation might mandate performances (for example, in terms of the desired effects of the organisation's operations on employees or customers) but the success or failure of such mandates needs to be understood in terms of their internal construction by the organisations concerned.

It is the case, then, that not only will function and performance be internally constructed, but the process of reflection, the organisation's autopoiesis, will strike an ongoing balance between function and performance. Certain balances will be selected in preference to others and this is dependent on the organisation's autopoiesis and not on external legal or regulatory mandates. Any hope, then, that the complications raised by the fragmentation of contracts among the functional systems might be mitigated in the context of the organisation is dashed by the realisation that, in systems terms, the organisation does not 'transcend the hermeneutic differences of the ... contractual chains emerging in different social contexts', rather it only adds 'yet another difference to the set: the one between different social levels', in this case between system and organisation (Teubner 2007: 57).

Analysing the Bond/CDS Example in Terms of Both System and Organisation

As an example of the way in which this multiple (horizontal and vertical) fragmentation of contracts can pose problems for policy, law, and regulation in terms of any predictability of outcomes, it is possible to consider the operation of the corporate bond/credit default swap contracts examined previously whilst taking account of the added complexity of the interplay between system and organisation. It is possible to see, for example, that the perfect hedge outlined in Figure 7.1 and then developed in systems terms in the following figures takes on a different character when understood in the context of the organisation's reflection. Recall that the CDS issuer will pay out in the event of the default of the bond issuer. The crystallisation of the credit risk will likely be an indication that the bond issuer is close to insolvency. The orientation of corporate insolvency law in jurisdictions such as the US or the UK is increasingly focused on corporate rescue – in other words, it seeks to protect the fragile entity from the precipitate efforts of creditors to recover their debts in such a way as would drive it to collapse and instead to give it breathing space to see whether recovery of all or least part of the business is possible (Insolvency Service 2009). In this respect, it may be said that insolvency law seeks to impose a performance on creditor organisations by requiring that they acquiesce in the corporate rescue of debtors. One could speculate, however, that there may be occasions when not for reasons of pure profit but rather for reasons of self-continuation the fact that a creditor organisation holds a CDS will mean that it is indifferent to the insolvency of a bond issuer.[10] Absent the CDS, the creditor organisation would have an interest in corporate rescue. One can thus begin to see how internally coherent decisions of organisations can have perverse effects on the economy as a whole. The presence of the internally differentiated subsystem of finance offers a means of achieving payments even when underlying economic transactions (commodities, loans, etc.) fail.

Not only are the limits of policy and regulation on performance exposed by a systems approach, however. The inability of policy and regulation to guarantee the fulfilment of organisational function is also laid bare – perhaps nowhere more so than in situations where there are multiple failures of economic transactions, with the result that the viability of the potentially exponentially greater number of financial transactions is called into question. In other words, a protection buyer who has sought to hedge credit risk through the purchase of a credit default swap may find itself confronting the crystallisation of counterparty risk against which there is no hedge. Add to that scenario the range of parties holding CDSs on a speculative basis and the potential for the problem to spiral out of control very quickly is clear.

Bearing in mind that CDSs were at the lower end of the scale of complexity of the instruments involved in the crisis, the scale of the challenge facing those seeking to avoid a repeat becomes obvious. The systems perspective reveals the extent to which the internal differentiation of the system of the economy to produce the subsystem of finance results in blind spots which mask significant risks while almost paradoxically offering simultaneously the amplification of payments and the effective removal of risk.

Regulatory Challenges

The next question to be considered is: What, if anything, can be done with this insight in order to inform the current policy and regulatory efforts that are the

---

10 Economists describe this as the 'empty creditor' problem. For a discussion, see the written testimony of Henry T. C. Hu, to the U.S. Senate Banking Committee – Subcommittee on Securities, Insurance, and Investment, 21 June 2009.

focus of so much debate in the context of the financial crisis? It is the case, after all, that the authorities in the US, for example, are actively considering whether and how to regulate the trade in OTC instruments such as CDSs (Department of the Treasury 2009: 46–9). Luhmann of course would be sceptical that we could do anything in this regard, whatever the analysis revealed. The very nature of autopoietic systems theory for Luhmann excludes a normative dimension (Luhmann 1992). As regards law, however, systems theory has been developed, especially by Gunther Teubner, in a way which, while continually downplaying any sense that old linear-casual ideas of regulation can be maintained, is based on the assumption that a normative reading of the theory is possible. Specifically, the proposal is for a *reflexive* orientation for law in this context, that is, an orientation where law is both aware of its own autopoiesis and that of the other social systems (Paterson 2006; King 2006).

Proceeding on the basis that such a normative reading is possible, the next question to address is the level at which such regulatory 'interventions' should best be directed. The foregoing analysis would suggest at first sight that there may be possible intervention points at the level of the organisation and at that of the system. On the face of it, insofar as the decisions of organisations turn out to be crucial in the development and spread of perverse effects, it looks as if this is the most promising starting point and further that the ideal point of intervention is the process of reflection. But systems theory immediately raises obstacles by pointing out that this is beyond direct control. Policy makers and regulators could try to structure processes of reflection, but all that would be achieved (assuming the organisation even noticed the 'intervention') would be a constructed image of that structured process which would, of course, itself emanate from an inevitably partial construction of the nature of the problem in the first place. In short, the opportunities for failure – or at best sub-optimal outcomes – are manifold. This does not, of course, stop legislators from attempting to structure organisational reflection (even if they would not use that terminology). Any codification of directors' duties, for example (as discussed above), represents such an effort. But even lawyers who are not viewing the issue from the perspective of systems theory are under no illusions as to the actual strength of any such effort (Keay 2007). The observations of non-systems theorists are in accord here with those of systems theorists.

With this in mind, the current proposals for regulatory reform do not appear to enjoy good prospects for success. The first recommendation emerging from the US Department of the Treasury in this regard is the promotion of the robust supervision and regulation of financial firms (Department of the Treasury 2009: 19). While this is based on the entirely reasonable observation that a crucial dimension of the financial crisis was the level of organisational decision making, the present analysis has revealed the difficulties facing any intervention aimed at this level. Mandating behaviours regarding an organisation's function or performance in respect of OTC instruments will be likely to fail if they ignore its reflection, but, in any event, efforts to structure reflection are at best risky. They either place an immense cognitive burden on the policy maker, legislator or regulator or they are so light-touch as to risk indifference on the part of the regulated (Teubner 1985: 386).

Given the obstacles in the path of interventions at the level of the organisation, are there opportunities that could be exploited at the level of functional systems? Here Teubner's more recent work on the hybridization of contract may offer fruitful possibilities. Recognising that systems theory in its autopoietic form offers an uncompromisingly fragmented picture of the contract among the systems of law, economics, and whichever productive system is in play, thus leaving no room for the contract as a unifying force beyond the limited role of structural coupling, it would appear that the only hope for the reappearance of any such unitary model of the contract will be in the context of another theory, complementary to systems theory, which could, as it were, illuminate the blind spot of functional differentiation and focus on the binding force of contracts that is precisely invisible to autopoiesis (Teubner 2007: 63). There is, of course, no naive assumption that the fragmentation of the contract is thereby miraculously cured. What is aimed for here is no more than the generation of a 'surplus value' by the orthogonal positioning of these two complementary theories, from the mutual illumination of blind spots. That surplus value is not a magic bullet, however – it is no more that an indication of the direction in which some alleviation of the detrimental effects of the fragmentation of contracts might lie. In this regard, Teubner himself is particularly struck by what appears to be the most troubling aspect of the fragmentation of contracts brought about by functional differentiation – namely, the monopolization by the market of 'the right to interdiscursive translation' and thus the imposition of the 'economic translation on the other discourses' (Teubner 2007: 67). He advocates accordingly a 'new freedom of contract', one which 'would destroy the project of an economic rationalization of the world and introduce the obligation of a necessary and simultaneously impossible translation amongst the different languages of the social world' (2007: 68). As to how this idea of 'contract as translation' would be put into effect, Teubner suggests that this would involve 'an extension of constitutional rights into the context of private governance regimes', something, however, that he realises would require a 'fundamental rethinking of the horizontal effect of constitutional rights' (2007: 71).

If these ideas might appear to some to be rather idealistic, it is surely true to say that they resonate more strongly now in the context of the financial crisis than at the time of their publication in early 2007. The question is, however, whether they offer any realistic guidance for policy makers and regulators in terms of interventions at the level of the system if the door seems so firmly closed at the level of the organisation. A fundamental rethinking of constitutional rights and their extension to private governance regimes is perhaps a more imaginable possibility in the context of crisis than otherwise, but it still looks remote when so much of the policy and regulatory effort is directed at the detail of financial transactions. It may be the case, however, that some of these efforts are in closer accord with Teubner's suggested project than first appears to be the case. If another of the proposed US interventions is considered, then a sense can be derived of their consonance with the notion of a new freedom of contract focused on the question of the hegemony of the economy over interdiscursive translation.

This second recommendation from the Department of the Treasury on the face of it looks just as unpromising as that directed at the level of the organisation discussed above insofar as it is to establish comprehensive regulation of financial markets. The detail is, however, perhaps more promising insofar as it includes requirements for *transparency* (Department of the Treasury 2009: 43). This seems at first sight to be the lightest of light touches, but crucially there has heretofore been *no* transparency in OTC markets. There are limits, of course. While it would already be advantageous to see who was doing what, which positions were becoming particularly risky, and so on, problems nevertheless remain. For example, valuing the risk associated with the most complex instruments is difficult. Similarly, all approaches to valuation raise some possibilities that they will produce perverse effects. Nevertheless, while transparency does not by itself break the monopoly of the economic system on interdiscursive translation, it is surely a necessary precondition.

This very brief review of the main thrust of the US proposals as they currently stand thus does little to engender too much enthusiasm insofar as one is looking for indications of some actualisation of contract as translation in response to the horizontal and vertical fragmentation of contract in conditions of functional differentiation. It is true, of course, that insofar as the diagnosis of the problem upon which the US proposals is built is not inspired by systems theory, such a finding is by no means surprising. It is equally true to say that there needs to be a clear appreciation of just how much weight can be borne by Teubner's ideas in this regard. For a start, his ideas on contract as translation and in particular on the constitutional dimension are at an early stage. He is very much pointing in the direction in which a solution might lie but not making any strong claims to have worked out what such a solution would look like. Beyond that, it must also be borne in mind that, as compelling a picture of the problem as systems theory reveals, the shift from diagnosis to prescription in such a setting is controversial. Teubner has always been at pains to downplay how much can be claimed for reflexive law, but even that modesty has invoked the ire of those who see his desire to do something about the fragmentation of society in conditions of functional differentiation as fundamentally at odds with the insights of systems theory itself.

Conclusion

In concluding, then, while this chapter has demonstrated that a systems theory perspective on the financial instruments involved in the crisis of the past two years can produce a distinctive analysis of the nature of the problems, it equally appears not to have been able to offer much that is concrete for those now seeking solutions. A proponent of reflexive law might have been expected to produce something more in this regard, but the analysis in this case appears not to warrant such a conclusion. In short, while this chapter is able, firstly, to offer support for Teubner's diagnosis of contractual fragmentation and, secondly, to add weight to the call for an orthogonally complementary theory to turn its spotlight on the unitary and unifying nature of contract that systems theory so completely masks behind its blind spot, it does these things to differing degrees, albeit for the same reason.

The analysis in the foregoing sections, by revealing the status of finance as an internally differentiated subsystem of the economy, if anything reinforces Teubner's conclusions on fragmentation. It is not just that contract is split between 'the triangle of contractual projects' (Teubner 2007: 70), that is, between law, economy and a productive system, but rather that it is further split between economy and finance. Thus, while in the context of financial contracts there is at first sight a reduction of the fragmentation insofar as a productive system is not in play, closer analysis reveals that what is important is the intensification of the fragmentation. The fact that the fragmentation takes place also within an internally differentiated subsystem serves to reinforce the degree of separation of that construction of the contract from others – and as a by-product to reinforce the differentiation of the economy itself. On the other hand, the weight lent to Teubner's prescription of contract as translation, of a constitutionalisation of contract, is more equivocal. There is no argument at the conceptual level, but the empirical domain of financial instruments has revealed the extent of the challenge facing a complementary theory which would purport to illuminate systems theory's blindness to the unitary and unifying nature of contract. Thus, the same intensification of fragmentation that supports Teubner's diagnosis places further obstacles in the path of his prescription. This is not to suggest that there is any more obvious solution, only that the surplus value that would need to be generated by the orthogonal juxtaposition of the theory of contractual fragmentation and the theory of contractual unity to produce a meaningful outcome appears to have to cross a very high threshold indeed.

The threshold is so high precisely because of the intensification of the fragmentation that finance as an internally differentiated subsystem is able to achieve. By simultaneously offering the amplification of payments and the mitigation of risk, finance allows the same contract to have a universal appeal, to appear irresistible from whichever direction it is viewed. By doing this also in a form that appears costless and riskless, it has been able to intensify the hegemony of the economic discourse and thus to render the need for contract as translation all the more necessary and yet all the more difficult to achieve.

As a consequence, if the new map of the landscape produced by a systems theory analysis does not question the direction in which we have been pointed by the idea of contract as translation, of the constitutionalisation of contract, it does nevertheless reveal that the journey will be longer and more arduous in the context of financial instruments.

If one were to baulk at the apparent pessimism of this conclusion, one might be tempted to take more drastic action. Transparency in formerly opaque markets is all very well, but stronger interventions are surely required. Why not simply mandate the transfer of currently OTC instruments to exchanges? No doubt there would be protests that this would involve the removal of a useful risk management tool from parties whose risk profiles do not match standardised instruments, but these can surely be dismissed as special pleading. Given what the current study has revealed about the internally differentiated subsystem of finance, however, it is surely also the case that the removal of one risk management (and payment generating) tool would simply serve to stimulate the search for new alternatives. Finance appears to be a subsystem with a particularly tenacious self-reproductive process. Thus, while this chapter has mentioned in passing two arms of Teubner's regulatory trilemma – namely, the size of the cognitive burden that attempted interventions in complex organisations and systems impose on regulators and the possibility of indifference on the part of the regulated to those attempted interventions – there does not appear to be a scenario in which attempted regulation would actually pose a risk to the internally differentiated subsystem of finance.

Does this mean that finance is an exception when it comes to the regulatory trilemma? Perhaps yes, if one reads the concept narrowly so as to encompass only the scenario where there is a destructive effect on the regulated system as a consequence of the attempted regulatory intervention. Perhaps no, if one reads the concept more widely to encompass a situation where the inability of the regulator to contain the system allows it to damage itself. It is after all possible to imagine a scenario where finance's own blind spot results in such an outcome. If finance were to succeed in the amplification of payments to such an extent that its internal constructions were wildly different from those of the system of the economy within which it is located, then there is a real possibility that payments could stop – all of them. Thus, the fact that the regulators face only a dilemma turns out not to exclude the third possibility of the destruction of the regulated system. It is simply that that alternative seems to lie in the hands of the system itself – a fact which nevertheless reveals all the more starkly the scale of the challenge facing the regulators.

References

Basel Committee on Banking Supervision, *International Convergence of Capital Measurement and Capital Standards: A Revised Framework* (Basel: Bank for International Settlements, 2004).

Berkshire Hathaway, *Annual Letter to Shareholders 2002* (Omaha, NE: Berkshire Hathaway Inc., 2002).

Berle, A.A., 'Corporate Powers as Powers in Trust', *Harvard Law Review* 44 (1931), 1049.

Chance, D.M., *An Introduction to Derivatives and Risk Management* (Sydney; London: Thomson/South-Western, 2004).

Clubley, S., *Trading in Oil Futures and Options* (Cambridge and Boca Raton: Woodhead/CRC, 1998).
Company Law Review, *Modern Company Law for a Competitive Economy: The Strategic Framework* (London: DTI, 1999).
____, *Modern Company Law for a Competitive Economy: Developing the Framework* (London: DTI, 2000a).
____, *Modern Company Law for a Competitive Economy: Completing the Structure* (London: DTI, 2000b).
____, *Modern Company Law for a Competitive Economy: Final Report* (London: DTI, 2001).
Culp, C.L., and M.H. Miller, *Corporate Hedging in Theory and Practice: Lessons from Metallgesellschaft* (London: Risk Books, 1999).
Department of the Treasury, *Financial Regulatory Reform – A New Foundation: Rebuilding Financial Supervision and Regulation* (Washington, DC: Department of the Treasury, 2009).
Dodd, E.M., 'For Whom Are Corporate Managers Trustees?', *Harvard Law Review* 45 (1932), 1145.
Errera, S., and S.L. Brown, *Fundamentals of Trading Energy Futures and Options* (Tulsa, OK: PennWell, 1999).
Financial Services Authority, *The FSA's Risk-based Approach: A Guide for Non-Executive Directors* (London: Financial Services Authority, 2006).
Financial Service Authority (FSA), *A Regulatory Response to the Global Banking Crisis* (London: Financial Services Authority, 2009).
Goldstein, M., 'Profiting from Mortality', *Business Week*, 30 July 2007, cover story.
Insolvency Service, *Encouraging Corporate Rescue: A Consultation* (London: Insolvency Service, 2009).
Keay, A., 's172(1) of the Companies Act 2006: An Interpretation and Assessment', *Company Lawyer* 28/4 (2007), 106–10.
King, M., 'What's the Use of Luhmann's Theory?', in M. King and C. Thornhill (eds), *Luhmann on Politics and Law: Critical Appraisals and Applications* (Oxford: Hart, 2006), 37–52.
Kolb, R.W., *Financial Derivatives*, 2nd edn (Cambridge, MA.: Blackwell Business, 1996).
Luhmann, N., 'Closure and Openness: On Reality in the World of Law', in G. Teubner (ed.), *Autopoietic Law: A New Approach to Law and Society* (Berlin: de Gruyter, 1989), 335–48.
Luhmann, N., 'Some Problems with Reflexive Law', in G. Teubner and A. Febbrajo (eds), *State, Law and Economy as Autopoietic Systems* (Milan: Giuffrè, 1992), 389–415.
____, *Social Systems* (Stanford, CA: Stanford University Press, 1995).
____, 'Limits of Steering', *Theory, Culture and Society* 14/1 (1997), 41–57.
McDonald, R.L., *Fundamentals of Derivatives Markets* (Boston and London: Pearson Addison Wesley, 2009).

Menkhoff, L., and N. Tolksdorf, *Financial Market Drift: Decoupling of the Financial Sector from the Real Economy?* (Berlin: Springer, 2001).

Paterson, J., 'Reflecting on Reflexive Law', in M. King and C. Thornhill (eds), *Luhmann on Politics and Law: Critical Appraisals and Applications* (Oxford: Hart, 2006), 13–35.

Paterson, J., and G. Teubner, 'Changing Maps: Empirical Legal Autopoiesis', *Social and Legal Studies* 7/4 (1998), 451–86.

Rottleuthner, H., 'The Limits of Law: The Myth of a Regulatory Crisis', *International Journal of the Sociology of Law* 17 (1989), 273–85.

Sas, B., 'Legal Aspects of Risk Management in Energy Markets', *Petroleum Economist, Energy Law Supplement* (July 1992), 50–59.

Teubner, G., 'After Legal Instrumentalism: Strategic Models of Post-Regulatory Law', in G. Teubner (ed.), *Dilemmas of Law in the Welfare State* (Berlin: de Gruyter, 1985), 299–325.

____, 'Regulatory Law: Chronicle of a Death Foretold', *Social and Legal Studies* 1/4 (1992), 451–75.

____, 'Company Interest: The Public Interest of the Enterprise "in Itself"', in R. Rogowski and T. Wilthagen (eds), *Reflexive Labour Law: Studies in Industrial Relations and Employment Regulation* (The Hague, London and New York: Kluwer Law International, 1994), 21–52.

____, 'Contracting Worlds: the Many Autonomies of Private Law', *Social and Legal Studies* 9/3 (2000), 399–417.

____, 'In the Blind Spot: The Hybridization of Contracting', *Theoretical Inquiries in Law* 8/1 (2007), 51–71.

Turner, Lord, *A Regulatory Response to the Global Banking Crisis*, (London: Financial Services Authority, 2009).

Viral, A., and M. Richardson, *Restoring Financial Stability: How to Repair a Failed System* (Hoboken, NJ: John Wiley & Sons, 2009).

Chapter 8
Values as Certain Uncertainties: The Paradox of Value Communication in Organisational Practice

Victoria von Groddeck

Introduction

Value-driven activities have become widespread in business organisations in recent years (Ethics Resource Center 2003, 2005, 2007). These activities define values as guiding principles, mission statements, and moral standards for leadership, and take a variety of forms, such as employees participating in corporate-sponsored volunteerism and new styles of leadership motivating employees not only by monetary incentives but also by value commitment.[1]

The rationale on which these developments are based is that (shared) values build an unconscious perception pattern that give orientation in complex situations and therefore support organisational control and improve ethical reasoning in management. The need for these activities is evident in the urge to develop new mechanisms of governance that can resolve conflicts between economic rationality and societal conditions (Conrad 1993, Frederick 1995, Seeger 1997, Schein 1991, Hofstede 2006, Kelly et al. 2005).

This characterisation of the motives of value-driven activities, however, is confronted with the fact that most of these activities do not deliver the required result. In our research interviews, employees describe how they do not feel supported in their work when high goals or values are set, and that they hardly see any changes in their daily business. In contrast, the introduction of value activities raises scepticism and disappointment. Both employees and the mass media react suspiciously, tending to accuse business organisations of window-dressing, using value semantics only for the organisational self-description and being essentially dishonest.

These empirical observations reveal that value communication seems to use its own rules: not only are the effects more complex as described in the causal manner by ethical management consultants (e.g. Kelly et al. 2005 Wieland 2004), but also the phenomenon of increasing value communication links organisational issues

---

1   An overview over value-driven activities in German business corporations is offered by Wieland (2004).

to societal issues. In this chapter, a system theoretical perspective will connect organisational and societal perspectives (Luhmann 1996, 1997).

Accordingly, several questions will be analysed and discussed in this chapter: Why is it plausible for business organisations to communicate on behalf of moral or social values? How is value communication influenced by the relation between organisational perspective and the environment of the organisation – or, to rephrase: Which role does society play?

Epistemological Premise

The basic task of this chapter is to understand how the contingent forms of value-communication stabilise themselves as organisational structure, as well as the functions of these specific communication structures. This research question excludes a pre-empirical definition of *value*; instead, value communication is understood as an element of organisational practice that follows a self-referential logic and not the logic of an academic idea. Therefore, the theoretical outline should enable research that can reflect the relationship between the theoretical preconditions of the research observation and the closed observation modes of the practice that is to be studied. From a system theoretical perspective this is a paradoxical venture. Because of the *closure of systems*, observation is unavoidably bound to the systemic, internal construction of an outside reality. In the context of perception this means that the 'reality is in the head' while simulating that 'the head is in reality' (Kneer and Nassehi 2000: 54, translated by the author). Accordingly, research observation is always self-referential and has to construct something outside that can be observed, described or analysed. Scientific insight is therefore, in this case, nothing more than a self-constructed observation.

But this is not a disadvantage. Moreover, if research starts with the epistemological perspective that all social processes of observation are operationally closed, constructionist research finds its strengths in describing the *contingency of closed social practice*. Thus, it is a practice which is improbable but not impossible: the task is to comprehend the specific selections of communications which are made in practice and to examine and understand how these selections are restricted by specific observer positions without forgetting that these analyses of communication practice are the product of the researcher's own closed observation practice (Nassehi and Saake 2002).

To show how a certain research perspective forms the analysis of the closed, self-referential communication practice (which is itself also a specific mode of observation), we will use the illustrative definition of observation of George Spencer-Brown, combining the idea of indication and distinction: 'We take as given the idea of distinction and the idea of indication, and that we cannot make an indication without drawing a distinction' (Spencer-Brown 1994: 1).

This definition of observation delivers a 'tool' to analyse differences in observation practices by defining observation as a communication that indicates something by simultaneously distinguishing it from something else. So two sides emerge by distinguishing: a marked and an unmarked space which is the explicit or implicit context of the marked side. Together with the third side – the distinction itself – these three sides build a specific *form* of observation. A form that can be illustrated as follows:

Figure 8.1 The form of observation

Exactly this perception of observation – as a three-part form – delivers an approach to describe and reflect closed observation perspectives by describing the practice of indicating and distinguishing.[2] By using Spencer-Brown's definition of observation it becomes possible to describe different observation forms heuristically – both one's own research perspective and the observation practice of the research phenomenon, which is formed by the research perspective.

We will first concentrate on the particular form of observation that enables the observation of a phenomenon by showing which contexts restrict the observation of the research object.[3] In the second part of this chapter we will show how communication practices that use value semantics form themselves as a contingent selection process.

---

2 Every observation has its blind spot because it can only observe what it can observe by the distinction. The observation cannot observe what it cannot observe by the particular distinction because reality exactly emerges by the particular distinction.

3 At this stage of research the construction of ontology is unavoidable. The difference to positivistic research is that the particular use of ontology is seen as contingent, open ontology, which is needed to create a phenomenon, but which has to be reflected during the research process (Åkerstrøm Andersen 2003a).

The Form of Research Observation

So far, the basic distinction for research observation is that the phenomenon of *value communication* is perceived as the marked side. It indicates what shall be of interest to the empirical analyses. The context (unmarked side), which influences the mode of observation of the phenomenon, is the theoretical perception that *all social operations are closed.*

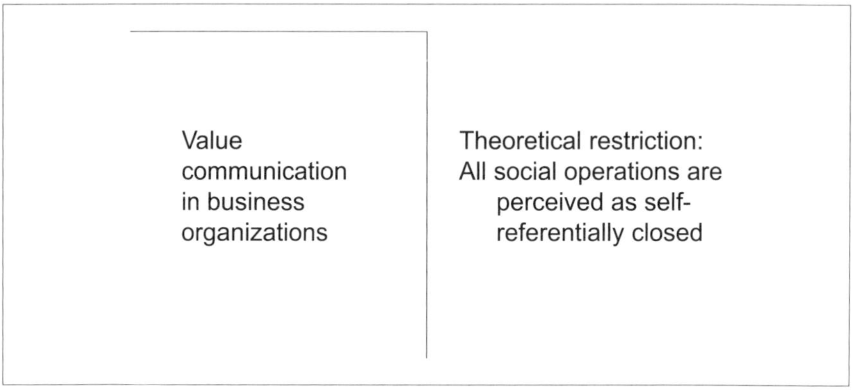

Value communication in business organizations	Theoretical restriction: All social operations are perceived as self-referentially closed

Figure 8.2 First form of research observation

The following outline concretises this basic distinction by showing how the form of research observation constructs the phenomenon of value communication in organisations.

1. Organisations in the Society as a 'Society of Presences'

As a further context of the form of research observation, the perception of organisation in society in general becomes extremely relevant, as without a concept of organisation and society, it is impossible to analyse organisational practice at all.

All social systems consist of certain communicative operations, or rather the connectivity of communicative events over time. The term 'system' is used to show how certain social formations emerge that are stabilised by the interrelations, feedback processes, and self-steering processes of communication.

This means that, by the real-time interrelation of certain communications, systems emerge by distinguishing themselves from their environment. In this context, systems – as already mentioned – are perceived as *operationally closed*. Closure in this respect does not mean that such systems are not able to experience contact with their environments. Although systems are not led by the idea that they work for a 'whole',[4] simultaneously systems are dependent on each other on a functional or informational level. They are only independent or closed on their operational level. The simultaneousness of both the self-referential, real-time operations of a system and the dependence on the capacity, logic, and function of a system in the environment, leads to a characterisation of society as a society of presences.

This simultaneity of dependence and independence sometimes turns society into a drama. This drama is due to the fact that a 'stage director' neither coordinates different 'roles' nor follows a certain 'script' that has to be fulfilled. Even more, on the 'stage' of society 'lay-actors' perform who have no opportunity to rehearse or correct their performance, because every social action takes place in real time. They have to improvise and self-stabilise the structures referring to the interdependence of operative independent functional systems. It is a fundamental *society of presences* (Nassehi 2003: 165; translated by the author).

Systems can be distinguished as interactions, societal functions, and organisations.[5] This theoretical differentiation builds empirical criteria for the observation of social practice. The distinction of three types of social systems allows the researcher not only to analyse an interaction as a situation where people meet in person but also to observe how an interaction might be structured by organisational decision-making or the logic of functional systems. The strengths of systems theory lie in the possibility to not only observe social practices but also to reconstruct the different systemic logics that determine the particular situation. This chapter studies business organisations, which means that systems theory allows observing the *certain restrictions* that influence the *concrete practice* in *business* organisations. Of interest are both the internal decisions of the particular business organisation and the restricting power of function systems like economy, law, and other societal systems (Nassehi 2005, Åkerstrøm Andersen 2003b, Åkerstrøm Andersen and Born 2007).

---

4   Exactly this was the conception of Talcott Parsons (e.g. 1960).

5   *Interactions* are social systems which use the co-presences of persons as their delimiting criteria. Interactions depend on the mutual perception of persons who respond to each other in real time. *Functional systems* structure themselves by specific communication media, such as money in economy, belief in religion, justice in the legal system or truth in science (Luhmann 1977, 1982). These communication media are able both to make improbable forms of connectivity less improbable and to facilitate the emergence of the functional systems themselves. Luhmann's observation of the emergence of different functional systems that are fostered by specific communication media leads to an understanding of society which emphasises differentiation instead of unity (Luhmann 1997, Nassehi 2003). *Organisations* for Luhmann are social systems which are able to stabilise forms of action and behaviour by the communication of decisions about both rules of membership and their practical doing (Baecker 2006). Since organisations perpetuate themselves by connecting decision to decision, they can be characterised as "decision machines" (Nassehi 2005).

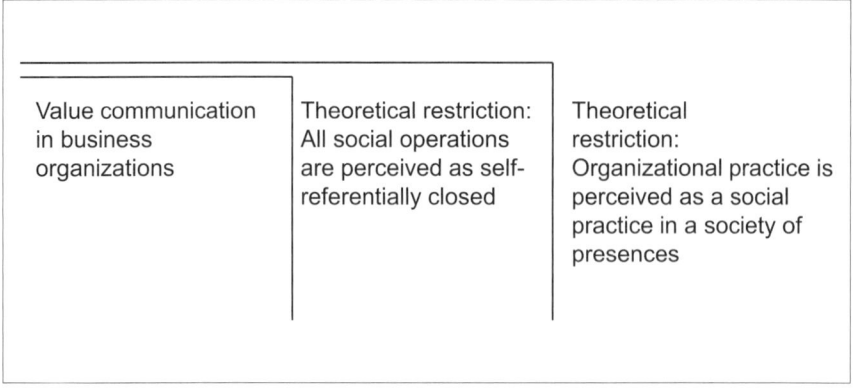

Figure 8.3 Second form of research observation

2. Values

After introducing the basic assumptions of the conception of society as a restricting context for a particular form of research observation, we will shift to the theoretical perspective on values as an extension of the form of research observation. The term 'value' has a long tradition in sociology, philosophy, and economics. The term 'value' grew very prominent at the end of the nineteenth century, when early sociologists used it to discuss the question of societal integration.[6] Because of an increasingly differentiated society with a less clear structure, the question arose as to what the society was holding together. The answer was seen in moral, social, and cultural values, not in religious beliefs as it had been in the pre-modern society (e.g. Durkheim 1973, Parsons 1960). Parsons formulates: 'Values in this sense are commitments of individual persons to pursue and support certain directions or types of action for the collectivity as a system and hence derivatively for their own roles in the collectivity' (Parsons 1960: 172).

This theoretical perception that values direct action and thereby secure a collective entity still forms the underlying principle for more applied research in the actual discussion of value activities in organisations, for example, business ethics or organisation studies (Conrad 1993, Frederick 1995, Seeger 1997, Schein 1991, Hofstede 2006, Kelly et al. 2005, Peters and Waterman 2006, Kotter and

---

6   The semantic history of the term 'value' is of course older. In the early Middle Ages the term was used to express appreciated characteristics of a person. From the thirteenth century onwards a splitting between an ideal and a material meaning was observable, but only in the nineteenth century, at the beginning of the modern age, did the plural 'values' emerge to express a certain relativism between values (Stollberg-Rilinger and Weller 2005). This development can also be reconstructed in the entry 'Würde' in Reinhart Koselleck's *Geschichtliche Grundbegriffe* (Brunner, Conze and Koselleck 1992).

Heskett 1992, Collins and Porras 1997). It should be evident that contemporary research on values in organisations relies on a theoretical conception that understands the function of values through its potential to integrate social entities by giving individual orientation for their action.

From a system theoretical perspective of society, which emphasises functional differentiation (Luhmann 1996), the common understanding of the function of value for integration and orientation is rather sceptical for both theoretical and empirical reasons.

Theoretically, a functionally differentiated society does not need values as integration mechanisms because social practice occurs in decoupled spheres, which build their own construction of the world (Nassehi 2003: 263–5). Furthermore, Luhmann argues that values are not able to direct action. He analyses values as a form of communication and not as a theoretical idea to explain a certain action (Luhmann 1990b, 1997). His argument is that values are too abstract to give orientation in specific decision situations, because for every value there is an opposite value, for example the antagonism between freedom and justice.

Each value merely precludes its antithesis (and not always even that). The resolution of collisions between values is thus unregulated. But decisions are only needed in the case of value collision. From this it follows that values are not able to regulate decisions. They may demand a consideration of the relevant values, but a conclusion does not follow from this as to which values are decisive in cases of conflict and as to which are set aside. All values may count as necessary, but all decisions remain, nevertheless, and for that very reason, contingent (Luhmann 1999: 66).

Here, Luhmann emphasises that values cannot solve conflicts or give orientation in complex situations, which is exactly the hope of business ethics researchers and managers who try to solve dilemmas through value management. Following Luhmann's argument, we can understand why the introduction of value activities can cause disappointments. The communicated values, which in the first place are communicated as expectation for the right management, cannot deliver orientation in conflict situations because these situations are constituted by unsolvable value conflicts. But despite Luhmann's argument, we cannot ignore the fact that value semantics – even if they do not deliver the desired effect – are empirically observed elements of organisational practice. Thus, the question of why value communication stabilises itself in organisational practice becomes even more relevant and interesting, especially from a system theoretical perspective.

Thus, in this chapter, values are not pre-empirically defined as an integration or orientation element, but solely as empirically observable elements of communication. The practices of value communication should therefore examine the contingent forms of indicating and distinguishing these practices.

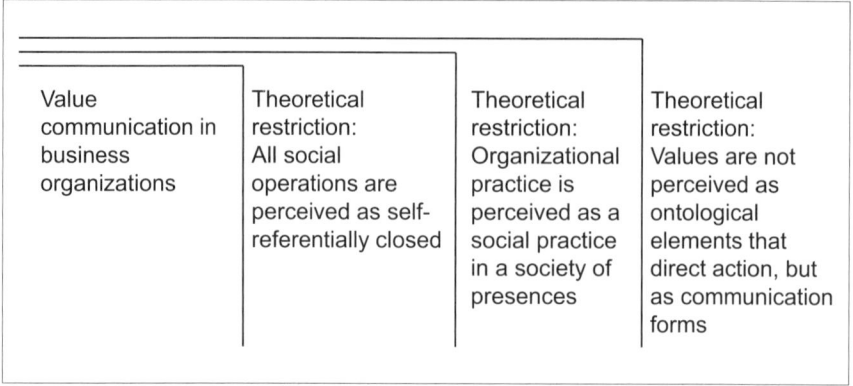

Figure 8.4 Third form of research observation

3. Analytical Strategy

Values are not presumed as an essential condition of individuals or social entities that influence action. They are empirically observable forms of communication that only *refer* to values as invisible aspects of individuals or societal entities. This conception of values and the general theoretical perspective of a system theoretical approach call for a methodology that employs communication practices as their starting point.[7] Organisational practice is perceived as lines of communications that deal with different systemic logics – interactional, organisational, functional – in real time. The challenge is to understand in what organisational contexts value communication is used and what role value communication plays in these organisational practices. The analytical strategy (Åkerstrøm Andersen 2003a) thereby combines a form analysis with a functional analysis. The form analysis (Luhmann 1997, Baecker 2006, Åkerstrøm Andersen 2003a) attempts to distinguish and describe different modes and locations of value communication in organisation. Reformulated in a system theoretical manner, this means that the aim of the form analysis is to observe the form of observation of the observed practice.

The functional analysis (Luhmann 2005a, 2005b) calls for the specific function of these particular observation forms, wherein *function* is not a term to describe causal effects of values. The functional analysis describes relational dependencies between problems and solutions. A specific phenomenon such as a form of value communication is perceived as an operational solution for an operational problem in an organisation. From a system theoretical perspective, the problem–

---

7   Although we start from a theoretical perspective (e.g. functionally differentiated society), the analysis should not be perceived as deductive, but as an oscillation between a theoretical horizon that offers meaning by establishing a frame of reference for empirical observations that in turn feed back into the theoretical frame (Åkerstrøm Andersen 2003a).

solution relationship is rooted in the need for the survival of the system, here the organisation. If we ask for the function of value communication, the task will be to relate the phenomenon of value communication to a particular referring problem that is solved by the practice of value communication. Thus this analytical strategy leads to insights as to why certain forms of value communication stabilise in organisations.

From this analytical perspective, the first task is to gain access to organisational practice and to communication that explicitly or implicitly uses values (semantics). To apply these considerations, a multi-case study approach (Yin 2005: 13–45) and a documentation analysis have been adopted with the aim of gaining access to the relevant empirical material, which means that as many as possible different communication practices in organisations have been observed. Involved are eight cases from global companies from different industries and 35 company documents that were publicly accessible.[8] In all case study companies, *narrative interviews* were conducted with a heterogeneous sample of employees (in gender, age, operational function, hierarchic status).[9] Furthermore, *protocols of participant observation* were produced and *internal and external documents* were analysed.[10]

We now switch perspective. In the following section, the closed forms of organisational observations and their functions, which emerge by the presented form of research observation, will be described.

Forms and Functions of Value Communication

The basic findings of the analysis of the empirical material is that value semantics are a communication media in business organisations that are able to cope with *uncertainty*. This means that the uncertainty of dealing with the complex organisa-

---

8   The industry sample consists of three companies from the financial service industry, one firm from the information technology industry, one from the insurance industry, one from the automobile industry and two companies from the engineering industry. As a selection criterion, the companies had to deal with corporate values in their organisational practice. Some of the companies were just introducing value programmes, where other companies had ten years of experience with a value programme.

9   The interviews were conducted in German; the cited passages have been translated into English for this chapter. No identifying information was elicited from the employees who were interviewed. The 'XXX' indicates these passages. Generally, as the structure of communication was the object of interest, the approach was to produce stories about the respondent's everyday working situation; this approach differs fundamentally from an approach that is interested in obtaining expert knowledge.

10   The process of the analysis of the data is threefold. First, all data was scanned for the emergence of values and the relevant passages were coded. Second, by searching for patterns and relationships, the codes were categorised into particular forms of value communication. Third, the identified forms were analysed for the specific function in the concrete social practice recorded in the empirical material.

tion and its environment can be semantically addressed by value communication. Values are a medium for organisations to cope with uncertainty, which is unavoidably produced by the simultaneity of a multitude of organisational operations.

In the following, three different forms of dealing with uncertainty by value communication are presented:

1. Form: The Uncertainty of Heterogeneous Expectations

The first form of value communication that was observable in the empirical material was dominant in official organisational self-descriptions (Seidl 2003a, 2003b) such as glossy brochures or annual reports. *Here, the essential observation is that self-description of organisations is only possible by a dominant use of values*. The following examples will illustrate this assumption.

The 2006 annual report of the German flight carrier Deutsche Lufthansa AG stated that the company wanted to grow by delivering 'excellent quality' and 'innovative service' and that this aim would produce opportunity for all stakeholders and thereby would 'create value' [*Wertschaffung*][11] for everybody (Deutsche Lufthansa AG 2006: 1).[12] In a similar way the automobile manufacturer BMW introduced its annual report with the phrase 'Assuming responsibility. Creating Values' (BMW AG 2006: 1); the German brand of the UniCredit Bank Bayerische HypoVereinsbank published a brochure with the title 'Live values – create value' [*Werte leben – Werte schaffen*] (Bayerische HypoVereinsbank 2007).

The sociological question that follows this observation is why business organisations refer to values when they describe themselves? This question links to the fact that organisations have to adapt to their environment in order to operate (Luhmann 2005c, Weick 1976, 1979, 1995). To survive, every organisation must coordinate its operations in a way that its outcomes interest at least some parts in the environment. Simultaneously, the organisation needs a degree of internal coordination (Luhmann 1964: 108).

Even if the idea of the essential need of adaptation and integration is accepted, the question of why the organisational self-descriptions of companies like Lufthansa or BMW do not refer to a factual purpose, like selling cars or flight tickets, but to abstract values, remains. The function of this abstract communication form lies in the need to secure the essential support of environmental and internal structures in situations where organisations have to react simultaneously to *heterogeneous expectations*. In situations with a heterogeneous audience, for example in an annual report or during an annual general meeting, it is difficult for an organisation to live up to all performance expectations. The factual purpose, like selling cars, might disappoint stakeholders who, for example, expect information about the

---

11 The original German expression is given to facilitate the understanding of the interpretation process.

12 The document analysis was based on documents written in German; for this chapter all passages from these documents have been translated by the author.

social engagement of an organisation. The solution to this problem is to use abstract semantics like values. This trick allows the organisation to express its identity without dismissing different or even contradicting expectations in the environment and without dismissing the simultaneously existing different parts of the organisation itself which all have divergent or even contradictory aims and purposes. To emphasise this point, the societal expectations that organisations must fulfil are so ambiguous, complex and heterogeneous that only abstract values are able to respond to all of them at the same time. This is possible because the meaning of a value is rather elastic (Luhmann 1990b).

The same can be said for the organisation itself. Only very abstract value communication makes it possible to address all internal differentiations with their different perspectives and references at the same time.

Therefore, values can address very complex and fuzzy configurations outside and inside the organisation. For example, in all analysed material, the organisations had to represent their merit with regard to economic, ecological and social references. To fulfil these complex expectations the only possibility is to use a very abstract communication form that can be read by all perspectives.

One can say business organisations change from 'monophonic' to 'heterophonic' (Åkerstrøm Andersen 2003b, Åkerstrøm Andersen and Born 2007), because even for the survival of business organisations the pure orientation towards the functional system of the economy is not sufficient, and interaction with different perspectives is essential. Therefore, to enlist environmental support for organisational issues, it is not enough to communicate in an economical manner, but other heterogeneous contexts must also be observed and positively influenced. This is precisely the function of value semantics: they have the power to communicate between heterogeneous logics. No part in the organisation or no stakeholder group outside the organisation would be disturbed by communicated values like quality and innovation or by value creation in general.

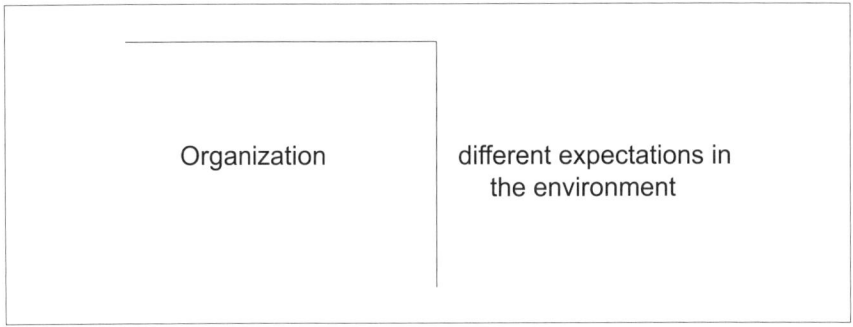

Figure 8.5 The uncertainty of heterogeneous expectations

2. Form: The Uncertainty of the Organisational Identity

It is clear that values are a capacitive communication media to address heterogeneous expectations both in the environment and within the organisation. Whereas in the previous section value communication is linked to the problem of simultaneously reacting to heterogeneous expectations from outside and inside of the organisation, this section shows how values play a role in the construction of an organisational identity. It will be shown that the presentation of organisational identity is only possible in reference to values. The form of value communication connected to the role of identity construction was mainly observable in the interview material of the study rather than in the analysed documents.

So far it has been shown that value communication has the function to balance different system logics by avoiding the exclusion of important perspectives from outside and inside the organisation. Value communication therefore enhances environmental support for the organisation's survival. In this section it will be shown how value communication reacts to the internal problem to simultaneously secure a certain state of integration and the differentiation of structures. Both are permanently needed to sustain the progress of organising. Here, values are a means of constructing an identity to conceal the fact that an organisation has never only one single or stable identity (Seidl 2003b, Weick 1995). This semantic 'trick' leads to identity construction that secures integration on a very abstract level, which does not necessarily affect the concrete situation. This identity construction should not be characterised as a deficit but as a very clever manoeuvre that both encourages a shared formal structure and gives flexibility to how an acute problem is solved. Again, this is possible because the meaning of values is elastic and therefore cannot direct concrete action.

Empirically, it is observable that this 'trick' is performed by the construction of an 'outside'. In the interviews, the identity of the organisation was described by emphasising the *uniqueness* of the corporate culture. This uniqueness, however, could only be described by comparing the company to something which appears significantly different. The following statement by a female employee illustrates this:[13]

> OK, it's our *culture* here at XXX, I'd say, before ... at XXX I didn't have a great insight, it was all a little chaotic, I had the feeling, nobody knew what the others were doing. I think the reason lay in the Chinese culture. After this experience I worked for a little agency, everything was loyal and informal and then I had completely different expectations ... the change to XXX, I thought everything would be more strict. And I had a lot of respect for such a big affair, for the people you meet and everything ... I was afraid whether I could meet expectations, because I thought the claims would be doubly high at this huge company compared to a small one.

---

13 Please refer to note 8.

The employee is only able to describe the uniqueness of her company by referring to the uniqueness of the corporate culture. However, mentioning the specific culture seems insufficient to give a clear picture. Comparing the present employer to the former sharpens the picture of the corporate culture. This mode of comparison is expressed in terms of values: the 'chaotic' structure of the Chinese company is compared to the 'loyalty' of the smaller company and the 'strictness' of the present employer.

This form of value communication has its function in constructing an organisational identity without revealing the complex and sometimes contradictory structures of the organisation. By semantically comparing the company to other organisations it becomes possible to make the relevant organisation appear more consistent or self-identical than it is, but, as said earlier, just a semantic identity is essential to coordinate the organisation's operations (Drepper 2005, Drucker 2001, 2002). This form of value communication makes it possible to transfer the internal complexity of an organisation and the uncertainty of dealing with it into a communicable form of an organisational identity.

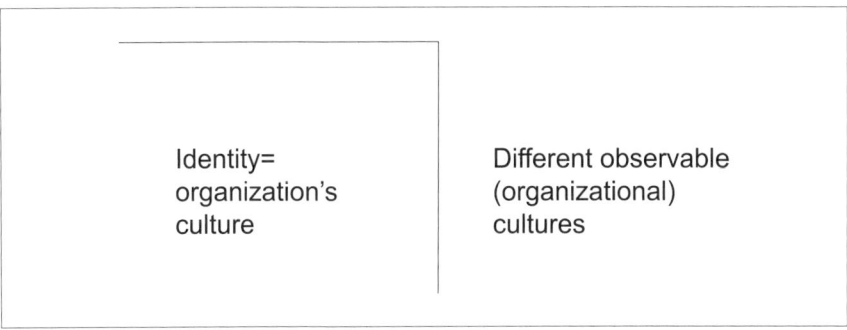

Figure 8.6 The uncertainty of the organisational identity

3. Form: The Uncertainty of the Organisational Future

So far the function of value communication lies in the potential to cope with uncertainty, 'caused' by, for example, the complexity and 'polycontexturality' (Günther 1979) of the societal environment or the multi-identity organisation. In the following we will see that values are also applicable to the uncertain construction of the *organisational future*.

Values in this context are communicated to describe the organisational future. As the future is an unclear and inaccessible horizon from the perspective of the present, it is impossible to describe it as a determinable matter of facts (Luhmann 1990a). Nonetheless, in many situations, organisations have to describe their future, for example in the annual general meeting or in a strategy workshop. Organisations then face the paradox of having to describe something that is not describable, because the future is always unknown. Values are a medium to describe the future. They create a satisfying picture of the future, which is simultaneously equipped with a degree of freedom. Values resolve the paradox to describe the indescribable, because values deliver elastic possibilities of meaning.

The annual report of Lufthansa illustrates this argumentation. At the beginning of the report, Lufthansa compares 'achievements' with 'objectives' (Deutsche Lufthansa AG 2006: 6). In the column of achievements the reader finds measurable facts about the last year (e.g. the share price rose by 66.6 per cent to €20.85 and a Corporate Value Added (CVA) of 552 billion was reached). In the column of objectives, the language differs considerably (e.g. the aim is to 'increase the corporate value' and to 'strengthen the confidence in a value-oriented growth strategy').

The example shows that the future is described by value semantics whereas the past is described by facts. This is not surprising, because the description of the future is a risky task for business organisations. The risk is that the difference between the past and a certain picture of the future in the present determines the company's scope of action and decision, although it is unclear what the future will bring. Describing the future in terms of abstract values has the advantages both defining the future and leaving it open.

Figure 8.7 The uncertainty of the organisational future

Conclusion: The Paradox of Value Communication

Three forms of value communication have been identified from the analysed material. All three of these forms respond to the problem of coping with uncertainty. In these situations, values are a communication means to provide the organisation stability, meaning and certainty for its actions, although the conditions under which the organisation has to act are very often unstable, ambiguous and uncertain

(Drucker 2001, 2002, Baecker 2007). In this context, value semantics change uncertainty into certainty by expressing the non-transparent observation in forms that allow both meaning and ambiguity.

The reason for the capacity of values to cope with uncertainty lies in the fact that values, on the one hand, are communication media which offer a very abstract semantic that makes it possible to address and describe very complex, ambiguous and uncertain situations and conditions. One the other hand, the use of value semantics transports a certain kind of meaning which suffices to build a base for organisational action. Value communication thereby helps organisations to act when it is unclear what to do.

This is precisely the point at which value communication becomes relevant for managerial control. Using value conditions, the urge for decision, action and change can be marked even when a numeric database is missing. But this aspect of managerial control by communication cannot be exploited in a causal manner because values transport meaning only on a very abstract, elastic basis that indicates a need for action but does not determine exactly how to act. This shortcoming of value communication is what constitutes the crucial point for the role of values with regard to management. Values, on one hand, establish media, which transform uncertain circumstances into meaning so that these circumstances can be managed in the organisation. On the other hand, the communicated meaning is so elastic that values do not have the power to control concrete situations.

This is not a paradoxical deficit but a modus of control which emphasises flexibility and creativity, as values only offer abstract points of reflection, but not strict instructions on how to act. This increases the chance to develop innovative forms of management that make the organisation more powerful – both with regard to ethical claims and to economic success.

References

Åkerstrøm Andersen, N., *Discursive Analytical Strategies: Understanding Foucault, Koselleck, Laclau, Luhmann* (Bristol: Policy Press, 2003a).
____, 'Polyphonic Organisations', in T. Hernes and T. Bakken (eds), *Autopoietic Organisation Theory: Drawing on Niklas Luhmann's Social Systems Perspective* (Copenhagen: Copenhagen Business School Press, 2003b), 151–82.
____, 'Heterophony and the Postponed Organisation: Organizing Autopoietic Systems', *Tamara Journal for Critical organisational Inquiry* 6/2 (2007), 176–6.
Baecker, D., 'The Form of the Firm', *The Critical Journal on Organisation, Theory and Society* 13/1 (2006), 109–42.
Baecker, D., *Studien zur nächsten Gesellschaft* (Frankfurt am Main: Suhrkamp, 2007).

BMW AG, Geschäftsbericht 2006. Available online at http://www.bmwgroup. com/d/0_0_www_bmwgroup_com/investor_relations/finanzberichte/geschaeftsberichte/2006/popup/_downloads/gb2006_gesamt.pdf [accessed 26 September 2007].

Brunner, O., W. Conze and R. Koselleck, *Geschichtliche Grundbegriffe*, vol. 7 (Stuttgart: Klett-Cotta, 1992).

Collins, J. C., and J. I. Porras, *Built to Last: Successful Habits of Visionary Companies* (New York: Harper Business, 1994).

Conrad, C. (ed.), *The Ethical Nexus* (Norwood: Ablex, 1993).

Deutsche Lufthansa AG, Geschäftsbericht 2006. Available online at http://konzern.lufthansa.com/de/downloads/presse/downloads/publikationen/lh_gb_2006.pdf [accessed 26 September 2007].

Drepper, T., 'Organization and Society', in D. Seidl and K. H. Becker (eds), *Niklas Luhmann and Organisation Studies* (Malmö: Liber, 2005), 171–90.

Drucker, P., 'The Next Society', *The Economist* 3 (2001).

____, *Managing in the Next Society* (New York: Truman Talley, 2002).

Durkheim, E., *On Morality and Society: Selected Writings* (Chicago: University of Chicago Press, 1973).

Ethics Resource Center, *National Business Ethics Survey: How Employees View Ethics in Their Organizations* (Arlington: ERC, 2003).

____, *National Business Ethics Survey: How Employees View Ethics in Their Organizations* (Arlington: ERC, 2005).

____, *National Business Ethics Survey: How Employees View Ethics in Their Organizations* (Arlington: ERC, 2007).

Frederick, W. C., *Values, Nature, and Culture in the American Corporation* (New York: Oxford University Press, 1995).

Günther, G., 'Life as Polycontexturality', in G. Günther (ed.), *Beiträge zur Grundlegung einer operationsfähigen Dialektik* (Hamburg: F. Meiner, 1979), 283–306.

Hofstede, G., *Culture's Consequences: Comparing Values, Behaviors, Institutions, and Organisations across Nations* (Thousand Oaks: Sage, 2006).

Bayerische HypoVereinsbank AG, *Werte leben – Werte schaffen*. Available online at http://www.hypovereinsbank.de/export/sites/aboutus/binaries/downloads/de/HVB_CSR_2007.pdf [accessed 21 June 2008].Kelly, C., et al., *Deriving Value from Corporate Values*. Available online at http://www.aspeninstitute.org/atf/cf/%7BDEB6F227-659B-4EC8-8F84-8DF23CA704F5%7D/VALUE%20SURVEY%20FINAL.PDF [accessed 21 June 2008].

Kneer, G., and A. Nassehi, *Niklas Luhmanns Theorie sozialer Systeme: eine Einführung* (Munich: Fink, 2000).

Kotter, J. P., and J. L. Heskett, *Corporate Culture and Performance* (New York: Free Press, 1992).

Luhmann, N., *Funktionen und Folgen formaler Organisation* (Berlin: Duncker and Humblot, 1964).

____, 'Differentiation of Society', *The Canadian Journal of Sociology* 2/1 (1977), 29–53.
____, *The Differentiation of Society* (Columbia: Columbia University Press, 1982).
____, 'Risiko und Gefahr', in N. Luhmann (ed.), *Konstruktivistische Perspektiven* (Opladen: Westdeutscher Verlag, 1990a), 131–69.
____, 'Tautology and Paradox in the Self-descriptions of Modern Society', in N. Luhmann (ed.), *Essays on Self-reference* (New York: Columbia University Press, 1990b), 123–43.
____, *Social Systems* (Palo Alto: Stanford University Press, 1996).
____,*Die Gesellschaft der Gesellschaft* (Frankfurt am Main: Suhrkamp, 1997).
____, 'Complexity, Structural Contingencies and Value Conflicts', in P. Heelas et al. (eds), *Detraditionalization: Critical Reflections on Authority and Identity* (Cambridge, MA: Blackwell, 1999), 59–71.
____, 'Funktion und Kausalität', in N. Luhmann (ed.), *Soziologische Aufklärung 1: Aufsätze zur Theorie sozialer Systeme* (Wiesbaden: VS Verlag, 2005a), 11–30.
____, 'Funktionale Methode und Systemtheorie', in N. Luhmann (ed.), *Soziologische Aufklärung 1: Aufsätze zur Theorie sozialer Systeme (*Wiesbaden: VS Verlag, 2005b), 31–53.
____, 'The Concept of Autopoiesis', in D. Seidl and K. H. Becker (eds), *Niklas Luhmann and Organisation Studies* (Malmö: Liber, 2005c), 54–63.
Nassehi, A., *Geschlossenheit und Offenheit: Studien zur Theorie der modernen Gesellschaft* (Frankfurt am Main: Suhrkamp, 2003).
____, 'Organizations as Decision Machines: Niklas Luhmann's Theory of Organized Social Systems', in C. Jones and R. Munro (eds), *Contemporary Organisation Theory* (Oxford: Blackwell, 2005), 178–91.
Nassehi, A., and I. Saake, 'Kontingenz: Methodisch verhindert oder beobachtet? Ein Beitrag zur Methodologie der qualitativen Sozialforschung', *Zeitschrift für Soziologie* 31/1 (2002), 66–86.
Parsons, T., *Structures and Process in Modern Societies* (Glencoe: Free Press, 1960).
Peters, T. J., and R. H. Waterman, *In Search of Excellence: Lessons from America's Best-run Companies* (New York: Harper Collins, 2006).
Schein, E. H., *Organisational Culture and Leadership* (San Francisco: Jossey-Bass, 1991).
Seeger, M. W., *Ethics and Organisational Communication* (Cresskill, NJ: Hampton Press, 1997).
Seidl, D., 'Metaphorical Self-description of Organisations', in A. Müller and A. Kieser (eds), *Communication in Organisations: Structures and Practices* (Frankfurt: Lang, 2003a), 165–84.
____, 'Organisational Identity in Luhmann's Theory of Social Systems', in T. Hernes and T. Bakken (eds), *Autopoietic Organisation Theory: Drawing on Niklas Luhmann's Social Systems Perspective* (Oslo: Copenhagen Business School Press, 2003b), 123–50.

Stollberg-Rilinger, B. and T. Weller (eds), *Wertekonflikte – Deutungskonflikte* (Münster: Rhema, 2005).

Spencer-Brown, G., *Laws of Form* (Portland, OR: Cognizer, 1994).

Weick, K. E., 'Educational Organisations as Loosely Coupled Systems', *Administrative Science Quarterly* 21/1 (1976), 1–19.

____,*The Social Psychology of Organizing* (Reading, MA: Addison-Wesley, 1979).

____,*Sensemaking in Organisations* (Thousand Oaks, CA: Sage, 1995).

Wieland, J. (ed.), *Handbuch Wertemanagement: Erfolgsstrategien einer modernen Corporate Governance* (Hamburg: Murmann, 2004).

Yin, R. K., *Case Study Research: Design and Methods* (Thousand Oaks, CA: Sage, 2005).

Chapter 9
Moralized Communications and Social Regulation

Diane Laflamme

Introduction

Social regulation can take many forms; conventional rules, legal frameworks, as well as claims of morality can be used to encourage the behaviors deemed socially desirable. Mere conventions, laws, and moral prescriptions can also intermingle, for example when a clergy makes certain dietary rules a religious and moral obligation, or when a government imposes a dress code as the required demonstration of one's morality. Such scenarios where morality is given the task of regulating for hidden purposes what one eats or wears are not unheard of even nowadays. Moralizing is an activity that seems more apt to promote conflicts in a given society than to encourage integration. In moralized conflicts, both sides usually claim to have a monopoly on what is good and right in order to publicly discredit and exclude the other side. Such a strategy can only put a stop to communications and further contacts.

Sociologist Niklas Luhmann warns us about morality, observing that it has become in the modern era "a disturbing factor" and "an attitude that cannot be observed without distrust and must be kept in check" (1995: 240). In Luhmann's theory of functionally differentiated societies, morality does not stand as a function system (1991a: 85; 1993a: 1001, n. 19). Religion and politics—as well as economy, law, science, education—are described as self-organized and fully differentiated functional systems.[1] Morality,[2]

---

[1] Various function systems emerge within a given society when "the orientation towards specific functions (or problems) of the social system catalyzes the formation of subsystems that dominate the face of society" (Luhmann, 2000: 133). On functional differentiation, see Luhmann 1989, where the following function systems are discussed: economy, law, science, politics, religion, education. The binary codes that have made possible over time the differentiation of these functional systems are: having-property/having-not-property (economy); legally right/legally wrong (law); true/untrue (science); having-official-power/ having-not-official-power (politics); transcendent/immanent (religion); good grades/bad grades (education). For more on the codes used by function systems, see 1977b and 1996a: 35. For a discussion of the limits to the applicability of the moral code in various function systems, see Rasch 2000: 90–92.

[2] The evolution of the Moral as Western societies have differentiated themselves over the past is described in Luhmann 1993b: 778–80.

though, did not succeed in establishing itself at the operative level as a distinct function system; the conditions under which morality could be expected to play on the side of the integration rather than the dissolution of social contacts did not stabilize enough to allow for such an emergence. It does not ensue that morality disappears in functionally differentiated societies; it rather becomes "multifunctional" (1995: 234). The social control of deviation or dissatisfaction can take a moral form in any function system. Communications can be moralized within any of them. For example, one can observe that religious values or political values are not necessarily also moral values. When communicating about values in a functionally differentiated society, one now has to distinguish the system's reference.

In Luhmann's view, "the human being lives in a meaningfully constituted world" (1985: 24). He describes how meaning-constituting systems operate and interpenetrate. With his theory of meaning-constituting systems we can examine how social regulation can be driven by the constitution of meaning. It will allow us to document what happens when communications are moralized, to explain how mutually constituted expectations are used by meaning systems for steering behaviors, and to briefly identify specific challenges for social regulation. We believe that Luhmann's theory of meaning-constituting systems can be best presented through an exegesis of his work and therefore we will extensively refer to his books and numerous articles available in English.[3]

Meaning Allows for Reciprocal Enabling

Luhmann's discussion of the Moral (1987a, 1991a, 1993a, 1994, 1996a) cannot be dissociated from his theory of meaning-constituting systems (1990a: ch. 2; 1995: ch. 2), namely psychic systems—where thoughts are produced out of previous thoughts—and social systems—where communications are produced out of communications.

A System Can Also Function as an Environment

Meaning-constituting systems presuppose life; for now at least, they have been observed where life is present. Life, consciousness, and communication are self-constituting.[4] Life only refers to life, and meaning only refers to meaning.

---

3 Meaning is discussed in *Essays on Self-reference,* where Chapter 2 is boldly entitled: "Meaning as Sociology's Basic Concept" and Chapter 3 is entitled "Complexity and Meaning," 1990a: 21–85. In *Social Systems*, Chapter 2 is entitled "Meaning," 1995: 59–102. See the references at the end of this chapter for more on Luhmann's books and articles where the constitution of meaning is discussed.

4 One could also say that they are autopoietic systems. Luhmann expresses it concisely: "They are autopoietic systems, and that means that they are their own product" (1997c: 71). Also: "We can define autopoietic systems by their ability to reproduce the

A meaningful operation can only connect to another meaningful operation, and this process is linear and sequential. When meaning inserts itself into a sequence that is bound to bodily feelings, it appears as "consciousness"; when meaning inserts itself into a sequence that involves others' understanding, it appears as "communication" (1995: 98). To maintain its existence, the system is continuously searching for connectivity. Each selection is a meaning event that has to be connected to the next meaning event, so the system can reproduce itself as self-constituting through its own operations.

A self-constituting system cannot operate in its environment. A selection is always an internal event for the system capable of making it. The meaning system is also capable of observing its own operations: When a selection event is attributed to the systems, it is distinguished as "action" from the perspective of the self-observing system; when a selection event is attributed to the environment, it is distinguished as "experience" (1995: 84).

In psychic systems, meaning is constituted on the basis of intentional acts of consciousness. An individualized psychic system is viewed as "the unity of a meaningfully related complex of actions and experiences" (1990a: 24) and as a unified and self-referential "nexus of conscious states" (1995: 59). In social systems, meaning is constituted on the basis of communications. Social systems can take various forms, namely interactions, organizations, and societies (see Table 9.1).

Table 9.1 Self-constituting systems

Self-constituting systems: To produce their elements, operations, and boundaries they use only their own elements, operations, and boundaries. They cannot operate outside their own boundaries.				
Cells, brains, organisms	**Psychic systems**	**Social systems** Their elements, operations and boundaries are communications produced out of communications		
		Interactions	Organizations	Societies
Life is self-produced, within physical boundaries	Their elements, operations, and boundaries are thoughts. Their operational mode is consciousness	They are constituted by the communications between those whose presence is perceived and recognized (1986b: 177; 1987b: 114)	They are constituted through membership, roles, and rules of admission (1995: 196)	They include all events which, for them, have the quality of communication (1986b: 176)
	Meaning-constituting systems Their boundaries are not physical in nature but are, instead, the boundaries of what may become relevant within given contexts of meaning (1987c: 176)			

elements of which they consist by using the elements of which they consist" (Luhmann 1987b: 113). Meaning and life are two different modes of autopoietic organization (Luhmann 1986b: 172).

It is the type of operations—consciousness or communication—that constitutes the system. Luhmann explains:

> If an operation of a certain type has started and is [...] capable of connectivity— that is, if further operations of the same type ensue from it—a system develops. [...] The system creates itself as a chain of operations. The difference between system and environment arises merely because an operation produces a subsequent operation of the same type. (2006: 49)

The identity of the system develops from its operations. Psychic and social systems are distinguished "according to whether consciousness or communication is chosen as the form of operation" (1995: 98).

Self-constituting systems function as an environment for one another. The environment of any system "is given to it as a confusedly complex structure of reciprocal system/environment relations" (1995: 18). The organic system functions as an environment for consciousness; the system of consciousness functions as an environment for communications; social systems function as an environment for an organic/psychic system; other psychic systems (alter) function as an environment for ego.

The environment is always more complex[5] than the system. Gains in complexity are made when the system increases "the number and the variability" of its elements (2002: 157). By increasing its complexity, the system also reduces the difference in the relative degree of complexity between system and environment. Meaning-constituting systems can be said to both reduce and preserve complexity, says Luhmann:

> What is special about the meaningful or meaning-based processing of experience is that it makes possible *both* the reduction and the preservation of complexity; i.e., it provides a form of selection that prevents the word from shrinking down to just one particular content of consciousness with each act of determining experience. (1990a: 27)

Because of its lack of complexity, a meaning system can fail to recognize the full complexity of its experiencing; this blindness might be temporary though, since the world will not shrink to accommodate such a narrow experiencing.

---

5 Luhmann presents the notion of complexity as follows: "When the number of elements that must be held together *in a system* or *for a system as its environment* increases, one very quickly encounters a threshold where it is no longer possible to relate every element to every other one. A definition of complexity follows from this: we will call an interconnected collection of elements 'complex' when, because of immanent constraints in the elements' connective capacity, it is no longer possible at any moment to connect every element with every other element" (Luhmann 1995: 24).

Since other psychic systems are seen as an environment from the perspective of a given psychic system, increases in complexity in a psychic system, as minimal as they could be, make the environment of other systems more complex. To enable another system, the first thing a meaning system has to do is increase its own complexity:

> Structural changes in individual systems make the environment of other systems more complex, and these react by exhausting new possibilities, or by adaptation or indifference—in any case, by increasing the selectivity of their state. Structural changes beneficial to the adapting system can, in turn, *leave the environment of other systems richer in possibilities* so that, although complexity does not necessarily increase for all systems or types of systems, it does for their relationship, which is then available to meaningful experience as the world. (1990a: 66; my emphasis)

The main point for the reciprocal enabling between meaning systems—and eventually for social regulation through reciprocal enabling—is to make the environment of other systems richer in possibilities. "A complex system can have a more complex environment and is capable of processing a greater amount of irritation internally, that is, it can increase its own complexity more rapidly." (2000: 158)

Luhmann indicates that communication can be stimulated only by the mind[6] and not by a state of fact brought about by any physical, chemical, biochemical, or neurophysiological operations as such. These "can have no effect on communication if it is not perceived, measured, and made conscious; only then can the fact stimulate the attempt to communicate about it" (2002: 177).

A human being is not a system and it is impossible to envision a concrete individual person as an "element" in the formation of a meaning-constituting system (1995: 40; 1990b: 30); the elements of these systems can only be their own operations. This has implications for social regulation and morality: Not being considered mere parts of society, human beings can enjoy more freedom. Luhmann explains:

> The distinction between system and environment offers the possibility of conceiving human beings as parts of the societal environment in a way that is both more complex and less restricting than if they had to be interpreted as

---

6 Only the mind is capable of perception (including the perception of communication), says Luhmann; "perception at first remains a psychological event without communicative existence. Inside the communicative occurrence, it is not connectable as it is. One can neither confirm nor refute, neither interrogate nor respond to what another has perceived. It remains locked up within consciousness and non-transparent to the system of communication as well as to every other consciousness." See Chapter 8, "How Can the Mind Participate in Communication?" in Luhmann 2002: 158.

parts of society, because in comparison with the system, the environment is the domain of distinction that shows greater complexity and less existing order. The human being is thus conceded greater freedom in relation to *his* environment, especially freedom for irrational and immoral behaviour. (1995: 212)

For the free human being, social regulation and morality are a challenge. For meaning systems, what is at stake is the reproduction of the system, namely the continuation of its existence from one meaning-constituting operation to the next one; when consciousness and communication try to coordinate their system/environment relationships, they do so in order to continue, nothing more.

Coordinating Relationships of Interpenetration

A meaning system cannot operate in its environment. Conscious operations can only happen within consciousness; communication operations can only happen within communications. It is the type of operations—consciousness or communication—that constitutes the system. As quoted previously, "if an operation of a certain type has started and is […] capable of connectivity—that is, if further operations of the same type ensue from it—a system develops," according to Luhmann (2006: 49).

It should be noted, though, that the relationship between systems of consciousness and systems of communication is asymmetrical. "Once it has come into existence, a system of consciousness can be active even without communication. It experiences this and that within itself, observes something, feels itself thinking, and even talks to itself. Communication, on the other hand, can hardly come into being without the participation of the mind" (Luhmann 2002: 171). If these asymmetrical meaning systems are to work together to both reduce and preserve complexity, as previously noted, each of them will have to make its own complexity available for constructing the other one. Luhmann proposes the concept of interpenetration[7] to describe how such a reciprocal enabling can take place: "Interpenetration can only mean: the unity and complexity (as opposed to specific conditions and operations) of the one is given a function within the system of the other" (2002: 182).

---

7   In *Social Systems* (1995; in German, 1984), the concept of interpenetration is abundantly discussed in Chapter 6 (45 pages). More than ten years later, Luhmann refers again to this concept in *The Reality of the Mass Media* (2000a; in German, 1996) in Chapter 10 entitled "Individuals," adding a specific reference to Chapter 6 of *Social Systems*. The concept of interhuman interpenetration is also discussed in *Love as Passion: The Codification of Intimacy* (1986a: ch. 16). In the article entitled "How Can the Mind Participate in Communication" (2002: Ch. 8) the concept of interpenetration is discussed in section VII. For a short explanation of the distinction Luhmann establishes between his concept of interpenetration and the same concept in Parsons, see note 5, in 1995: 546–7. For a discussion of interpenetration in Parsons and in Luhmann, see Rempel 2001; Leydesdorff, 2003, 2001: 21–7.

In penetration, "one can observe how the *behavior* of the penetrating system is co-determined by the receiving system." Adding the prefix "inter" indicates a reciprocal process. Interpenetrating systems "enable each other" (1995: 213). Reciprocity and codetermination are key words for describing interpenetration, and no causal link is created in such process.

Relationships of interpenetration between self-constituting systems[8] establish an "operative and structural link" between them (2002: 182). This is not a causal link. To better grasp the nature of this link, it is necessary to remember three things about structures and operations. First, a self-constituting system does not consist of two different kinds of entities, namely structures and operations. Luhmann explains: "Rather the system uses the same type of operations [...] in the dual function of (1) producing subsequent operations; and (2) confirming or changing the structure used to select the next operation" (1991b: 1440). Second, the structures of a self-constituting system are the result of the system's own operations; they "condense" (1991b) as the system moves from one operation to the next one. And third, self-constituting systems are environments for each other, so the operations of one system cannot be the cause of a change in the structure of another system since a system cannot operate in the environment.

Structural couplings are necessarily implied in the system/environment relationship between self-constituting systems: "Of course, structural couplings between system and environment are presupposed. Without such couplings, the system could not exist" (2000b: 50). The concept of structural couplings describes only a part of what is happening in interpenetration. To refer to structural coupling when discussing interpenetration allows us to underline the noncausal aspect of the link created between interpenetrating systems, since structural couplings are "forms of simultaneous (and therefore not causal) relations" (1991b: 1432).

Luhmann has abundantly described how fully differentiated function systems (politics, economy, law, etc.) are structurally coupled[9] among themselves and how

---

8   According to Luhmann, "interpenetration permits a relation between autonomous autopoiesis and structural coupling." (1995: 221) In this chapter, we did not introduce the concept of autopoiesis, but the description we provide for the notion of "self-constituting systems" in Table 9.1 also fits autopoietic systems. With the concept of autopoiesis, the focus is on the reproduction of the system rather than its constituting capacity. Both constitution and reproduction require a search for connectivity. Briefly stated, for a social system, autopoiesis "is nothing more than this constant process of reduction and opening of connective possibilities." (Luhmann 2002: 172). On the one hand, autopoiesis continuously reproduces the elements of the system (operations and structures are elements of autopoietic systems); on the other hand, structures are discontinuously changing through coupling (1995: 220).

9   Up to now, most of the discussions on structural coupling versus interpenetration have not been focused on relationships between psychic systems and social systems on the one hand and relationships among human beings on the other hand—as Luhmann intended for interpenetration—but rather examine relationships between function systems (politics, law, economics; culture, urban systems, etc.); for example, see King and Thornhill 2003,

functional systems are structurally coupled to society as a whole—what Luhmann designates as "the societal system" (1991b: 1419). But let us not forget that all the functional subsystems of society are meaning-based communicative systems. Something crucial happens when meaning systems interpenetrate: Meaning is constituted. Luhmann writes: "What we call interpenetration reaches further; it does not connect performances but *constitutes* connections" (1995: 218; my emphasis).

The concept of interpenetration describes an "operative and structural link," as mentioned previously, and this linkage happens through meaning-constituting operations. The key event here is the constitution of meaning. It is meaning "that enables psychic and social system formations to interpenetrate" (1995: 219); when psychic systems and social systems interpenetrate, it is meaning that "simultaneously enables consciousness to understand itself and continue to affect itself in communication, and enables communication to be referred back to the consciousness of the participants" (1995: 219).

Luhmann distinguishes between two forms of interpenetration.

The relationship among human beings is described as *interhuman interpenetration*, or intimacy (1995: 224). The concept of interpenetration is built from a very simple observation: "the complexity of a human being has significance for another human being and vice versa" (1995: 223). The concept also allows for taking into account the incommunicability between human beings: "Interhuman interpenetration exceeds the possibilities of communication. This refers not only to the boundaries of linguistic possibilities and not only to the meaning of bodily contact. Instead, intimacy includes what is incommunicable and therefore includes the experience of incommunicability. Alter is significant for ego in ways that ego cannot communicate to alter" (1995: 228).

The relationship between organic/psychic systems and social systems is designated as *social interpenetration*. Social interpenetration refers to the "possibility of taking account of the complexity of the formation of individual consciousness within social communication" (2000a: 73, with note 2 referring to *Social Systems*, Chapter 6). In social interpenetration, Luhmann indicates, there is simultaneously inclusion and exclusion: The complexity of the contributing systems is used by the receiving systems, but to make this possible, "a multiplicity of interpenetrating systems must distinguish themselves from one another," asserting their own identity and, by so doing, excluding each other (1995: 220). Luhmann explains how this oscillation between inclusion and exclusion works within communication:

> The individual who participates in communication is, in one way or another, simultaneously individualized and de-individualized, that is, standardized

---

Philippopoulos-Mihalopoulos 2007. The constitution of meaning through interpenetration is generally ignored, except in Leydesdorff 2001, 2003, 2010 and Leydesdorff and Franse 2009.

or fictionalized such that communication can continue to make reference to individuals without being able to include the operations which cause each individual for itself to come into being as a unique, operationally closed system. (2000a: 74)

Standardization and fictionalization allow for some inclusion, although the human being, in his or her uniqueness, is excluded.

Morality has a role to play for the reciprocal enabling between meaning systems. More precisely, morality is given the function of coordinating these "two distinct relationships of interpenetration" (1995: 235): the interpenetration between organic/psychic systems (interhuman interpenetration) and the interpenetration between organic/psychic systems and social systems (social interpenetration). Again, with the introduction of morality in the picture, interpenetration reaches further than a mere structural coupling: What is at stake when a system chooses to moralize communications is the constitution of meaning. As Luhmann explains: "We are faced by the question, what is the meaning of accepting or rejecting the freedom which is anyway given in all communication, of morally recoding it, even if it only amounts to a distinction, whose values good, bad likewise produce in communication the freedom of acceptance or rejection" (1991a: 91).

Social regulation will not necessarily want to enroll morality in its endeavors, but could be tempted to do so when better coordination is needed between relationships of interpenetration among human beings and between psychic systems and social systems. To moralize communications can have a powerful impact because the mind is fascinated by communication and language. In social interpenetration, for instance, the reciprocal initiation of changes between systems of communication and systems of consciousness is driven by this fascination:

> Communication fascinates and occupies the mind whenever, and as long as, it continues. [...] It is apparently possible to link communication to communication and in so doing to activate the necessary and indispensable states of consciousness, even though the required environment, the systems of consciousness, is made up of highly unstable, self-dynamic, diffuse mental states that (aside from individual consciousness) cannot be hooked up directly to one another. (2002: 172)

As noted before, interpenetration creates an operative and structural link between meaning systems. Observing how human societies, over the ages, have invested in the fascinating power of communication could shed some light on their capacity for a "mutualistic constitution" of meaning (1995: 110).

Language is not a requirement for communication, notes Luhmann: "communication takes place in all situations where one willingly or unwillingly allows another access to the meaning of his experience" (1990a: 32). Language brings a definite advantage though: "Only thus can meaning be freed from the concrete situation and itself made a content of the processes of consciousness in such a way that meaning can also regulate the selectivity of meaning" (1990a: 32). Over centuries, human beings have strongly invested in the new experiences opened to them by language and its derivatives.

Luhmann describes the main steps in the evolution of this linkage between interpenetrating systems:

> The evolution of social communication is possible only in a constantly operative link with states of consciousness. This link was first achieved through language, then more effectively through writing, and finally through printing. Decisive in this process is [...] the differentiation of special experiential objects that are either extraordinary or fascinating. They have no similarity to anything else that can be experienced and are constantly in motion or (as in reading) usable only in motion. Language and script fascinate and preoccupy the mind and thereby secure its participation, even though this is in no way required by the internal dynamics of the mind and diversions are always held at the ready. (2002: 175)

Each emergence of more technologically advanced form of languaging can be seen as a threshold in the coevolution between psychic systems and social systems, feeding their attempts to simultaneously reduce and preserve complexity: "changes in the forms in which language becomes comprehensible to the mind, from simple sounds to pictorial scripts to phonetic scripts and finally to print, mark thresholds of societal evolution that, once crossed, trigger immense impulses of complexity in a very short time" (2002: 174). We could now add another threshold to this list with the emergence of virtual languaging devices: Internet--cell phones transmitting sounds, texts, and pictures; e-books. With these new developments, language makes itself more and more fascinating for the mind. This could eventually help language to also become more and more comprehensible to the mind. If it happens, it would be an example of the reciprocal enabling made possible by the interpenetration between social systems and psychic systems. These new developments also bring new challenges for social regulation, among others: the choice to regulate or not the communication, and the choice to moralize or not the communications thus produced.

How Meaning Is Constituted in the Factual, Temporal and Social Dimensions

Psychic systems and social systems have evolved together (1995: 97, 271; 2002: 167) and it shows in their common use of meaning. The constitution of meaning, a favorite topic for philosophers since Husserl, is given a central place in Luhmann's sociological theory. Luhmann designates meaning as "sociology's basic concept"[10] (1990a: Ch. 2).

---

10   In an interview with David Sciulli in 1994, Luhmann confirms this statement, originally formulated in 1969: "My 'solution' at this point was to show that the concept

A Phenomenological Perspective on Meaning and Communication

A system is not an object, and meaning is not an object either. To attempt a definition of meaning as a substantial object would get us nowhere; Luhmann warns us: "It is impossible to find a 'supporting substance' for meaning" (1995: 98). Luhmann then chooses to describe meaning as "processing according to differences", namely the difference between actuality and potentiality. Meaning processing "constantly shapes anew the meaning-constitutive difference between actuality and potentiality" (1995: 65). This is how meaning is constituted: "At any time, meaning can gain actual reality only by reference to some other meaning" (1995: 61).

Luhmann refers also to the notion of horizon, derived from Husserlian phenomenology, to describe the constitution of meaning:

> Because meaning can be meaning only as the difference between what is actual at any moment and a horizon of possibilities, every actualization always also leads to a virtualization of the potentialities that could be connected up with it. The instability of meaning resides in the untenability of its core of actuality; the ability to restabilize is provided by the fact that everything actual has meaning only with a horizon of possibilities. (1995: 65)

Meaning-constituting systems cannot command their environment as they please but any operation of the system can push back its horizon still further, under the constraints imposed by the system's own capacity for connectivity. The system's horizon "always recedes when it is approached, but only in accordance with the system's own operations. It can never be pushed through or transcended because it is not a boundary. It accompanies every system operation when this refers to something outside the system" (1995: 17; see also 1989: 22).

When a distinction distinguished "this and not something else," the other side of the distinction is not erased, it is also "co-presented along with the distinction" (2000: 59). The system is oscillating between the two sides of a distinction. The other possibilities do not disappear; they are preserved and they could reappear in a subsequent actualization of meaning, as the system will keep searching for a better connectivity between its operations. Luhmann insists:

---

of meaning could integrate systems theory and hermeneutical (phenomenological) descriptions because of its built-in circularities. The main essay making this point, 'Meaning as Sociology's Basic Concept', was written in 1969" (quoted in Sciulli 1994: 37). When discussing meaning-constituting systems, in books and articles, Luhmann refers extensively to Husserlian phenomenology, for example: 1990a: 23–5; 1995: 82, 106; 1996b: 343; 1998: 110; 2000: 55, 139; 2002: 55, 83. For more on the constitution of meaning according to Luhmann, see Laflamme 2011.

> It is important to note here that although the selection of one particular use or aspect of meaning does neutralize or even negate other possibilities for the moment, it does not simply eliminate them as such, as possibilities. The world is not reduced to only what is actually being attended to each time a selection is made; it still remains as the horizon of references, as the horizon of further possibilities, and thus as the domain from which follow-up selections and further choices are made. This makes it possible to refer acts of selection to one another, to coordinate them, and thus to increase selectivity, even though the actually given potential for attention remains unchangingly small. (1987c: 177)

Meaning is constituted through the distinctions made by consciousness and communication systems: by selecting, referring to selections, coordinating selections, increasing selectivity.

Meaning systems can both reduce and preserve complexity because their selections always refer to the world[11] as the "ultimate horizon of all meaning" (1995: 69). As meaning, the world is accessible everywhere: "in every situation, in any detail, at each point on the scale from concrete to abstract," but at a given time only very little can form the actual focus of the conscious attention of a psychic system or be treated as an actual theme of communication by a social system (1989: 17; see also 1995: 70).

Luhmann explains that he has chosen the term "constitution" to describe the "being-possible-only together" of meaning and the world:

> Meaning always appears within some delimitable context and yet at the same time always points beyond this context and lets us see other possibilities. What I want to understand and to describe with the term constitution is this relationship between a selectively restricted order and the openness of other possibilities, a relationship of mutual interdependence, of being-possible-only-together. (1990a: 25)

Husserlian phenomenology describes as "constitution" the operation required of the mind when it aims at distinguishing a specific object given in the world.[12] Briefly stated, constitution requires the emergence of a unifying synthesis rather than the appearance in the mind of an approximate representation of the object.

---

11   "Systems that constitute and use meaning presuppose a world. [...] The world does not designate a (total, all-encompassing) sum of facts, an *universitas rerum* [...] Originally and phenomenologically, the world is given as an ungraspable unity [...] In both regards the concept of a world designates a unity that becomes actual only for meaning systems that can distinguish themselves from their environments" (Luhmann 1995: 207, 208).

12   Luhmann criticizes Husserl's use of the term "constitution" as "ambivalent in at least two regards" because it "fluctuates in its meaning, namely between the having of immediate evidence and performance on the one hand and between receptive clarification and creative production on the other" (Luhmann,1990a: 69).

In Luhmann's theory, the concept of communication is described as such a unifying synthesis: "communication requires the production of an emergent unity that has the capacity to integrate and disintegrate the internal states of more than one operationally closed system" (1993b: 774). In a communication meaning is constituted as the "synthesis of three selections" (1986b: 183): information, utterance and understanding. "An utterance is chosen from various behaviors; information is chosen from various facts" and the distinction between the two is "constitutive" (2002: 181). Communication takes place "only when a difference of utterance and information is first understood. This distinguishes it from a mere perception of other's behaviour. By understanding, communication grasps a difference between the information value of its content and the reasons for which the content is being uttered" (2002: 157). This synthesis of three constitutive elements is an event that "has to be recreated from situation to situation by referring to previous communications and to possibilities of further communications which are restricted by the actual event" (1986b: 175). Thus communication "constantly shapes anew the meaning-constitutive difference between actuality and potentiality" (1995: 65), as quoted previously when we attempted to define the concept of meaning.

The constitution of meaning in communication is a focal point for the observation of morality since, according to Luhmann, "the range of application of the moral should reasonably be limited to communicative operations." He explains: "Neither life as such, nor the functions of the brain, nor the conscious operations of perception and thinking have intrinsic moral quality. […] It fully suffices for us to assume that psychic systems are impressionable through participating in moral communication" (1993a: 1000).

In the Western philosophical tradition, regulation of the individual conscience has been the main task given to morality rather than reciprocal enabling. A society made of rational individuals acting in accordance with a universally defined moral sense was thus expected to emerge.

In Luhmann's theory of meaning-constituting systems, the communications are moralized, not the system:

> A communication presents itself as being moral, if it suggests or explicitly states that self-esteem or the esteem accorded to others relies upon the fulfillment of certain conditions. He who communicates morally in this manner implies that he cannot respect others, if they do not adhere to the communicated conditions; and he also puts his own self-esteem in jeopardy, he binds himself to the communicated morality and makes it more difficult for himself to revise his opinion in retrospect. (1987a: 92)

Moralized communications are meaning-constituting events made possible when psychic systems and social systems interpenetrate. Communications, moralized or not, can be stimulated only by the mind: "The mind has the privileged position of being able to disturb, stimulate and irritate communication. The mind cannot instruct communication, because communication constructs itself. But the mind is a constant source of impulses for the one or the other turn of the operative process inherent in communication" (2002: 176–7). Psychic systems and communication systems have the capacity to reciprocally enable each other thanks to the meaning reference of all their operations.

The Constitution of Meaning: Oscillation in a Double Horizon, in Three Dimensions

Psychic systems and social systems experience meaning as a difference, more precisely "the difference between what is *actually given* and what can *possibly* result from it" (1995: 74). This process of differentiation is circular, closed, and self-referential: Meaning only refers to further meaning (1995: 69), but the self-reference of meaning can be "re-specified dimensionally" (1995: 75). Luhmann describes how meaning is constituted in three dimensions of the system's experience: the "Fact dimension" (1995: 75), also translated as "the Material or Object dimension" (1990a: 36), the Time or Temporal dimension, and the Social dimension.

The system can differentiate between these three dimensions of meaning. In each one of them, the selections made by the system are framed by a double horizon allowing for oscillation between the two sides of a distinction. The Factual, Temporal and Social constitution of meaning requires a pulsation: A meaning system "pulsates, so to speak, with the constant generation of excess and selection" (2002: 160). Luhmann also describes this phenomenon as an oscillation[13] between the two sides of a distinction. This oscillation will be observed between self-reference/hetero-reference in the Fact dimension,[14] between past/future in the Time dimension, and between ego's perspective/alter's perspective in the Social dimension (see Table 9.2).

In the Fact dimension, the two-sided distinction self-reference/hetero-reference allows consciousness to distinguish itself from its contents, and social system to distinguish themes in communication. Thus, "two horizons cooperate in the Factual constitution of meaning" and "twofold descriptions giving internal and outer profile are necessary to fix the meaning of an object" (1995: 77).

Meaning-constituting systems also distinguish between two Temporal horizons which meet and are linked together in the present: that of the past and that of the future. The system can operate only in the present, of course, but it can also recursively refer backward or forward to previous perceptions or

---

13 "An oscillating system can preserve the undecidability of whether something is inside or outside a form. It can preserve and reproduce itself as a form, that is, as an entity with a boundary, with an inside and an outside, and it can prevent the two sides from collapsing into each other" (Luhmann, 2002: 84).

14 For a detailed description of the oscillation between self-reference and hetero-reference, see Luhmann, 1998: 10–17.

thoughts (psychic systems) or to other communications (social systems). The actualization of meaning is time-related: It happens in an instant of experience or of communication. Meaning-constituting systems use the actuality of their operations as starting point and connecting point to further meaning references that extend in the past and the future (2000: 139). The two-sided distinction past/future also allows meaning systems to build a memory and to orient themselves towards the next operation. In the present, meaning extending into the past or the future can be presented to the system (e.g. the steps necessary to realize a future goal can be chosen in the present). In communication, themes and contributions to a theme can be recursively "recalled and anticipated." Themes are "old or new"; themes can become "obsolete" (1995: 156; see also 1976).

In the Social dimension, the two-sided distinction ego/alter allows the system, in its various encounters, to establish if alter is experienced as another experiencing system.[15] The Social dimension "concerns what one at any time accepts as like oneself, as an alter ego (1995: 80). One can ask of every meaning whether somebody else experiences it in exactly the same way he or she does. The Social dimension of experience and meaning is constituted "by a non-ego being recognized as another ego, being experienced as the bearer of its own albeit different experience and perspective of the world" (1990a: 37).

Table 9.2 The three dimensions of meaning and their double horizon

	The constitution of meaning in the three dimensions of the system's experience		
	Factual constitution	**Temporal constitution**	**Social constitution**
Meaning is constituted within a dual horizon:	– Horizon of self-reference – Horizon of external reference	– Horizon of the past – Horizon of the future	– Horizon of ego – Horizon of alter ego
Oscillation allows for orientation:	Among the different contents experienced and among various themes in communication	At other points in time than the present	With various participants in communication

---

15 In this respect, Luhmann notes that "only in highly developed societies are all persons (and only persons) included" (1990a: 38). Anthropologists have amply documented how dead ancestors, out-of-this-world deities or nature-linked entities can be included as Alter in a communication system.

To moralize communications is to impose a condition to the oscillation between the two sides of a distinction. This condition is expressed as a binary schematism (a code) that knows only two sides and excludes anything else.[16] The code used to moralize communications is a dual one: good/bad and esteem/disesteem.[17]

Codes are "mobile structures that are applied differently from situation to situation" (2000: 187). A code is a strictly internal structure; it is a construct. The meaning system is "an open-ended, ongoing concern structurally requiring itself to decide how to allocate its positive or negative value. The bifurcation necessitates decisions and thereby further operations" (1991b: 1428). With the moral code, for example, whoever or whatever is held to be good is not bad. The positive value (good) allows the connecting up of the system's operations. The negative value (bad) indicates that there is no possibility to connect up because the imposed condition was not met. This binary coding allows a meaning-constituting system to move more rapidly from one selection to the other.

This capacity to use a binary scheme in order to condition the link between selections is also what comes into play when meaning systems interpenetrate. As mentioned previously, in relationships of interhuman interpenetration a psychic system makes its own complexity available for constructing the other psychic system, and in relationship of social interpenetration, a psychic system makes its own complexity available for constructing a social system. How is it possible to use the complexity of another system to construct one's own? In Luhmann's words: "For the domain of psychic and social systems, that is, the domain of meaning-processing systems, the answer is by binary schematization" (1995: 229)

Morality is defined by Luhmann as a binary schematization: "Morality is to be understood as the coding of communication by the binary scheme of good and bad" and the moral code "is always applicable when the behavior that is the subject of communication is sanctioned by the bestowal or withdrawal of esteem or contempt" (1989: 139). The moral code presents the special feature of linking together the sweeping generalization good/bad with a distinction based on the emotions[18] of esteem or disesteem (also translated as "contempt/disdain").

---

16   For more on morality as a coding that excludes the third, see Laflamme 2008 and Winter 2008. On moral invention as a process requiring the reinclusion of the previously excluded third, see Laflamme 2006.

17   As previously noted, morality did not develop into a fully differentiated function system. Function systems succeeded in differentiating themselves on the basis of their binary code; these codes are listed here, in n. 1. Morality functions only as one code among others. It is impossible to make it so that the positive side of a code always coincides with the positive side of another code. Each function system uses its own code and thus operates within its own system-specific rationality; for a discussion and some examples, see Dallmann 1998, section 4.

18   On emotions, Luhmann writes: "Emotions are not representations that refer to the environment but *internal* adaptations to *internal* problem situations in the psychic system that concern the ongoing production of the system's elements by the system's elements." Luhmann also notes that emotions "can augment and weaken without direct reference to

It was also mentioned previously that morality has the "function" to coordinate interhuman interpenetration and social interpenetration (1995: 235). Morality can assume this function simply by conditioning the distribution of esteem/disesteem, and also the distribution of self-esteem since there is one necessary condition for the moral conditioning to work, that is "the interdiction of self-exemption" (1996a: 29). To coordinate relationships of interpenetration is then described in the vocabulary of social regulation:

> Social regulation of the market for esteem takes place through conditioning the process of distribution of esteem and disesteem. It is taken for granted that these distributions hold good for self-esteem as well as for esteem of others. The socially integrative function of the moral rests upon this prevalent conditioning. This means that whoever expresses moral judgments gambles his self-esteem at the same time. (1993a: 999)

When morality is used for the purposes of social regulation, the process is driven by emotions, namely emotions of esteem or disesteem for ego and for alter.

Luhmann warns us that moral conditionings also create something artificial: "Morality resides in conditioning the attribution of esteem or contempt. In this way 'morality' is an artificial aggregate because it is never necessary or possible for communication that the totality of the conditioning viewpoints be available in a way that sharply distinguishes one from another" (1989: 139). The binary schema of morality reduces the full complexity of experiencing another human being to two sides only, one side excluding the other one. Those meaning references not attended to for now will inevitably reappear in the experiencing of the meaning systems as they will continue to interpenetrate. The full complexity of the world is always accessible to meaning systems in different kinds of situations and with various themes in communication (Fact dimension), at other points in time (Time dimension), and with other possible partners of communication (Social dimension).

Moralized Distinctions: Self-steering Relying on Expectations that Are Expected

Meaning systems oscillate between the two sides of their distinctions. This oscillation allows for steering. Luhmann uses the notion of steering to designate "a very specific use of distinctions, namely the attempt to *reduce the difference*" (1997b: 43). Steering is an operation among others in the system, but as described by Luhmann it is always self-steering, "regardless of whether the steering refers

---

occurrences in the environment, depending on consciousness's own experience of itself." As far as the steering of the system is concerned, Luhmann observes how emotions, in the face of problems that arise, "use simplified procedures of discrimination, which permit decisions without considering the consequences" (1995: 274).

to the system itself by an internally constructed distinction of self-reference and outside reference or whether the steering refers to the environment of the system"[19] (1997b: 46).

Steering becomes possible because the system imposes conditions to its meaningful selections. Steering "does not fix the system upon a future overall state of affairs, but changes only some of its conditionings," says Luhmann; only differences "are projected, i.e. fixed as conditions of possible oscillation" (1997a: 368). Since the operations of a meaning system can only take the form of a distinction, the system always refers to a difference (dual horizon) in each one of the three dimensions of meaning.

As previously mentioned, meaning systems use rough generalizations and condensations of meaning references in order to increase the connectivity of their operations. Such generalizations are useful since they provide the system with guiding differences for steering behaviors, but they also carry a risk: When they are using generalizations, meaning systems "buy the possibility of treating what is dissimilar as similar, and vice versa" (1995: 327). The repertoire of possibilities for meaningful selections becomes narrower, the system knows what to expect. Expectations will be open to revisions because they will constantly be challenged by the complexity of the environment, the system being always less complex than its environment. Again adopting the point of view that any operation of a meaning system posits a difference, Luhmann says: "an expectation reconnoiters unknown terrain using a difference it can experience within itself: it can be fulfilled or disappointed, and this does not depend on itself alone" (1995: 268).

Especially when meaning references are bundled together and condensed into an expectation, and when the next operation of selection is made conditional to the fulfillment of one side only of a binary schema called a code, steering is simultaneously facilitated and impaired. Facilitated, because the repertoire of expected meaningful selections has been narrowed; impaired, because the rough generalizations needed to make a distinction between a positive side and a negative side make it so that the system treats what is dissimilar as similar. When the moral code is applied, for example, the system can orient itself more rapidly between what is expected to be good and estimable, rather than bad and contemptible, but this rigid binary schema also makes it more difficult afterwards, in the next meaningful connections, to simultaneously reduce the difference between good/bad and between esteem/disesteem—which would be the aim of steering according to Luhmann's definition of the term.

In the dual binary schema of morality, the distinction good/bad is linked to the distinction esteem/disesteem. This linkage brings the emotion of esteem in the building of a behavioral expectation since esteem is defined as a "generalized recognition and

---

19   Luhmann explains it with the following example: "In the external world there are no temperatures—although I do not want to deny that one is irritated, starts to feel cold and finally checks why the heating is not working in winter" (1997b: 46).

evaluation which honors the fact that others accord with the expectations one believes must be assumed for social relations to continue" (1995: 235).

Steering at the Level of Expectational Structures

Luhmann introduces the concept of expectation to account for the fact that the referential structure of meaning can only be used in a condensed form: "Without this condensation, the burden of selection would be too great for connecting operations." He describes a feedback loop between generalizations and expectations: On the one hand, generalizations "condense the referential structure of every meaning into expectations, which indicate what a given meaning situation foresees"; on the other hand, "the requisite expectations and proofs of worth in concrete situations guide and correct generalizations" (1995: 96).

Expectations acquire a structural value inasmuch as they improve the connectivity of the meaning-constituting operations (1995: 309).The system can test its expectations and retains only the ones that have proven their worth.[20]

The two processes of interpenetration between meaning systems—interhuman interpenetration and social interpenetration—are fuelled by the testing of expectations. As previously noted, the relationships of interpenetration between meaning systems establish a structural and operative link; the system can only change its own structure, but meaning systems use each other for a reciprocal initiation of structural changes (2002: 177). Moralized communications will come into play at this point since it was also indicated that the function of morality is the coordination of two distinct relationships of interpenetration, namely interhuman and social (1995: 235).

Expectations "pre-structure" (1995: 268) the connection between thoughts in psychic systems, and between communication[21] events in social systems. What is to be noted is how the distinctions used for steering become more abstract with the condensation of expectational structures in the Factual, the Temporal and the Social dimensions of meaning (Table 9.3, first two rows).

In the Fact dimension, expectations are condensed along four perspectives
Selection events pass away; they have no permanence. The Fact dimension of meaning refers to the need meaning systems have to stamp an identity on those selections that feed their connectivity, thus keeping them available for further use.

---

20 Leydesdorff and Franse (2009: 112–13) describe, with references to Luhmann's theory of expectations, how strongly anticipatory systems construct their own future states and how "horizons of meaning" are thus generated. Simulation models showing how meaning-processing systems construct their expectations are discussed in Leydesdorff 2005 and 2010.

21 Communication is a process fed by expectations: Communication "is determined in its elemental events by the expectation of a reaction and the reaction to an expectation" (Luhmann 1995: 443).

In the Fact dimension of meaning, expectational selections can be distinguished according to the persons to whom they refer, to roles, programs, or values.[22] Using these four perspectives, the meaning-constituting system can identify faster and more easily in an expectational nexus which selection offers a better chance for connectivity (1995: 315). With each one of these four perspectives, meaning systems move their distinctions to more abstract levels.

The concept of "person" is not proposed here as a synonym for "psychic system" or human being. A person is "constituted"; a person is a "collage of expectations" (1995: 127). Person is a concept used "to indicate the social identification of a complex of expectations directed toward an individual human being" (1995: 210). When we refer to somebody as a person, we mainly refer to expectational structures—constituted through meaningful selections—that make sense for ourselves and for the designated person:

> One can be a person for oneself and for others. Being a person requires that one draws and binds expectations to oneself with the help of one's psychic system and body, including expectations about oneself with regard to others. The more expectations and the more different type of them that are individualized in this way the more complex the person. (1995: 315)

The challenge for social regulation will then be to allow for the integration of these more and more complex persons into viable societies.

The next level of abstraction is the introduction of roles. Roles can be distinguished from the person when building expectations since "only a portion of a human being's behaviour is expected in the form of a role" (1995: 316). For example, to participate in communication within more than one system of interaction makes it so that a human being has various commitments and role obligations, and could be seen in a certain way as a different person in each interaction system because his or her personal identity is connected there with different histories and expectations (1995: 419). At the level of roles, persons can be enlisted to contribute to social regulation.

In the Fact dimension of meaning, the system can also move to the abstract level of programs for the conditioning of expectations. "A program is a complex of conditions for the correctness (and thus the social acceptability) of behavior" (1995: 317). Conditions are made easily reusable:

> So far as relationships between meanings are concerned, the problem of selection appears to reside in the reusability of the points of view that guide selection, that is, in an identification that simultaneously varies and confirms these points of view. Such identifications require that operations are observed not only as

---

22 These four levels of abstraction do not correspond to Parsons' four "levels of normative culture," namely roles, collectivities, norms, and values. See Luhmann 1995: 576, n. 99.

a series of situation-dependent chance events but also as the realization of a program. (2000: 228)

Moral programs, for example, will organize the assignment of good/bad and esteem/disesteem according to criteria that are subject to consensus or dissent among the participants in communication (1989: 127). The code is stable, but we can observe how moral programs have varied over the history of human societies. At the level of programs, persons that are acting according to their role will be expected to fulfill specific goals.[23]

On the "highest attainable level of establishing expectations," meaning systems will use values for the factual constitution of meaning. Values are "general, individually symbolized perspectives which allow one to prefer certain states or events" (1995: 317). In the communication process, values serve as a kind of probe: "Values are indisputable; they are not even in need of explicit communication. They can be taken for granted," says Luhmann. "They are stable because they are ambivalent. They produce a semantic cover for unresolved conflicts" (1996a: 31–2). Values stabilize motivations (1990a: 134) so they can be used for observation and more importantly for orientation: "Values improve the depth, accuracy, and range of observation and orientation," indicates Luhmann, and they introduce the possibility of criticizing since "they invite others to observe one's observations and orientations" critically (1990a: 134). To sum it up: Reference to values will make sure a program acquires the capacity to motivate the person to act according to its expected role.

Technologies also have an impact on values. It is to be taken into account in relationship with the new challenges facing social regulation when more technologically advanced forms of languaging become available, as noted earlier. Technologies reduce complexity in a peculiar way: They transform what Luhmann calls "future presents" into "a string of anticipated presents."[24] Thus the future is "defuturized" by technology. This is where values come into the picture: "to justify this whole procedure of technical defuturization we use values. Values, then, have the function of guaranteeing the quality of present choice in spite of technical defuturization" (1976: 144).

Any attempt at social regulation will need to take into account these four levels of abstraction (persons, roles, programs, values) available to meaning systems for the Factual constitution of meaning. They provide meaning systems with successfully tested guiding viewpoints instead of a set of rules, thus allowing psychic systems and communication systems to show more sophistication when they condition their own selections: "The mere opposition of actual behaviour

---

23   For more on goal programs and conditional programs in Luhmann's theory, see Brans and Rossback 1997.

24   To effect this transformation of future presents into a string of anticipated presents, technologies "postulate and anticipate causal or stochastic links between future events in order to incorporate them into the present present" (1976: 143).

and normative, morally charged rules for correct behaviour with which earlier societies could manage is broadened" (1995: 318).

Norms are constituted in the Temporal dimension of meaning The present is "temporalized"; for Luhmann, it means that the present is "conceived as a difference between past and future" (1995: 310). In the Temporal dimension of meaning, steering is made possible through expectations: "As soon as one can establish what is anticipated, one can calculate futures and pasts. Time becomes flexible through anticipation" (1995: 308).

Expectations also "establish terminable episodes" in the course of consciousness and in the course of communication (1995: 268). By referring to episodes in consciousness[25] and episodes in communication,[26] meaning systems can differentiate and discontinue their operations "so that a leap to entirely different guiding structures always remains possible" (1995: 268).

Norms are constituted when behavioral expectations become stabilized over time (1995: 315; 1985: 33). They split reality into the difference between conformity to expectations and deviation, so the system can warn itself against disappointment and choose to maintain or not a normative expectation that was disappointed. Since norms are constituted in the Temporal dimension of meaning, leaps are always possible: Norms are contingently maintained or replaced over time.

The contingency of norms and the possibility to leap from present normative expectations to different ones in the future amplify insecurity. The "interpenetration of entire human beings into the social order" in the Temporal dimension of meaning is "decisive" for sociocultural evolution. Luhmann explains:

> One must treat human beings as if they were reliable and at the same time secure expectations against disappointment. One can form riskier expectations if one can guarantee that disappointments remain tied to specific events and do not trigger accumulations that would endanger security. Viewed in this way, evolution is an ever-new incorporation of insecurities into securities and of

---

25   That is to leap "from one context of linguistic thought to the next without [...] preventing the possibility of further thoughts becoming conscious. It (the psychic system) can equip the difference between before and after in the succession of thoughts with an immense and constantly changing capacity for exclusive operations" (Luhmann 1995: 273). Through its own operations, a psychic system can distinguish "linguistic, programmatic and goal-directed episodes" (1995: 600).

26   For example, communications can leap from one theme to the other in the Factual constitution of meaning, communication can leap from one interaction to the other in the Temporal constitution of meaning ("the ending of an interaction need not be interpreted as the destruction of its meaning"), and from one commitment to the other in the Social constitution of meaning (1995: 418–20).

securities into insecurities without an ultimate guarantee that this will always succeed at the level of complexity. (1995: 310)

Meaning systems constitute their own Time horizons and, in the course of their coevolution, they keep using norms for orientation, although observation has proven over and over how present norms are continuously challenged and carry the risk of becominge obsolete.

In the Social dimension, claims are expectations that play on emotions Finally, in the Social dimension of meaning, expectations can be condensed into claims. Claims appear when "the self-commitment and the vulnerability established and put into play in the difference between fulfillment and disappointment" of expectations is strengthened. Luhmann points out that "the transition from expectations to claims increases the chance and the danger that emotion will form, just as one can, conversely, cool down emotions by retreating to mere expectations" (1995: 269). Since the code of morality also draws on emotions, as previously noted, moral claims will often carry a strong emotional content in addition to their normative meaning references.

Steering at the Meta-level of Expectations that Are Expected

Expectations are constructed from generalizations and, as such, they also have the function of "bridging the multiplicity of meaning dimensions and keeping them accessible at each specific moment of meaning" (1995: 95), and of bridging "discontinuities in Fact, Temporal, and Social regards, so that an expectation can still be used when the situation changes" (1995: 97). The generalization of meaning references is constantly tested: The system will select expectations that "extend across discontinuities and can thereby prove themselves as generalizations" (1995: 97).

In order to do this expectations themselves will have to become generalized, that is to become expectations that are expected. "Expectation must become reflexive; it must be able to relate to itself, not only in the sense of a diffuse accompanying consciousness but so that it knows that it is anticipated as anticipating" (1995: 303). Social order is built on the fact that meaning systems can anticipate that their expectations will be expected. "This is how expectation can order a social field that includes more than one participant," explains Luhmann. "Ego must be able to anticipate what alter anticipates of him to make his own anticipations and behavior agree with alter's anticipation" (1995: 303).

At this meta-level of expectations that are expected, meaning systems condense previously generalized expectations into "symbolic abbreviations representing highly complex expectational situations"; these symbolic abbreviations serve "as a surrogate for a tedious investigation, enumeration, and publication of the actual expectations implied in any given situation" (1995: 306).

Morality[27] is a symbolic generalization of meaning (1995: 236) that uses the symbolic dual code good/bad and esteem/disesteem as a sweeping abbreviation to move from one meaning selection to the next one. For the purpose of the communication process, meaning is "symbolized" as a code (1977a: 520). We have to remember here that, for Luhmann, symbols "*are themselves* what they perform," rather than designating something else (1995: 94).

Morality works at the meta-level of expectations that are expected (last row of Table 9.3). This meta-level of expectation of expectations "offers additional means of integrating expectations as a means of steering behavior." Meaning-constituting distinctions become reversible. Meaning-constituting operations are sequential events, and such a sequence is linear and irreversible; conversely expectations that are expected are reversible. "In principle, structures formed on the level of the expectation of expectations, that is, ones established *only* by the *expectation* of expectations, provide a chance of reversibility." Corrections can be made, not at the operational level but at a more abstract level: "The reflexivity of anticipation makes corrections (and even a struggle for corrections) possible on the level of expectation itself. This is an inestimable advantage because expectations provide structures with a content that can be revised. One has not yet acted, but only toys with the possibility" (1995: 305).

As mentioned previously, the function of morality is to coordinate relationships of interpenetration between meaning-constituting systems. Because they are operating at the meta-level of expectations that are expected when they moralize their communications, interpenetrating meaning systems are challenged to move to more abstract levels when distinguishing persons, roles, programs, values, norms, and claims.

How do we recognize the success of morality as a reciprocally enabling device for meaning-constituting systems? Morality succeeds:

> [...] if it succeeds in binding the conditions under which one can relate to one another as a person and as a human being back to the construction of a common social system (or to having already lived in such a social system), and if, conversely, the continuation of such a system's operations is inconceivable without considering *what human beings personally think of each other* and how they include each other's complexity and freedom of decision into their own self interpretation. (1995: 238; my emphasis)

---

27 Not only morality, but most of the abstractions used by meaning systems for their ongoing orientation, that is "stipulations of what should be done, values, concepts of obligation, and references to custom, normality, or what is usual" are symbolic generalizations (Luhmann 1995: 306).

Table 9.3 Morality: Steering at the level of expectations that are expected

	The **Fact dimension** of meaning	The **Time dimension** of meaning	The **Social dimension** of meaning
Oscillation within a double horizon:	– Self-reference – External reference	– Past – Future	– Ego – Alter
Steering at the level of **expectational structures:**	Four perspectives allowing for increasing levels of abstraction : *Persons, Roles, Programs, Values*	*Norms:* behavioral expectations stabilized over time	*Claims:* Linkage between expectations and emotions
Steering at the **meta-level of expectations that are expected** by moralizing communications:	– The moral code esteem/disesteem is used to make distinctions between more complex *Persons*, occupying more diversified *Roles* – Moral *Programs* are reversible – Moral *Values* are reversible	Moral invention: – *Normative* expectations are reassessed if disappointed – new *Normative* expectations are built to deal with the increase in complexity	Moralized *Claims*: – are reversible – can be inflamed by the expression of emotions

To express esteem or disdain for a fellow human being and to link it to the binary distinction good/bad is a mechanism based on the generalization of meaning. It reduces the full complexity of ego/alter relationships to the level of complexity exhibited by the systems, thus negating for now the full complexity of those relationships. It looks like evolution at the level of meaning-constituting systems could be "an evolution of the technique of generalizing," says Luhmann (1990a: 69).

The expectational structures of meaning systems are constantly challenged because they are constructed with rough generalizations and binary conditionings. As said before, the world will not shrink and complexity will not be erased in order to accommodate the fact that a meaning-constituting system is not yet capable to increase its level of complexity. Deviation from expectations and innovation are possible in matters of social regulation and in matters of morality:

> If society becomes more complex it increasingly creates and reacts to effects that are not steered by established structures of expectation but emerge freely and of themselves, as it were. Correspondingly, it is very likely that such production will be classified as deviant and/or innovative because only thus can it establish a relationship with existing structures. (1995: 398)

Applying or not applying the moral code to a given communication has become a contingent choice (1993a: 1009); that is, a choice that is neither necessary nor impossible. Since expectations that are expected are reversible, to moralize communication will stop neither deviance nor innovation. Contingency also means that, in functionally differentiated societies, morality—and social regulation in general—has a more challenging task ahead of it: to become increasingly reflexive. Interpenetrating meaning systems are in a position to enable each other. They can aim at simply stabilizing that which already morally counts by allowing it to reproduce itself. Alternatively, they could observe the shortcomings of their expectational structures and demonstrate their capacity for moral invention[28] by taking more and more into account in their meaning-constituting operations the full complexity of the relationships between human beings.

Conclusion

Meaning allows for a reciprocal enabling between self-constituting systems that function as an environment for each other. Any increase of complexity in one meaning system leaves the environment richer in possibilities for other meaning systems. The Factual, Temporal, and Social constitution of meaning is based on sequential operations of distinctions: The system distinguishes this and not something else, but the distinction is open to an oscillation between these two sides. To improve the connectivity between their operations, meaning systems use

---

28   On moral invention in meaning-constituting systems, see Laflamme 2006.

generalizations and conditionings: Meaning references are bundled together and the next meaning selection is made conditional to a binary choice that excludes the third.

Meaning references can be condensed into behavioral expectations. Moreover, meaning systems can operate at the meta-level of expectations that are expected. The reflexivity of the expectation gives it a reversibility that the sequential operations of a system do not have. Morality works at this meta-level. We can observe over time how moral claims, moral norms, moral values, and moral programs show reversibility. As for persons and roles, the moral code is open to more oscillation when persons are experienced by meaning systems as more complex human beings, individualized and occupying diversified roles. Meaning systems have then fewer possibilities to use sweeping generalizations to bestow esteem or disesteem to the whole person as a participant in communication. Moral coding is always a coding of communication. Since participants can only use language and its evolved forms (script, writing, virtual languaging) to bring into a communication system their own perceptions and their interpretation of the situation, new technologies capable of linking in a virtual space psychic systems and systems of communication will continue to fascinate them and will initiate new forms of reciprocal enabling between them. What counts morally does tend to reproduce itself, but moral invention is also possible since meaning systems simultaneously reduce and preserve complexity, with the world as the ultimate horizon of all meaning.

Hence there are four challenges for social regulation when it is driven by the constitution of meaning: to keep generalizations in check since what is not being taken into account by the system will reappear in enlarged horizons; to use binary coding reflexively since those fast connections have a fascinating effect and blind the system to the full complexity of its environment; to invest in the reciprocal enabling allowed at the meta-level of expectations that are expected, since reversibility is needed for innovation; and, on a more practical note, to monitor the effects of the technologically advanced languaging devices already at work since they create new structural and operational links between psychic systems and social systems.

References

Brans, M., and S. Rossbach, "The autopoiesis of administrative systems: Niklas Luhmann on public administration and public policy," *Public Administration* 75 (1997), 417–39.

Dallmann, H.–U., "Niklas Luhmann's systems theory as a challenge for ethics," *Ethical Theory and Moral Practice* 1/1 (1998), 85–102.

King, M., and C. Thornhill, *Niklas Luhmann's Theory of Politics and Law* (Basingstoke: Palgrave/Macmillan, 2003).

Laflamme, D., "The constitution of meaning according to Niklas Luhmann," in Margarita Maass Moreno (ed.), *Sociology on the Move* (Mexico: UNAM, Centro de Investigaciones Interdisciplinarias en Ciencias y Humanidades, 2011).

____, "Moral coding and programming as evolutionary achievements," *Journal of Sociocybernetics* 6/2 (Winter 2008), 69–83.

____, "Ethics and the interplay between the logic of the excluded middle and the logic of the included middle," in B. Nicolescu (ed.), *Transdisciplinarity: Theory and Practice* (New York: Hampton Press, 2008).

____, "Moral invention in meaning-constituting systems," *Kybernetes* 35/7–8 (2006), 1210–22.

Leydesdorff, L., "The communication of meaning and the structuration of expectations: Giddens' 'structuration theory' and Luhmann's 'self-organization,'" *Journal of the American Society for Information Science and Technology* 61/10 (2010), 2138–50.

____, "Anticipatory systems and the processing of meaning: a simulation study inspired by Luhmann's theory of social systems," *Journal of Artificial Societies and Social Simulation* 8/2 (2005). Available online at http://jasss.soc.surrey.ac.uk/8/2/7.html.

____, *A Sociological Theory of Communication: The Self–organization of the Knowledge-based society* (Boca Raton, FL: Universal Publishers, 2003).

Leydesdorff, L., and S. Franse, "The communication of meaning in social systems," *Systems Research & Behavioral Science* 26 (2009), 109–17.

Luhmann, N., "System as difference," *Organization* 13/1 (2006), 37–58.

____, *Theories of Distinction* (Stanford: Stanford University Press, 2002).

____, *Art as a Social System* (Stanford: Stanford University Press, 2000).

____, *Observations on Modernity* (Stanford: Stanford University Press, 1998).

____, "The control of intransparency," *Systems Research & Behavioral Science* 14 (1997a), 359–71.

____, "Limits of steering," *Theory, Culture & Society* 14/1 (1997b), 41–57.

____, "Globalization or world society?: How to conceive of modern society?" *International Review of Sociology* 7/1 (1997c), 67–79.

____, "The sociology of the Moral and ethics," *International Sociology* 11/1 (1996a), 27–36.

____, "Membership and motives in social systems," *Systems Research & Behavioral Science* 13 (1996b), 341–48.

____, *Social Systems* (Stanford, CA: Stanford University Press, 1995).

____, "Politicians, honesty and the higher amorality of politics," *Theory, Culture & Society* 11 (1994), 25–36.

____, "The code of the Moral," *Cardozo Law Review* 14 (1993a), 995–1009.

____, "Deconstruction as second-order observing," *New Literary History* 24 (1993b), 763–82.

____, "Paradigm lost: on the ethical reflection of morality," *Thesis Eleven* 29/1 (1991a), 82–94.

____, "Operational closure and structural coupling: the differentiation of the legal system," *Cardozo Law Review* 13 (1991b), 1419–41.
____, *Essays on Self-reference* (New York: Columbia University Press, 1990a).
____, *Political Theory in the Welfare State* (Berlin and New York: W. de Gruyter, 1990b).
____, *Ecological Communication* (Chicago: University of Chicago Press, 1989).
____, "The morality of risk and the risk of morality," *International Review of Sociology* 3 (1987a), 87–101.
____, "The evolutionary differentiation between society and interaction," in J.C. Alexander, B. Giesen, R. Munch, and N.J. Smelser (eds), *The Micro–Macro Link* (Berkeley, Los Angeles, and London: University of California Press, 1987b), 112–31.
____, "Modern Systems Theory and the theory of society," in M. Volker, D. Misgeld, and N. Stehr (eds), *Modern German Sociology* (New York: Columbia University Press, 1987c), 173–86.
____, *Love as Passion: The Codification of Intimacy* (Cambridge, MA: Harvard University Press, 1986a).
____, "The autopoiesis of social systems," in F. Geyer and J. van der Zouwen (eds), *Sociocybernetic Paradoxes: Observation, Control and Evolution of Self-steering Systems* (London: Sage, 1986b), 172–92.
____, *A Sociological Theory of Law* (London: Routledge & Kegan Paul, 1985).
____, "Generalized media and the problem of contingency," in J.J. Loubser, R.C. Baum, A. Effrat, and V.M. Lidz (eds), *Explorations in the General Theory in Social Science* (New York: The Free Press, 1977a), 507–32.
____, "Differentiation of society," *Canadian Journal of Sociology* 2/1 (1977b), 29–53.
____, "The future cannot begin: temporal structures in modern society," *Social Research* 43/1 (1976), 130–52.
Philippopoulos-Mihalopoulos, A., *Absent Environments: Theorising Environmental Law and the City* (London: Routledge-Cavendish, 2007).
Rasch, W., "Immanent systems, transcendental temptations, and the limits of ethics," in W. Rasch. W., and C. Wolfe (eds), *Observing Complexity: Systems Theory and Postmodernity* (Minneapolis: University of Minnesota Press, 2000), 73–98.
Rempel, M., "On the interpenetration of social subsystems: a contemporary reconstruction of Parsons and Luhmann," in F. Geyer and J. van der Zouwen (eds), *Sociocybernetics: Complexity, Autopoiesis, and Observation of Social Systems* (Westport: Greenwood Press, 2001), 89–107.
Sciulli, D., "An interview with Niklas Luhmann," *Theory, Culture and Society* 11/2 (1994), 37–68.

PART III
Beyond Legal Positivism: Norms, Rights and Constitutions

Chapter 10
Making Law Together? On Some Intersystemic Conditions of Judicial Cooperation

Jan Winczorek

Introduction

Musical metaphors enjoy a peculiar place in the stylistic repertoire of academic legal writing. Even though papers and books in this domain refer sometimes to musical concepts, conservative ones are more likely to be cited: melody (Postema 2004), harmony (Krotoszynski 2006), ouvertures (Zumbansen 2004: 1499), or counterpoints (Maduro 2003). Consequently, the image of music that can be reconstructed from these citations evokes a stereotypical vision of just one genre—classical music. Other musical styles, particularly jazz or modern musical experimentalism (with their different takes on the idea of improvisation), do not speak much to lawyers' imagination, not to mention such plebeian genres as rock or pop.

Should that bias be regretted? Maybe. Apart from being informative about law professors' dominant aesthetic preferences, this choice of metaphors is also quite revealing as to how they think about the law. It shows that the law is believed to be structured like a harmonious tune whose tone is determined by a composition—a text prepared in advance by a single author: trained, consistent and talented. Like a musical performance, the application of law is supposed to reflect this artfully crafted base material to do justice to its coherence and wisdom. It is a matter of harmony and order, not chaos. Even such innocent elements of musical composition as dissonances are acceptable in law only as long as they are thoughtfully placed in the desired scheme. Cacophony of dissonant voices is something to be feared, not an artistic technique that might be purposefully utilized.[1]

Alfred Schütz remarks in his "Making Music Together," a classic of sociological writing about music, that musical score, despite its apparent precision, is in fact a very vague medium of communication (Schütz 1964: 166). The music is, he argues, just as much written in advance as it is created by musicians in the course

---

[1] See, for example, the title of the symposium "Diversity or Cacophony?: New Sources of Norms in International Law," published in the *Michigan Journal of International Law* in 2004.

of their interactions on the stage. It is implausible to think, therefore, that music actually exists before it is performed. To the contrary, it is made while it happens and ceases to exist immediately afterwards. Performance presupposes a lot of room for musical interaction and interpretative discretion and requires musicians to "tune in" and to mutually adjust their ways of understanding the tune during the very process of playing. Therefore, to maintain that music is about intellectual, advance interpretation of the score, is to miss its most important, social element, something that makes the final result truly unpredictable.

By relying on a stereotypical vision of classical music, by stressing the necessity of performative fidelity and by emphasizing the duty of conformity to others' past performances. lawyers obfuscate the very same aspect of the law: its processual, unpredictable, social nature, the fact that it changes while it happens.[2] An alternative interpretation is thus ruled out, according to which it is performance, application, interpretive creativity and conflict that are decisive for the actual shape of the law. It is unthinkable for lawyers that the content of the law cannot be ascertained in advance, and that no overarching legal coherence, other than in individual interpreters' own interpretations, can be expected.

To be sure, such assumptions are not just a matter of style and they are not unimportant. They fuel some of the discussions in legal academia and by doing so they contribute to the uncertainty and confusion that had accompanied recent developments in the legal system. One example is the anxieties concerning the plurality of the law. The multiplicity of contemporary legal sources, the multitude of law's effects and contexts as well as the diversity and interconnectedness in its institutional infrastructure (Slaughter 2004: 66ff.) have all become an object of increased attention in different areas of legal scholarship. This concern is visible both in public law, where it is an obvious consequence of contemporary shifts in distribution and scope of political power (see, for instance, Sand 2001) and private law, where new private law regimes and regulations are discussed (Teubner 2000).

Characteristically, the terms used to describe these phenomena are also many: diverse in their exact meanings, sometimes overlapping and not always precise. Deliberations on such matters are filed under labels as different as legal pluralism, legal polycentricity, polycentrism, multicentrism, interlegality, departmentalism, judicial dialogue, juridical pluralism, pluralistic universe of law, judicial cross-fertilization, multilevel legal systems, or even legal globalization. Their evaluations are also highly divergent. One can hardly avoid the impression that the plurality of the object of study is mirrored in the discourse that deals with it. And, to return to music, it comes to one's mind that this apparent difficulty in finding an adequate and agreed-upon terminology signifies the hardships of abandoning the smooth vision of a harmonious law, coherent and pre-interpretable.

---

2 G. Postema, in his paper utilizing melody as a metaphor of law puts it straight: "Law's modus operandi is to offer guidance and a framework for the interaction of rational self-directing agents. This requires at a minimum a kind of normative coherence over time" (Postema 2004: 223).,

Theoretical difficulties are particularly visible when it comes to a narrower problem that is considered in this chapter: the possibilities of cooperation between adjudicating bodies having competing jurisdictions. Such courts and para-courts are mushrooming on the global level; their proliferation is also acutely visible on the regional scale. Still, no established methods of coordinating their adjudication exist. The dissimilarity between this state of affairs and the traditional, hierarchical organization of the judiciary provokes many questions. How, it is asked, given such a multiplicity of competing adjudicating bodies, can some degree of coordination in the application of the law be secured? How is the ultimate value of legal certainty to be realized if no clear hierarchy of courts exists and if there are many institutions eligible for issuing final opinions, not just one (something that traditionally contributed to such effect)? How can different adjudicating theories, methodologies of interpretation, cultures of decision-making produce a single, coherent legal order? How can the different instruments of the judicial orchestra be tuned so that they all play one melody when there is no conductor?

Lawyers and All That Jazz

Such questions sound alarming, and the search for a global conductor is already under way. Proposals range from the sociopolitical and the legislative to methodological.[3] Still, there is room for an alternate, perhaps unorthodox, take. Couldn't the solution be found in the methodology of adjudication, in how judges interpret the law at hand, thereby independently producing a legal order? Is any conductor needed at all if judges agree on some rough standards of interpretation of the law, just like jazz musicians who accept some general rules for collective performance—including some "standards" to be interpreted—and leave the rest to be clarified in the spontaneous process of on-stage interaction?

As a prelude to further discussion, one can note that, contrary to a belief expressed sometimes in said legal literatures, the phenomenon of diversity in law is not new, and that conservative musical metaphor has been wrong from the very start. Legal pluralism has been around for centuries and this despite decades-long efforts to create a "legal system" that is logically coherent and as rational as possible. Although the persistence of legal pluralism has been largely repressed from legal conscience and theory, its many traces have made its way even into European jurisprudence. It has been noted, for instance, that the idea of "legal pluralism" can be, paradoxically, traced back to Montesquieu (Macdonald and Kleinhans 1997: 30). One could also seek inspiration in the historical school of early nineteenth century with its hostility toward the movement toward codification and such conceptions as associations and their law (see Pospisil 1967: 5). Later on, early opposition to the positivist paradigm in legal scholarship from figures such as Leon Petrażycki in Russia and Poland (Kojder 2006; Motyka 2006) and Eugen

---

3   See, for instance, theories of Maduro, Kumm (2005) or Sauer (2008).

Ehrlich in Austria (see, for instance, the essays in Hertogh 2009), expressed the view that the law should be seen in pluralist terms, as a composite of, respectively, "unofficial" or "living law" and "official" and "statutory" law.

Moreover, empirical evidence of legal pluralism was available as soon as empirical methodology started being used in the legal context. As early as the 1930s, Polish legal scholars Bronisław Wróblewski and Witold Świda (1938) demonstrated, using the results of polls conducted among criminal judges, that even within a highly hierarchical, unitary legal system operating on the basis of a freshly enacted code interpretations of the same law might vary wildly, suggesting that it is not the code, or not only the code, that determines judicial decisions. However, unlike Ehrlich or Petrażycki, Wróblewski and Świda did not welcome this result. Instead, they (and their followers after the Second World War) treated it as a challenge and tried to pinpoint the psychosocial factors responsible for the diverse decisions of judges and judicial panels (Kaczmarek 1972 and 1987; Giezek 1989).

The same story of legal multiplicity has been retold, in different ways and languages, in the social sciences dealing with the law. The sociology of law owes its very existence to said early opposition to the view that a logically coherent normative system can guide human conduct. The idea of pluralism was still present in the discipline in the postwar period,[4] even if it was not directly expressed at a time of unfavorable trends in social theory. In the empiricist legal sociologies of the 1950s, 1960s, and early 1970s, one can easily find the view that ideally identical legal norms are usually different in their actual application, depending on context,[5] which on a theoretical level led to ideas like those of Theodor Geiger or Donald Black on the gradual validity of the law. Even functionalism eventually evolved into a form more supportive of the idea of concurrent plurality of legal orders. Similarly, legal anthropology developed the concept of legal pluralism as a tool to discuss the interactions between indigenous and colonial law (see, for instance, Benton 2002), and then later extrapolated it to encompass legal phenomena as such. Here, too, the law is viewed as indispensably plural, as a social entity that cannot be reduced to just one of its many appearances (for a classical articulation of this view, see Moore 1973).

Against this background, contemporary interest in the plurality of law in mainstream jurisprudence appears as an odd, and badly informed, departure from established theoretical pathways. In the two centuries following Jeremy Bentham and John Austin it was the state that was seen as the main player of the law's melody, the conductor who has disappeared from today's chaotic orchestra. Even if the historical development of legal theory can be seen as a slow dilution of the ideas of hard positivism through consecutive concessions toward the ever-expanding (and itself changing) social thesis formulated by Hart and later Dworkin

---

4   See the summary of views expressed by Adam Podgórecki from the late 1950s (Podgórecki 1991, ch. 1) or the theories of Masaji Chiba (1989).

5   For one well-known illustration of this, see Blankenburg 1976.

or neo-institutionalism, one can hardly imagine how the idea of the multiplicity of legal orders can fit with the rest of the picture sketched by (post)positivism. After all, the social thesis presupposes a mythical, ontological social, a position that is nowadays extreme even in sociology (for a somewhat exaggerated critique of this view in a legal context, see Latour 2010: 254ff.) and contradicts the assumption of the normative incoherence of society, strongly expressed in theories of legal pluralism. More importantly, the softened version of the idea of law's hierarchy is still present even in those authors who explicitly postulate some elements of legal pluralism.

A claim that the transition to legal pluralism is just another step in the evolution of mainstream legal doctrines can, therefore, hardly be accepted. Rather, for a pluralist view of law to be correct, state-centered legal theorizing must be considered dead and the quest for legal theory should be started anew, this time on realistic premises.[6]

Too Many Notes or Too Many Conductors?

Leaving aside this petty-minded interdisciplinary reckoning, one must admit that something has changed in the institutional framework of contemporary law. It is true that many new legal actors have emerged, as shown most notably by the globally and regionally operating courts and court-like conflict-resolving institutions. It is also true that state-run adjudicating bodies are now but an element of a larger picture of conflict resolution. It is, finally, true that no overarching mechanism exists that could coordinate them all and that, in many such cases, courts enjoy (to extend the term used mostly in a European context) *Kompetenz-Kompetenz*—the ability to define their own competences—which adds to the danger of conflicts.

Yet again, this recognition of truthfulness of lawyers' observations comes at a cost of a fundamental reservation. It is one thing that the law—its sources, interpretation, and application —is diverse and pluralized and yet another that the institutions that apply it are not hierarchically organized. Whenever one speaks about judicial multicentrism and dialogue, one should be precise and careful not to confuse these two phenomena. It is true that in Western cultures of modern times the institutional design of the judiciary has been controlled politically and conceptually. Still, it is hard to maintain that the law has not been pluralistic anyway because of its informal and lay dimensions and because of obvious discrepancies in legal interpretations—and these even in the same jurisdiction. Consequently, when one speaks of the plurality of courts today, one in fact means the lack of

---

6   For a recent example of the evolutionary doctrine, see Haack 2008. Interestingly, even though Haack admits that the law is an evolving, cultural phenomenon and distances herself from attempts to define its substance, she still defines the notion of law in state-related, highly ethnocentric, and rather substantive terms, denying this name to such phenomena as indigenous law (Haack 2008: 461–2).

coordination of their activity, not "legal pluralism" in a strong anthropological or sociological sense. Legal pluralism in the latter meaning persists, but is not new—it has long been there, irrespective of changes in the organization of the judiciary.

For more clarity, a typology of legal and judicial systems can be produced by cross-tabulating the distinctions of unicentric and multicentric forms of organization of the judiciary on one hand and of pluralistic and monistic legal systems on the other (for details, see Winczorek 2009). This allows us to distinguish unicentric–pluralistic legal systems (where institutions are coordinated hierarchically, but legal norms are not coherent), multicentric–pluralistic ones (where no hierarchy of institutions exists and where legal pluralism persists), multicentric–monistic ones (with multitude of institutions relying on a conceptually and factually coordinated, homogeneous legal order[7]), and unicentric–monistic ones (with hierarchical coordination in both legal institutions and the law). It is dubious, of course, whether *any* legal order can be wholly and completely monistic; one can, however, have an approximation of such when one limits the temporal, factual, and social scope of the analysis (far) below the level of a nation state.[8]

Analytical as it might be, this typology opens up a new space for dealing with the problem at hand. It is possible now to reformulate the question of today's judicial multiplicity in terms of institutional cooperation and thus to detach it from legal pluralism. In this way, the matter becomes compatible with two levels of analysis, suggested by systems theory: the level of functionally differentiated social systems (here: the law) and the organizations in their environment (here: the courts).[9] From yet another angle, but still in the tradition of systems theory, the law can be seen as a symbolically generalized medium of communication, mediating the activities of courts (see, generally, Luhmann 1976 and Luhmann 1997: 190ff.). To communicate a verdict is, in this sense, to make a distinction in the law-medium. Consequently, to refer to someone else's judgment is to reconstruct (observe) the meaning mediated by the legal communication by producing one's own distinctions in the very same medium.

The question of judicial cooperation is thus reformulated as follows: How should the judicial environment be observed by the legal system so that the principal function of the law—maintaining normative expectations—is preserved and legal communication is continued? In terms of media theory, the question is: Is it possible to create such a law-medium that allows for legal communication at a time when politically backed hierarchies of courts are no more?

---

7   An example could be a community based on shared values allowing for the maintenance of a coherent law despite the lack of coordination in the sphere of decision-making.

8   Consider, for example, a secluded traditional community with ad hoc conflict-resolving "bodies."

9   The observation that the legal system should not be identified with the organizational dimension of the judiciary or the legal profession is stressed by Luhmann (1993: 329–33)

It also follows that even if the structure of the legal system is of the highest importance, legal pluralism is not necessarily an answer to the problem of judicial pluralism. Of course, legal pluralism must be taken into account. It is a factor that might—or might not—help in dealing with the problem of coordination in the judiciary. It influences the operation of the law-medium and contributes to how the system observes the environment, but is not decisive for judicial multiplicity. It will persist regardless of the ultimate changes in law's observation of the environment.[10] Thus, a choice—if there is space for any—should not be made between legal pluralism and legal monism but between different possible forms of observation of the law's environment.

In more conventional terms, the problem is not how to bring national and supranational legal orders (complete with courts embedded in them) into conformity when traditional means of doing so are not available, but rather how to coordinate the courts and other judicial bodies without superimposing upon them an unattainable hierarchy and without utopian attempts to unify the law.[11] Conversely, what is sought is not legal coherence obtained by means of judicial cooperation, with courts putting themselves in the place of the missing global or regional political unifier, but the possibility of continuing legal communication despite conflicts and *because* of them.[12]

Second Life of the Band

In this difficult situation, lawyers can, as in the case of music, benefit from interactions with the social sciences. Suspicions about monocentric, hierarchical social structures have been expressed in the latter for a long time. The observation that formalized, bureaucratic organizations require, in order to survive, a second

---

10 While Luhmann (1993: 333ff.) stresses that the center/periphery distinction determines the role of courts in the legal system, he admits that, viewed "operationally," this does not preclude the possibility of ad hoc legal communications in the periphery nor does it guarantee cohesion of the system.

11 The inability to notice this difference is apparent in some contemporary attempts to theorize the problem of judicial conflicts and judicial cooperation. See, for instance, Maduro (2007: 17), who goes as far as stating that "to take full advantage of this idea of legal and constitutional pluralism we need to conceive forms of reducing or managing the potential conflict between legal orders," or Snyder, who speaks of legal pluralism as involving "institutions, norms and dispute resolution-processes" (Snyder 2002: 10) or some examples of the "constitutional borrowing" debate where coherence of legal orders is desired while judicial dialogue flourishes (Lollini 2007).

12 Of course, from a strictly jurisprudential point of view this observation requires clarifications concerning its impact on many important concepts in contemporary legal thinking, such as rule of law or legal certainty. This cannot be discussed here. For some arguments on how nonhierarchical institutional structures of adjudication can contribute to rule of law, see Stith 2008.

life of informal interactions is indeed a classic of the sociology of organization. In this vein, organizations grow out of social roots that supply them with resources that they need but are unable to produce themselves. Since Max Weber defined bureaucratic organization, a multitude of studies has been conducted that aim to demonstrate that specialization, formalization, hierarchy, and other features of such entities must be supplemented by counterbalancing elements. They undermine bureaucracy to some extent, but also provide it with informal information flows or casual leadership, thereby eliminating its many deficits. It follows that in reality formal organizations are not, and cannot be, truly formal (see, classically, Selznick 1949 and the wealth of subsequent literature).

This squares neatly with wisdom stemming from sociolegal and anthropological research. As in organization studies, it is possible to think of legal institutions as institutions depending on a second life of their own and on the second life of unofficial law, but still officially organized as if they were exclusively formal and rational and as if the law were a coherent system.[13] Informal law allows them to resolve conflicts and regulate behaviour, limit the inflow of cases, control the parties involved and determine the outcomes—something they would not be able to do if they had to rely only on their official codes. This also holds for the relationships between individual courts in national adjudication systems, where adjudication strategies are influenced by such informal factors as likelihood of reversal or the argumentation culture.

Does that mean that effective adjudication is also possible without hierarchy? One can turn for inspiration to P. G. Herbst, the author of the pioneering book *Alternatives to Hierarchies*, who maintained that traditional bureaucratic organizations are but one possible form. Also nonhierarchical organizations are thinkable and practicable, and these two types can be distinguished by five features (Herbst 1976: 22f.). First, it is the assumption that every task can be split into smaller segments and distributed among members of an organization—in non-bureaucratic organizations this division of labour is replaced by a networked system of cooperating peers. Second, it is the existence of a single, rigid hierarchical structure which links all members of an organization versus the adjustable, constantly changing structure in non-bureaucracies. Third, it is a fixed system of hierarchical relationships between individual members, as opposed to more flexible and interchangeable links that allow for leaders to be changed depending on the task. Fourth, it is a clearly defined boundary between organizational units versus flexible and changing relationships between entities. Fifth, and finally, it is the fact that organizational boundaries create permanent gulfs between units, whereas in non-bureaucratic organizations they are dictated by the task in hand. According to Herbst, organizations that follow the second set of principles can

---

13   To be sure, one must distinguish between courts as bureaucratic institutions and the second life within each of them (a problem that is not discussed here), and courts as elements of a broader legal landscape.

be more effective than bureaucratic ones, and still allow for a measure of healthy democratic labour relations.

In a more contemporary discourse an observation is made that hierarchies are produced whenever knowledge disparity exists between positions in organizations pertaining to the accomplishment of certain tasks (Garicano 2000). The more difficult it is to acquire knowledge, and the easier it is to delegate solution-finding, the more likely it is that a hierarchy emerges based on unequal distribution of knowledge.[14] On such grounds formulae are devised for establishing efficient organizational structures, given some starting assumptions. Yet, it also follows, consistently with what Herbst had claimed, that a group of equally competent workers does not need to be organized hierarchically in order to be effective.

The lessons derived from Herbst's call for flexibility and from the thesis of knowledge disparity is thus twofold. First, both suggest that courts must be equally equipped with knowledge as to how adjudicate. Knowledge disparities may lead to an informal hierarchy, with some courts interested in transferring some of their cases. It is also possible for an intellectual dependence on others' theories and concepts to emerge, and, most likely, for the phenomenon of forum shopping to become more acute. All this might in the end lead to bandwagon effects and to the hardening of knowledge disparities into competing camps.[15]

Interestingly, knowledge disparities do not occupy lawyers much. It is stressed sometimes that international judges' networks are being established, helping to "exchange experiences" and to create common understanding of relevant matters (Slaughter 2003). Yet, some degree of exclusivity can be registered, at least in some areas of dispute resolution (see Dezalay and Garth 1996). It is also a matter of extralegal resources that are at the disposal of the judiciary in different parts of the world. It might be, therefore, that "judicial dialogue" can only be enjoyed by the well-equipped judiciary in the well-off North, whereas the poorer and less well-organized adjudicative bodies in the South will only be passive recipients of ideas (and conflicts) produced elsewhere. This question cannot be investigated here. It puts, however, an important restraint on everything that can be said: The range of solutions is limited by resources available to all. If one is not willing to accept hierarchies, one should adhere to low-cost and culture-independent proposals.

---

14   The reasoning behind this claim is simple: Workers situated at the front line of production deal with a number of standardized problems and their ability to cope with more complicated ones is limited by the relative unlikeliness of their appearance. Consequently, the competence required for solving such problems is delegated to some specialized problem-solvers, who deal only with nonstandard cases, ones that cannot be solved by regular employees. They in turn are differentiated according to their skills. This division is further repeated, so that a hierarchical structure emerges.

15   These observations are to some extent confirmed by the results of American research on predictors governing the citation of other courts' verdicts, which suggest that the stronger predictor is "the perceived prestige of the cited source" (Black and Epstein 2007: 799f.). However, see Slaughter 1999–2000 for an enumeration of reasons for which judicial dialogue can be maintained between peers.

Second, it follows that there must exist some method of communication between courts, allowing them to coordinate their efforts, while preventing the development of an informal hierarchy. Courts must therefore be able to learn from one another but they should not be able to transfer cases at will, nor be forced to do so. In legal discourse a distinction is made in this context between hard (formal) types of "judicial dialogue"—for instance based on prejudicial questions—and soft ones, based on persuasion, arguments, and prestige. From the proposed perspective, only a subsection of such soft methods appears acceptable.

On the other hand, this does not necessarily mean that courts must intentionally seek agreement with their peers. To the contrary, persistent effects may also be achieved when the cooperation is an unintended or even latent consequence of courts' daily adjudication. In particular, this does not contradict the observation, repeatedly formulated by many authors, that informal relationships between justices are focal to cooperation of their courts, nor the idea of "judicial comity" (Slaughter 2003), at least if it is understood as an effect of courts' actions rather than a description of the actions themselves.

In terms of systems theory, this necessity of restructuring the communication in the legal system can be perceived as yet another incarnation of the paradox of self-description. In this vein, competence conflicts can be viewed as a symptom of the inability of the legal system to produce an overarching perspective, a second-order observation that allows for describing all of the communication in it as something that belongs to that system, yet still in the system's own terms (Luhmann 1987 and 1993: 73ff.; Clam 2000). In the past, one way of resolving the paradox was to point at the system's environment, to take advantage of an external observer. The adjudicating institutions of final instance were treated as deparadoxalization devices of legal communication (Luhmann 1993: 297ff.). Today, this solution is insufficient because the external reference is itself multiplied due to overlapping competences. If many courts can be used for the task, who is to give the final answer?

This reformulation of the problem is helpful, because it draws attention to the fact that the impossibility of hierarchy pertains not only to the institutional solutions, such as the establishment of a global court to resolve competence-conflicts. In many proposals for ways of escaping the paradox of coordinating courts, it is overlooked that not only legal institutions, procedures or material norms but also legal theories and concepts can be viewed as second-order observations of the legal system, performed from within that very system (Luhmann 1993: 496ff.; Winczorek 2009a, ch. 4). They are advertised as solutions to the paradox, while in fact they reproduce it. In other words, they fail to provide an answer as to why they should be accepted by individual courts if they put a limit on their self-proclaimed autonomy.

This is well illustrated by the idea of counterpunctual law. Its proponents lay down directives for conflict-avoidance (Maduro 2003), yet make no justification as to why this particular theory—out of many conceivable theories—should be accepted by courts, particularly given that this would produce a hierarchy. Similar remarks hold for the concept of constitutionalism beyond the state, where "political morality" is believed to be the mediating force that might mitigate conflicts (Kumm 2005: 268).[16] In all such voluntary solutions the problem of multitude of *Kompetenz-Kompetenz*-enjoying bodies is not resolved, but merely transformed into a question of (author's own) *Kompetenz-Kompetenz-Kompetenz*, which might easily slip into *Kompetenz-Kompetenz-Kompetenz-Kompetenz* etc.

In Search of Instruments

As extensively discussed by Luhmann and other authors, problems of this sort are by no means new. Questions of self-reference are claimed to be a distinctive feature of modern, functionally differentiated society (Luhmann 1997: 748ff.). The solutions are well recognized as well: When one encounters a paradox within one's communicative realm, one is inclined to look for a deparadoxalization outside of it (see, for instance, Luhmann 1993:.168ff.). Yet, as it were, the possibility of escaping the paradox of self-reference utilized in the theoretical tradition of Western law—the structural coupling between law and politics through constitutions (Luhmann 1993: 440ff.)—is insufficient when it comes to contemporary judicial multicentrism.

It is plausible to ask if this link could be reestablished so that nonhierarchical communication is somehow supported politically. This requires that the structural coupling is modified in such a way that legal expectations of political decisions serve as a go-between in courts' discourse. Thus, such decisions need to be conceived as providers of "virtual" collision norms or perhaps as the norms themselves. Put simply, the decision as to who is right in courts' disputes would have to be made—directly or indirectly—politically. Of course, this traditional approach has its obvious limitations, as it presupposes a high degree of organization of world politics. It is clear that certain solutions remain impossible precisely for that reason. For instance, it is highly unlikely that a single "world court" dealing with competence disputes will be established (cf. Oellers-Frahm 2001), or that a single decision-making body will be created to establish and enforce universally binding collision norms.[17]

Still, such limitations do not rule out political solutions. Some political changes can trigger desired changes in the judiciary and facilitate information exchange. Consider, for example, proposals elaborated by Inger-Johanne Sand (2004) in the context of European law.[18] She postulates extending the repertoire

---

16   Even Teubner (2004) uses, when discussing similar matters, a misleading language of "commandments" (pp. 1018ff.)

17   This also holds on the regional scale. For instance, a vision of the European Court of Justice as an "umpire" is clearly wrong, merely as a statement of fact.

18   To be sure, Sand is one member of larger number of voices who have announced such a possibility. A solution is often sought in simply adding a political dimension to

of social steering by techniques of governance. Not only political and legal means of regulating social relations should be used but economic and technological ones as well. Consequently, the traditional method of linking politics and law—the constitution—must also be changed in order to reflect this new situation. In this vein, Sand postulates "creativity" in reestablishing the structural coupling. Beside traditional political institutions, devices such as "European identity", market, expert participation in problem-solving committees, or deliberative democracy should also be utilized to rebuild the relationships between law and politics.

When reviewing these proposals in the context of the institutional design of the judiciary one can easily see the new possibilities that they would bring. As opposed to the crude positivist approach where decisions are expected to be determinate and courts are thought to be mere mouthpieces of the statute—applying political decisions rather than "adding to them"—governance perspective leaves plenty of room for legal interpretation. If the results of the political debate are never final but based on under-determinate conditions, and if they require that a judgment is made on rationality of actions driven by changing assumptions, one is not just allowed to express one's own interpretations but required to do so.

This is visible in every dimension of meaning, as defined by Luhmann (1984: 112): temporal, social, and factual. First, courts may not ignore changes in politics and continue treating political decisions as if they were issued by sovereign states, because their temporal dimension is much more demanding. The time horizon for making decisions is now much shorter, because the assumptions governing political decisions perish at a much quicker pace. Second, the coalitions and pressure groups behind decisions change rapidly, making it difficult to look for legislative intentions as a guideline for interpretation of the law. Third, connections between different social subsystems cause changes in definitions of problems at hand. What yesterday appeared as environmental problems might today be defined economically or legally, or the other way round (cf. Luhmann 1989). All in all, it is impossible to treat "soft law" or "regulations" in the same manner as statute proper.

From the point of view of legal positivism it is as if the courts had to deal with hard cases every time they pass a judgment. They face a much more open-

---

courts' activities—that is, treating them as a link between law and politics. In the European context it has been repeatedly pointed out that the very existence of the European Union owes much to the fact of the European Court of Justice having taken over some political roles during the process of integration. In the USA an interesting discussion has been going on at least since mid-1990s concerning the possible and desired scope of citations of foreign courts by American judges. It has been observed that the agenda of at least some scholars promoting "judicial dialogue" in this context was to persuade American judges to participate in the process of international policymaking and foreign relations by referring to foreign judgments more frequently (Black and Epstein, 2007). In both cases, a political solution intertwines with the legal one, setting anew the relationships between law and politics and adding a new dimension to the understanding of both.

textured law and the medium that they use to communicate is able to encompass more information. Consequently, they are both allowed to increase the information capacity of their judgments and forced to do so. Their opinions must be richer in order to make sense of increasingly blurry political decisions. Consequently, since more creativity is required; judgments are more difficult to compare and confront. On the other hand, the same reasons allow judges to both borrow from their peers and to symbolically distance themselves from them—but still do not force them to perform any of those operations.[19]

Thus, governance-oriented politics is conducive to court cooperation. Courts can learn from one another but still avoid conflicts by refusing to refer to their peers when they find it necessary. Yet, they may not rely completely on either of these options, because they will not be able to pass a satisfying verdict. Moreover, it can be expected that a court's relative reluctance to cite its peers can negatively influence its own chances of being cited. In this sense, the new freedom of the courts is not unlimited: It finds its boundaries in external conditions in which they operate, in the medium affected by altered structural coupling with politics.

Despite these interesting possibilities, the reliance on the political has its disadvantages. In a sober reply to Sand's argument, Fisher-Lescano (2004) raises an important point about looking for help in the political realm. The links between law and politics run in both directions, making these social systems mutually dependent. Stability of the political system depends, among other things, on it being coupled with the law. This presupposes the existence of certain structural conditions in the legal system which in turn depend on a particular structuring of politics. In other words, in order to maintain its own stability and resolve its own paradoxes, the political system must *first* rely on the stability of the law. History knows too many examples of catastrophes caused by the political escaping the limits superimposed on it by the law.

If politically induced change in courts' communication appears too risky, too close to a strange loop, one might look for support elsewhere. One of the options is progress in the media of dissemination, most importantly the spread of modern information technologies. Studies in this field suggest that new ways of communicating the law and views about it have tremendous impact on the possibilities of its critical analysis. It has been noted, for instance, that the concept of precedent only came about thanks to the communication technology of print (Katsh 1989: 35ff.), which allowed for the credible dissemination of verdicts. The same can be said regarding the development of the conceptual method of steering the complexity in the legal system (Luhmann 1993: 120f.). Legal doctrine as it

---

19   It has been noted that precedents—understood as binding grounds for decisions—can only exist when the number of cases which can be cited is limited. If they are too many, the power of a single judgment becomes much smaller because there are many alternatives (Katsh 1989: 45). *Mutatis mutandis*, the same can also be said about decisions issued in situations of uncertainty, where the next decision can be constructed on the grounds of more general theories or by referring to more diverse contexts.

is known today would not have come into existence without the possibility of comparing judgments and distributing commentaries. This has been possible only since case reports became broadly available.

If a link between methods of adjudicating and technologies of communication indeed exists, it is rational to believe that the recent emergence of electronic technologies of communication has an impact on how courts operate and cooperate. Perhaps such technologies can help establish new relationships between courts by enabling another level of observation in the legal system. It also follows from the knowledge/hierarchy concept that good access to information should be a facilitator, if not a precondition, of mutual learning (see similar remarks and examples in Slaughter 2005).

Yet, little research exists to corroborate or falsify this intuition (for rare examples, see Cerrillo, Martínez, Fabra, and Abat 2008; Aas 2005). Nonetheless, it is indirectly confirmed by empirical and theoretical work in organization studies and education. One of the trendy notions utilized in these fields, "community of practice" (CoP), referring to informal information networks, coordination capabilities, social bonds, and identity creation mechanisms in organizations, has been used in the context of information retrieval and storage systems.[20] It is suggested that utilization of properly designed information systems facilitates the establishment of a community of problem-solvers who coordinate their activities, find solutions, and build professional identities by utilizing that very system. They may be able to establish a professional community through mediated interaction, allowing them to communicate and share experiences with their peers working in completely different physical settings. Information technology becomes here a flexible and easily scalable medium, through which more than just technicalities of a trade are efficiently communicated.

One could be moderately optimistic about possibilities of establishing a "community of practice" among global courts and justices, given that many of their verdicts can now be remotely retrieved from different database systems. With some effort and financial input, even the language barrier can be overcome (McAuliffe 2008). One example of such international cooperation is the databases and other information retrieval systems utilized in the process of "European judicial cooperation." They do not only allow for the dissemination of decisions and reasons, but also enable judicial dialogue in the strict sense: the common elaboration of solutions to shared problems (Jimeno-Bulnes 2003).

Still, community of practice literature teaches that mere utilization of a database is by no means a sufficient condition for the establishment of such communities. Modern IT tools can be used to foster their development, yet it is the willingness of the participants in the process and their ability to use that opportunity that are

---

20 For a short overview of concepts and empirical examples, see Cox 2005. Some insights on CoPs in the context of information technology are provided by Kling and Courtright 2003 and Hara and Kling 2002. The original concept was formulated by Lave and Wenger (1991) in an extremely well-circulated book.

decisive for the existence of communities of practice. There is no reason why this observation should not also hold in the case of courts. Again, then, the solution boils down to the question of how the courts will produce their judgments and whether their practices will be open to the possibilities offered by database technologies. Technological change is only an external incentive for the legal system to restructure, but it is by no means sufficient. As in politically induced solutions, context-rich adjudication is needed to produce the desired effect.

Moreover, databases have their threats. To name some, one might fear their being utilized merely mechanically, thereby hampering rather than promoting mutual learning and allowing for the strategical uses of references to other courts. The very way in which the database is organized might also debilitate the process of communication and contribute to production of hierarchies, because it allows for circulation of information only in a rigidly prescribed way, much closer to a standard "expert system" than a collaborative work environment (see, in this respect, Aas 2005).

Rehearsals

Two briefly discussed possibilities of recreating the self-description of the legal system so that it becomes compatible with dispersion of the judiciary should suffice as a demonstration that in every case the willingness to resolve the paradox presupposes changes in the operation of courts and in justices' habits. The broadening of structural coupling with politics is not a sufficient condition for changing the way the legal system is organized, nor is utilization of technology. Some other shifts in the structure of the legal system allowing for the establishment of new interdependencies between courts in the systems' environment are thus necessary. They must allow for proper deparadoxalization of the legal system on grounds other than that of structural coupling itself. In other words, structural changes should only come about as a result of transformation of already existing ways of adjudication, not thanks to external revolutions or steering.

The question is now whether such opportunities for change are indeed offered by the methodology of adjudication. The paradigmatic, positivist view in the European context is that the scope of legal interpretation is limited by the possibilities of coordinating the literal interpretation of a legal text and its underlying purpose. The relative weight of the latter is lower, making linguistic interpretation the default: the law cannot be interpreted beyond its literal wording as long as such a reading is congruent with the law's purpose. Only when a certain threshold of conflict between conclusions stemming from linguistic and purposive interpretation is exceeded can the latter be used (Feteris 2008). This, of course, brings to the fore the problem of distinguishing between acceptable and unacceptable conflicts. The concept of the rationality of the legislator is normally used as a yardstick for their measurement (Feteris 2008) and, consequently, as a regulative idea of the legal system. If particular interpretations can be viewed as congruent in the light of a counterfactually assumed rationality of the legislator, literal interpretation cannot be abandoned.

This observation is relevant for judicial dialogue because it suggests that the paradigmatic method of legal argumentation is conducive to the authoritative announcement of one's position. It leaves little room for a critique or commentary, allowing only for confrontation. Even if arguments between courts emerge for reasons other than diverging choice of interpretive methods (for instance because of law's natural vagueness, thereby producing inconsistent results even if the same method of interpretation is used by individual courts), one of their major sources is certainly incongruent methodology of interpretation. Thus, different answers to a legal question may be produced by a different—explicit or implicit—evaluation of the legislator's rationality in a particular case. Such an evaluation depends in turn on the reconstruction of the legislator's set of values, which is a highly problematic intellectual activity. Therefore, the court's true reasons for arriving at a particular verdict are more likely to be obfuscated than explicated. Thus, as long as the concept of the rational legislator is fuzzy and no methodology is developed to determine his or her values with certainty, it serves as an apt disguise for the interpreter's real views rather than helping to specify them. For that reason, unless a "logical" error in the court's reasoning is discovered, the argument must be either taken for granted or rejected on symmetrical grounds.

On the other hand, it has been pointed out that contemporary judicial dialogue—where it is successful—owes its existence to the discourse of human rights (Barak-Erez 2004). In this discourse, quite consistently with what has been said, the balance between linguistic and teleological interpretation is heavily weighted in favor of the latter. The vagueness of human rights as legal standards makes linguistic methods extremely difficult, if not impossible. This is particularly visible when such standards are used as a subsidiary tool of legal interpretation—that is, when agreement between a norm being applied and a human right standard must be secured (for instance in *verfassungskonforme Auslegung*). Consequently, the reference to human rights makes it more improbable for a direct conflict to emerge, because tracing a discrepancy in views is much more difficult when vague standards are involved. Such apt terms as the "hermeneutic effect of human rights" and the "in-depth interpretation of law" are used in a similar context to describe this ability to escape clashes (Cartabia 2007: 14ff.).

It follows that a multi-contextual, rich and principle-based interpretation of law can be helpful in promoting judicial dialogue. It may contribute to the establishment of new types of external references in the legal system and to the creation of an alternative method of self-description. By doing that it may also help to establish a nonhierarchical, but still completely functional, relationship between *Kompetenz-Kompetenz*-capable courts. This may be possible, because an open model of interpretation allows for reference to be made to other courts' verdicts even if the contexts of decisions and their ultimate conclusions differ. Natural vagueness of such reasoning is a great facilitator, allowing for "cherry-picking" as well as for using citations as "distancing devices" (McCrudden 2000) or for utilizing foreign references as sources of legitimization (Barak-Erez 2004: 627). Even if from the perspective of argumentative purity such strategic manoeuvres and instrumental usages of interpretation are not welcome; they help to promote the ultimate goal discussed in this chapter. Moreover, they might produce such effects even if they are not deliberately used for that purpose.

It is good to notice that this argument is consistent with more abstract observations provided by systems theory. In *Das Recht der Gesellschaft* (1993: 347ff., 400ff.; Winczorek 2009a: 267ff.), Luhmann observes that two types of legal argumentation can be distinguished: referring to logic and to principles. The former leads to the reduction of complexity of the legal system by eliminating possible irritations, the latter opens the system to external influences by enhancing irritability and increasing complexity. While one produces redundancies, the other delivers variations. The two types of adjudication, one based on the assumption of legislative rationality and the other relying on human rights, obviously correspond to these two types of argumentation. While in the case of the paradigmatic methodology logical reasoning and linguistic interpretation are expected, in the nonorthodox case a broader scope of arguments is admissible.

This, in turn, suggests that the intuition suggesting a positive link between human rights and judicial dialogue is theoretically justified. First, human rights allow for deparadoxalization of the system by a means of a mechanism similar to that of justice. While in the case of the standard paradigm opposites produced by self-reference are logically sharpened and require external (political) reference to be resolved, human rights mediate them by means of their intrinsic vagueness. Second, the law-medium through which courts cooperate is more complex in the latter case than it is in the former, thus reducing the probability that communicated meanings are categorized as identical or contradictory due to awkwardness of their go-between. To return to the musical metaphor: To expect courts bound by paradigmatic methodology to produce a "judicial dialogue" is like expecting a jazz band to improvise on Coltrane's "Love Supreme" with only four notes.

Of course, even if systems theory registers the opportunities for judicial dialogue, its emergence is by no means obvious or guaranteed. It is, as it were, a matter of social evolution, not external design and imposition, and that requires more than just an intellectual possibility— it requires actual evolutionary potential. In this context it must be noted that a clear conflict exists between said two traditions in legal methodology. Will the forces supportive of open-textured interpretation prevail or is the paradigmatic methodology strong enough to persist? What is worse, one of these options may be politically inconvenient. It might be argued that the more context-independent the interpretation and the fewer factors taken into account in its course, the easier it is to steer it by changing the legislation. In this sense, political interests in adjudication conflict with strictly legal ones. On the other hand, the utilization of broader normative material and nonorthodox interpretation methods might be seen as yet another case of judges' unwanted political activism.[21]

Such dependencies suggest that the question of possible legal evolution towards judicial dialogue might be empirical. Two methodologically different examples can be offered as a preliminary answer to this question. First, one might look at the much-discussed relationships between the European Court of Justice (ECJ) and the national courts of the member states, particularly constitutional courts. A model of their relationships that avoided direct conflicts is some 20 years old and does not need to be reconstructed here in detail (see Sadurski 2008; Slaughter 1999–2000). Suffice to say that the Solange judgments, the reactions to them on the part of the ECJ and the inspirations that were taken from this conversation elsewhere, for instance in the dialogue between the ECJ and the European Court of Human Rights—historically in Defrenne (Jacobs 2003: 511f.; Besson 2008) or recently in Kadi—fall quite well into the categories described above. Human rights—an extremely vague standard—have been used as a yardstick for determining which of the courts is competent to decide cases where their competences overlap (judicial review of Community law). Moreover, both the German Constitutional Court and ECJ relied on comparative and functional methods of interpretation. Famously, in one of the cases the ECJ went so far as to make general references to "indications provided by the constitutional rules and practices of the nine member states," treating them as if they were consistent and precise.

Judicial exchanges can also be observed in a handful of verdicts delivered on the occasion of the introduction of the European Arrest Warrant (EAW). Yet, if these judgments are any way analogous to the Solange discourse, it is only by the fact that in both cases the competence of the ECJ is denied by constitutional tribunals (Sadurski 2008). First, literature dealing with this matter draws attention to the fact that constitutional courts, facing the danger of the unconstitutionality of domestic laws introducing the EAW, have stuck to a literal interpretation and gone as far as interpreting constitutional principles as Dworkinian rules. Second, it is noticed that in most cases the possibility existed to interpret these laws in a non-formalistic fashion, avoiding the conflicts between judgments of the ECJ and the constitutional courts on the matter of the required meaning and procedure of the EAW (Komarek 2005). Third, it is pointed out that political pressures can be traced in at least some EAW decisions (Sadurski 2008). It follows that whenever authoritative judgment is expected, literal interpretation is used, which leads to the impossibility of a "follow up" by future partners in a hypothetical dialogue. Of course, a battle of contradicting opinions is still possible (if, for example, the ECJ finds it necessary to "answer" the German Constitutional Court's disregard for the Pupino judgment), but this is not the type of "dialogue" that is expected.

---

21   Yet, it is doubtful if this argument is convincing when it comes to demonstrating that formalistic adjudication is not political—rather, it might only point to the shift in the sources of power.

An interesting contribution to the latter observation can be found in the second example, provided by a natural social experiment conducted on the flesh and blood of the Polish judicial system (for details, see Stawecki, Staśkiewicz, and Winczorek 2008). It came about as a result of a succession of structural reforms. First, the early 1980s saw, as an element of long-fought-for legal reform the establishment of two new adjudicative bodies: the Supreme Administrative Court (SAC) and the Constitutional Tribunal (CT). At first, their competences were clearly delimited and, for political reasons, compromised. The two new bodies were meant to supplement the Supreme Court (SC), the main court in then-existing system, rather than to compete with it. The SAC was even subordinate to the SC in cases involving public administration, due to the possibility of an extraordinary appeal from its decisions to the Supreme Court. Similarly, a judgment of the CT could be overturned by a qualified majority in parliament. Yet, the political changes at the end of the decade, the structural reforms of the 1990s, and successful activities of both new institutions led to significant elevation of their positions. This, in turn, sparked clashes between members of the CT and the SC regarding direct implementation of constitutional provisions by regular courts and the binding force of interpretative decisions of the CT.

The conflict was partially induced by the fact that, in the process of reinforcing the positions of the CT and CAS, it was simply taken for granted that their competences and those of the SC could be clearly delimited. This assumption quickly turned out to be wrong, because in some contexts a reaction to decisions of other courts is not only desired (i.e. in cases of CT's interpretation of some constitutional principles) but also formally required (i.e. in cases of renewal after CT rules on unconstitutionality of a provision of a law being a basis for past court decisions).

This case is interesting in the current context because adjudicating methodology played an important role in it. The study of the mutual impact of decisions of the CT, SAC and SC, conducted on a large sample of verdicts (Stawecki et al. 2008) reveals that they paid very little attention to the normative theories and concepts elaborated by their peers. This is demonstrated by the finding that courts cited their own judgments much more frequently than decisions of other adjudicative bodies, irrespective of the nature of the matter at hand. Also, the research showed that even in similar cases the three institutions used their own adjudicative methodologies but still shared a strong tendency toward formalistic adjudication—based on literal or systematic interpretation rather than functional or comparative. This allowed them to achieve a peculiar equilibrium: They did not draw from their peers but did not push them to do so either. In this way they eliminated the danger of external intrusion into their autarchic adjudicative empires. Thus, formalistic interpretation served as a tool of conflict avoidance.

The lesson to be drawn here is, therefore, contrary to the one that follows from the European example. The more formalistic lesson is in adjudication, the more likely one is to succeed in creating tight boundaries of one's own adjudicative empire. The same factor is also likely to contribute to the preservation of one's autonomy.

Such an outcome might seem positive; at least, no open conflicts are to be expected. However, such an equilibrium comes at a cost. First, whenever cooperation is required—for instance in cases of interpretative decisions or grand theories in constitutional adjudication—a competence conflict is likely to emerge. Courts will expect that only their concepts are used, but the degree of interpretive flexibility offered by formalistic methodologies and required to avoid clashes, will be insufficient. If little creative interpretation is allowed, no possibility exists even to "cherry-pick" or make other strategic use of other courts' interpretations. This might become even more acute over time, when formalistic interpretation sediments into established interpretive tradition.

Second, such a situation is undesirable for practical reasons. If it occurs, arguments relying on concepts and ideas from a particular judicial realm may not be used in other contexts. Theories of constitutional principles, elaborated by the CT, will not have any effect when referred to in proceedings before the SAC or SC. It is not just that the judges will not be bound by views of other courts—it is that they will ignore them altogether. The legal certainty that emerges in such a situation is surely strongly compromised.

Coda

Conclusions stemming from these deliberations are complex. First, it seems that the apparent multicentric organization of the judiciary must be accepted. There is little chance of a return to the simple world of the hierarchical organizational structure of the courts, with a single court "on top," whose decisions are binding for everyone else and can be enforced when necessary. There are many external conditions that contribute to this impossibility: both political and technological conditions as mentioned in this chapter, and also economic ones, which were not discussed. Second, any attempts to structure the global judiciary according to hierarchical models, be they formal or informal, perpetuated by knowledge distribution or rigid meta-theoretical assumptions, will eventually produce a conflict. Theoretical proposals in this domain must be formulated carefully so that no arbitrary meta-level is proposed. Third, nonhierarchical solutions must be sought, allowing *Kompetenz-Kompetenz*-capable courts to treat other as peers. Fourth, nonhierarchical cooperation between courts can be achieved by different methods. One of them is by effecting changes in the adjudicating methodology. A transition from formalistic to multi-contextual interpretation can facilitate references to decisions of other courts. Fifth, some results might also be reached by other means. Lack of conflict can be produced by avoiding contact. In this case, however, legal certainty is compromised by conflicts emerging from courts' "forced" encounters. Sixth, legal pluralism—as opposed to institutional pluralism—will persist, irrespective of the prevailing model of adjudication. Consequently, the issue of nonhierarchical construction of the legal order concerns only the relationships between adjudicating institutions, not between legal orders or legal norms. The interest in legal pluralism is therefore redundant for the question of judicial interactions.

Metaphorically speaking, the courts of overlapping jurisdictions are like jazz musicians entering onstage. Some rehearsals have been done, and a degree of understanding of what can be played has been gained. Still, nobody can decide on the repertoire, actual pace, and tone of the music. It is the actions of every musician, reactions to these actions, and reactions to these reactions, that will allow the sound to emerge. Enjoyable and exciting when it comes to music, such situations can indeed be difficult from the point of view of a court. A decision to make an "open-ended" verdict presupposes reciprocity on the part of every other court with possibly overlapping jurisdiction—but precisely this reciprocity is not certain. On the other hand, taking an authoritative position might be rewarding, at least in the short-term, but might also have devastating consequences in a longer perspective.

References

Aas, K. F., *Sentencing in the Age of Information: From Faust to Macintosh* (Cavendish: Routledge, 2005).

Barak-Erez, D., "The International Law of Human Rights and Constitutional Law: A Case Study of an Expanding Dialogue," *International Journal of Constitutional Law* 4/2 (2004), 611–32.

Benton, L. A., *Law and Colonial Cultures: Legal Regimes in World History, 1400–1900* (Cambridge: Cambridge University Press, 2002).

Besson, S., "Gender Discrimination under EU and ECHR Law: Never Shall the Twain Meet?" *Human Rights Law Review* 8/4 (2008), 647–82.

Black, R. C., and L. Epstein, "(Re-)setting the Scholarly Agenda on Transjudicial Communication," *Law & Social Inquiry* 32/3 (2007), 789–807.

Blankenburg, E., "The Selectivity of Legal Sanctions: An Empirical Investigation of Shoplifting," *Law & Society Review* 11/1 (1976), 109–30.

Cartabia, M., "'Taking Dialogue Seriously': The Renewed Need for a Judicial Dialogue at the Time of Constitutional Activism in the European Union," Harvard Jean Monnet Working Paper 12 (2007).

Cerrillo, A., A. C. Martínez, P. Fabra, and P. F. Abat, *E-Justice: Information and Communication Technologies in the Court System* (Hershey etc.: Information Science Reference, 2008).

Chiba, M., *Legal Pluralism: Toward a General Theory through Japanese Legal Culture* (Tokyo: Tokai University Press, 1989).

Clam, J., "Die Grundparadoxie des Rechts und ihre Ausfaltung: ein Beitrag zu einer Analytik des Paradoxen," in G. Teubner (ed.), *Die Rückgabe des zwölften Kamels: Niklas Luhmann in der Diskussion über Gerechtigkeit* (Stuttgart: Lucius & Lucius, 2000), 109–45.

Cox, A., "What Are Communities of Practice? A Comparative Review of Four Seminal Works," *Journal of Information Science* 31/6 (2005), 527–40.

Dezalay, Y., and B. G. Garth, *Dealing in Virtue: International Commercial Arbitration and the Construction of a Transnational Legal Order* (Chicago: University of Chicago Press, 1996).

Feteris, E. T., "The Rational Reconstruction of Weighing and Balancing on the Basis of Teleological-evaluative Considerations in the Justification of Judicial Decisions," *Ratio Juris* 21/4 (2008), 481–95.

Fischer-Lescano, A., "Themis Sapiens: Comments on Inger-Johanne Sand," in G. Teubner, I.-J. Sand, and C. Joerges (eds.), *Transnational Governance and Constitutionalism* (Oxford: Hart, 2004), 67–81.

Garicano, L., "Hierarchies and the Organization of Knowledge in Production," *The Journal of Political Economy* 108/5 (2000), 874.

Giezek, J., *Okoliczności wpływające na sędziowski wymiar kary* (Wrocław: Wydaw. Uniwersytetu Wrocławskiego, 1989).

Haack, S., "The Pluralistic Universe of Law: Towards a Neo-classical Legal Pragmatism," *Ratio Juris* 21/4 (2008), 453–80.

Hara, N., and R. Kling, "Communities of Practice with and without Information Technology," *Proceedings of the American Society for Information Science and Technology* 39/1 (2002), 338–49.

Herbst, P. G., *Alternatives to Hierarchies* (Leiden: M. Nijhoff, 1976).

Hertogh, M. L. M., *Living Law: Reconsidering Eugen Ehrlich* (Oxford: Hart, 2009).

Jacobs, F. G., "Judicial Dialogue and the Cross-fertilization of Legal Systems: The European Court of Justice," *Texas International Law Journal* 38 (2003), 547.

Jimeno-Bulnes, M., "European Judicial Cooperation in Criminal Matters," *European Law Journal* 9/5 (2003), 614–30.

Kaczmarek, T., *Sędziowski wymiar kary w Polskiej Rzeczypospolitej Ludowej w świetle badań ankietowych* (Wrocław: Zakład Narodowy im. Ossolińskich, 1972).

———, *Decyzja sędziego w sprawie wymiaru kary i jej psychospołeczne uwarunkowania* (Wrocław: Wydaw; Uniwersytetu Wrocławskiego, 1987).

Katsh, E. M., *The Electronic Media and the Transformation of Law* (New York: Oxford University Press, 1989).

Kling, R., and C. Courtright, "Group Behavior and Learning in Electronic Forums: A Sociotechnical Approach," *The Information Society* 19/3 (2003), 221–35.

Kojder, A., "Leon Petrazycki's Socio-legal Ideas and Their Contemporary Continuation," *Journal of Classical Sociology* 6/3 (2006), 333.

Komarek, J., "European Constitutional Pluralism and the European Arrest Warrant: Contrapunctual Principles in Disharmony," Jean Monnet Working Paper 10 (2005).

Krotoszynski, R. J., "'I'd Like to Teach the World to Sing (in Perfect Harmony)': International Judicial Dialogue and the Muses: Reflections on the Perils and the Promise of International," *Michigan Law Review* 104 (2006), 1321.

Kumm, M., "The Jurisprudence of Constitutional Conflict: Constitutional Supremacy in Europe before and after the Constitutional Treaty," *European Law Journal* 11/3 (2006), 262.

Lave, J., and E. Wenger, *Situated Learning: Legitimate Peripheral Participation* (Cambridge etc.: Cambridge University Press, 1991).

Latour, B., *The Making of Law: An Ethnography of the Conseil d'Etat* (Cambridge: Polity 2010).

Lollini, A., "Legal Argumentation Based on Foreign Law: An Example from Case Law of the South African Constitutional Court," *Utrecht Law Review* 3/1 (2007), 60–74.

Luhmann, N., "Generalized Media and the Problem of Contingency," in J. J. Loubser, R. C. Baum, A. Effrat and V. M. Lidz (eds.), *Explorations in General Theory in Social Science: Essays in Honor of Talcott Parsons* (New York: Free Press, 1976), 507–32.

____, *Soziale Systeme: Grundriss einer allgemeinen Theorie* (Frankfurt am Main: Suhrkamp, 1984).

____, "Tautologie und Paradoxie in den Selbstbeschreibungen der modernen Gesellschaft," *Zeitschrift für Soziologie* 16 (1987), 161–74.

____, *Ecological Communication* (Cambridge: Polity Press, 1989).

____, *Das Recht der Gesellschaft* (Frankfurt am Main: Suhrkamp, 1993).

____, *Die Gesellschaft der Gesellschaft* (Frankfurt am Main: Suhrkamp, 1997).

Macdonald, R. A., and M.-M. Kleinhans, "What is a 'Critical' Legal Pluralism?" *Canadian Journal of Law and Society* 12/2 (1997), 25–46.

Maduro, M. P., "Contrapunctual Law: Europe's Constitutional Pluralism in Action," in N. Walker (ed.), *Sovereignty in Transition* (Oxford: Oxford University Press, 2003).

____, "Interpreting European Law: Judicial Adjudication in a Context of Constitutional Pluralism," *European Journal of Legal Studies* 1/2 (2007).

McAuliffe, K., "Enlargement at the European Court of Justice: Law, Language and Translation," *European Law Journal* 14/6 (2008), 806–18.

McCrudden, C., "A Common Law of Human Rights? Transnational Judicial Conversations on Human Rights," *Oxford Journal of Legal Studies* 20 (2000), 499–532.

Moore, S. F., "Law and Social Change: The Semi-autonomous Social Field as an Appropriate Subject of Study," *Law & Society Review* 7/4 (1973), 719–46.

Oellers-Frahm, K., "Multiplication of International Courts and Tribunals and Conflicting Jurisdiction Problems and Possible Solutions," *Max Planck Yearbook of United Nations Law* 5 (2001), 67–104.

Motyka, K., "Law and Sociology: The Petrażyckian Perspective," in M. Freeman (ed.), *Law and Sociology* (Oxford: Oxford University Press, 2006).

Podgórecki, A., *A Sociological Theory of Law* (Milan: Giuffrè, 1991).

Pospisil, L., "Legal Levels and Multiplicity of Legal Systems in Human Societies," *Journal of Conflict Resolution* 11/2 (1967).

Postema, G. J., "Melody and Law's Mindfulness of Time," *Ratio Juris* 17/2 (2004), 203–26.

Sadurski, W., "'Solange, Chapter 3': Constitutional Courts in Central Europe, Democracy, European Union," *European Law Journal* 14/1 (2008).

Sand, I.-J., *Changes in the Functions and the Relations of Law and Politics: Europeanization, Globalization and the Role of the New Technologies*, vol. 1 (Oslo: ARENA, 2001).

____, "Polycontextuality as an Alternative to Constitutionalism," in G. Teubner, I.-J. Sand and C. Joerges (eds.), *Transnational Governance and Constitutionalism* (Oxford: Hart, 2004), 41–64.

Sauer, H., *Jurisdiktionskonflikte in Mehrebenensystemen* (Berlin: Springer, 2008).

Schütz, A., "Making Music Together: A Study in Social Relationship," in A. Brodersen (ed.), *Alfred Schütz. Collected Papers*, vol. II (The Hague: M. Nijhoff, 1964), 159–78.

Selznick, P., *TVA and the Grass Roots* (Berkeley: University of California Press, 1949).

Slaughter, A.-M., "A Brave New Judicial World," in M. Ignatieff (ed.), *American Exceptionalism and Human Rights* (Princeton: Princeton University Press, 2005), 277–303.

____, "Judicial Globalization," *Virginia Journal of International Law* 40 (1999–2000), 1103–24.

____, "A Global Community of Courts," *Harvard International Law Journal* 44/1 (2003), 191–219.

____, *A New World Order* (Princeton, NJ: Princeton University Press, 2004).

Snyder, F., "Governing Economic Globalisation: Global Legal Pluralism and European Law," in F. Snyder (ed.), *Regional and Global Regulation of International Trade* (Oxford; Portland, OR: Hart, 2002), 1–48.

Stawecki, T., W. Staśkiewicz, and J. Winczorek, *Between Polycentrism and Fragmentation. The Impact of Constitutional Tribunal Rulings on the Polish Legal Order* (Warsaw: Ernst & Young, 2008).

Stith, R., "Securing the Rule of Law through Interpretive Pluralism: An Argument from Comparative Law," *Hastings Constitutional Law Quarterly* 35/3 (2008), 401.

Teubner, G., "Contracting Worlds. The Many Autonomies of Private Law," *Social and Legal Studies* 9/3 (2000), 399–19.

Teubner, G., and A. Fischer-Lescano, "Regime-collisions: The Vain Search for Legal Unity in the Fragmentation of Global Law," *Michigan Journal of International Law* 25 (2004), 999–1046.

Winczorek, J., "Between Triviality and Triviality: Legal Multicentrism from Systems," Theoretical Point of View," in M. Zirk-Sadowski, B. Wojciechowski and M. J. Golecki (eds.), *Multicentrism as an Emerging Paradigm in Legal Theory* (Frankfurt am Main: P. Lang, 2009).

____, *Zniknięcie dwunastego wielbłąda. O socjologicznej teorii prawa Niklasa Luhmanna.* (Warsaw: Liber, 2009a).

Wróblewski, B., and W. Świda, Sędziowski wymiar kary w II Rzeczpospolitej. Ankieta (Vilnius: Wydawnictwo Uniwersytetu Stefana Batorego, 1938).

Zumbansen, P., "Globalization and the Law: Deciphering the Message of Transnational Human Rights Litigation," *German Law Journal* 5 (2004), 1499–520.

Chapter 11
Rights in Niklas Luhmann's Systems Theory[1]

Pierre Guibentif

Introduction

Niklas Luhmann's contribution to the theory of law is well acknowledged: his account of the legal system as an autopoietic functional social system has had considerable impact on the discussion of modern law, in legal theory as well as in sociology of law. His thoughts on the phenomenon of—subjective—rights, however, also deserve attention.[2] In his writings of the 1990s this topic is approached within the framework of an intriguing broader problematic: the relationship between social and psychic systems, that is between social communication and individual perceptions; more precisely, the issue of the structural coupling between these two types of systems. An issue referred to for example in the following quotation: "[If] a violation of subjective rights is [a condition] for litigation, a structural coupling of individual consciousness and irritations in the legal systems is [assured]" (Luhmann 1993/2004: 490/419).[3]

A possible way of taking advantage of Luhmann's work on rights is to reconstruct his theory of the relationship between social and psychic systems and to revisit the notion of rights in the light of this theory. These two steps could provide us with the foundations required to analyze some recent trends concerning precisely the phenomenon of rights, and revealing, possibly, changes in this relationship. In the present chapter, we shall limit ourselves to some methodological reflections with

---

1   Earlier versions of this chapter were presented first at the workshop "Niklas Luhmann e os direitos fundamentais" organized in October 2008, by Germano Schwartz and Leonel Severo da Rocha, at UNISINOS in São Leopoldo (Brazil, Rio Grande of the Sul), where my participation was sponsored by the International Institute for the Sociology of Law (Oñati, Spain), and later at the international meeting "Sociedade, Direito e Decisão em Niklas Luhmann" organized in November 2009 in Recife (Brazil, Pernambuco) by the research unit "Moinho Jurídico," under the coordination of Artur Stamford da Silva.

2   Papers that focus precisely on this topic are Verschraegen 2006, Menke 2008, and Ladeur 2008.

3   Original text, to justify the changes proposed in the translation (in brackets): "Soweit eine Verletzung subjektiver Rechte Klagevoraussetzung ist, ist auch in dieser Hinsicht für eine strukturelle Kopplung von individuellen Bewusstseinslagen und Irritationen im Rechtssystem gesorgt."

the view to future researches on these trends. Such future researches could allow us to continue on the line traced by Luhmann when referring to the "problem in the relation between the social system of the world society and its human environment" (Luhmann 1997b).

The present essay does not pretend to be more than a framework proposal for further research and discussion. These future steps will necessarily require contributions from fields other than social theory and sociology of law, in particular organization theory, cognitive sciences, and—as Ladeur (2008: 121) reminds us— systems theory as developed by other authors than Luhmann.

The Relations between Social and Psychic Systems

Luhmann is already tackling the issue of the differences and the relationship between social and psychic systems in his early sociological writings—for example, in the last section of *Legitimation durch Verfahren* (1969), about "the Separation between social and personal systems." The relevance given by Luhmann to this issue in these early works is certainly due, to a significant extent, to the influence of Talcott Parsons, who aimed at including in his concept of social action the subsystems of the personality and of the behavioral organism.[4] Later on, the topic opens the first chapter of *Social Systems* (1984/1995), and it becomes more important in his last books. The title of the sixth—and last—volume of the series *Soziologische Aufklärung* (Luhmann 1995) is *Die Soziologie und der Mensch* (Sociology and the Human Being). It includes notably an extensive essay, originally published in 1985, about the "Autopoiesis of consciousness" (Luhmann 1985/1995). The year of first publication of this essay indicates the existence of a working effort that parallels over several years the main research of Luhmann, on the functional differentiation of society. As we know, this research structured his publication strategy from *Social Systems* (1984) on, dictating the priority given to the books successively dedicated to the different functional systems. These books, however, include important chapters addressing the relationship between social and psychic systems.[5] And many other papers published in the 1990s deal with this

---

  4   This theory of social action—the "action frame of reference"—is summarized in Parsons 1961; on Luhmann's interpretation of Parsons' theory, on this particular point, see Luhmann 1991–2/2002: 39.

  5   See "Bewusstsein und Kommunikation" (Consciousness and Communication), first chapter of *Die Wissenschaft der Gesellschaft* (1990), "Wahrnehmung und Kommunikation: Zur Reproduktion von Formen" (Perception and Communication: The Reproduction of Forms), first chapter of *Art the a Social System* (1995/2004), "Mensch und Gesellschaft" (Human Being and Society), first chapter of *Das Erziehungssystem der Gesellschaft* (2002); as well as "Individuen", chapter 10 of *Die Realität der Massenmedien* (1996) and chapters 3 and 9 of *Organisation und Entscheidung* (2000): "Mitgliedschaft und Motive" (Membership and Motives) and "Personal" (Staff).

topic, in particular several articles on art and pedagogy,[6] the texts gathered in the fourth volume of the series *Gesellschaftsstruktur und Semantik* (1995a), as well as an important lecture on the phenomenology of Husserl held in Vienna, also in 1995 (Luhmann 1996b).

Thus, the architecture of Niklas Luhmann's work may be interpreted as the result of a decision to give priority to the discussion of the theoretical tools required for analyzing the social systems, while the relationship between social and psychic systems is treated in a more fragmentary and essayistic way. Two justifications for such a decision may be derived from the writings of that time. On the one hand, the fact that, on the level of social systems, one finds a limited set of clearly differentiated and typified entities—functional systems and organizations—that offer a more comfortable basis than the—roughly counted—five thousand million psychic systems that Luhmann was encountering on the level of individual minds, when it came to the choice of a systems reference as starting point for his research (Luhmann 1990a: 63). On the other hand, there is also the concern expressed in the following quotation:

> The physical, chemical, biological and social conditions of possibility of knowledge cannot be enlightened by the self-analysis of consciousness. On the contrary, consciousness works better without being aware of these conditions of possibility of knowledge, because such awareness would drown it with information; its functioning would be slowed down and, eventually, completely stopped. (Luhmann 1995a: 165)

The present chapter could be justified in the following way: The phenomena that Luhmann, as a third-order observer of social reality eschewed, might be tackled with some chances of success by a fourth-order observation—a work based on the reading of Niklas Luhmann.

In this sense, we shall summarize Luhmann's reflections firstly, in general terms, on the relations between social and psychic systems (A); secondly, more specifically, on the psychic systems (B); and thirdly, on the mechanisms of structural coupling between these two types of systems (C).

(A) The thesis that cuts across Luhmann's discussion of the relationship between social and psychic systems—and that underpins in particular the papers collected in the volumes *Gesellschaftsstruktur und Semantik*—is that these two types of systems are the result of a common evolutionary process, a process that gave rise, in parallel, to a certain type of individual consciousness—a certain type of individuality—as well as to a certain type of communication—social systems with certain characteristics. The model of autopoietic systems suggests that each of these two realities is the result of a process of operational closure; that is, a process of closure of individual minds, on the one hand, and on the other a process by which communication was led to communicate with itself.

---

6 Papers recently republished in Luhmann 2004 and Luhmann 2008a.

But while these two realms of reality became more differentiated, structural relations developed between them. Consciousness makes use of a tool shaped in communication processes: language. And communication relates to its—psychical and material—environment thanks to the perceptions of consciousness. These relations indicate that there are mechanisms of structural coupling between the two types of systems, mechanisms—to be discussed below (section C)—whose performances explain, on the one hand, the evolutionary success of the device formed by the articulation between communication and consciousness. These mechanisms favored the subsistence of the two types of systems here at stake (applying here the presumption, derived from the theory of evolution, according to which a system only can survive if it is structurally coupled with its environment, while this survival is highly improbable in the absence of such mechanisms). On the other hand, they explain the current dynamics of the systems of the two kinds: The autopoiesis of one kind of system stimulates, through the structural coupling, the autopoiesis of the other (Luhmann 1990: 49).

However, the thesis of the coevolution of psychic systems and communication is complemented by the thesis of the prevalence of the evolution of communication, over that of consciousness. This second thesis derives from the two following statements. The fact that communication systems only relate to material reality in a mediate way, with the help of minds, allows them to produce a knowledge more distanced towards the world, less conditioned by material constraints. It also makes it possible for the social systems to have their own evolutionary dynamics ("evolutionäre Eigendynamik"; Luhmann 1990: 56). Under these conditions, transformations of communication could have an impact upon the reproduction of individual consciousness. We shall have to come back to this later in the chapter.

One result of the coevolution of psychic and social systems, in recent times, is that the differentiation of social systems may be interpreted, among other points of view, as meeting the needs of a better coupling between communication and consciousness. Certain social systems did differentiate because they were in a condition to perform a more effective role in this coupling. Communication communicates with communication, and with communication only, but it requires the "participation"[7] of consciousness. Notably, the distinction between information (*Information*) and expression (*Mitteilung*) requires, from the part of *ego*, the notion of a communicative intention from the part of *alter*, which implies the notion of *alter* as bearing a consciousness. In more general terms, the "double contingency" that any communication has to deal with corresponds to the experience of two minds[8] unable to access each other. Under such circumstances, communication

---

7   Luhmann uses the word in the following title of an article: "Wie ist Bewusstsein an Kommunikation *beteiligt*?" (our emphasis; Luhmann 1988/1995: "How does consciousness participate in communication?"). At the roots of *Beteiligung* is the word *Teil*, which means "part." So *Beteiligung* has precisely the same metaphorical potential as "participation."

8   Latin languages have no direct equivalent to the English word "mind"; on the other hand, they allow the plural form for the word corresponding to "consciousness". These

will be easier to process if each consciousness involved has been trained to cope with the inaccessibility of other consciousness. This is the function of the *education system*: to create a communicative context in which the minds involved are trained to imagine what could possibly happen in the consciousness of the other (Luhmann 2002: 81). *Law*, by stabilizing certain normative expectations, allows the individual consciousness to presume that the consciousness of other people will take for granted the same expectations (we shall come back to this topic later). In general terms, any communication is likely to take advantage from a communication specialized in the discussion of the fact that the perceptions of one person are not accessible to others. This is the function of *art*.

Despite the statement, repeatedly formulated by Luhmann, according to which communication only communicates with communication, he recognizes that it requires, as one of its material conditions of possibility, minds aware of what is being communicated. Therefore, narrow connections have to be established between certain kinds of communications and certain kinds of consciousness, the latter being adequately trained to react to more concrete situations of double contingency, and, if necessary, to simulate the necessary consensus (Luhmann, 2002: 81). The establishment of such connections is a function of one type of social systems in particular, that is, *organizations*, which link modes of communications to categories of people by means of the member/non-member distinction.

(B) A more detailed analysis of the relationship between psychic and social systems has to focus on the mechanisms of structural coupling between consciousness and communication. However, in order to properly reconstruct these mechanisms, we first have to introduce Luhmann's characterization of psychic systems.[9] This will be done here in three steps discussing successively: (a) the basic operations of consciousness and the main features of the systems generated by the autopoiesis of consciousness; (b) the structures of consciousness—that is, what could be named knowledge;[10] and (c) the variety of what could be named the regimes of consciousness autopoiesis.

(a) Luhmann seeks to analyze consciousness by means of his theory of autopoietic systems. Actually, this intellectual tool has the potential to create a distance between the author who carries out the analysis and his own thoughts, which can now be viewed as objects. Indeed, the thinker here faces a typical autologic challenge, similar to the one faced by society when it develops self-observation devices. Society has to get a distance from itself, but at the same

---

differences deserve an inter-linguistic discussion and interpretative effort that transcend the framework of this essay.

9   On Luhmann's conceptualization of social systems as communication, see King and Thornhill 2003: 14ff.; Guibentif 2004.

10   Luhmann refers here to *Wissen*, a word that can easily be translated in Latin languages by *savoir, saber*, etc., and means the ability to behave adequately in a certain context or to carry out adequately a certain activity, as distinct from *Kenntnis/connaissance*, which suggests a sharp differentiation between subject and object of cognition.

time, it is obliged to remain within its own frontiers (the communication necessary to the observation of society will always be a part of society too; Luhmann 1997a: 1128f.). Making use of concepts shaped in completely different contexts, autopoiesis theory allows us to approach the phenomenon of consciousness—usually experienced as one of the most familiar realities—from a new angle.

To begin with, let us briefly recall the essentials of the theory of autopoietic systems, and apply them to the phenomenon of consciousness. A system is a reality that subsists because a distinction is continuously being made, forming, for some time at least, an uninterrupted chain of operations: the distinction between this system and its environment. The question that derives from this starting point is: What exactly is the distinction that, continuously applied, forming a chain of operations, generates consciousness?

Luhmann, when discussing the operations that constitute social systems, qualifies them without hesitation, as the readers of his work know well, as communications. Communications, indeed, trace here and now the distinction between what makes sense and what does not. A communication, reacting to another communication, may signalize acceptance or refusal of it, thus continuing or interrupting the interaction. On this ground, Luhmann introduces the reader to the diversity of social systems, which results from the diversity of distinctions likely to be added to this foundational distinction (sense/no sense); additional distinctions that yield different types of communication. Consciousness is not approached in a comparably direct way. We actually do not find, in Luhmann's writings on consciousness, such a structured model as the one of communication analysed in its three components: information, expression and comprehension. Even more, he admits that, in the realm of consciousness, there are not necessarily sharp distinctions.[11] Consciousness, it seems, proved to be much more difficult to grasp than communication. Attempting to summarize his analysis of this domain, we should point out at least three different motives.

The most constant is that consciousness is said to be operating by means of the distinction between self-reference and hetero-reference; between what it is itself and what is outside of it (Luhmann 1985/1995: 64; 1995c/2000: 18/8; 1996: 34). This description can easily be combined with the main features of consciousness. Its operations would permanently and separately produce two "things": reality, perceived as what is outside there, and another world that may be qualified, in a first approach, as "interior." On the other hand, this description does not allow us to grasp the specificity of consciousness. According to Luhmann's theory, the distinction between self- and hetero-reference is a characteristic of all processes of autopoiesis.

A second motive concerns, more substantively, the nature of consciousness operations. The difficulty met here by the reader is some hesitation, on the part of

---

11 For a synthesis of Luhmann's theory of communication formulated in the framework of his discussion of consciousness, see Luhmann 1995/2000: 22–3/11–12; in particular, for perception as *diffus* (elusive), see p. 36/20.

Luhmann, between two ideas. In his 1985 essay on the autopoiesis of consciousness, he focuses on thoughts (Luhmann 1985/1995: 60f.); in *Art as a Social System* (Luhmann 1995/2000: e.g. 14/6.) he often refers to perceptions (*Wahrnehmung*). On several occasions he refers to the trilogy perception/thought/communication,[12] a motive that suggests that "perception" and "thought" would belong to the same conceptual level. Should we admit that psychic systems, contrarily to social systems, are characterized not by one but by two types of operations? Or should we acknowledge that the operations of consciousness are a combination of these two types of operations? Exactly this idea is expressed in the following sentence: "To process perceptions and to guide them by thoughts [*durch Gedachtes zu steuern*] is the primary performance [*die primäre Leistung*] of consciousness."[13] This formulation might be compared with this other one: the "type of operation" of consciousness is said to be the "process […] of steering attention" (1996b: 48). Luhmann's concepts here are quite similar to those of phenomenology, and Luhmann recognizes this affinity (Luhmann 1996b). Consciousness is constituted by acts of perception; that is, of distinguishing certain items against the background of other, less differentiated, perceptions, and of experiencing in this act of distinction our intention of perception. This experience corresponds to a thought, and such a thought may, under certain circumstances, be formulated in words.

This leads us to a more concrete notion of what could be a "combination" of self- and hetero-reference: a perception requires at the same time a more precise demarcation of the perceived object (hetero-reference) and a better formulation of its—possibly verbal—qualification in the realm of thought (self-reference). In Luhmann's words: "consciousness operates intentionally, permanently paying attention both to things in the world out there, and to itself" (Luhmann 1995a: 180), and is "combining self-reference and hetero-reference in [its] ongoing operations" (Luhmann 1995/2000: 18/8). What remains is to formulate what characterizes consciousness as an autopoietic process. Autopoiesis here arises from the fact that each of these two different processes—demarcation of objects and formulation of its qualification—gives impulses to the other. A concrete example in the optic domain: the vision of a form different from a form initially perceived obliges us to revise our qualification; the intuition of another qualification suggests new views on the things. In both cases, a difference has been perceived because a distinction could be made between what is perceived (hetero-reference) and its qualification (self-reference), and because these two elements could be related in a comparative operation (here we meet the paradox of the difference's unity, frequently mentioned by Luhmann).

---

12   Luhmann 1995b: 251; Luhmann 1995/2000: 27/15.

13   Luhmann 1995c/2000: 27/14: the concrete and direct way of referring to thought and perception, and of linking these two notions, achieved by the German phrase "Wahrnehmung durch Gedachtes zu steuern" gets lost in the—however elegant—translation: "cognitively focusing perceptions."

The third motive is the distinction between medium and form. According to Luhmann's terminology, a medium is a set of elements loosely coupled, while a form is a set of elements strictly coupled. Consciousness, from this point of view comparable to communication, is said to be an ongoing production of medium and forms. Indeed, the demarcation of a perceived object can be reconstructed as the strict coupling of a set of perceptions. The formulation of a certain qualification may be the result of a composition—set of strict links—of notions arising from previous perceptions. Obviously, the link between the object and a certain qualification itself constitutes a form, too. The medium where consciousness finds elements loosely coupled, likely to be strictly coupled by its operations, is what Luhmann calls "meaning" (*Sinn*; Luhmann, 1995/2000: 173/107).

(b) Let us remember that, according to Luhmann's systems theory, in order for autopoiesis to take place, operations have to produce their own tools for distinguishing their own distinction. This means that the "basic operations" (*basale Operation*: Luhmann 1984/1995) of the system—the application of the distinction characterizing the system—have to be paralleled by operations checking whether the distinction applied is the one of the system, thereby enabling the system to identify itself, distinguishing its own operations from other events. These parallel operations are—in Luhmann's terminology—"observations." In other words, autopoiesis requires self-observation. Consciousness—which autopoiesis we experience at any time—has to be equipped with mechanisms of self-observation. Indeed, we are capable of focusing our attention on our perception of external phenomena, as well as on our own thoughts. Luhmann calls this kind of operations "representation" (*Vorstellung*: Luhmann 1985/1995: 62). We can represent to ourselves, on the one hand, an object, thinking about the perception we had of it; on the other hand, a thought, being aware of the fact that we had it in our mind.

This notion of representation allows to characterize the structures of consciousness. Structures are strict couplings that are maintained throughout successive operations. Perceived phenomena may undergo changes at any time, and the same applies to the thoughts that seek to qualify these objects. Representations of phenomena or of thoughts on them, on the other hand, may be evoked—represented—in the same terms several times. Such repeated evocations may be favoured by similar perceptions, but these perceptions will never be identical. Applying the terminology of medium and forms, such evocations create forms. To the extent that such forms stabilize, they constitute structures of consciousness.

The notion of self-observation of consciousness, allied to the one of structure, enables Luhmann to develop his theory of memory. The theory of autopoietic systems does not admit the possibility of travelling back into the past in order to find past perceptions. Indeed, consciousness is the current ongoing process of its operations, and nothing else. Past processes of conscience have to be actually represented. This is possible if we succeed in establishing strict links between certain thoughts and certain perceptions, on the one hand, and on the other, if we have a notion of a certain moment as belonging to the past. This enables us to relate, here and now, certain perceptions with certain thoughts (for instance the vision of a certain face with a certain name), and to compare this relationship with relationships established in other past circumstances (we gave that name to that person on several occasions in the past). In this sense, Luhmann describes memory as a process of consistency checking (Luhmann 1990a: 62). The set of forms likely to be used in memory operations is called *Wissen* (knowledge).

The mechanisms generating memory and knowledge allow us to construct, anytime we encounter situations in which we make perceptions similar to those made in other situations, an imaginary version of the world out there and, possibly, an anticipation of what will happen in that world. In other words, memory and knowledge give rise to expectations (*Erwartungen*; Luhmann 1990a: 58). Here Luhmann revisits a concept already discussed in several papers of the 1960s and 1970s, at that time within a conceptual framework more similar to the sociological tradition.[14] He is now in condition to offer a more detailed model, in which he tries to draw a distinction between the psychic and the social level. He emphasizes that the mental structures that constitute psychic expectations are by no means directly accessible to communication, and that there will always be a gap between them and the expectations thematized in communication.

(c) As we know, Luhmann clearly distinguishes in the realm of communication several different types of social systems with the typology of these systems—mainly: interactions, organizations, functional systems, world-society—being a central component of his theoretical work. In the realm of psychic systems, however, he seems to be reluctant to draw sharp distinctions. This is partly due, certainly, to his concern about developing a theory able to cope with the diversity of thousand of millions of psychic systems. Nevertheless, one piece of his theory of consciousness deserves to be related—however "loosely"—to the differentiation of the social systems: the recognition of the fact—which he actually does not emphasize—that the autopoiesis of consciousness may happen in different ways. We could speak here about "regimes" of consciousness.

In the first place, one can distinguish between consciousness with and without reflection. Using the above introduced terminology, the observation of the operations of consciousness can be more or less intense.[15] The perception of a certain object can be more or less intensively observed, and thereby more or less narrowly controlled (certain perception may be improved, or, on the contrary, suppressed). The same applies to thoughts triggered by certain perceptions, which can be more or less attentively reworked, in the sense of grasping more precisely these perceptions, or giving them a more accurate qualification. In a more general sense, Luhmann uses the wording "consciousness as a medium," suggesting that

---

14   See, in particular, Luhmann 1969/2008; Luhmann 1972/1985: ch. 2.

15   On the other hand, Luhmann refuses the notion of the unconscious, considering that everything that happens in the mind that is more or less controlled deserves to be included in the notion of consciousness (Luhmann 1995/2000: 15/6).

there may be moments of less strict coupling between events of consciousness, and moments when there is a more strict concatenation of events (Luhmann 1995a: 146).

Other distinctions used by Luhmann in the characterization of regimes of consciousness are not easy to order and could possibly overlap to some extent. Three of them deserve a special mention:

1. Thought can be verbal, using words, or not;
2. We can pay attention to what surrounds us, or to our own thoughts;
3. We can represent the world as we assume that it is actually in reality, or, on the contrary, we can evoke a fictitious reality, from which we know that it does not correspond to what happens out there.[16]

Relating to these two last distinctions, Luhmann reminds us of this strategy of consciousness, which consists in concentrating on our thoughts—on a fictional reality or (why not?) on theory—in order to evade perceptions of the world out there.

Arguably, the different regimes of consciousness characterized by these variables can be related—even if loosely—to the differentiation of social systems. Indeed, different types of social systems are more or less demanding in terms of verbal communication. They may ask for a more or less focused attention on the part of the participating psychic systems. They may favour the perception of reality as a fiction (as is the case in certain artistic communication). Or they may oblige us to focus on our own thought, as is the case for communication on theories in science.

(C) For the autopoiesis of consciousness to take place, certain material conditions have to be fulfilled, for it depends on the functioning of organisms and nervous systems. The participation of consciousness, in turn, is a necessary condition of communication. The reverse relationships are equally relevant. Living organisms are more likely to survive if they can take advantage of the perceptions and means of orientation supplied by a consciousness aware of the world that surrounds it. And the chances of survival will benefit from the possibility of joining the material forces of different organisms, which requires not only the perception of other organisms, but communication. Consciousness itself takes advantage from what is generated by communication, language first of all; but also, and perhaps in the very first place, the stimulus of being recognized as consciousness, a recognition that only communication can provide.

Thus the relationship between these systems of different types—nervous systems, consciousness, communication—is necessary to all of them. Since they are of different kinds, the relations between them cannot be direct, but have to be established by mechanisms of structural coupling. And since systems of these three

---

16 On fictional reality, see Luhmann 1995/2008.

types actually exist, we are allowed to presume that such mechanisms exist and are somehow efficient; otherwise, all these systems hardly would have survived.

Luhmann makes almost no mention of the mechanism of structural coupling between consciousness and nervous systems, and between nervous systems and the living organisms of human beings. He just alludes to the fact that our five senses act as filters, limiting the range of stimulus that actually reach our attention. This discussion of the relationship could be further elaborated by analysing how we got used to focusing our attention on what is perceived by our eyes, more than by any other means of perception. As far as the present author's knowledge of Luhmann's work goes, neither the neuronal processes that parallel the operations of consciousness are discussed, nor the way these processes could be related to these operations.[17] In abstract terms, in line with a reasoning applied elsewhere, one could admit that there is "repression" of the major part of the sensations processed by the nervous system, below a certain threshold corresponding to what is experienced as pain. Thereby, only a limited part of the flow of sensations likely to be experienced by a living human organism reaches consciousness, which makes it more probable to appreciate differences and similarities in the sensations. Here recent advances in neurophysiology and cognitive sciences certainly would help us to go beyond the point reached by Luhmann in the works here under scrutiny. And the concepts of autopoiesis and of structural coupling could help to develop interdisciplinary approaches that would avoid any kind of presumptions as regards a direct impact of the nervous system on consciousness.

On the other hand, Luhmann is very interested in the mechanisms of structural coupling favouring the relationship between psychic systems and social systems. However, the discussion of these mechanisms is spread over several papers. One prominent argument is the existence of a phenomenon located between consciousness and communication: meaning (*Sinn*), which can be qualified as a medium common to both types of systems (a). This medium, in turn, allows the differentiation of certain forms able to fulfill specific functions in the relationship between consciousness and communication (b).

(a) Luhmann characterizes meaning as the result of the coevolution of consciousness and communication.[18] This reasoning may be formulated in more concrete terms by referring to the differences between consciousness and communication pointed out by him on several occasions. Let us remember that consciousness and communication are conceived as the result of concrete operations, that is, concrete events. By definition, events have a limited duration. Communication events are said to last longer than consciousness events. The formulation of information and its display, in order for it to be adequately perceived

---

17   One possible reason for Luhmann's reluctance to discuss these questions could be his notion of the distribution of scientific roles to be maintained between him and his colleagues Humberto Maturana and Francisco Varela.

18   On meaning as emerging both in communication and in consciousness, as the generation of a common medium, see, notably, Luhmann 1990: 53ff.

as an expression ("here there is an intention to communicate!"), take time. And this is even more the case for the concatenation of successive communications. Indeed, it should be possible to interpret each of them as the comprehension of a previous communication, and this requires the time needed, successively, for the expression first of the previous communication and then of the communication reacting to it. Processes of consciousness, on the other hand, are said to be less time consuming. They even require a kind of contraction, or merging of operations, necessary to the narrow articulation between self- and hetero-reference. As mentioned above, Luhmann is very careful in his characterization of the psychic processes, but his analysis suggests the notion of a rapid oscillation between perception and qualification, and an almost simultaneous confrontation, in the representation, with perceptions and qualifications memorized. Thus, the difference between the pace of the operations of communication and the pace of the operations of the psychic systems might have favoured the emergence of meaning.

What "makes sense" is the fact that we are able to relate some meaning to a certain object, which implies that it is also possible to relate the same object to other meanings. Luhmann insists on this point; in order to produce sense, we have to be able to evoke virtually those meanings that do actually not apply at a given moment. The word "yes" makes sense because we can oppose it to "no." The difference in the pace of consciousness and of communication favours the production of meaning in the following way. On the one hand, while one of the terms is communicated, consciousness involved in the communication, taking advantage of its rapid pace of processing, evokes virtually at the same time the other possible alternative terms. And each consciousness involved may assume that the oscillatory evocation of alternative meanings takes place in the other psychic systems involved. On the other hand, the oscillation in the realm of consciousness could hardly have produced, as such, the clear differences required for the production of meaning. These differences are experienced in the communication, made obvious by the slow pace of alternation—required for their expression—between the terms, when referred to successively.[19]

This mechanism, however, only works if, on both levels, the level of consciousness and the level of communication, there is the same notion of a possible link between a certain sign and a certain meaning. The paradigm of this kind of link is supplied by language, which identifies a universe of things likely to be related to one word, and not to another. What makes possible the sharing of this notion could be the fact that both processes are constructed, as already mentioned, each with reference to the other. Communication requires the notion of a consciousness that has chosen a sign, for example a word (information), in order to display a certain message (expression). Consciousness is able to use signs as far as it has the memory of their successful use in communication, and the notion of a similar memory in other minds.

---

19   Close to this form of presentation of consciousness and communication; Luhmann 1990: 50.

(b) With the notion of meaning as a common medium for consciousness and communication as a starting point, Luhmann discusses different mechanisms of structural coupling between consciousness and communications. Let us remember at least some of them, and briefly describe how they actually work.

One is language, as already mentioned. Language may be used to communicate as well as to formulate thoughts. We should not forget, however, that both, consciousness as well as communication, are able to use other means. This explains the function of art, where means of expression other than verbal are used, and where artists seek to transmit messages unlikely to be transmitted by words. Art claims, more precisely, to re-inject into the communication nonverbal impressions triggered by nonverbal communication, sometimes using words, but trying to give them meanings that go beyond their ordinary meaning. In this sense, art is a mechanism of structural coupling between consciousness and communications complementary to language; in other words, art is a functional equivalent to language (Luhmann 1995/2000: 36/19, 39/22). Both in art as well as in verbal communication, what is at stake is to make probable the emergence of new meaning in communication as well as in consciousness.

Another mechanism is the notion of person (Luhmann 1995b: 153), which allows consciousness to become an issue of communication; and, conversely, to sharpen, in the consciousness of the people involved in a communication process, the attention to aspects of the world more directly relevant to this process, and thereby to the practical activity that it orients. One way of reinforcing and focusing the impact of personal experiences on communication is precisely the notion of subjective rights, which will be discussed in the next section.

Whatever the specific mechanism, we have to better analyse how structural coupling between consciousness and communication works. Here we have to make use of the concepts of form and medium, of how elements belonging to a universe where they loosely connect to other elements are likely to be strictly coupled with some of them. Meaning is likely to feed both thoughts and communication. Words, in particular, may be used in the communication—where they refer to what has been referred in former communication—as well as in consciousness—where they refer what is perceived or represented. A language shared by two psychic systems favours parallel processes of specification of the uses of words, as tools for thought as well as for communication. That is, parallel processes of establishment of strict couplings between elements, of creation of forms: of perception in one case, of communication in the other. In a more complex manner, the notion of person favours parallel construction processes of a certain type of subjectivity, and of certain communicative practices based on the assumption that they address or concern one person in particular. These parallel processes facilitate the coupling between these two realities, the person as perceiving him/herself as individuality, and the person as a role emerging in communication.[20]

Here it is worth coming back to the phenomenon of the differentiation between social systems. As stated above, some functional differentiations of social systems do contribute to the structural coupling between psychic and social systems: The educational system, with its vocation of forming persons; organizations, by giving a status to the people involved in a certain activity; art, by thematizing the perception of persons, and the possibility for this perception to lead to meanings different from those usually accepted. But beyond these specific functions, all social systems are likely, at any moment, to impact on consciousness, and this impact will vary according to the specific features of the different social systems. Every system corresponds to a certain type of communication, revealed by a certain language. Each one of these languages will induce the emergence, within psychic systems, of a different kind of specific reasoning. There will be no such clear mental differentiation processes as those that take place in the realm of social systems. But it may happen that the same person adopts alternatively quite different modes of reasoning, according to which system he/she currently participates in.

Towards a Systemic Concept of Rights

Luhmann tackles the issue of rights as early as his first sociological works and discusses it throughout his entire intellectual career. We shall recall (A) here how this line of thought evolves until the moment at which he starts to work on the theory of the relationship between psychic and social systems, outlined in the previous section. A mature version of this theory is available when he finalizes *Law as a Social System* (1993/2004) and underpins the reflections on subjective rights included in this book, and these reflections at the same time introduce several new theoretical elements, and put forward a more integrated systemic concept of rights (B).

(A) There is one motive of reflection constant throughout the whole period analysed here: the link between the concept of rights and functional differentiation. What changes is the attention paid to persons.

(a) The first book dedicated by Luhmann mainly to the law is *Grundrechte als Institution:Fundamental Rights as an Institution* (1965).[21] Let us recall the main argument of this book, still strongly influenced by the theory of functional differentiation developed by Talcott Parsons: The fundamental rights are worth being studied from the viewpoint of their societal function. This function,

---

20   There are here affinities between the possible development of systems theory and the work of Foucault. For a comparison between these two lines of theoretical work, see Guibentif 2010.

21   For an introduction to this book, see Verschraegen 2006: 102f.

indeed, is to assure functional differentiation. The main fundamental rights correspond to four differentiated social systems that remind us of the four subsystems of the action frame of reference: dignity and liberty would favor the differentiation of the system of personality; liberty of expression, the "civilization in the behavioural expectations" (a domain that could be compared to the subsystem of "community" in the work of Talcott Parsons); the protection of property and of professional activity, the differentiation of the economy; and the right of political participation, combined with the principle of equality, the differentiation of the political sphere.[22] In this discussion of the fundamental rights, the concept of subjective rights is discussed only in marginal terms. What is at stake is to attenuate the practical relevance of this legal concept. In the final discussion on how fundamental rights are to be enforced, Luhmann recalls that they are subjective rights, and that their enforcement depends on the action of courts, that is, in a first step, on the will of the citizens to have their rights enforced and to act in court in the pursuit of them. He argues that it is highly problematic for such a crucial device to depend exclusively on the initiative of ordinary people. Legislative measures should be taken in order to implement the fundamental rights, measures to be designed by the political decision-makers with a view to their societal function (Luhmann,1965: 209). Here we meet the optimistic attitude of Luhmann at the beginning of his career, in the early 1960s, concerning the contribution of sociology to government. What matters is society, and society itself has the cognitive means for its own enlightenment—sociology—and the organizational means to take the necessary measures—politics.[23] There is little room left for ordinary people and their subjective rights in such an intellectual framework.

(b) Over the next years, the concern of Luhmann is not so much anymore to explain how functional differentiation is maintained, since its effectiveness raises little doubt. What is at stake is to appreciate its consequences. Having observed that the distinction between *objektives Recht*—law—and *subjektive Rechte*—rights—is a typical feature of modern law, he tries, in his paper on "The function of subjective rights" (1970/1981/2009), to connect the emergence of the concept of subjective rights with the process of functional differentiation. As a starting point, he analyses the differences between the notion of rights and comparable older notions, such as, in particular, the Roman *ius*. These older notions have in common that they are always based on reciprocity: we can claim something from the part of somebody under the condition that this person received something from our part. What is new with rights is that they cease to require reciprocity. They are based only on the complementarity of expectations (Luhmann 1970/1981/2009: 362/§5 s.): *ego* expects *alter* to do something, and *alter* expects *ego* to have

---

22 This thesis structures Luhmann 1965, where each system is treated by a separate chapter. For a compact formulation of it, see, for instance, p. 200.
23 This interpretation of Luhmann's evolution is presented in some detail in Guibentif 2010.

precisely this expectation. Here Luhmann makes use of a terminology where the concept of expectation plays a central role, a terminology recently developed in his paper "Norms in sociological perspective."[24]

The success of such a notion of subjective rights is due to the fact that functional differentiation brings about complex networks of interpersonal relations—the wording used in the article here analysed is "encounter of partners" (Luhmann 1970/1981/2009: 367/§13)—too complex to allow, in a given relationship, to find obligations that would correspond to rights in a way assuring reciprocity. On the one hand, who enters into a relationship does it in relation to a specific role, among other roles that he/she has to play at the same time in other contexts, and he/she knows that the same applies to his/her partners. Under these circumstances it is almost impossible to evaluate the burdens related to the commitments of our partners outside the relationship in which we meet them, and, therefore, impossible to appreciate the real efforts required for them to fulfill their obligations within this relationship. So the evaluation of reciprocity is almost impossible. On the other hand, complex organizational arrangements are more frequent, where we find what could be named chains of commitments. A simple example is a product offered in a shop or a meal served in a restaurant. In most cases, the client pays the service to the owner, and expects the employee to serve him/her correctly, while the employee is paid by the owner. An additional argument of Luhmann is that arrangements based on reciprocity need time to stabilize and to convince the people involved of the effectiveness of reciprocity. To change them requires time, which is not compatible with the demands of a functionally differentiated society—demands due to the fact that each differentiated system works and evolves according to its own logic, ignoring the others, which makes it probable for all systems to suffer interferences from the part of other systems, requiring rapid adaptive answers.

In the same article of 1970, Luhmann also mentions briefly an argument that anticipates the works published after 1980 under the title *Gesellschaftsstruktur und Semantik*. The success of the notion of subjective rights would have to do with the prominence given, for reasons not directly connected to the evolution of law, to the notion of subject in domains like arts and politics.

(c) Another article is specifically devoted to the issue of subjective rights, published ten years later: "Subjective rights: on the reconfiguration of legal consciousness in modern society" (Luhmann 1981b). This article takes up and develops further the reasoning of 1970, on the basis of a broader range of references. There is, however, a new motive: The concept of subjective rights would strengthen the position of human beings in their relation to the legal system. Such strengthening is in need at a time when the process of functional differentiation tends to deprive persons from their concrete places, making them run the risk of losing their means of orientation, and their chances of

---

24   Luhmann 1969/2008. The main arguments of this paper are also to be found in Chapter II.2 of Luhmann's *Rechtssoziologie*, published a few years later (1972/1985).

obtaining recognition.[25] Indeed, in other types of human societies, segmented in subunits defined by the people who belong to them—for example the Indian castes or the social orders in the Middle Ages — social differentiation as such provided persons with a clear notion of their place in the social universe. In a society structured by functional differentiation, functional systems no longer define places for persons. Strictly speaking, functional systems tend to dispense with human beings. The notion of subjective rights would express a kind of commitment of the social systems to re-establish places for human beings (Luhmann 1981b: 84).

Significantly, subjective rights assume in this last argumentation a specific function in the relationship between society and its human environment, and not only the function of facilitating the operations of other social systems. Law, including the notion of subjective rights, is no longer considered only as a structure of other social systems; it is now recognized as one more differentiated functional social system among others, with its own functions in the management of the relationship between the whole set of social systems, on the one hand, and the world of psychic systems, on the other.

(d) Over the 1980s, one theoretical motive acquires increasing weight in Luhmann's work: paradoxes.[26] Several texts published at that time seek to take advantage of this motive in the discussion of law. Among those articles, a first one addresses specifically the notion of rights: "The theory of order and the subjective rights" (Luhmann 1984/2009). The starting point of this article is the paradox that we meet when it comes to defining law. On the one hand, when law shows its validity in the most obvious way, that is, when it is enforced, what is applied is violence—the exact contrary of law. On the other hand, semantically, the word "law" makes no sense unless we evoke, at least virtually, its contrary, *Unrecht* in the original German texts of Luhmann. One could say that, in both cases, it is just a matter of recognizing the difference between the two terms. But by recognizing the difference, we lose sight of what constitutes the difference—what relates both terms and makes the link between them necessary; that is, in the words of Luhmann, the unity of the difference. If we try to grasp the law in rigorous terms—a task for a theorist of the law, or for a sociologist, or else for an artist (Luhmann, at that point

---

25 Not all sociologists would follow Luhmann without hesitation on this track. Bourdieu (1994/1997; in particular pp. 53f.: "Espace social et champ du pouvoir" [Social space and field of power]), for instance, insists on the importance of the notion of social space, considering that we all occupy places rather precisely defined in their relation to the places occupied by other people. One has to recognize, however, that the representations of the social space vary significantly from individual to individual, and that there are no mechanisms clearly specialized in warranting the congruence between these different representation of the social space (for a comparison between these two authors, see Guibentif 2010).

26 On the paradoxes in the thought of Luhmann, see Clam 2000 and 2001, as well as Menke 2008. For an article published originally in English, where Luhmann applies the notion of paradox to law, see Luhmann 1988.

of his exposition, likes to quote José Luís Borges)—we unavoidably face such paradoxical circles. Despite these paradoxes, however, the notion of law plays an important role in social life. This means that we have succeeded in making invisible, in forgetting, the paradox. Therefore the question for the sociologist has to be: How did we succeed in making the paradox invisible? On this ground, the functionalist reasoning of Luhmann becomes the following: If a social structure survives, it is because it fulfills successfully some relevant functions, and, among other possible functions, that of making paradoxes invisible. This is the reasoning applied at that time by Luhmann when tackling the issue of subjective rights.

In the paper of 1984, several potentialities of the notion of rights are surveyed, from the point of view of the need to make law's original paradox invisible. In a first stage of the evolution of mankind, this notion would have allowed the construction of narratives eschewing the opposition *Recht/Unrecht* by starting with the notion of "appetites" (Luhmann 1984 /2009: 135/§4). Since we accept these appetites, we recognize the notion of subjective rights, necessary for the concept of "natural rights".[27] This narrative, however, has to be further elaborated, because the natural rights of some persons will collide, naturally, with those of others. There the notion of order comes in, in the form of the concept of—objective—law, which has precedence over the subjective rights.[28] This notion of objective order is most clearly formulated, says Luhmann, at a historical time when it also corresponds to a concrete experience: the eighteenth century, when absolutist monarchs were able to impose an effective order in the territories under their jurisdiction (ibid.: 44/§20). Furthermore, the opposition and link between—subjective—rights and—objective—law makes it possible to shape the sense of the opposition between rights and obligations. This creates conditions for another mechanism that contributes to hide the paradox of law. The notion of right, as opposed to the one of obligation, establishes a distinction that doubles the distinction *Recht/Unrecht*, distracting our attention from the foundational paradox of law (ibid: §13).

At the very beginning of this paper, Luhmann briefly mentions an idea that anticipates his last works:

> From a practical point of view [the fact that subjective rights were embodied in constitutions in terms of fundamental rights] has essentially the following meaning: to provide the constitutions with specific sensors, able to notice social change. To put it boldly: if historical conditions change, do not forget the human beings! (Luhmann 1984/2009: 133/§1)

---

27 One could base on this hypothetical original reasoning the etymology of the Basque word *eskubidea*, which means "subjective right," and literally the "way of the hand." By a gesture of my hand, I show what I am willing to catch something, thus affirming the right to take it.

28 A comparable reasoning is presented in the article "Am Anfang war kein Unrecht" (Luhmann,1989).

The author does not come back to this idea in the following text. A similar thought appears, however, at its very end:

> A society that authorizes subjective rights and even admits them to be defined by contracts will be confronted with the consequences of that imbalance [between different claims arising without reciprocity being required]. And if the natural law of God or His "*invisible hand*" are not enough, claims will have to be addressed to the political system. (ibid.: 149/§28; English in the German original)

(e) Rights are given a more developed treatment in a paper published in 1989: "Individuum, Individuality, Individualism."[29] This paper, probably written after *Social Systems*, makes use of an advanced version of the autopoietic systems model, structured around the notion of paradox. Here we find precisely the analysis of psychic systems as autopoietic systems, elaborated, as we saw, approximately since the mid-1980s (see the first section of the present chapter). Subjective rights are discussed in direct relation, not to the topic of functional differentiation, but to the phenomenon of the differentiation of individual consciousness, a process linked to functional differentiation, but worth considering for its own characteristics. Modern individuals, with the features that functional differentiation favored, are supposed, each of them, to identify themselves with a unique personality, an identity that cannot be backed by anything but itself. The challenge here is comparable to the one faced by the law, mentioned in point (d) above. How can the individual deal with this paradox? Luhmann's hypothesis on this point is the following. The autologic nature of subjectivity confronts the individuals with what distinguishes them from the rest of world. To escape this paradoxical confrontation, individuals need another distinction, likely to double—that is, possibly to make invisible—this foundational distinction. This other distinction is the one between, on the one hand, the individual as he/she is, here and now, and, on the other hand, the individual as he/she ought to be; the distinction between the real and the ideal individual. Subjective rights are part of the set of devices—among which morality plays an important role[30]—that provide us with an image of what we ought to be, ideally (Luhmann 1989: 242).

(B) We shall analyze here only two chapters of *Law as a Social System* (1993/2004) where the issue of rights is tackled: the discussion of the mechanisms of structural coupling between law and the other social systems (a); and the discussion of law as a functional system of the world society (b).

---

29   Luhmann 1989: 149–258; on the same issue, see also, in English, Luhmann 1986; for a later development of this line of work: Luhmann 1997c. On individualism and rights in Luhmann, see Verschraegen 2006: 113f.

30   On this point, see the collection of articles of Luhmann on morality, recently published in German (Luhmann 2008); on morality and inviduality in Luhmann, see Pires 2005.

(a) Rights are a prominent issue in Chapter 10 of *Law as a Social System*, about the mechanisms of structural coupling. The main theoretical innovation in the discussion of the phenomenon of rights, compared with the above summarized papers, is the use of the concept of structural coupling. This concept emerges in Luhmann's work at the end of the 1980s,[31] the probable first mention being found in a paper of 1989 on the relationships between economy and law (Luhmann 1990b). This concept allows a more precise formulation of—and a better constructed link between—two motives until that moment discussed separately: the relationship between rights and the phenomenon of functional differentiation, and the role of rights in the coupling between social and psychic systems. This relationship is at stake in the following quotation:

> In the form in which subjective rights are provided, namely as objective rights, the legal system alerts itself to the problematic nature of the inclusion of individual human beings in the legal system. This problem results from the very fact that the fusion of psychological operations and social operations in one system [*durch Systembildungen*] is impossible.
>
> If this applies, it can explain—independently of the historical terminologies which were used to engineer the change—that the yet to be developed forms of coupling which connect the separate functional systems also [are] coordinated with the legal institution of individual rights. The constitution, apart from its function as an "*instrument of government*", was introduced explicitly in order to implement a "*Bill of Rights*". It has also been widely observed that property law was reconstructed individualistically in the eighteenth century. [...] Accordingly, the legal system functions largely, or at least initially, to cushion [*fungiert als Auffangssystem*] the consequences that the restructuring of society towards functional differentiation has on the individual.[32]

The thesis according to which rights would be a device adequate for a functionally differentiated society—in particular because they do not require reciprocity—was first formulated in 1960–70. Now, the concept of structural coupling allows Luhmann to complement this formulation by supplying a detailed model of what happens at the borderline between the law and other functional systems. The issue of the relationships between psychic and social systems is already referred to in 1981. Now the role of law in this relationship can be analyzed in more precise

---

31   For additional references on the concept of structural coupling in the writings of Luhmann, see Guibentif 2010. For a critique of the role played by this concept in Luhmann's theory, see Ladeur 2008: 113.

32   Luhmann 1993/2004: 487/416f. (English in the German original). One change proposed to the published translation, considering the sense of the German phrase : "*[...] dass [...] die neuen Kopplungsformen [...] mit dem Rechtsinstitut der individuelle Rechte abgestimmt sind.*" (our emphasis).

terms. Moreover, the two motives can now be linked: Rights fulfill under better conditions their function of structural coupling between consciousness and communication if they serve, at the same time, for the structural coupling between law and other social systems. This makes it possible for them to couple psychic systems, beyond law, with society in general.

In the first section of this chapter, we saw that, exactly during the period when Luhmann was finalizing *Law as a Social System*, he also was devoting a considerable effort to the development of concepts apt for grasping the autopoiesis of consciousness, and its coupling with social systems. The discussion of rights as a mechanism of structural coupling here summarized is a direct result of this effort. However, what we find in *Law as a Social System* is just a short and sketchy indication of how this conceptualization could be embodied in the systems theory of the law. In particular, it would be worth better taking into account Luhmann's last reflections on structures and expectations in the reconstruction, on the one hand, of psychic processes, and, on the other hand, of communication concerning legal issues. Such conceptual advancements could enable us to construct more detailed models of the emergence and of the performances of mechanisms of structural coupling based on the notion of rights.

Luhmann wanted to give priority to another line of his theoretical work: the appreciation of the probability of these mechanisms to perform effectively. It seems that, having outlined the perspectives of the necessary theoretical work, he felt the need to emphasize the aims of such work. In the discussion of the effective performances of these mechanisms, Luhmann picks up an argument already formulated in *Grundrechte als Institution* (1965): The problems arising from the fact that the enforcement of subjective rights depend on steps taken by the holders of these rights. Many of them will not have an easy access to justice, or will not consider the judicial way as preferable for the defense of their rights. What changes is the attitude of Luhmann towards this fact. He abandons the optimistic solution of the 1960s, consisting in handing this problem over to the government, which would be better in condition to appreciate the needs of a functionally differentiated society. On the contrary, the coexistence of, on the one hand, individual reactions and, on the other, political efforts of regulatory intervention appears now to be one more problem that modern society has to deal with (Luhmann 1993/2004: 490/418).

Another phenomenon—perhaps related to the above evoked problematic coexistence—is the trend towards political responses that avoid measures requiring the recognition of subjective rights. Luhmann refers here to the environmental domain as an example. The notion of risk cannot easily be combined with the one of rights, and leads preferably to the notion of responsibility. If this trend persists, it could have consequences on the structural coupling between psychic and social systems:

> The delicate balance [between the subjective rights of protected people and the freedom of those who are legally entitled to oppose these rights] could

be dislodged under the massive pressure of ecological threats. It is more probable that it will be diminished in its importance and replaced with, or at least complemented by, increased regulatory activity on the part of the states to which the constitution increasingly yields by way of amendments or supplements. However, the consequence of this would be that law would lose its importance for the structural coupling of individual consciousness and social communication. And then law would lose the certainty of being able to mobilize consciousness for legal purposes when it needed to, for instance if there were a political need. Then the legal system would require scandals, which attract high levels of publicity or huge "Amnesty International"-type reports, in order to maintain its rule of law [*den Rechtsstaat*], in which individually nobody any longer has an interest. (Luhmann 1993/2004: 488f./418)

(b) In the last pages of *Law as a Social System*, Luhmann comes back to the issue of human rights as a semantic that compensates the fact that the process of functional differentiation did challenge the place of persons in the social universe. As we saw, this topic appears in Luhmann's work in 1981. It is now revisited under the perspective of the notion of paradox.[33] The original paradox is the one that characterizes, as a consequence of functional differentiation, the relationship between society and communication, on the one hand, and human beings and consciousness on the other. Functional differentiation radicalizes a notion of communication that only communicates with itself, but, at the same time, it cannot dispense consciousness that permits the distinction, in communication, between information and expression. Here we meet, as inherent to the operations of communication, the paradox of the unity of the difference between society and human beings. If society and human beings can be thought of as distinct realities, it is because we have the notion of something these two realities have in common. Perhaps something that could be named "humanity." But, as we try to grasp this common reality, we are led back to our point of departure, the difference between society and human beings.[34] In a first step, this paradox is made invisible by deviating attention towards another difference, that between—subjective—rights and—objective—law. But thereby we are confronted with another paradox: How can we speak about rights, about subjective claims—of human beings—without using the notion of an objective order that would give foundations to the validity of these claims? And how can we construct the notion of a valid order, without

---

33 *Law as a Social System* (1993/2004), pp. 574/482f. This part of the book should be read in conjunction with the following two papers: "Das Paradox der Menschenrechte und drei Formen seiner Entfaltung" (1993/1995) and "Braucht unsere Gesellschaft noch unverzichtbare Normen?" (1993/2008), where the same reasoning is presented, with emphasis on different aspects of the problematic. Specifically on this topic, see Verschraegen 2006: 122f.

34 For a discussion of this paradox inspired by Derrida's deconstruction, see Menke (2008: 104), who locates at this point the "force" that generates persons and society.

using the notion of a claim—made by many human beings—for the validity of this order?

Luhmann seeks to reconstruct how this paradox has been dealt with in recent times. During some periods, it has been through the positivization of human rights, notably by the means of official declarations and constitutions. Today, this management of the paradox is no longer satisfactory, since it is experienced on a planetary scale. Now that systems as economy and science function worldwide, the issue of people coexisting with these systems has to be tackled at that planetary scale. So we may observe two kinds of paradox management. On the one hand, efforts toward a positivization of human rights at a global level, by means of international treaties, and international agencies in charge of their implementation; and, on the other hand, the focusing of public attention, facilitated by the media, on cases where fundamental human rights are severely violated.

This second mechanism could favor legal communication, but on the condition that the distinctions applied in the perception and communication of actual events are adequate and precise enough. Just to be horrified by an event does not per se generate an experience of law. What is required is what Luhmann calls "exemplary experience of the negation of social injustice."[35] Even if the concept of structural coupling is not used in this context, one could argue that what is at stake here is the coupling between the consciousness of addressees of the media, and a legal communication that would, to a significant extent, be processed by the media.

Perspectives for Empirical Research

The work of Niklas Luhmann on subjective rights invites developments of the most advanced versions of systems theory. Such developments, however, are only tentatively outlined by him, and he had no time to fully take advantage of the potentialities of the reasoning initiated. A perceptive reader will hardly escape the feeling that it is now urgent to take over and to continue this line of work. This task would take the form of both developments of the theoretical proposals and gathering empirical data. The increasing relevance of empirical research for the future development of systems theory corresponds to an evolution in the work of Luhmann himself (A). With a view to future works in specific domains of rights, I shall try to show here how the above-introduced theoretical proposals could inspire the construction of tools for collecting and interpreting empirical data (B).

(A) Luhmann himself admits that the development of systems theory is to an important extent a matter of empirical research. Let us remember that the series

---

35 Luhmann 1993/2004: 578/485; Luhmann 1993/2008: 250; on this point, Luhmann quotes Bielefeldt 1988 and Brugger 1989. With the English translation, much of the suggestive potential of the German original expression had to be abandoned: "exemplarische Unrechtserfahrung" connects directly to the *Recht/Unrecht* distinction identifying the legal system.

of books most directly addressing the relationships between consciousness and communication—*Gesellschaftsstruktur und Semantik*—is presented as a set of studies on empirical material (Luhmann 1989: 9). Two characteristic evolutions of Luhmann's theory justify the argument that his work evolves in the sense of a reinforcement of its empirical component. One is the increasing sophistication—one could say "fine-tuning"—of his concepts, which favours their use as tool for empirical research. The most obvious illustration of this evolution is the fact that the concept of operation—a concept comparatively easy to be mobilized in empirical research—becomes central in the architecture of systems theory. The other is the trend towards more attention paid to consciousness and to the processes of perception. The more the evolution of his theory convinces Luhmann of the relevance of psychic perception for communication, the more he recognizes the relevance of empirical research in science. The need to take more data into account to feed and to back his theory might also be due to his perceptions of world society in his last years of life. These perceptions made it urgent for him to evaluate more precisely—that is, with more empirical data—the nature and orientation of the processes observed. Let us remember that many of the explanations on subjective rights included in *Law as a Social System* (1993/2004) end up in ambivalent statements. This invites the reader to collect data on the basis of which different hypothetically opposed trends could be measured and compared.

(B) It is possible to derive from the above outlined theory of rights a fairly detailed model of the processes of mobilization of these rights (a).[36] Systems theory may also contribute to the methodological discussion concerning the collection of data (b). Finally, Luhmann formulates several hypotheses on societal evolution that could be objects of empirical research; and these hypotheses could today be further elaborated, in view of trends that we have witnessed in recent years (c).

(a) The starting point of the construction of a model concerning the mobilization of rights is the assumption that rights are part of a set of mechanisms ensuring the structural coupling between individual consciousness and communication, mechanisms that proved, over the evolution, to be apt to facilitate the maintenance—the autopoiesis—of both consciousness and communication, and the reciprocal stimulation of these two processes.

In the realm of consciousness we may, in abstract terms, distinguish two phenomena. On the one hand, we have to consider situations of reading.[37] There are discourses on rights—in the media, in legal texts and in other official documents. These discourses are part of a communication that creates a fictitious reality, addressing individual readers—the audience of the media and of official publications—that suggests elements of a representation of the individual as an

---

36   This brings us back to a concept defended some time ago by Blankenburg 1995.

37   The precise characterization of the reading process, which combines communication and perception, must still be worked out. In Luhmann's papers on art (see, in particular, Luhmann 1995/2008) the topic is discussed, but only briefly and in passing.

entity entitled to have certain expectations, or that should expect, on the part of others, certain expectations. This representation makes us as individuals aware of the fact that we may—or must—assume a certain identity, an identity that is constructed in the ongoing confrontation between what we expect to happen and what actually happens (see the above point (e) in the second section above).

On the other hand, we have to consider situations in which we experience disappointments of our expectations. Certain events may be perceived as significantly departing from what we expected, triggering a more specific succession of thoughts. Some unpleasant perception—a disturbing noise caused by a neighbour; defaults in a product we recently acquired, etc.—calls for the representation of the deception of the expectation, an effort to qualify the expectation challenged: "Should it be maintained? Or should I learn to abandon it?" And, in the case of the normative option—"Expectation maintained!"—the anticipation of certain steps likely to be taken in order to re-establish the world as it was expected to be before the disappointing event—to stop the noise; to obtain a product without default, etc.

The relationships between these two types of processes must be discussed cautiously. They are likely to cross over—"What happens to me right now is exactly what never should have happened to me, according to what I recently had the occasion to read"; or else, the other way round: "If such a thing happens to me, which contradicts my expectations, and if my reactions have no success, I had better forget that official document whose reading generated that expectation." But these two kinds of mental processes—reading and disappointment—have different temporalities. Events that contradict my expectations are brief events in the course of daily life. On the other hand, the formation of that imaginary personality that I ought to/have the right to be is a long-lasting process that may parallel the whole life of a person, structured notably by experiences of involvement in the education system or in specific organizations, or of being informed by the media.

One may argue, however, that specific situations—in particular situations defined by the functioning of certain organizations—may favor the forming of links between different psychic processes. When starting a formal procedure, a lawsuit, or an arbitration procedure, participant individuals will have several opportunities to formulate in an articulate way his/her identity—of plaintiff, of citizen applying for intervention from the part of a public agency—and the way he/she analyzes recent events.

Favored or not by specific organizational processes, such links are likely to strengthen structures of consciousness—that is, strict links between certain perceptions and certain thoughts. These structures are strengthened in particular by the following mechanisms: the representation of these links (self-observation of consciousness, according to Luhmann 1985/1995: I am aware of a certain perception, and of the fact that it elicits a certain reaction from me); and the link between this specific representation and a more general representation of myself, in a process that may be called identification.[38] These structures form what Luhmann calls "expectations," in the sense this term receives within the framework of the theory of psychic systems.

The processes that have now been reconstructed hypothetically will obviously happen, at the same time, in the minds of all the people involved in a given situation (the neighbor who wanted to carry out a noisy repair; the shopkeeper who acquired certain products from suppliers whom he considers liable for the faults in these products, etc.).

In parallel to these processes of consciousness, at a certain moment elicited by the above hypothetically described perceptions and anticipations, communication processes are going on. A possible sequence is the following. *Ego* addresses *alter*, opening an interaction, and communicating that his expectations were disappointed by a fact presumably caused by *alter*, and asking for action in the sense of recreating a world that would correspond to his expectations (the noise has to cease; the product has to be replaced, etc.). There are at least three mechanisms of structural coupling between this interaction and the psychic processes of the participants, according to the hypotheses supplied by Luhmann. In the first place—language. Perhaps the dialogue that later took place between *ego* and *alter* had been anticipated in the mind of *ego*, an anticipation in which certain wordings were mentally tested as corresponding more or less accurately to the event experienced, or to the anticipated interaction ("I have to complain; I have to tell him/her that is awful; I have the right to tranquillity, to the quality of the products I buy! etc."—wordings that later on will be understood more or less precisely in the communication. A second mechanism is the notion of person, which will facilitate the interpretation of the initial contact, and the interpretation of the signs used in the later communication, as expression of a message giving information about something experienced by somebody. And a third mechanism is the notion of subjective rights, which correspond both to the expectation perceived by *ego*, and to the expectation communicated in the interaction.

Let us admit that, in a concrete case, this interaction does not lead to results corresponding to the expectations of *ego* (the interaction is terminated by the refusal of *alter* to communicate with *ego*; or the interaction is continued by a reply of *alter* refusing to do what is claimed by *ego*). In this case, *ego* may consider the prospect of demanding an intervention from the authorities. He/she may have anticipated mentally such steps too, possibly inspired by past experiences and by his/her knowledge of the available relevant procedures.[39] Now *ego* may

---

38 See, in particular, the essay "Individuum, Individualität, Individualismus," in Luhmann 1989: 149ff.

39 I must admit some Eurocentrism in the situation here reconstructed. The model proposed, however, allows the discussion of very different situations, too—where it could lead to identify the mere absence of legal autopoiesis, or else, possibly, provide some hints for the appreciation of what hinders this autopoiesis. An extreme example in this sense is the one evoked by Schwartz (in Rocha et al. 2009: 113) in describing the brutal death of

initiate contacts with organizations supplying legal information (there might also be a moment of autonomous surveying of the available legal information). The next step, which admittedly will take place in only a small proportion of cases (Santos et al. 1996: 44f.), is to take the case to court. Such a judicial procedure will intertwine communications belonging to interactions and to organizations, as well as communications belonging to the legal system. All these communications will be structurally coupled with psychic systems, by the mechanisms of the language, the notion of person, and the rights, just as discussed in the case of the above reconstructed interaction. More specifically, one may argue that in these communications, taking place in more or less central, or more or less peripheral parts of the legal system,[40] the notion of subjective rights will facilitate the structural coupling between, on the one hand, the consciousness of people not specialized in law—having acquired some knowledge in the interaction between non-specialists, or in training programs including modules on legislation for non-jurists, etc.—and legal communications involving legal professionals. This coupling will be facilitated, at least to some extent, by the fact that important words in the legal vocabulary have an obvious sense in common language. This point would deserve a careful comparison between languages. In Latin languages, for instance, the word *droit/diritto/derecho/direito/drept* and so on is used in the legal language to formulate the notions of both law and rights, and is used in many popular expressions. Therefore it is apt to play a crucial role in the linguistic coupling between discourses. Similar linguistic structures in English should be appreciated and commented on by native English-speaking researchers.

Judicial procedures that would take place, especially if there were many similar cases, or if they involved people known to the public, or if they related to situations of a very peculiar kind, would likely be considered "informative" by the media (and this informative value will increase if the rights at stake may be considered by the addressees of the media as being one of their rights, too). With or without such moments of media coverage, judicial procedures, more than the mere multiplication of informal interactions on the same issues, are likely to "irritate" in particular political, and possibly economic, communication. The structural coupling between the legal system and these systems will take advantage, again, of the notion of subjective rights. The expectations of tranquillity, or of quality of products available on the market, beyond the experiences of certain persons in particular, may correspond to expectations of the citizenry, and may thus be translated in the political arena in terms of quality of life, or of consumer protection, notions that are likely to orient public policies or to structure debates between

---

João Hélio, as a result of an act that included—by no means its most shocking aspect—a total refusal of communication ("Other drivers tried to alert them [...]").

40   For a critique of the qualification by Luhmann of parts of the legal system as central or peripheral, see Ladeur 2008: 113. Against this critique one could argue, however, that "peripheral" does not necessarily mean "less relevant".

government and opposition.[41] As far as the structural coupling with economy is concerned, one could evoke the loss of prestige of a brand, as a consequence of clients' disappointed expectations, which will have an impact on the market, triggering reactions in form of new marketing strategies.

(b) The model here outlined should not lead to research that would attempt to take into account all contemporary communication on rights. On the contrary, it shows the need to research very different contexts of communication and their relationship with very different individual experiences. It teaches that in any case research has to focus on well-delimited domains. On the other hand, it also offers a frame of reference that may help to justify the identification of possible fields of research to locate the possible contributions of certain specific researches to a broader knowledge, beyond the field studied, and to develop strategies of connecting the results obtained in those different sectorial researches.

The theory of the relationships between psychic and social systems might also help to deal with an important obstacle to the execution of this kind of research. Indeed, empirical work has to approach two types of reality. Communications are easy to observe, apart from obvious difficulties of access to certain situations, and from the appropriate consideration of the diversity of the different communication spheres observed—social systems—and also apart from the relationship between scientific communication and the systems observed. Perceptions of the people involved, on the other hand, cannot be accessed directly. To solve this problem, one could take advantage of the lessons of evolution and create, in the scientific communication, differentiated spheres where individual perceptions are thematized. This is what social sciences already do in the format, for instance of open-ended interviews. The problems here identified by systems theory, by the means of its own terminology, have already given rise to methodological debates, not only in abstract terms, but with reference to concrete tools of observation. Actually, this also applies to the observation of communications (direct observation, participant observation, discourse analysis, etc.). The methodological discussion of these techniques cannot be ignored, but it can possibly benefit from a systemist contribution. This contribution could consist of the application of the model outlined in point (a) before a specific type of interaction such as that between researchers and people experiencing certain situations. This could allow us to refine our notion of the communication that actually produces this interaction, particularly in light of the notion of structural coupling between consciousness and communication. This could also help us take into account, in this reflection, the relationship between this interaction and on the one hand, the scientific

---

41 In this sense, it is worth considering the link between rights constitutionally recognized and rights recognized by other legal texts, as well as the consequences of these links on the citizens' experience of frustration of their normative expectations. Another question is why there is, among jurists, a debate about the distinction between fundamental and other rights. For a discussion of this second issue, which requires a definition of what are fundamental rights, see Schwartz 2007 and in particular p. 50.

organizations like research centers and projects and, beyond these organizations, its relationship to scientific communication in the more precise sense of that expression, and on the other hand, the social contexts where study is at stake.

(c) Systems theory, in its version worked out by Luhmann, whatever the criticism it may deserve, allows the construction of a tool of empirical observation of a phenomenon that Luhmann, as well as many authors who seek to go beyond his proposals, would like to grasp more firmly: an emergence of a "new legal culture" (Rocha in Rocha et al., 2009: 40). We are definitely not ready at the end of the present chapter to formulate substantive conclusions on this point. But two general hypotheses may be submitted to the debate.

The first is that empirical research on legal consciousness inspired by the systemic approach here summarized will lead us back to a phenomenon that Luhmann, fascinated by functional differentiation, did not want to study further: The fact that certain cognitive structures, certain expectations, are more probably to be found in the answers of persons belonging to certain social categories. The most radical contribution on this point comes from Marcelo Neves, who wants systems theory to take into account the opposition between those who are in a condition to use legal notions when reflecting their life experiences and orienting their acts, and those excluded form the spheres where legal communication is being processed, who have neither material means or nor perceptual frames needed to access the law.[42]

The second hypothesis regards specifically the notion of rights. As we saw, Luhmann himself suggests that in the future this notion might lose the relevance it has today. Indeed, there are organizations that set up strategies aiming at reducing the probability of people experiencing the situations in which they are involved in light of normative expectations corresponding to rights. That is: rights on the grounds of which they could take action against other persons, in the sense of the fulfillment of their expectations. Among various types of strategies, let us remember two very different examples. One is the promotion of mediation for the resolution of conflicts. What is at stake here is not to discuss the potentialities of mediation in general terms; it is to draw attention to a possible side effect of such procedures—to reduce the perception of situations in terms of rights. This may be beneficial from the point of view of the restoration of a peaceful social fabric; benefits from the viewpoint of the development of citizenry are less obvious. Another example is the strategy adopted by companies that subcontract the management of their staff to another company, while that other company is under their direct control. Generally speaking, such arrangements make it difficult to apply labor law. But they also have in particular the effect of dissolving a clear perception on the part of the workers of an entity to which to address the claims

---

42   See, in particular, Neves 2003: 266. For a hypothetical reconstruction of less extreme inequalities, nevertheless likely to have a significant impact on legal communication in European societies, see Guibentif 2004.

arising from their workers' rights. The absence of a clear reference as regards the addressee of the claims is likely to erode the notion of rights itself.[43]

The systemist model of the autopoiesis of psychic and social systems leads to the hypothesis of links between the evolution of the mechanisms of structural coupling—here, rights—and the evolution of the systems concerned by these mechanisms—here, psychic and social systems. According to this assumption, if the notion of rights loses part of its relevance, it might have, in the long run, an impact on the autopoiesis of the psychic and social systems involved: on individualities, and, on the side of the social systems, in the first place the legal system. We shall have to pay attention in the empirical work to be carried out on the basis methodology sketched above to processes of the kind to which Luhmann alludes in the last lines of *Law as a Social System*: the loss of centrality of law as a functionally differentiated social system; but also, on the other side of the structural coupling, transformations of our experiences of individualities. These transformations deserve special attention, taking into consideration the trend, as pointed out by Catherine Colliot-Thélène (2009), as a result of which persons as legal subjects would become the most important players in the politics of world society. If such a trend exists, we also observe trends in the sense of the dilution of precisely that individual political instance.[44] Such trends should urgently be surveyed and, as far as possible, precisely measured. This research work should also be underpinned by an effort to better connect two hypotheses separately formulated by Luhmann: the loss of significance of subjective rights on the one hand, and the role of media coverage of gross violations of human rights on the other. Evoking the concept of "exemplary experience of the negation of social injustice"/"exemplarische Unrechtserfahrung," Luhmann suggests—and this idea is worth further development—that scandals reported by the media may contribute to the autopoiesis of law, providing there is some link between the appreciation of the extreme cases, and the appreciation everyone is in a position to make of his/her own situation. The theory of the unity of the human rights as rights of the human beings (Menke 2009: §30) could find here an unexpected supporter: systems theory. It would be a disenchanted and distanced supporter, however, which limited itself to remembering that rights are a necessary feature of the humanity formed by the distinction of subjectivity and society, a kind of humanity that may be maintained, or not.

---

43 Recent trends in our notions of rights could also be related to transformations in the debates on the legitimacy of states' activities, and to the loss of relevance of the very notion of legitimacy itself. See Ashenden and Thornhill 2010 and Guibentif 2010b.

44 Trends to which corresponds the notion of "liquid society" put forward by Bauman 2000. See Guibentif 2007.

References

Bauman, Z., *Liquid Modernity* (Oxford: Polity Press, 2000).
Bielefeldt, H., "Die Menschenrechte als Chance in der pluralistischen Weltgesellschaft," *Zeitschrift für Rechtspolitik* 21 (1988), 423–32.
Blankenburg, E., *Mobilisierung des Rechts: Eine Einführung in die Rechtssoziologie* (Berlin etc.: Springer, 1995).
Bourdieu, P., *Raisons pratiques* (Paris: Seuil, 1994).
Brugger, W., "Stufen der Begründung von Menschenrechten," *Der Staat* 31 (1992), 19–38.
Clam, J., "Die Grundparadoxie des Rechts und ihre Ausfaltung: Ein Beitrag zu einer Analytik des Paradoxen," *Zeitschrift für Rechtssoziologie* 21 (2000), 109–43.
____, "The Specific Autopoiesis of Law: Between Derivative Autonomy and Generalized Paradox," in J. Přibáň and D. Nelken (eds), *Law's New Boundaries : The Consequences of Legal Autopoiesis* (Aldershot: Ashgate, 2001), 45–79.
Colliot-Thélène, C., "Pour une politique des droits subjectifs: la lutte pour les droits comme lutte politique,"*, Année sociologique* 59 (2009), 231–58.
Guibentif, P., "Le chameau dans le laboratoire. La théorie des systèmes et l'étude de la communication juridique quotidienne," *Droit et société* 47 (2001), 123–53.
____, "The Liquidity and Solidity of Contemporary Social Reality: The Example of Social Inclusion Policies," in J. Přibáň (ed.), *Liquid Society and Its Law* (Aldershot: Ashgate, 2007), 173–97.
____, *Foucault, Luhmann, Habermas, Bourdieu. Une génération repense le droit* (Paris: Lextenso-Librairie générale de droit et de jurisprudence, 2010).
____, "Sociology among the Third-order Observers in Legitimization Processes," in S. Ashenden and C. Thornhill (eds), *Normative and Sociological Approaches to Legality and Legitimacy* (Baden-Baden: Nomos, 2010).
King, M., and C. Thornhill, *Niklas Luhmann's Theory of Politics and Law* (Basingstoke; New York: Palgrave Macmillan, 2003).
____ (eds), *Luhmann on Law and Politics: Critical Appraisals and Applications* (Oxford: Hart, 2006).
Ladeur, K.-H., ,"Das subjektive Recht und der Wunsch nach Gerechtigkeit als sein Parasit," *Zeitschrift für Rechtssoziologie* 29 (2008), 109–24.
Luhmann, N., *Grundrechte als Institution: Ein Beitrag zur politischen Soziologie* (Berlin: Duncker & Humblot, 1965).
____, "Normen in soziologischer Perspektive," in N. Luhmann, *Die Moral der Gesellschaft* (Frankfurt am Main: Suhrkamp, 2008), 25–55 (orig. publ.: 1969).
____, *Legitimation durch Verfahren* (Darmstadt; Neuwied: Luchterhand, 1969).
____,"Zur Funktion der 'subjektiven Rechte.'" in N. Luhmann, *Ausdifferenzierung des Rechts: Beiträge zur Rechtssoziologie und Rechtstheorie* (Frankfurt am Main: Suhrkamp, 1981), 360–73. French trans.: "De la fonction des droits subjectifs" *Trivium—Revue franco-allemande de sciences humaines et*

sociales 3 (2009). Available online at http://trivium.revues.org/index3265.html (accessed: November 2010).

―――, *Rechtssoziologie* (Reinbek bei Hamburg: Rowohlt, 1972); Engl. trans.: *A Sociological Theory of Law* (London and Boston: Routledge & Kegan, 1985).

―――, *Ausdifferenzierung des Rechts: Beiträge zur Rechtssoziologie und Rechtstheorie* (Frankfurt am Main: Suhrkamp, 1981a).

―――, "Subjektive Rechte: Zum Umbau des Rechtsbewusstseins für die moderne Gesellschaft", in N. Luhmann, *Gesellschaftsstruktur und Semantik* 2 (Frankfurt am Main: Suhrkamp, 1981b), 45–104.

―――, Soziale Systeme. Grundriss einer allgemeinen Theorie (Frankfurt am Main: Suhrkamp, 1984); Engl. trans.: *Social Systems* (Stanford: Stanford University Press, 1995).

―――, "Die Theorie der Ordnung und die natürlichen Rechte," *Rechtshistorisches Journal* 3 (1984), 133–49. French trans.: "La théorie de l'ordre et les droits naturels," Trivium—Revue franco–allemande de sciences humaines et sociales 3 (2009). Available online at http://trivium.revues.org/index3277.html (accessed: November 2010).

―――, "Die Autopoiesis des Bewusstseins,", in N. Luhmann, *Soziologische Aufklärung, 6:Die Soziologie und der Mensch* (Opladen: Westdeutscher Verlag, 1995), 55–112.

―――, "The Individuality of the Individual. Historical Meanings and Contemporary Problems," in T. Heller et al., *Reconstructing Individualism. Autonomy, Individuality, and the Self in Western Thought* (Stanford: Stanford University Press, 1986), 313–25.

―――, "Wie ist Bewußtsein an Kommunikation beteiligt?" in N. Luhmann, *Soziologische Aufklärung* 6 (Opladen: Westdeutscher Verlag, 1995), 37–54.

―――, "The Third Question: The Creative Uses of Paradoxes in Law and Legal History," *Journal of Law and Society* 15 (1988), 153–65.

―――, *Gesellschaftsstruktur und Semantik*, vol. 3 (Frankfurt am Main: Suhrkamp, 1989).

―――, *Die Wissenschaft der Gesellschaft* (Frankfurt am Main: Suhrkamp, 1990a).

―――, "Economia e diritto: Problemi di collegamento strutturale," in Centro Nazionale di Prevenzione e Difesa Sociale, *L'informazione nell'economia e nel diritto* (Milan: Cariplo, 1990b), 27–45.

―――, Einführung in die Systemtheorie (Vorlesung Wintersemester 1991–92) (Heidelberg: Carl Auer, 1991–92).

―――, *Das Recht der Gesellschaft* (Frankfurt am Main: Suhrkamp, 1993); Engl. trans. *Law as a Social System* (Oxford: Oxford University Press, 2004).

―――, "Das Paradox der Menschenrechte und drei Formen seiner Entfaltung," in *Festschrift Werner Krawietz* (Berlin: Duncker & Humblot, 1993), 539–46.

―――, *Gibt es in unserer Gesellschaft noch unverzichtbare Normen?* (Heidelberg: C.F. Müller, 1993).

―――, "Literatur als fiktionale Realität" (unpublished paper of 1995), in N. Luhmann 2008a, 276–91.

____, *Gesellschaftsstruktur und Semantik*, vol. 4 (Frankfurt am Main: Suhrkamp, 1995a).

____, *Soziologische Aufklärung 6. Die Soziologie und der Mensch* (Opladen: Westdeutscher Verlag, 1995b).

____, *Die Kunst der Gesellschaft* (Frankfurt am Main: Suhrkamp, 1995); Engl. trans.: *Art as a Social System* (Stanford: Stanford University Press, 2000).

____, *Die Realität der Massenmedien* (Opladen: Westdeutscher Verlag, 1996a).

____, Die neuzeitlichen Wissenschaften und die Phänomenologie (Wiena: Picus, 1996b).

____, *Die Gesellschaft der Gesellschaft*, 2 vols. (Frankfurt am Main: Suhrkamp, 1997a).

____, "Globalization of World Society. How to Conceive of Modern Society?" *International Review of Sociology* 7/1 (1997b); also available in French: "Globalisation ou société du monde: comment concevoir la société moderne?" in D. Kalogeropoulos (ed.), *Regards sur la complexité sociale et l'ordre légal à la fin du XXème siècle* (Brussels: Bruylant, 1997), 7–31.

____, "Selbstorganisation und Mikrodiversität: Zur Wissenssoziologie des neuzeitlichen Individualismus," *Soziale Systeme* 3 (1997c), 23–32.

____, *Organisation und Entscheidung* (Opladen: Westdeutscher Verlag, 2000).

____, *Schriften zur Pädagogik* (Frankfurt am Main: Suhrkamp, 2004).

____, *Schriften zur Kunst und Literatur* (Frankfurt am Main: Suhrkamp, 2008a).

____, *Die Moral der Gesellschaft* (Frankfurt am Main: Suhrkamp, 2008b).

Menke, C., "Subjektive Rechte: Zur Paradoxie der Form," *Zeitschrift für Rechtssoziologie* 29 (2008), 81–108.

____, "De la dignité de l'homme à la dignité humaine: le sujet des droits de l'homme," *Trivium* 3 (2009). Available online at http://trivium.revues.org/index3303.html (accessed November 2009).

Neves, M., "Von der Autopoiesis zur Allopoiesis des Rechts," *Rechtstheorie* 34 (2003), 245–68.

Parsons, T., "An Outline of the Social System," in T. Parsons, E. Shils, K. Naegele, and J. Pitts (eds), *Theories of Society* (New York: Free Press, 1961), 30–79.

Pires, E. B., "O pensamento de Niklas Luhmann como teoria crítica da moral," in J. M. Santos (ed.), *O pensamento de Niklas Luhmann* (Covilhã: Universidade da Beira Interior, 2005), 253–79. Also available online at http://www.lusosofia.net/textos/o_pensamento_de_niklas.pdf (accessed November 2009).

Přibáň, J. (ed.), *Liquid Society and Its Law* (Aldershot: Ashgate, 2007).

Přibáň, J., and D. Nelken (eds), *Law's New Boundaries: The Consequences of Legal Autopoiesis* (Aldershot: Ashgate, 2001).

Rocha, L. S., M. King, and G. Schwartz, *A verdade sobre a autopoiese no direito* (Porto Alegra: Livraria do Advogado, 2009).

Santos, B. de S. et al., *Os tribunais nas sociedades contemporâneas: o caso português* (Porto: Afrontamento, 1996).

Schwartz, G., "A autopoiese dos direitos fundamentais," in E. H. Macedo, L. Ohlweiler and W. Steinmetz (eds), *Direitos fundamentais* (Canoas: Editora da ULBRA, 2007), 41–56.

Verschraegen, G., "Systems Theory and the Paradox of Human Rights," in M. King, C. Thornhill (eds), *Luhmann on Law and Politics: Critical Appraisals and Applications* (Oxford and Portland, OR: Hart, 2006), 101–25.

Chapter 12
Jurisprudence and Intersystemic (Mis)communication[1]

Katayoun Baghai

Reflecting on the peculiar paucity of empirical research in the sociology of law, Luhmann (1985) took note of the failure of sociology to take law and jurisprudence seriously. If autopoietic theory aspired to be a remedy, little has since changed. Leaving the study of law and jurisprudence to legal scholarship, sociology remains confined to investigation of law-*related* phenomena. Disparate empirical investigations (on, for example, the legal profession, judicial behaviour, opinion about the law, or differential access to it) tend to rest on ad hoc theorising and common-sense conceptions of law, with little bearing for a general theory of society. As a result, the sociology of law remains marginal, not only to the discipline of sociology, but also, and to their detriment, to sociolegal studies.[2] In many respects, Friedman's (1986) appraisal of sociolegal studies still rings true:

> To many observers, the work done so far amounts to very little: an incoherent or inconclusive jumble of case studies. There is (it seems) no foundation ... nothing cumulates. The studies are at times interesting and are sporadically useful. But ... [n]othing adds up. Law and economics offers hard science; CLS [Critical Legal Studies] offers high culture and the joy of trashing ... Grand theories do appear from time to time, but they have no survival power; they are nibbled to death by case studies. There is no central core. (p. 779)

The missing core is law as a self-describing and functionally differentiated communication system.

---

1   This chapter is a revised version of a paper presented to the conference on Applied System Theory, Niklas Luhmann's Theory of Self-referential Systems: Theoretical and Empirical Research, Inter-University Centre, Dubrovnik, Croatia (2009). With gratitude to the participants and to James Porter and Steven Rytina for their helpful comments.

2   On the troubled relation between sociology and law, the tension between theory and empirical research, and the eclipse of the sociology of law by sociolegal studies in the second half of the twentieth century, see, e.g., Cotterrell 1986, 2002, and 2006; Deflem 2008; Freeman 2006; and Paterson and Teubner (1998).

A sociological attempt at empirical legal autopoiesis, this chapter engages jurisprudence – that is, the self-description of the legal system – as normative structure, but conducts its investigation from the vantage point of a central problematic of the discipline of sociology: functional differentiation. The aspiration is to facilitate structural couplings between sociology and reflexive theories of law.[3]

Rights-based judicial review of legislation in the United States is reformulated in systems-theoretic terms. The Supreme Court's jurisprudence on abortion and homosexuality, two morally charged and politically divisive issues of American law and politics, is examined at the juncture of functional differentiation and legal autopoiesis. While variation in Court rulings is often seen as politically and/or ideologically influenced, rather than legally determined, this chapter shows how legal doctrines allow the former without undermining the latter. Two rival methods of constitutional interpretation, Originalism and Living Constitutionalism, rather than expressions of American exceptionalism, emerge as universal and complementary strategies for dealing with increasing complexity of law and its environment. A case is made for investigating jurisprudence of rights at the level of world society.

Judicial Review and Sociolegal Studies

Since the passage of the Judiciary Act of 1789, the judicial power of the United States is vested in one Supreme Court at the summit of a system of independent courts. In 1803 the Court for the first time used this power to declare an act of Congress unconstitutional,[4] thereby establishing its judicial oversight over legislative and administrative action.[5] Since then American jurisprudence has grappled with the legitimate foundation, proper scope, and actual exercise of power by the Supreme Court, an unelected and

---

3   See Luhmann (1988).

4   *Marbury v. Madison*, 5 U.S. (1 Cranch) 137 (1803). Marbury had been appointed Justice of Peace by John Adams before the latter's presidential electoral defeat by Thomas Jefferson. Upon the withholding of his commission by James Madison, Jefferson's Secretary of State, Marbury petitioned the Court to force delivery of his commission. The Court acknowledged a violation of the law, but denied relief by holding the section of the Judiciary Act of 1789, on which the petition was based, unconstitutional. The Court thus established its power of judicial review by denying Congress the right to extend the Court's jurisdiction beyond what was initially determined by the Constitution!

5   Judicial review has a more ancient root in the English practice of reviewing corporate by-laws to ensure they are not 'repugnant' to the laws of England. This practice was extended to the American colonies in as much as some colonial legislatures were merely directorates of chartered trading companies. In a sense, the Judiciary Act only shifted the reference for 'repugnancy' from the laws of England to the American Constitution. For a short historiography, see Bilder 2008.

unaccountable body, over representative government.[6] Sociolegal studies seem to have mostly followed suit.

In the early twentieth century, adoption of the 'substantive due process' doctrine by the Court and the rise of Legal Realism in American jurisprudence augmented emphasis on the political, rather than judicial, function of the Court.[7] In tune with Legal Realism, since the 1950s social scientific investigations of judicial review have mostly disregarded the difference between *political* and *judicial* decision making and primarily focused on identifying and measuring extra-legal determinants of judicial behaviour.[8] The success of such studies in predicting Justices' votes superseded concern for investigating jurisprudence in relation to structural transformations of modern society.

In recent years, and perhaps in accord with greater emphasis in legal scholarship on the constitutive, rather than instrumental, role of law, a variety of new institutionalist approaches to judicial review have tried to 'bring the law back in'. Such investigations have drawn attention to institutional norms, procedures and missions as endogenous variables in guiding and limiting possibilities of meaningful action, and highlighted the role of 'jurisprudential regimes' and 'argumentation frameworks' in judicial decision making.[9]

Yet, insofar as the primary focus remains prediction of judicial behaviour, such studies fall short of a radical break with prevalent behavioural approaches in the field.[10] Jurisprudence is brought back in, but only as one variable among others regulating or coordinating Justices' actions or policy preferences. What is ignored

---

6   Often the debate is cast in terms of questions of democracy, popular sovereignty, separation of powers, and the counter-majoritarian role of the Court. See, e.g., Corwin 1910, 1911; Dworkin 1977, 1990; Goldstein 1986, 1987; Harel 2003; Rostow 1952; Stephenson 2003; Tribe 1983; Tushnet 1999, 2008.

7   The Fifth and Fourteenth Amendments prohibit the national government and the states from depriving any person of 'life, liberty, or property without due process of law'. The doctrine of 'substantive due process' extended the power of judicial review from oversight of procedures to approval of contents of legislation, mostly regarding un-enumerated rights. The doctrine was used during the Lochner era (1897–1937) to strike down labour laws in the name of freedom of contract.

8   Judicial decision making is examined in relation to variety of extra-legal factors such as Justices' party affiliations, ideological commitments, and attitudes (Lim 2000; Segal and Cover 1989; Segal and Spaeth 1993); strategic decision making and panel composition (Cross and Nelson 2001; Lindquist et al. 2007); public opinion, congressional balance of power, and the social status and ideological positions of litigants (George and Epstein 1992; Harvey and Friedman 2006; Howard and Segal 2004; Mishler and Sheehan 1996; Songer and Sheehan 1993).

9   See Gillman 2006; Marlowe 2011; Richards and Kritzer 2002; Sweet 2002.

10   On the degree to which behavioural approaches to judicial review, best exemplified in Spaeth and Segal's (1993) 'attitudinal model', can incorporate new institutionalist perspectives, see Segal 1999. For an empirical example, see Lindquist and Klein 2006.

is the significance of jurisprudence in regulating the relation between the legal system and its environment.

Rights-based Judicial Review: Law at a Crossroad

No party to the debate denies a law-making moment in adjudication, especially by the highest court of the land. At issue is whether an irreducibly legal element sets such episodes apart from policymaking by the legislature; if there is something in adjudication that distinguishes judicial decisions from mere exercises of power. The answer, at least in part, lies in the condition of exercising judicial power.

Like the legislature, the Court can make and unmake the law. But, unlike the legislature, the Court cannot exercise this prerogative at will. It can only do so in settling cases between adversarial parties. Cases find their ways to the Court not according to electoral cycles, changes in the composition of the Court or public opinion, but according to unpredictable litigations and procedural mechanisms for their resolution. The Court cannot initiate law making for politically expedient purposes; nor, once a hearing is granted, can it postpone law making until favourable political conditions obtain. It cannot issue advisory opinions, rule on questions the political nature of which is already established,[11] or decide issues it deems 'premature' or 'moot'. In other words, the buffer between the Court and its environment is not the unwavering commitments of Justices to law and justice, but temporal disjuncture between a functionally differentiated legal system and its environment.

Although the Court cannot anticipate which conflicts are litigated and which make their way to the chamber, since passage of the Judiciary Act of 1925 which substantially reduced the range and number of cases over which the Court had obligatory appellate jurisdiction, the Court has exercised almost complete discretion in accepting cases for review. Not obliged to provide reasons for granting or denying a hearing, in allowing itself to be influenced by one conflict and not another, the Court is sovereign. It can ignore many conflicting claims to legal validity in its environment and continue its operation.

Granting a hearing, however, acknowledges that in response to a particular conflict legality can have more than one answer *within* the legal system. Like 'hard cases', such momentary exposures of the paradox of law, the unfounded character of law's foundational distinction, disrupt the ordered complexity of the law and necessitate its reconstitution.[12] On the one hand, 'existing, doubtlessly valid, legal

---

11 Constitutional courts in Europe are bound by the same consideration with respect to political questions. See Sweet 2000: 90.

12 These moments are not limited to Supreme Court cases. As Hart (1958: 607) suggests: 'Fact situations do not await us neatly labeled, creased, and folded, nor is their legal classification written on them to be simply read off by the judge.' Legal reasoning is never reducible to logical deduction from premises to conclusions or empirical induction

norms applied with logically correct deductive methods do not lead to unequivocal decisions'; on the other, the Court is legally obliged to decide the case lawfully (Luhmann 2004: 281, 287). This does not necessarily suggest a lag between the 'law in the books' and the 'living law'. It does not mean that law is lacking or information insufficient. Quite the contrary, what makes an 'authoritative legal ruling' necessary is that 'there is *too much law*', an excess of simultaneously plausible, yet contradictory, grounds for legal decision making (Cover 1983: 53).[13]

To impose a temporary hierarchy upon the law, a simple decision is not enough. The Court is obliged to provide an account – that is, legally valid arguments that present the decision as grounded in and governed by the law.[14] While decisions are able to 'change the position of the law', it is by means of legal arguments that the legal system seeks to ensure its operations continue 'in one direction (and not the other)' (Luhmann 1995: 286). On its own, a *decision* is a simple application of the code 'legal/illegal'; a single selection with no ground for connection to the past or retention in the future. It is the *opinion* that makes rediscovery of this selection in future and past cases possible. That is why 'what judges say is even more important than how they vote' (Shapiro and Sweet 2002: 98). It is the opinion which provides 'the constraining directions to the public and private decision makers who determine the 99 per cent of conduct that never reaches the courts' (Shapiro 1968: 39). The primary function of Court opinions, therefore, is not to 'deceive' internal or external observers of the legal system concerning the 'discovery' rather than 'invention' of the ruling law. Rather, it is to tailor connective potentials of decisions to past and future decisions.[15]

In other words, a legal decision – that is, a *first-order* observation by the legal system as to the legal quality of a normative expectation in its environment – requires

---

from evidence to proposition. That is why the domain of law is not a realm of necessity, demonstration and proof, but one of plausibility, argumentation and persuasion. The focus here on Supreme Court cases is primarily due to the Court's obligation to complement its decisional response to such indeterminacies with written opinions; i.e., to observe its own observations. It is at the level of second-order observations that the normative closure of the legal system is produced and maintained.

13   Hart (1994 [1961]) and Dworkin (1963, 1975, 2004) have provided two contrasting influential views of adjudication in their discussion of 'hard cases'. For Hart, in hard cases the law is at least partly indeterminate. Therefore, such decisions involve some degree of judicial discretion to 'make' the law appropriate for the case. For Dworkin, however, each hard case has only one correct answer, which is discovered according to antecedent legal principles and collective moral principles of the community; and justified by means of publically accessible reasons. Nonetheless, both agree that hard cases cannot be brought under clear rules of law already laid down by statutes or precedent.

14   The same applies to Constitutional Courts in Europe. See Sweet 2000: 46.

15   Of course, as the history of the Court's jurisprudence clearly shows, such attempts are never fully successful. In every iteration past judicial decisions are cast in a new horizon; new legal justifications for them are discovered; and new possibilities for connecting them to further decisions are brought to light.

a *second-order* observation to establish the validity of the first by reference to legal communications. In this *self-observation*, the Court has to exhibit the highest degree of autonomy, or normative closure. It can turn what is legal into illegal and vice versa. Yet, it cannot use a code other than 'legal/illegal' to manage such alterations. While the legislature can make contradictory decisions by simply announcing new policy preferences, the Court is bound to adjudicate consistently by reference to established law and its own precedents, departure from which requires legal, rather than moral or political, justification.

Judicial review, in short, is externally induced self-inspection of the law. It is triggered at the juncture of two sets of conflicts: one in the environment of the legal system, between two sets of normative expectations; another within the law itself, between different ways of identifying the ruling law and applying it to the case. The Court can respond to the former only through the latter. Yet, sociolegal studies have failed to analyse judicial review at the juncture of the two. Concerned with social inclusion, the social sciences tend to focus on what the Court 'does' – that is, its *decision*; preoccupied with normative validity, legal theory engages what the Court 'says'– that is, its *opinion*.

As a sociology of self-describing systems, social systems theory offers a conceptual apparatus to bridge this divide and examine judicial review as the legal system's external-reference *through* self-reference. This shifts the focus of investigation concerning normative closure, or autonomy, of the law from judicial behaviour to jurisprudence. Undoubtedly, the Court cannot operate without individual Justices. Yet, their interests, thoughts and commitments remain inconsequential to the judicial process unless expressed in legal communications.[16] Once so communicated, however, they take on a life of their own and become evocable in diverse and unexpected contexts, possibly in support of positions and goals radically different from their original contexts and authors' intentions. Only when that which sets the law apart from other social systems – that is, the specific form of its recursive communications – is recognised, can the nature and extent of mutual influences between the law and its environment be adequately examined.

Abortion and Homosexuality as Critical Challenges

The Court's jurisprudence on abortion and homosexuality offers a good example for such investigation. Conflicts over abortion and homosexuality have produced political, religious, moral and scientific communications in the environment of the legal system, and induced repeated self-inspections of the latter as to the legal boundaries of these communication systems. Absent explicit protection in the Constitution, and in the context of a doctrinal divide on the bench over constitutional interpretation, the Court's response has been inconsistent and contradictory.

---

16   See Nobles and Schiff (2009).

Since decriminalising abortion in 1973,[17] the Court has annulled requirements of parental and spousal consent for abortion;[18] upheld denial of Medicaid for non-therapeutic abortions;[19] upheld prohibition of using public employees, funds and facilities for counselling, referring and performing abortion;[20] and both annulled[21] and upheld[22] prohibition of the so-called partial birth abortion without a health exception. Yet, to date it has refused to recriminalise abortion.[23] With regard to homosexuality, the Court upheld criminal sodomy laws in 1986[24] and struck them down in 2003.[25] In between the two, it annulled a state constitutional Amendment precluding equal protection to homosexuals;[26] and denied them equal protection against discrimination in membership associations.[27]

To examine the Court's handling of these variations an analytic distinction is made between Court *decisions* and Court *opinions*: Court decisions are analysed as responses to external conflicts over social inclusion – that is, they constitute the legal system's *external-reference*.[28] Their implications are examined with

---

17   *Roe* v. *Wade*, 410 U.S. 113 (1973).

18   *Planned Parenthood of Central Missouri* v. *Danforth*, 428 U.S. 52 (1976); *Bellotti* v. *Baird*, 443 U.S. 622 (1979).

19   *Harris* v. *McRae*, 448 U.S. 297(1980).

20   *Webster* v. *Reproductive Health Services*, 452 U.S. 450 (1989); *Rust* v. *Sullivan*, 500 U.S. 173 (1991).

21   *Stenberg* v. *Carhart*, 530 U.S. 914 (2000).

22   *Gonzales* v. *Carhart*, 550 U.S. 124 (2007).

23   *Planned Parenthood of Southeastern Pennsylvania* v. *Casey*, 505 U.S. 833 (1992). Court refusal to overrule *Roe* came as a surprise, as four Justices had expressed their willingness to do so, and two Justices were leaning in that direction. Relying on the doctrine of *stare decisis*, the plurality called overruling 'under fire' a serious subversion of its legitimacy. Since then, the anti-abortion lobby has focused on limiting late-term abortion. The term 'partial birth abortion' was coined to galvanise support against abortions due to foetal abnormality, something which offends many constituencies including disability groups. After legislatures in 30 states banned partial birth abortion, the Congress passed the Partial Birth Abortion Act of 2003 in which the procedure was called 'gruesome', 'inhumane' and 'morally wrong'. Presently 38 states have foetal homicide laws that were initially intended to protect pregnant women and their foetuses against violent attacks by third parties. In recent years such laws are evoked against pregnant women themselves. On the medicalisation and moralisation of abortion on the road from *Casey*, through *Stenberg*, to *Gonzales,* see, e.g., Gee 2007 and Heffernan 2001.

24   *Bowers* v. *Hardwick*, 478 U.S. 186 (1986).

25   *Lawrence* v. *Texas*, 539 U.S. 558 (2003).

26   *Romer* v. *Evans*, 517 U.S. 620 (1996).

27   *Boy Scouts of America* v. *Dale*, 530 U.S. 640 (2000). The Court denied relief on the ground that the Boy Scouts of America could exclude homosexuals based on its members' right to free speech and association.

28   External references of the legal system still belong to the system. They are references of the system to its environment, without exact equivalent in the latter. Since law cannot operate beyond its own boundaries, it cannot determine the boundaries of other

respect to functional differentiation of social systems in the law's environment. Court opinions are analysed as responses to internal conflicts over constitutional interpretation – that is, they constitute the legal system's *self-reference*. Their implications are examined with respect to legal autopoiesis.

But first, a brief discussion of the conditions of emergence of conflicts over equality and privacy is in order.

Equality, Privacy and Functional Differentiation

The Fourteenth Amendment to the United States Constitution (1868) provided all persons within its jurisdiction with equal protection of the laws.[29] Since then, the substance of equality and the nature and scope of State responsibility for its protection have remained contentious.

Equality as Selective Indifference

Briefly, as long as social inclusion is automatically guaranteed by virtue of fixed social position, individuals are not 'rights-bearing entities', and the right to equality has no place in regulating social life. Dissolution of the stratified order puts an end to homogenous, total, and ineluctable social inclusion and exclusion. '*It is no longer groups of people that are being differentiated but types of communication*' (Verschraegen 2002: 264, 266). In this context, the right to equality functions as a 'principle of *selective indifference*'. It renders irrelevant all qualities and characteristics except those pertinent to role expectations in the function system in question. Thus, all with the ability to pay expect equal access to the market; all within a certain jurisdiction expect equal access to the law; and all with the ability to learn expect access to public education regardless of faith, political affiliation, skin colour, gender and the like. Of course, contracts go to lowest bidders; prior convictions affect sentencing; and university admissions depend on examination scores; at least, that is the expectation.

---

social systems in its environment. But it can determine where they should be according to the law. The promise of legal redress in case of violation of such boundaries stabilises generalised normative expectations and in so doing participates in the structural drift of system boundaries.

29 Section 1 of the Fourteenth Amendment reads: '... No State shall make or enforce any law which shall abridge the privileges or immunities of citizens of the United States; nor shall any State deprive any person of life, liberty, or property, without due process of law; nor deny to any person within its jurisdiction the equal protection of the laws.'

Privacy as Withdrawal and Inclusion

A 'radical privatisation' plays an essential role in this process. Leaving to the individual certain decisions concerning property, ultimate belief, occupation and marriage undermines ascription of entire persons or households to only one stratum and further compartmentalises the economy, religion, politics and family. Thus, capital accumulation can continue with no regard to religious or moral expectations about surplus distribution or fear of arbitrary political acquisition (Luhmann 1982: 129). Private rights are also essential to functional differentiation of the political system and centralisation of the State, as they prevent politicisation of religious and economic activities (Thornhill 2011: 164–7).

There is no expressed guarantee for a right to privacy in the US Constitution. Conceptual ambiguity and doctrinal incoherence with respect to the exact meaning and legal ground of privacy persist. Nonetheless, the legal system has recognised the right to privacy as a ground for claims-making, legislation, and adjudication.[30] As functional differentiation proceeds, requirements of communication in interaction systems, organisations, and societal systems increasingly diverge (Luhmann 1982); and selective attribution of communication to social systems becomes more complex and contingent. Leaving to the individual making sense of action and experience in a 'zone of privacy',[31] reduces this complexity in each social system and allows for greater complexity at the societal level. More than simply a right to be let alone, the right to privacy is also a right to social inclusion irrespective of decisions concerning private matters. That is why privacy claims are often interwoven with claims to equality.

Rights to equality and privacy are emergent properties of functional differentiation. Their contours remain in flux not merely due to changing balances of power between conflicting groups, but more fundamentally due to the shifting boundaries of functionally differentiated societal systems.[32] In the absence of a unified hierarchy among societal systems, and with each system able to cast the entire world in its own image, it is not always clear where the economy, politics, law, morality, science, religion, etc., begin and end. The Supreme Court intervenes when such intersystemic boundary tensions in the environment of the legal system

---

30   The earliest legal recognition of the violation of the 'sacred right to privacy' was made in *DeMay* v. *Roberts*, 46 Mich. 160, 9 N.W. 146 (1881), when a doctor brought an unqualified assistant into a woman's bedchamber in childbirth. Since then the Court has dealt with the concrete meaning of privacy in various issues including interracial marriage, contraception, termination of medical treatment, and collection and disclosure of personal information. For a useful survey of various conceptions of privacy and their shortcomings, see Solove 2009. For a systems-theoretic analysis of privacy as structural coupling between social communication systems, see Baghai 2012.

31   *Griswold* v. *Connecticut* 381 U.S. 479 (1965).

32   On the relation between legal indeterminacies in private law and conflicts between societal systems, see Teubner 1993: 100–122.

reverberate within the law exposing ambiguous boundaries of societal systems in legal provisions.

Judicial review of legislation concerning abortion and homosexuality, therefore, rests at the juncture of a circular relationship between functional differentiation and legal autopoiesis. Triggered by conflicting expectations in the environment of the legal system over social exclusion, a hearing exposes a conflict in the law with respect to their normative validity. Each decision gives rise to further boundary tensions between societal systems, and hence future cycles.

Decision: Social Exclusion and Functional Differentiation

In reviewing legislation concerning abortion and homosexuality, the Court must decide whether or not the social exclusion in question denies the equal protection of the laws. Equal protection jurisprudence has evolved so that today, to make a decision about the constitutionality of a legislative or administrative act, the Court responds to some or all of the following questions:

- Is there a liberty interest involved? Yes/No
- Is the liberty fundamental?[33] Yes/No
- Is the classification suspect?[34] Yes/No
- Is the State interest non-compelling? Yes/No
- Is the law or policy overbroad? Yes/No
- Is the burden imposed on the affected individuals undue?[35] Yes/No
- Is partial revision to the law or policy insufficient? Yes/No

To recognise a constitutional violation and strike down a statute, the Court needs to consistently respond in the affirmative: It has to recognise a liberty interest in the case; declare that liberty fundamental; find the affected class suspect – that is,

---

33   A right is fundamental when its infringement by the State requires extraordinary justification. Whether fundamental rights are strictly limited to those expressed in the Constitution and enjoyed by Americans at the time of its ratification, or whether new rights can be recognised as fundamental by the Court is a central contention in rights-based reviews.

34   The US Supreme Court holds certain bases of classification, such as race and religion, as inherently suspect for legislation, and thus subject to a 'strict scrutiny' test. In such cases the government carries the burden of proof and has to show the indispensability of the statute to achieve a 'compelling state interest'. If the basis of classification is not 'suspect', a 'rational basis' test and only a reasonable ground for legislation may suffice. Classifications based on sex and sexual orientation are examined with an 'intermediate' level of scrutiny.

35   A burden is undue if it is calculated to place a substantial or absolute obstacle or severe limitation before the exercise of a right. Of course, these concepts do not have coherent legal bases. Nor are they applied consistently.

a victim of past discrimination; establish the non-compelling character of State interest in limiting that liberty through appropriate tests; demonstrate the burden of the statute on affected individuals as undue; and find partial revisions inadequate to bring the law or policy in line with constitutional standards.

Such consistencies, however, presuppose agreement on application of further distinctions.[36] In the absence of a norm hierarchy, and in the context of a doctrinal divide on the bench over constitutional interpretation, it is no surprise that the history of Court engagements with abortion and homosexuality has been one of ongoing variation, from partial recognitions and retreats to full reversals of position. One negative response is enough to break the chain of attribution in one network of communication and set in motion another chain in which the statute could be upheld by its positive connection to other legal provisions. Yet, focusing on the 'selective indifference' in question, we can examine how each decision slightly alters system boundaries as understood by the law.

For example, criminal abortion laws make access to pregnancy-related medical services, – that is, inclusion in the healthcare system – dependent on a woman's choice to carry a fetus to term. Thus, religious/ethical views on the value of life, rather than medical need, are made legally relevant to reception of care. Likewise, denial of Medicaid to abortion services turns some pregnancy-related health services into commodities, access to which depends on economic status. Since the public healthcare system per se is expected to be indifferent to characteristics not concerning health and illness, the question is whether the political system can use the law to limit access to the healthcare system based on religious or economic criteria.

In contrast, rejecting compelling State interest in categorical protection of the unborn renders religious and scientific definitions of life irrelevant to the legal meaning of abortion.[37] Rejecting the requirement of parental or spousal consent renders family status irrelevant in access to abortion services.[38] Rejecting regulation of abortion services and medical procedures in violation of accepted

---

36 Liberty can be understood as expressed or implicit; determined by reference to individual happiness or collective goals; fundamental can mean ancient or essential; strict scrutiny can be applied to State intention or to the consequence of its action; undue burden can be imposed negatively or positively, etc., etc.

37 While the abortion controversy is often attributed to the rise of the religious Right, the role of science should not be overlooked. According to the Court's brief account of the history of abortion regulation, in the common law and British statutory law, before quickening or viability the fetus was part of the mother and its destruction was not considered homicide. 'Quickening' disappeared from American law in the latter part of the nineteenth century mainly due to the efforts of the American Medical Association. Recognising the life of the fetus before quickening, the AMA criticised the State for failing to protect the unborn; called for revision of abortion laws; and requested the support of medical societies and the clergy for that cause. See *Roe v. Wade*, 410 U.S. 113, 141–2 (1973).

38 'The State does not have the constitutional authority to give a third party an absolute, and possibly arbitrary, veto over the decision of the physician and his patient

medical practice renders non-medical considerations irrelevant to delivery of abortion services.[39] In recognising the right to make decisions about abortion 'without public scrutiny and in defiance of the contrary opinion of the sovereign or other third parties',[40] the law treats the person as 'belong[ing] to himself, and not others nor to society as a whole'.[41] This protects the individual not only against the political system, but also all other societal systems, including the family, and prevents de-differentiation of the latter.

Likewise, criminal sodomy laws make enjoyment of liberty in intimate relations, property and equal protection of the laws dependent on moral values concerning sexual conduct. Decriminalisation of homosexuality, on the other hand, relieves the political system of scrutinising people's conduct in their homes,[42] further differentiates religion, morality, politics and intimate relations, and provides a ground for equal access to all societal systems regardless of sexual orientation. This could provide legal grounds for further right-claims concerning military service, marriage, adoption, etc., and further protection of individuals, as biological and psychic systems, against all social systems. Each such decision can serve as irritation for the law and function systems in its environment.[43]

Opinion: Normative Validity and Legal Autopoiesis

By its *decisions* the Court selectively transfers legal validity to contested normative expectations in its environment. Re-establishment of the ordered complexity of the law through connection of past and future decisions, however, is the task of its *opinions*. As self-descriptions of the legal system, they appear when the

---

to terminate the patient's pregnancy ... The State cannot relegate the authority it does not have' *Planned Parenthood of Central Missouri* v. *Danforth*, 428 U.S. 52, 74 (1976).

39   Invalidating several Pennsylvania abortion regulations including delivery of detailed information about abortion and its alternatives, the Court held 'a rigid requirement that a specific body of information be given in all cases, irrespective of the particular needs of the patient', to constitute intrusion 'upon the discretion of the pregnant woman's physician' *Thornburgh* v. *American College of Obstetricians & Gynaecologists*, 476 U.S. 747, 762 (1986). *Akron* v. *Akron Center for Reproductive Health*, 462 U.S. 416, 431 (1983).

40   *Bellotti* v. *Baird*,443 U.S. 622, 655 (1979) (Stevens, J., Concurring).

41   *Thornburgh* v. *American College of Obstetricians & Gynecologists*, 476 U.S. 747, 777 (1986) (Stevens, J., Concurring).

42   'In our tradition the State is not omnipresent in the home. And there are other spheres of our lives and existence, outside the home, where the State should not be a dominant presence' *Lawrence v. Texas*, 539 U.S. 558 (2003).

43   Decriminalisation of abortion in 1973 inadvertently demobilised the feminist movement and contributed to the creation of the 'Moral Majority', with harmful consequences for civil rights; while severe restrictions on abortion in 1989 mobilised the pro-choice movement and led to electoral changes and favourable results for civil rights. On the irony of 'juridicalisation of politics', see, e.g., Rosenberg (1991) and Shapiro (1994).

law observes its own observations, not its environment. Setting aside the often idiosyncratic logics of discovery, opinions describe logics of justification. They explain how the judgment 'could have been arrived at on the basis of logical, step-by-step reasoning' (Posner 2008: 110). At issue is how to ground the decision in the law and tailor its connective capacity to past and future decisions.

The US Supreme Court has not adopted a specific theory of constitutional interpretation. Each case has produced a slightly different interpretation of precedents and uncovered somewhat new grounds for past decisions.[44] These inconsistencies are broadly understood by the legal system in terms of a doctrinal divide between Originalism and Living Constitutionalism. Yet, as we shall see, despite their spirited mutual attacks, they provide complementary strategies for self-referential operations of the legal system; two strategies for producing variety/redundancy in the law and its environment.[45]

Variety/redundancy, as a form, is a measure of complexity. Variety refers to the number and diversity of events to which a system reacts by activating its information processing mechanisms. The more variety within a system, the more operations it can recognise as its own, and thus the higher its irritability and responsiveness to its environment. Redundancy, on the other hand, refers to rules or generalisations of already processed events that enable indifference towards new events, thereby reducing surprises for the system. This allows the system to determine the meaning of a new situation by means of a small amount of information (Luhmann 1995: 291–2). To manage the pace of information processing, a differentiated legal system requires an effective organisation of its memory – that is, a balance of variety/redundancy. The two sides of this form are not in an inverse relationship. In fact, different levels of abstraction in producing redundancy can produce different degrees and kinds of variety and create different potentials for doctrinal combination. Thus, both redundancy and variety can increase at the same time. The key is the particular relation between them (Luhmann 2004: 320–22). The concern here is to see how Originalism and Living Constitutionalism process right-claims concerning abortion and homosexuality; what type of variety/redundancy relation they produce; and to what effect for law and its environment.

Originalism

Originalism describes itself as advocacy of judicial restraint and popular sovereignty. It claims to treat the original meaning of the Constitution, as

---

44 This, of course, is not a failure of the law but a function of the inherent instability of meaning as the unity of the difference between the possible and the probable, what is actually given and the potentiality that lies beyond it.

45 On the evolution of Originalism and Living Constitutionalism and their many strands, see, e.g., Ackerman 2007; Grey 1975; McBain 1927; O'Neill 2005; Rehnquist 2005; Scalia 1989; Strauss 2010; Whittington 2004.

understood by reasonable persons at the time of its adoption, as authoritative in constitutional interpretation. Thus, it opposes the use of judicial review to extend constitutional protection to rights neither enumerated in the Constitution nor widely recognised at the time of its adoption. In dealing with abortion and homosexuality, Originalism interprets constitutional rights, statutes, and the case at hand at the most concrete level.

> Liberty includes only those practices, defined at the most specific level, that were protected against government interference by other rules of law when the Fourteenth Amendment was ratified.[46]

Limiting fundamental rights to those explicitly guaranteed in the Constitution, Originalism denies the information value of statutory restrictions on other rights for the Court. Thus, violation of implicitly protected rights by legislative or administrative action, while clearly political, cannot trigger connective events in the legal system. For example, as no fundamental right to abortion is explicitly guaranteed by the Constitution, a reasonable State objective is held sufficient to criminalise or regulate it.[47] Likewise, denial of public funding for abortion services is held constitutional, because when Medicaid was enacted abortion was already illegal;[48] and there is no limitation on State authority to value childbirth over abortion.[49]

In fact, according to Originalism, the State may 'choose not to operate any public hospitals at all' and not be found in violation of constitutional standards.[50] The fact that such measures deprive poor women of the exercise of their right is legally irrelevant, because the poor are not legally recognised as a 'suspect class', and the Constitution 'imposes no obligation on the State to pay the pregnancy-related medical expenses of indigent women'.[51] According to Originalism, 'Due Process Clauses generally confer no affirmative right to governmental aid, even where such aid may be necessary to secure life, liberty, or property interests of which the government itself may not deprive the individual.'[52] The same strategy is used to adjudicate criminal sodomy laws:

> There is no such thing as a fundamental right to commit homosexual sodomy ... Decisions of individuals relating to homosexual conduct have been subject to state intervention throughout the history of Western civilization. Condemnation

---

46 *Planned Parenthood v. Casey*, 505 U.S. 833 (1992) (Scalia, J.).
47 *Roe v. Wade*, 410 U.S. 113, 174 (1973) (Rehnquist, J., Dissenting).
48 *Beal v. Doe*, 432 U.S. 438 (1977).
49 *Maher v. Roe*, 432 U.S. 464, 474 (1977); *Poelker v. Doe*, 432 U.S. 519, 521 (1977).
50 *Webster v. Reproductive Health Services*, 492 U.S 450, 509 (1989).
51 *Maher v. Roe*, 432 U.S. 464, 471 (1977).
52 *Webster v. Reproductive Health Services*, 492 U.S. 450, 507 (1989).

of those practices is firmly rooted in Judeo-Christian moral and ethical standards
... This is essentially not a question of personal 'preferences', but rather of the
legislative authority of the State.[53]

Since this right is not deeply rooted in the history and tradition of the United States, a governing majority's belief about its immorality is deemed sufficient for its regulation.[54] Expansion of fundamental rights beyond what was explicitly recognised at the time of the Constitution's adoption, Originalism argues, requires a political rather than a judicial decision.

Living Constitutionalism

Living Constitutionalism understands the broad language of the Constitution as an invitation for its dynamic interpretation with reference to both precedent and contemporary standards of justice and equity. It construes both the Constitution and the statute or policy in question at a higher level of abstraction. Thus, statutory or common law violations of implied rights can acquire information value, activate constitutional provisions, and potentially lead to judicial recognition of new right-claims. While the Constitution does not explicitly mention any right to abortion or homosexuality, 'the concept of personal liberty ... [is understood as] broad enough to encompass a woman's decision whether or not to terminate her pregnancy[55]... [as well as one's] decisions concerning intimate relationships.'[56] Legislative prohibition of funding elective abortion is unconstitutional because it affects pregnant women's exercise of choice.

> Her choice is affected not simply by the absence of payment for the abortion, but by the availability of public funds for childbirth if she chooses not to have the abortion.[57]

Criminal sodomy laws are unconstitutional not because they prohibit a particular sexual activity but because they violate 'the most comprehensive of rights and the right most valued by civilized men ... the right to be let alone.'[58] This level of abstraction requires introducing new concepts and further distinctions in making decisions.[59] In the case of abortion, the Court introduced two distinctions to differentiate abortion from homicide, and yet authorise its regulation or prohibition: viable fetus/non-viable fetus; and person/non-person. The first left the

---

53 *Bower v. Hardwick*, 478 U.S. 186, 196 (1986) (Burger, C.J., Concurring).
54 *Lawrence v. Texas*, 539 U.S. 588 (2003) (Scalia, J., Dissenting).
55 *Roe v. Wade*, 410 U.S. 113, 154 (1973).
56 *Bower v. Hardwick*, 478 U.S. 186, 200 (1986) (Blackmun, J., Dissenting).
57 *Maher v. Roe*, 432 U.S. 464, 483 (1977) (Brennan, J., Dissenting).
58 *Lawrence v. Texas*, 539 U.S. 588 (2003).
59 On the creative use of paradoxes in the law, see Fletcher 1985 and Luhmann 1988.

law cognitively open to the changing state of medicine and technology, and thus regulation and proscription of abortion in progressively earlier stages of pregnancy.[60] The legal definition of personhood, however, has remained normatively closed to external irritations. To date, the Court has refused to recognise the unborn as a person entitled to similar legal protections.

Criminal sodomy laws were invalidated by means of a distinction between intimate relations and some of its forms, such as marriage/non-marriage, procreation/non-procreation, and heterosexual/non-heterosexual relations. Extending legal protection to intimate relations as a medium for development of self-identity makes inconsequential the side of the form on which a relationship lies. Legal protection of certain decisions concerning marriage, procreation and certain heterosexual relations is grounded, not in their particular virtues against their opposites, but in the central role of intimate relations in individuals' free definition of self-identity and happiness:

> We protect the decision whether to have a child because parenthood alters so dramatically an individual's self-definition, not because of demographic considerations or the Bible's command to be fruitful and multiply ... We protect the family because it contributes so powerfully to the happiness of individuals, not because of a preference for stereotypical households ... [for] the ability independently to define one's identity that is central to any concept of liberty.[61]

Statutes that prohibit a conduct between adult and consenting sexual partners are held 'demeaning' and 'controlling' of the 'existence' and 'destiny' of individuals and in violation of due process.[62]

---

60 One can say that most abortion jurisprudence has been in part responsive to the Court's self-created problem, i.e., *Roe*'s trimester timetable, according to which before the end of the first trimester the right of privacy was held supreme; in the second trimester the right to privacy was balanced against State interest in protecting a woman's life; in the third trimester, especially after fetus viability, the State was allowed to restrict and even proscribe abortion to protect potential life. In response, state legislatures enacted more restrictive abortion regulations to provoke test cases that would eventually lead to the overruling of *Roe*. Improvement in medical technology proved paradoxical as well: late-term abortions became increasingly less risky for the woman, while early abortions raised questions of fetus viability at progressively earlier stages. Thus, the trimester framework overburdened the Court and turned it into the 'country's *ex officio* medical board with powers to approve or disapprove medical and operative practices and standards throughout the United States' *Planned Parenthood of Central Mo.* v. *Danforth*, 428 U.S. 52, 99 (1976) (White, J., Concurring in part and dissenting in part). This has become increasingly the case in dealing with the so-called 'partial birth abortion' legislation.
61 *Bower* v. *Hardwick*, 478 U.S. 186, 205–6 (1986) (Blackmun, J., Dissenting).
62 *Lawrence* v. *Texas*, 539 U.S. 558 (2003).

Friendship of Foes?

Despite mutual rebuttals, Originalism and Living Constitutionalism provide the legal system with complementary strategies to deal with its own increasing complexity and that of its environment.[63] By concrete interpretations of the Constitution and the case at hand, Originalism reduces decisions to disparate events without a unifying principle.[64] In the absence of an abstract meaning, no generative rule for dealing with similar situations can emerge and no constitutional ground for new right-claims can be established. This can radically reduce the legal system's sensitivity to changes in its environment. That is what Living Constitutionalism tries to avoid. An excessive level of abstraction, on the other hand, can introduce into the legal system a surplus of innovations beyond its assimilative capacity, and undermine its ability for self-direction or normative closure. That is what Originalism claims to prevent. Nonetheless, their interplay increases the internal complexity of the legal system, albeit with different implications.

By limiting constitutional protections to explicitly guaranteed rights, Originalism permits more disparity among states with respect to implied rights. Thus, the evolution of the legal system is made subject to dynamics of local politics, rather than functional differentiation of law at the national level, let alone that of world society. Unlike the Court, which has to decide cases with some semblance of consistency, legislatures can compromise coherence for political expediency.

> One of the benefits of leaving regulation of this matter to the people rather than to the courts is that the people, unlike judges, need not carry things to their logical conclusion. The people may feel that their disapprobation of homosexual conduct is strong enough to disallow homosexual marriage, but not strong enough to criminalise private homosexual acts – and may legislate accordingly.[65]

Deference to state legislatures subjects legal recognition of new right-claims to the temporality of local politics. To the degree that statutes remain incongruent and yet constitutional, more variety is produced in the legal system without enabling the Court to offer legal solutions to their potential conflicts.

---

63   While initially perceived as radical opposites, in recent years some patterns of combination have emerged both on the bench and in legal scholarship. Originalism's judicial restraint has turned out to be highly selective (see, e.g., Howard and Segal 2002; Post and Siegel 2006; Siegel 2008); while attempts are made to recover the Originalist foundations of Living Constitutionalism (see, e.g., Balkin 2007). This, of course, is not the first time that conventional wisdom in legal scholarship about internal divides in American jurisprudence has been questioned. See Duxbury 1995; Hart 1977; and Tamanaha 2009 on the Realist/Formalist divide. See Sarat and Kearns 1995 on the instrumental/constitutive divide.

64   This is what Rubenfeld calls 'compartmentalisation of precedent', whereby one knows some rights are protected but does not know why (1989: 749).

65   *Lawrence v. Texas*, 539 U.S. 558 (2003) (Scalia, J., Dissenting).

Living Constitutionalism, however, allows for harmonisation of legal decisions at the national and, at times, global level.[66] By recognising some legal communications from other jurisdictions as its own, thus allowing them to trigger connective events in American law, it too produces variety in the legal system, but of a different kind. This time it is dynamics of local politics that are made subject to functional differentiation of law. By granting constitutional protection to implied rights, the Court produces irritations for local politics both inside and outside the legislature. Either way, the asynchrony between the law and social systems in its environment produces more conflict than consensus, as indicated by endless legislative efforts to supersede or circumvent judicial decisions not preferred by the governing party.

Neither side, however, appeals to extra-legal grounds to resolve these legal episodes. Legal communications from both sides of the bench are fully self-referential.[67] Even when morality is recognised or rejected as a legitimate ground for legislation, support for that position is found in law and precedent not in morality. This is well illustrated by comparison of *Bowers* (1986), which upheld the constitutionality of criminal sodomy laws, with *Lawrence* (2003), which overruled it.

In *Bowers* the Court denied that its prior judgments concerning family, marriage and procreation construed the Constitution to 'confer a right of privacy that extends to homosexual sodomy'. The basis for this assertion was the Court's own criterion for identifying implied rights and liberties that may qualify for heightened judicial protection (i.e., their 'deep roots' in the 'history and tradition' of the United States). Claiming 'ancient roots' for criminal sodomy laws, the Court refused to extend constitutional protection to homosexuality by means of 'judge-made constitutional law ... with no recognizable roots in the language or the design of the Constitution'.[68] With the right-claim failing the test of fundamentality, criminal sodomy laws were said to require only a 'rational basis' for their constitutionality. The Court recognised that rational basis without passing judgment on the morality of homosexual conduct. Rather, the question before the Court was whether morally grounded legislation had a strong enough rational basis to be upheld as constitutional. In a 5 to 4 decision the Court responded in the positive:

> The law, however, is constantly based on notions of morality, and if all laws representing essentially moral choices are to be invalidated under the Due Process Clause, the courts will be very busy indeed. Even respondent makes no such claim, but insists that majority sentiments about the morality of homosexuality

---

66 On the long history of the Court's use of 'foreign' law in constitutional decisions, which is strongly rejected by Originalism, see Farber 2007.

67 This is not necessarily true about legal commentaries on Court judgments. That may, in part, explain the limited influence of sociolegal scholarship and normative constitutional theory on Court decisions. See Balkin 2004: 1574–6); Posner 2008: 204–29.

68 *Bowers v. Hardwick*, 478 U.S. 186, 191–3 (1986).

should be declared inadequate. We do not agree, and are unpersuaded that the sodomy laws of some 25 States should be invalidated on this basis.[69]

Criminal sodomy laws were upheld, not on the ground of immorality of sodomy, but because there are many morally motivated and uncontested laws on the books:

> Countless judicial decisions and legislative enactments have relied on the ancient proposition that a governing majority's belief that certain sexual behaviour is 'immoral and unacceptable' constitutes a rational basis for regulation ... State laws against bigamy, same-sex marriage, adult incest, prostitution, masturbation, adultery, fornication, bestiality, and obscenity are likewise sustainable only in light of Bowers' validation of laws based on moral choices.[70]

In *Lawrence*, the Court overruled *Bowers* in a 6 to 3 decision rejecting both the ancient roots of criminal sodomy laws and the rational basis standard for their judicial review:

> There is no longstanding history in this country of laws directed at homosexual conduct as a distinct matter ... Early American sodomy laws were not directed at homosexuals as such but instead sought to prohibit non-procreative sexual activity more generally ... Laws prohibiting sodomy do not seem to have been enforced against consenting adults acting in private ... It was not until the 1970's that any State singled out same-sex relations for criminal prosecution, and only nine States have done so.[71]

Whereas *Bowers* required ancient roots for homosexuality to grant it constitutional protection, *Lawrence* required ancient roots for criminal sodomy laws to exempt them from strict scrutiny. The fact that the statute under scrutiny only concerned sodomy between homosexuals and not sodomy per se played an important role in selective ordering of legal communications. Concurring with the opinion of the Court in *Lawrence,* Justice O'Conner, who had previously voted for *Bowers* clarified the issue further:

> In Bowers ... [w]e rejected the argument that no rational basis existed to justify the law, pointing to the government's interest in promoting morality ... The only question in front of the Court in Bowers was whether the substantive component of the Due Process Clause protected a right to engage in homosexual sodomy ... Bowers did not hold that moral disapproval of a group is a rational basis under the

---

69   *Bowers v. Hardwick*, 478 U.S. 186, 196 (1986).
70   *Lawrence v. Texas*, 539 U.S. 558 (2003) (Scalia, J., Dissenting).
71   *Lawrence v. Texas*, 539 U.S. 558 (2003).

Equal Protection Clause to criminalize homosexual sodomy when heterosexual sodomy is not punished.[72]

In *Lawrence*, the Court explicitly acknowledged that many hold profound convictions about the immorality of homosexual conduct. Yet, it refused to grant the majority a right to 'use the power of the State to enforce these views on the whole society through operation of the criminal law'.[73]

> That certain, but by no means all, religious groups condemn the behavior at issue gives the State no license to impose their judgments on the entire citizenry. The legitimacy of secular legislation depends, instead, on whether the State can advance some justification for its law beyond its conformity to religious doctrine … The Constitution cannot control such prejudices, but neither can it tolerate them. Private biases may be outside the reach of the law, but the law cannot, directly or indirectly, give them effect.[74]

Bowers was overruled not as a lapse in moral judgement, but as an *error* in the law.

> Bowers was not correct when it was decided, and it is not correct today. It ought not to remain binding precedent. Bowers v. Hardwick should be and now is overruled.[75]

The dissenting opinion in *Bowers* became the majority opinion in *Lawrence* without a single moral argument for or against homosexuality. Instead, another selective history of constitutional and common law regulation of sexual conduct was offered and a different horizon was opened to connect criminal sodomy laws to the body of legal norms such that criminal sodomy laws lost their ground in the law and the Constitution.

In *Lawrence*, not only did the Court deny the immediate and intrinsic value of morality for legal decision making, but it also provided a way to judge the constitutionality of morally grounded legislation: it required legislatures to provide a ground for such legislation beyond the moral judgement of the majority. This confirms Cover's (1983) suggestion that contrary to conventional wisdom, in the United States some moral beliefs of minorities are entitled to constitutional protection. Thus, the law cannot simply announce the majority opinion as *the* morals of the nation.[76]

---

72 *Lawrence* v. *Texas*, 539 U.S. 558 (2003) (O'Conner, J., Concurring).
73 *Lawrence* v. *Texas*, 539 U.S. 558 (2003).
74 *Bowers* v. *Hardwick*, 478 U.S. 186, 211–12 (1986) (Blackmun, J., Dissenting).
75 *Lawrence* v. *Texas*, 539 U.S. 558 (2003).
76 A comparative historical analysis of the Court's jurisprudence on morally grounded legislation can yield interesting research questions for the normative closure thesis and

Seen as political practice (i.e., vehicles for conservative and liberal mobilisations),[77] Originalism, Living Constitutionalism and their interplay would be understood *primarily* in terms of changing balances of political forces in the United States; an example of American exceptionalism. The present analysis, however, draws attention to the world societal context of their emergence and invites investigations into their functional equivalents around the world.[78]

Judicial Review: Beyond Legal vs. Political

By taking jurisprudence seriously, social systems theory takes sociolegal studies beyond the old dichotomy of the Court's claim to autonomy, on the one hand, and the political character of its decisions, on the other. Despite, or perhaps because of, the interdependence of law and politics in constitutional states, neither system is reducible to the other. The constitution represents a form of structural coupling between the legal and political systems. It makes positive law the primary instrument for political organisation, and at the same time provides legal means for the disciplining of politics. The result is a higher degree of freedom and an acceleration of the internal dynamics of both law and politics. Restricting their influence on one another to channels provided by the constitution increases their mutual irritability immensely (Luhmann 1985: 404). The legal system and the political system remain autopoietic. Yet, constitutions provide an instrument for dissolving the circularity of their self-reference. They protect the illusion that politics can be legally constituted and limited, while at the same time exposing the legal system to political influences through legislation.

Not hierarchy, but centre/periphery, provides the proper model for understanding the relation between legislation and adjudication. As the centre of the legal system, the Court is the site of the emergence and unfolding of the paradox of law. The task of supervising the consistency of legal decisions belongs solely to the Court. The organisation and professionalisation of juridical competence, and formally equal access to the legal system, are to sustain generalised normative expectations about judicial independence and equality before the law. It is at the Court that we expect the highest degree of autonomy of the legal system. All other areas of law, including legislation, lie at the periphery of the legal system, and thus are more sensitive to disparate external irritations. The importance of this distinction between the Court and the legislature becomes more apparent if one considers that political motives are considered sufficient for legislation, but not for adjudication. A judiciary open to external pressures is considered corrupt by modern standards

---

provide empirical irritants for Luhmann's categorical understanding of autopoiesis and Teubner's (1993) graduated conception.

77   See Post and Siegel 2006.

78   Hirschl points to a similar divide over the interpretation of sacred texts in what he calls "constitutional theocracies" (2010: 218–26).

(Luhmann 2004: 292–304). That is why the thorny question of autonomy is raised with respect to the Court more than the legislature, the openness of which to influences of constituencies, corporations, lobbyists, etc., is common knowledge.

Conclusion

Social scientific and legal engagements with jurisprudence have mostly talked past each other. Descriptive and explanatory accounts of external-references of the legal system have remained at odds with the normative character of its internal-references. Recognising the indispensable role of the latter in the former, autopoietic theory has the potential to bridge this divide and emerge as a form of structural coupling between reflexive theories of law and the social sciences, particularly sociology. This would allow sociology to seriously engage self-descriptions of the legal system, while providing legal theory with relevant conceptual achievements of social systems theory.[79] Realising this potential requires research programmes that engage problematics concerning both. The unfolding of legal paradox in rights-based judicial review is one such problematic. Others remain to be constructed.

If the normative closure of the legal system is a requirement of functional differentiation, and if this closure is achieved at the level of second-order observations, then evolution of legal doctrine and jurisprudence could be examined in terms of coevolution of law and its environment. If fundamental rights are safeguards against de-differentiation, then variation in the order of emergence, development and scope of constitutionally guaranteed rights can be examined in terms of stages and dynamics of functional differentiation. Such investigations may in turn serve as irritations for reflexive theories of law in conceptual and doctrinal innovations. This is particularly important in the context of proliferating transnational regulations and fragmentation and incoherence of global law;[80] increasing importance of judicial and constitutional review concerning fundamental rights;[81] and the inadequacy of previous attempts to understand the significance of these developments without a sociological theory of society.

References

Ackerman, B., 'Oliver Wendell Holmes lectures: The living constitution', *Harvard Law Review*, 120 (2007), 1737–812.
Baghai, K., 'Privacy as a human right: a sociological theory', *Sociology* 46 (2012), forthcoming.

---

79 See Luhmann 2004: 459.
80 See, e.g., Cotterrell 2009; Fischer-Lescano and Teubner 2004; Gessner 1995.
81 See, e.g., Hirschl 2008; Shapiro and Sweet 2002; Sweet 2000.

Balkin, J. M., 'Abortion and original meaning', *Constitutional Commentary* 24 (2007), 292–352.

____, 'What "Brown" teaches us about constitutional theory', *Virginia Law Review* 90 (2004),1537–1577.

Bilder, M. S., 'Idea or practice: A brief historiography of judicial review', *Journal of Policy History* 20 (2008), 6–25.

Corwin, E. S., 'The establishment of judicial review I', *Michigan Law Review* 9 (1910), 102–25.

____, 'The establishment of judicial review II', *Michigan Law Review,* 9 (1911), 283-316.

Cotterrell, R., 'Law and sociology: Notes on the constitution and confrontations of disciplines', *Journal of Law and Society* 13 (1986), 9–34.

____, 'Subverting orthodoxy, making law central: A view of socio-legal studies', *Journal of Law and Society* 29 (2002), 632–44.

____, *Law, Culture and Society: Legal Ideas in the Mirror of Social Theory* (Aldershot: Ashgate, 2006).

____, 'Spectres of transnationalism: Changing terrains of sociology of law', *Journal of Law and Society* 36 (2009), 481–500.

Cover, R., 'The Supreme Court 1982. Foreword: Nomos and narrative', *Harvard Law Review* 97 (1983), 4–68.

Cross, F. B., and Nelson, B. J., 'Strategic institutional effects on Supreme Court decision making', *Northwestern University Law Review* 95 (2001), 1451–7.

Deflem, M., *Sociology of Law: Vision of a Scholarly Tradition* (Cambridge: Cambridge University Press, 2008).

Duxbury, N., *Patterns of American Jurisprudence* (Oxford: Oxford University Press, 1995).

Dworkin, R., 'Judicial discretion', *The Journal of Philosophy* 60 (1963), 624–38.

____, 'Hard cases', *Harvard Law Review* 88 (1975), 1057–109.

____, *Taking Rights Seriously* (Cambridge, MA.: Harvard University Press, 1977).

____, 'Equality, democracy, and Constitution: We the people in the Court', *Alberta Law Review* 28 (1990), 324–46.

____, 'Hart's postscript and the character of political philosophy', *Oxford Journal of Legal Studies* 24 (2004), 1–37.

Farber, D. A., 'The Supreme Court, the law of nations, and citations of foreign law: The lessons of history', *California Law Review* 95 (2007): 1335–65.

Fischer-Lescano, A., and G. Teubner, 'The vain search for legal unity in the fragmentation of global law', *Michigan Journal of International Law* 25 (2004), 999–1046.

Fletcher, G. P., 'Paradoxes in legal thought', *Columbia Law Review* 85 (1985), 1263–92.

Freeman, M., (ed.), *Law and Sociology: Current Legal Issues* (Oxford: Oxford University Press, 2006).

Friedman, L. M., 'The law and society movement', *Stanford Law Review* 38 (1986), 763–80.

Gee, G., 'Regulating abortion in the United States after *Gonzales* v *Carhart*', *The Modern Law Review* 70 (2007), 979–92.
George, T. E., and L. Epstein, 'On the nature of Supreme Court decision making', *The American Political Science Review* 86 (1992), 323–37.
Gessner, V., 'Global approaches in the sociology of law: Problems and challenges', *Journal of Law and Society* 22 (1995), 85–96.
Gillman, H., 'Regime politics, jurisprudential regimes, and unenumerated rights', *Journal of Constitutional Law* 9 (2006), 107–19.
Goldstein, L. F., 'Popular sovereignty, the origins of judicial review, and the revival of unwritten law', *The Journal of Politics* 48 (1986), 51–71.
____, 'Judicial review and democratic theory: Guardian democracy vs. representative democracy', *The Western Political Quarterly* 40 (1987), 391–412.
Grey, T. C., 'Do we have an unwritten constitution?' *Stanford Law Review* 27 (1975), 703–18.
Harel, A., 'Rights-based judicial review: A democratic justification', *Law and Philosophy* 22 (2003), 247–76.
Hart, H. L. A., 'Positivism and the separation of law and morals', *Harvard Law Review* 71 (1958), 593–629.
____, 'American jurisprudence through English eyes: The nightmare and the noble dream', *Georgia Law Review* 11 (1977), 969–82.
_____, *The Concept of Law*, 2nd edn (Oxford: Oxford University Press, 1994 [1st edn 1961]).
Harvey, A., and B. Friedman, 'Pulling punches: Congressional constraints on the Supreme Court's constitutional rulings, 1987–2000', *Legislative Studies Quarterly* 31(2006), 533–62.
Heffernan, L., '*Stenberg* v *Carhart*: A divided US Supreme Court debates partial birth abortion', *The Modern Law Review* 64 (2001), 618–27.
Hirschl, R., 'The judicialization of mega-politics and the rise of political courts', *Annual Review of Political Science* 28 (2008), 93–118.
____, *Constitutional Theocracy* (Cambridge: Harvard University Press, 2010).
Howard, R. M., and J. A. Segal, 'An original look at originalism', *Law & Society Review* 36 (2002), 113–38.
____, 'A preference for deference? The Supreme Court and judicial review', *Political Research Quarterly* 57 (2004), 131–43.
Lim, Y., 'An empirical analysis of Supreme Court Justices' decision making', *The Journal of Legal Studies* 29 (2000), 721–52.
Lindquist, S. A., and D. E. Klein, 'The influence of jurisprudential considerations on Supreme Court decision making: A study of conflict cases', *Law & Society Review* 40 (2006), 135–62.
Lindquist, S. A., and R. S. Solberg, 'Judicial review by the Burger and Rehnquist Courts: Explaining Justices' responses to constitutional challenges', *Political Research Quarterly* 60 (2007), 71–90.
Luhmann, N., *Differentiation of Society* (New York: Columbia University Press, 1982).

____, *A Sociological Theory of Law* (London; Boston: Routledge & Kegan Paul, 1985 [1971]).
____, 'The third question: the creative use of paradoxes in law and legal history', *Journal of Law and Society* 15 (1988), 153–65.
____, 'Legal argumentation: An analysis of its form', *The Modern Law Review* 58 (1995), 285–98.
____, *Law as a Social System* (Oxford: Oxford University Press, 2004).
Marlowe, M., *Jurisprudential Regimes: The Supreme Court, Civil Rights, and the Life Cycle of Judicial Doctrine* (LFB Scholarly Publishing LLC, 2011).
McBain, H. L., *The Living Constitution: A Consideration of the Realities and Legends of Our Fundamental Law* (New York: Macmillan Company, 1927).
Mishler, W., and R. S. Sheehan, 'Public opinion, the attitudinal model and Supreme Court decision making: A micro analytic perspective', *Journal of Politics* 58 (1996), 169–200.
Nobles, R., and D. Schiff, 'Why do judges talk the way they do?', *International Journal of Law in Context* 5 (2009), 25–49.
O'Neill, J., *Originalism in American Law and Politics: A Constitutional History* (Baltimore; London: The Johns Hopkins University Press, 2005).
Paterson, J., and G. Teubner, 'Changing maps: Empirical legal autopoiesis', *Social and Legal Studies* 7 (1998), 451–86.
Posner, R. A., *How Judges Think* (Cambridge, MA: Harvard University Press, 2008).
Post, R., and R. B. Siegel, 'Originalism as political practice: The Right's living Constitution', *Fordham Law Review* 75 (2006), 546–74.
Rehnquist, W. H., 'The notion of a living constitution', *Harvard Journal of Law and Public Policy*, 209 (2005), 401–15.
Richards, M. J., and H. M. Kritzer, 'Jurisprudential regimes in Supreme Court decision making', *The American Political Science Review* 96 (2002), 305–20.
Rosenberg, G. N., *The Hollow Hope: Can Courts Bring about Social Change?* (Chicago: The University of Chicago Press, 1991).
Rostow, E. V., 'The democratic character of judicial review', *Harvard Law Review* 66 (1952), 193–224.
Rubenfeld, J., 'The right of privacy', *Harvard Law Review* 102 (1989), 737–807.
Sarat, A., and T. R. Kearns, 'Beyond the great divide: Forms of legal scholarship and everyday life', in A. Sarat and T.R. Kearns (eds), *Law in Everyday Life* (Ann Arbor: The University of Michigan Press, 1995), 21–6.
Scalia, A., 1989. 'Originalism: the lesser evil', *University of Cincinnati Law Review* 57 (1989), 849–65.
Segal, J. A., and A. D. Cover, 'Ideological values and the votes of U.S. Supreme Court Justices', *The American Political Science Review* 83 (1989), 557–65.
Segal, J. A., and H. J. Spaeth, *The Supreme Court and the Attitudinal Model* (New York: Cambridge University Press, 1993).

Segal, J.A., 'The Supreme Court deference to Congress: An examination of the Marxist model', in Clayton C. W. and H. Gillman (eds), *Supreme Court Decision Making: New Institutionalist Approaches* (Chicago and London: The University of Chicago Press, 1999), 237–53.

Shapiro, M., 'Juridicalization of politics in the United States', *International Political Science Review* 15 (1994), 101–12.

Shapiro, M., and A. S. Sweet, *On Law, Politics & Judicialization* (Oxford: Oxford University Press, 2002).

Siegel, R. B., 'Dead or alive: Originalism as popular constitutionalism in Heller', *Harvard Law Review* 122/1 (2008). 191–245.

Solove, D. J., *Understanding Privacy* (Cambridge, MA: Harvard University Press, 2009).

Songer, D. R., and R. S. Sheehan, 'Interest group success in the courts: amicus participation in the Supreme Court', *Political Research Quarterly* 46 (1993), 339–54.

Stephenson, M. C., '"When the devil turns …": The political foundations of independent judicial review', *The Journal of Legal Studies* 32 (2003), 59–89.

Strauss, D. A., *The Living Constitution* (Oxford: Oxford University Press, 2010).

Sweet, A. S., *Governing with Judges: Constitutional Politics in Europe* (Oxford: Oxford University Press, 2000).

____, 'Path Dependence, Precedent, and Judicial Power', in M. Shapiro and A. S. Sweet, *On Law, Politics & Judicialization* (Oxford: Oxford University Press, 2002), 112–35.

Tamanaha, B. Z., *Beyond the Formalist–Realist Divide: The Role of Politics in Judging* (Princeton: Princeton University Press, 2009).

Teubner, G., *Law as an Autopoietic System* (Oxford: Blackwell, 1993).

Thornhill, C., *A Sociology of Constitutions: Constitutions and State Legitimacy in Historical–Sociological Perspective* (Cambridge: Cambridge University Press, 2011).

Tribe, L. H., 'A constitution we are amending: In defence of a restrained judicial role', *Harvard Law Review* 97 (1983), 433–45.

Tushnet, M., *Taking the Constitution Away from the Courts* (Princeton: Princeton University Press, 1999).

___, *Weak Courts, Strong Rights: Judicial Review and Social Welfare Rights in Comparative Constitutional Law* (Princeton: Princeton University Press, 2008).

Verschraegen, G., 'Human rights and modern society: A sociological analysis from the perspective of systems theory', *Journal of Law and Society* 29 (2002), 258–81.

Whittington, K. E., 'The new originalism', *Georgetown Journal of Law and Public Policy* 2 (2004), 599–613.

Cases Cited

Akron v. *Akron Center for Reproductive Health*, 462 U.S. 416 (1983).
Beal v. *Doe*, 432 U.S. 438 (1977).
Bellotti v. *Baird*, 443 U.S. 662 (1979).
Bowers v. *Hardwick*, 478 U.S. 186 (1986).
Boy Scouts of America v. *Dale*, 530 U.S. 640 (2000).
DeMay v. *Roberts*, 46 Mich. 160, 9 N.W. 146 (1881).
Gonzales v. *Carhart*, 550 U.S. 124 (2007).
Griswold v. *Connecticut*, 381 U.S. 479 (1965).
Harris v. *McRae*, 448 U.S. 297(1980).
Lawrence v. *Texas*, 539 U.S. 558 (2003).
Maher v. *Roe*, 432 U.S. 464 (1977).
Marbury v. *Madison*, 5 U.S. (1 Cranch) 137 (1803).
Planned Parenthood of Central Missouri v. *Danforth*, 428 U.S. 52 (1976).
Planned Parenthood of Southeastern Pennsylvania v. *Casey*, 505 U.S. 833(1992).
Poelker v. *Doe*, 432 U.S. 519 (1977).
Roe v. *Wade*, 410 U.S. 113 (1973).
Romer v. *Evans*, 517 U.S. 620 (1996).
Rust v. *Sullivan*, 500 U.S. 173 (1991).
Stenberg v. *Carhart*, 530 U.S. 914 (2000).
Thornburgh v. *American College of Obstetricians & Gynaecologists*, 476 U.S. 747 (1986).
Webster v. *Reproductive Health Services*, 452 U.S. 450 (1989).

Chapter 13

Structural Coupling between the Systems of Law and the Media: The Contrasting Examples of Criminal Conviction and Criminal Appeal

Richard Nobles and David Schiff

Introduction

Luhmann tells us that the 'mass media are not media in the sense of conveying information from those who know to those who do not know. They are media to the extent that they make available background knowledge and carry on writing it as a starting point for communication.'[1] Background knowledge is stored in the system's memory:

> For the social system, memory consists in being able to take certain assumptions about reality as given and known about in every communication, without having to introduce them specifically into the communication and justify them. This memory is at work in all the operations of the social system, that is, in every communication, it contributes to the ongoing checks on consistency by keeping one eye on the known world, and it excludes as unlikely any information that is too risky.[2]

The Legal System in the Memory of the Media

Memory requires the grouping of experiences into consistent frameworks of meaning, and their retention as the basis of comparison for further experience. Each functioning social subsystem (law, politics, media, etc.) communicates by actualising its memory, and assuming that there is a reality that can be known and represented by utilising that memory. However, each functioning system has a different memory and set of consistent frameworks, and makes different assumptions about the reality which it represents in its communications. The mass media observes events and then relies on its programmes to determine which events

---

1 Luhmann 2000: 66.
2 Luhmann 2000: 65.

should be represented as meaningful. In other words, as with all functioning social subsystems, it constructs its version of reality. But what has become commonplace in the modern world is the extent to which the constructions of reality of the mass media can have a momentum that 'irritates' other functioning systems. The mass media might or might not have a self-reflective grasp of this, understanding how their constructions alter the reality that they construct. Thus, for example, Luhmann observes that the political system and the mass media system 'irritate' each other a great deal (2000: 67–8). Political actors will regularly attempt to be mentioned in the media, while what is constructed by the media as political news will commonly be responded to immediately by political actors.

The situation seems to be very different between the legal system and the media system. What is routinely apparent is either deafness or stability of expectations, rather than irritation.[3] Of course, law can be irritated by the media, but despite stories that might be expected to provoke reaction many nevertheless tend to be responded to with either deafness or self-reflective closure. Newspaper reports about trials can have particular consequences in the law relating to contempt of court,[4] unless they conform to the legal rules. But the law specifically and determinedly sets itself against 'trial by media'. The more usual relationship between law and the media is that of stable expectations that are expressed in the memory of the assumptions that underpin the particular communications made. The example of the assumptions that lie behind the communication of the event of criminal conviction can illustrate this, despite the different meanings constructed around those events within law and the media. The legal system self-observes its construction of convictions in terms of the procedures that produce them, and the rights of defendants to trials conducted in accordance with those procedures. Within the media, convictions are understood as events with factual meaning: that the persons convicted have actually committed their crimes. These differences in meaning are productive for both systems. The media is provided with a constant supply of authoritative and 'objective facts' with which to generate newsworthy stories. The legal system attracts resources as a body which treats defendants fairly as well as 'solving' crimes.

Criminal Conviction and Media Stories

The legal system, in the memory of the media, is an acknowledged and important source of facts and stories. In a world of contested moral values and many other uncertainties, it both defines crimes and establishes who has committed them.

---

3 A communication that requires some response, alteration or reconstruction by the system that is perturbed.

4 Contempt of court rules determine the conditions under which 'unacceptable' reporting about trials or pre-trial might be liable to sanction, or could even have the effect of determining that a defendant has not had a 'fair trial' due to adverse press publicity. (See Luhmann's reference to these rules, 2000: 24)

Criminal conviction allows media stories to move from allegations and the examination of evidence, and contested interpretations of events, to the fact that a particular person has committed a particular crime. Writing after conviction, the media not only has the fact of who committed this crime, it often can extract, usually from the prosecution evidence or comments by the judge, what are presented as facts about how the crime was committed, and with what motive. The media's memory assumes that what does not need to be justified is the fact of conviction which can be checked for consistency with the many other stories about those who have committed crimes, stories about the impact on victims, the dangers for society in general, etc. It is 'risky' to attempt to write a story about how a conviction might not represent the truth. It is risky not because the legal system has any rules about such a story being written after the end of a trial (the rules of contempt of court apply pre-trial or during a trial but rarely after it), but rather because it disturbs the memory of how stories have been and are being written – so many other stories that rely on the factual guilt of an accused person would need to be rephrased, and the themes that those stories address (such as what it means for society that such crimes are committed, and by such offenders) would need to be rewritten or not written at all. What the legal system offers to the media is news, namely new information about a real event, a trial, in which an offender has become liable to punishment because they did what they were accused of doing. This news is a staple diet for actualising the media's memory and the many potential themes associated with that memory.

This understanding of the end result of a criminal trial, a criminal conviction, differs from the internal legal understanding of trial and conviction – the legal system's memory. The legal system, as the system which has generated the conviction, is more aware of itself, and the processes by which that conviction has been produced: charges, pleadings, evidence, discovery, examination, cross-examination, summing up, jury deliberation (for legal systems that rely on juries) and verdict. Each of these stages may be viewed by its participants as making a contribution to the establishment of the truth of a conviction, but each is also understood in terms of legal rules and due process. Any of these stages may go wrong, not in terms of a demonstrable reduction in the accuracy of an eventual conviction, but simply in terms of what, according to the standards and procedures of the system, ought to have occurred.[5]

At the moment of a criminal conviction both the media and the legal system are likely to address a defendant in similar terms. Even though there may be journalists who are well informed about the processes of trial, and lawyers who are completely sceptical about the ability of their system to identify factual guilt, at the point of conviction it is rarely possible, within either system, to communicate on any basis other than an acceptance of factual guilt. The judge has to accept the verdict, as does the defence lawyer, who must now move from demonstrating their clients' innocence to mitigating their sentences – a speech in which there will

---

5   For a fuller statement of these different priorities, see Nobles and Schiff 2006.

be no reference to their clients' innocence. The journalist is similarly constrained – the conviction as an authoritative statement of guilt will usually offer the only possibility for a story.[6]

One can conclude that the media has an enormous investment in convictions, and that, by comparison, the media has relatively small investment in the processes, particularly trial processes, which produce convictions. By investment we mean simply that conviction is a communication that the media can use over and over again, in a relatively stable manner. A conviction identifies who has committed a crime. It produces a fact, an authoritative fact, around which a news story can be constructed. But the stable manner in which conviction is used by the media is what produces the lack of commitment to the particularities of the legal procedures which produce it. The news story which is available directly upon conviction is in terms of the guilt of the person convicted. The manner in which the conviction has been produced can be plundered for details of the motive and actions of the guilty individual. But otherwise the manner in which this decision has been reached is unlikely to form part of this news; indeed, if anything, it has the capacity to reduce the newsworthiness of the story.

The Legal System and the Media: An Example of Structural Coupling

The stability of the structural coupling between the legal system and the media which exists at the moment of conviction is, however, not duplicated when the legal system communicates about convictions in the processes of criminal appeals. The latent differences in memory of the two functioning systems can generate a sustained and hostile media reporting on the legal system, based on the legal system's inability to reproduce the media's understanding of convictions in terms of factual guilt. From the perspective of the media, criminal appeals which succeed on the basis of due process are 'technical acquittals',[7] whilst appeals that fail in the face of widespread media reportage that prisoners are factually innocent, can result in further reporting in terms of reduced public confidence in the criminal justice system (or even a 'crisis of public confidence').[8] From the perspective of the legal system, which understands its own operations as justice, such media attacks (irritations) threaten the ability of the legal system to deliver criminal justice on a routine basis (they perturb the routine operations of the legal system).

---

6   For a detailed analysis of media reporting at conviction in one particular high-profile case, and then its reporting on the first and second appeal, see Nobles and Schiff 2004. For an analysis of the 'values' (including entertainment values) involved in media reporting about crime, see Schlesinger and Tumber 1994, especially chs 7–9.

7   This perspective is also a common basis for criticism by political actors.

8   We have demonstrated how this theme arose in media reporting of criminal appeals in the UK between 1989 and 1992 (Nobles and Schiff 2000: ch. 4).

The difference in the memories of the legal system and the media system built on their different understandings of trial processes and the resultant meaning of a criminal conviction – the one almost wholly committed to convictions as the expression of factual truths, the other divided between ideas of truth and ideas of rights and due process – become apparent at the point at which the media tries to represent what a successful appeal amounts to as a newsworthy story. From a starting point that conviction represents the truth of an individual's factual guilt, a successful appeal should represent an individual's factual innocence (and what is newsworthy about that is the tragedy of false imprisonment, the deficiency of the legal system or some part of it, the desperation of the victim or their family, etc.). However, if for the legal system the condition of those who are not convicted, or whose convictions are quashed on appeal, is not factual innocence, but only a presumption of innocence, then the legal system's memory will have organised its frameworks of meaning in very different ways. The usual[9] basis for quashing a conviction is not simply an acceptance of the factual innocence of the prisoner, but the demonstration of an error in the processes that led to the conviction – a breach of the appellant's rights. Where the media accepts a version of the legal system's own understanding of the nature of appeals, that is, that the successful appellant has not been declared innocent, but has been released, or sent for retrial, on the basis of some error of procedure, then the media has very little to say. Within the media, if there is any story here, it is that large numbers of convicted prisoners are freed on the basis of legal technicalities. This is, of course, not a significant 'irritation' for the legal system, however it may irritate the political system and encourage a political response (a change to the law). In other words, such a story opens the legal system to political initiatives. A recent example in the UK was the government's consultation paper 'Quashing Convictions'.[10] The consultation paper relied on a case that had received considerable media coverage, and which was utilised by the media, and in this political initiative, as an example of a successful appeal described as a 'technical acquittal'[11] of a terrorist offender.

---

9 Factual innocence as a statement made by the Court of Appeal on quashing a conviction is a very rare occurrence. Its rarity is why it is possible for media stories about such rare events to be run in terms of why a particular miscarriage is 'one of the worst examples'. Although rare, there are contemporary examples which are reported on invariably by referring back to previous cases of factual innocence. For a recent example, see the reporting in all UK newspapers on 28 March 2009 of the successful appeal of Sean Hodgson. When such an appeal arises, the form of the media report is consistent – there is an easy story to tell.

10 See, especially, the foreword by the then Home Secretary John Reid and the strong reactions to it: http://www.nio.gov.uk/response_to_quashing_convictions_consultation_paper_october_2007.pdf. This recent history is succinctly analysed by Elks 2008: ch. 2.

11 The *Mullen* case. However, abuse of process is hardly 'technical' for the legal system. And, more significant, the legal system's approach to appeals does not accept that 'technical acquittals' arise. Their memory always involves the relationship between

The media story and political initiative both represented a 'memory' which is not consistent with the legal system's self-observations of its own operations, but clearly significant to those of the media and politics. That memory involves stories and political argument about what the public want: namely a populist view that the criminal justice system may be too lenient or favour the rights of defendants over those of their victims. However, these proposals were in the end dropped after unanimous criticism from all sections of the legal system. Those criticisms taken together amounted to a clear expression of the impossibility of being able to operate these proposals within the legal system. It was at this point that an impasse was reached. The legal system, it would appear, is organised to consider the relationship between rights, due process and truth rather than to consider each separately. As such 'technical acquittals' do not occur, a breach of a suspect's rights is an opportunity to consider to what extent that breach might or might not have been significant in relation to the trial and the likelihood that the defendant was guilty of the crime alleged.

A further difficulty for the structural coupling between the legal system and the media arises from the media's understanding of cases in which appeals do not succeed. These may be cases in which the media has become engaged in the campaign of the appellants concerned, or their families. Such involvement may establish as part of the media's 'memory' a predisposition to believe in the appellant's factual innocence. Here a successful appeal will be reported as if it represented, or ought to represent, a declaration of innocence: that is the easy story. But if the appeal is unsuccessful then a different story may arise.[12] The predisposition to believe in the appellant's factual innocence will have been generated by processes, and communications, which arise outside of the legal system, and which cannot be duplicated by the legal system. Examples may assist. Part of the media's willingness to believe in the innocence of prisoners is the status of persons who declare similar beliefs. Thus when campaigns result in public figures declaring their support, which is likely to attract a media story, the appeal process is more likely to be reported as a vindication of innocence, and not a procedural error. As one of the Maguire Seven (a famous terrorist case of the 1970s), Giuseppe Conlon's campaign received a particular boost from the support of Archbishop of Westminster Basil Hume, who was convinced that a devout Catholic would not risk eternal damnation by maintaining a false claim of innocence to his priest on his deathbed. This is not something that the legal system can reproduce. For legal purposes, it is simply not evidence. Another example is

---

due process and factual guilt; their programmes adopt that relationship; their operations represent it.

12   It appears that there are times when the media is interested in such stories, but times when they are rare, suggesting that editorial policies make a significant difference to whether such stories are considered newsworthy (remembering that there will always be some appellants who will continue to protest their innocence despite the failure of their appeals, or further applications to relevant bodies).

Chris Mullin's interview, on a confidential basis, with members of the IRA who confessed to the bombings for which the Birmingham Six (another of the famous 1970s terrorist cases) had been convicted.[13] Again, whatever its plausibility, this was not information that could be accessed by the legal system. These are extreme examples, but they do make an important point: there is no realistic possibility for the appeal processes of the legal system to be redesigned so as to be able to take account of all the information that can be utilised by the media in forming a view that prisoners are factually innocent. If one tried, one would be chasing a mirage. The size of the legal system's difficulties becomes even more apparent if one moves to more mundane forms of information. Belief in the innocence of some of those who only succeeded in their appeals after many years of imprisonment and failed appeals, such as the well-known 1970s IRA terrorist cases of the Maguire Seven,[14] Guildford Four[15] and Birmingham Six was largely a consequence of biographical enquiries. The more one learned about these persons, the less likely it seemed that they would have been chosen by the IRA as mainland operatives. Admittedly, part of the power of this evidence is the media's changing reporting of the nature of this organisation, which had changed over two decades, from that of a threat located within a suspect Irish immigrant community to that of a tightly organised and disciplined body. But neither the changing perception of this organisation, nor the personal history of these defendants, comes within what the Court of Appeal treats as evidence capable of justifying a successful appeal.

Alongside the use of information and materials that are not accessible to the legal system, one finds the media making use of material that was accessible to the legal system at trial but is not, or at least not in the same way, available on appeal. Within the media, the plundering of the prosecution case, which is often used to flesh out the story on conviction, is replaced by a plundering of the defence case, once the media has decided to give credence to claims of factual innocence. This process cannot be repeated on appeal, not simply because any retrial by an appeal court would have to be more impartial, and give credence to both prosecution and defence evidence, but because appeals are not retrials; they operate only as reviews of the original trial. In their review of a conviction, the Court of Appeal does not start looking at all the evidence afresh. Instead, it begins by identifying what evidence the jury must be taken to have believed in forming the decision to convict. Having identified what facts they believe were accepted by the jury in order to find the prisoner guilty, the appeal court will not disagree with those findings, simply because alternate judgments are possible. They presume them to be true. From this starting point, errors of procedure, and new evidence, are then considered to see if they might have made a jury reach a different conclusion. If one compares this with the kind of exercise carried out by investigative journalists, one would say that an appeal to the Court of Appeal is both more liberal and more conservative than its

---

13   Mullin 1997.
14   Kee 1989.
15   McKee and Franey 1988.

media counterpart. On the one hand, a successful appeal only requires that the Court of Appeal believe that the error or new evidence 'might' have made a difference to the jury. In cases of procedural error, this is easy to translate in the media as 'getting off' on appeal due to a technicality. On the other hand, this is an incredibly conservative approach. New evidence or procedural errors have far less potential to overturn a conclusion that a prisoner is guilty if you start from the presumption that the facts accepted by the jury are true, than by looking at all the evidence afresh. The difference between these two approaches is caught in the claim that appellants face a reverse burden of proof at the Court of Appeal.

The gap between a media and legal construction of a miscarriage case grows larger when one looks at the full panoply of restrictions that surround appeals. Evidence available at trial, even if not led, is generally not accepted at any appeal.[16] This restriction is justified within the legal system by the need for finality. The accused must not be allowed to run two defences, one at trial and another on appeal. But this commitment is not part of the media's framework of reference – it is difficult to think of what within the media's memory mirrors such an approach. A further significant contribution to the gap between the two systems arises from the actual processes of extracting evidence. A reporter writes, or films, and edits. A trial and appeal involve examination and cross-examination. The same witness may appear completely reliable within one process, and not so within the other.

Conclusion

As systems that not only observe the world but also themselves, and organise their observations into frameworks which allow them to construct their realities, the media system and the legal system structurally couple. The meanings that they give to events are never the same, but might well create stable expectations. Criminal convictions as events allows this, most of the time. Indeed, criminal convictions are a staple diet of newsworthy news for the media. But that stability is not built on the same memory, the same taken for granted reality, or the same risks. The recognition of 'uneducated' media reporting has led to the development of press officers for courts, programmes geared toward educating the public, cross-system organisations that are sensitive to the internal understandings of different systems, and attempts to produce greater symmetry between them. But, not only can this never be 'successful' but it also tends to lead to changes that reflect subtle and complex patterns of communication. To operate self-reflectively enables the development of this subtlety and complexity. However, that brings with it new problems and further misunderstanding.

---

16   There are, of course, exceptions about which there is a significant amount of technical case law, but case law of such technicality that it is not likely to be available to journalists as a story that will interest their readership.

The legal system and the media structurally couple over the meaning of criminal convictions, not by operating with the same meanings, but by relying on each other and thus producing stable expectations. However, those different meanings have implications for this structural coupling when events of, or leading to, the outcome of criminal appeals arise. The legal system does not 'create' the meanings of miscarriage of justice generated by the media, and has great difficulty in developing responses that can control those meanings and their attendant stories. Indeed, in many ways, it finds the task impossible. This does not mean that attempts will not be made, but their success is contingent on factors that the legal system can neither control nor create.

References

Elks, L., *Righting Miscarriages of Justice?* (London: Justice, 2008).

Kee, R., *Trial and Error: The Maguires, the Guildford Pub Bombings and British Justice* (Harmondsworth: Penguin, 1989).

Luhmann, N., *The Reality of the Mass Media*, trans. K. Cross (Oxford: Polity Press, 2000).

McKee, G. and R. Franey, *Time Bomb: Irish Bombers, English Justice and the Guildford Four* (London: Bloomsbury, 1988).

Mullin, C., *Error of Judgement: The Truth about the Birmingham Bombings* (Dublin: Poolbeg Press, 1997).

Nobles, R. and D. Schiff, *Understanding Miscarriages of Justice* (Oxford: Oxford University Press, 2000).

____, 'A Story of Miscarriage: Law in the Media', *Journal of Law and Society* 31 (2004), 221–44.

____, 'Theorising the Criminal Trial and Criminal Appeal: Finality, Truth and Rights', in A. Duff et al. (eds), *The Trial on Trial*, vol. 2 (Oxford: Hart Publishing, 2006), ch.14.

Schlesinger, P. and H. Tumber, *Reporting Crime: The Media Politics of Criminal Justice* (Oxford: Clarendon Press, 1994).

Chapter 14
Constituting Constitutions beyond the State: Polycontextural Constitutionalism of the World Society

Lasha Bregvadze

From Observing Systems to Constituting Constitutions

The metaphor of "observing systems," initiated somehow as a strange but undoubtedly innovative idea, has been transformed into a fruitful and even stimulating concept. Already the title of the collection of essays by Heinz von Foerster—*Observing Systems*—declares the whole essence of cybernetics of cybernetics, second-order cybernetics.[1] The interplay of first- and second-order observations, mutual interdependence and self-reference of subject and object, opening up the possibility of observing observers and systematizing systems, leads to new questions and formulates new answers. Both the conceptual strength and the beauty of the metaphor of "observing systems" with its double meaning has inspired and attracted many scholars from different branches of the sciences, including "sociological observers of the legal system."[2]

The general purpose of this chapter is to apply the idea of "observing systems" to modern constitutional theory, especially as presented within the current sociolegal debates which form the core of the emerging hybrid discourse—the *sociology of constitutions*. The aim is to observe how new *forms* of constitution are being constructed within the different sectors of functionally differentiated

---

1 The volume was edited by Francisco J. Varela in 1982. The second collection of essays by von Foerster from 2003 continues the tradition as well, this time pushing the cognitive mechanisms even further with the title *Understanding Understanding*.

2 Notably N. Luhmann and G. Teubner. Luhmann, while developing the paradoxical idea about the production of the unity of the system by the system itself and making a distinction between internal and external reference, employs the metaphor developed by von Foerster "in the double sense of the English -*ing* form" (Luhmann 1992: 1420), the word "observing" meaning the observer as a subject but also as the object of the observation at the same time. Teubner, examining the idea about foundation of law placed by the deconstructionist tradition on the arbitrary violence of law itself, proposes an alternative vision using the concept of second-order observation, symbolized by the metaphor of "observing systems" as a first answer made by systems theory to the challenge posed by deconstruction, "paradoxificaton" being the second answer (Teubner 1997a: 764).

world society and how they are themselves constructing, and paradoxically even constituting, social reality, the environment of meaningful societal communications and the unity of world society. Empirical facts demonstrating the emergence of new constitutional forms and even constitution-building processes beyond the control mechanisms of the nation-state and public polity presuppose and indicate the actual state of the problem. Certain needs of the societal environment to constitute its functionally structured unity due to the particular, internal constitutional logic can also be detected. The paradoxical unity of the world society based on its functional differentiation and structural schematization raises questions about the constitutional stability of the global system in the sense of maintaining balance between certain subsystems and organizational orders and protecting from the dominance of concrete functional rationalities in the environment. How are the conditions for dynamic stability, leading toward reflexive evolution, reached within the pluralistic world society? How does society reinforce the order of its structural constituencies based on normative closure and autopoietic self-reproduction of the fragmented totality? Can the concept of constitution be productively used in the discourse of social evolution? Is this the case where concepts like composition, structuration, construction, and constitution merge, complement, and reinforce each other?

The idea of *constituting constitutions* is an attempt to adopt the original argument of Heinz von Foerster for observing current constitutional transformations within the different sectors of social environment simultaneously as objects and subjects of evolutionary processes. Constitutions being produced within the different sectors of the world society at the same time reproduce their own meaningful boundaries and constitute the unity of world society, structuring internal components of social interactions, organizations, and functionally differentiated subsystems, reinforcing balance, stability, and "division of functions" between different forms of social systems and societal communications. Constitutions constitute and are constituted.

The Problem of the Emerging Constitutional Forms

"The Basic Law of the State"—in general, this is an accepted formulation of the concept of constitution within dogmatic jurisprudence. Thus, the constitution of the nation-state—i.e. a basic law of a certain sovereign state—is recognized as a conventional model of the constitution. It is actually unimaginable within established constitutional dogmatics to think about constitutions without a corresponding nation-state: indeed, for traditional legal doctrine, it could be taboo. State-centered constitutionalism, based on the principles of legal monism, implicitly excludes the very idea of legal pluralism. According to the doctrine of legal positivism, the law is defined as the system of norms established and enforced by the state and the constitution—the set of supreme, highest norms.

On the other hand, in the epoch of postmodernism, due to the processes of fragmented globalization and pluralization of autonomous social spheres, accompanied by the rapid privatization of the lifeworld, a new "reading" of societal reality emerges, followed by a reconsideration and reinvention of conventional concepts and standards, demolition of the classical narratives, and, in general, a deconstruction of social reality. Emerging and all-encompassing processes of globalization and privatization within the global society presuppose the reconsideration of the basic modern evolutionary achievements, such as the model of the nation-state, liberal legalism, ideals of the legal and social state, rule of law, differentiation of the center and the periphery, private–public dichotomy, and the concept of the constitution of a sovereign state itself. The old concepts have to be adapted to the modern global social dynamics. From this point of view, in the sense of determination of social changes, *globalization* has to be understood as the process (or the totality of the processes) determining the dynamics of functionally differentiated social communications and, through the reproduction and generalization of local spaces, creating a global unity, an all-encompassing system of the world society.[3] And *privatization*, as the second basic trend of the postmodern epoch, has to be defined broadly as the shift of the mechanisms of legitimacy and social control from the public to private actors and networks, as the replacement of the dominant political players or institutions by the private organizational structures, as the shift from "political government" to "private governance," and the replacement of public legal control by private justice.[4] The shift from "hierarchical to circular models" (Febbrajo 1988) in regulation exerts its influence even on science describing new evolutionary processes.

The processes of globalization and privatization, undoubtedly also accompanied by the spread of digitalization, exert their influences upon such an important product of the public-political sphere as the constitution. In a modern world, the role of constitution as a mechanism for political legitimacy, the area of constitutional validity, and the essence of constitution itself are rapidly changing. In the sense of social integration, modern political constitutions are less effective, which presupposes the emergence of functional equivalents of the classical constitutions, characterized by increasing social flexibility and capability of adaptation to modern social dynamics. Without looking at the fact that orthodox jurisprudence based on the legal positivism, as the dominant source of legal education and legislative processes, grants constitutional validity exclusively to the "basic laws" of certain nation-states, the modern legal reality

---

3   About the earlier definition of the concept of "world society", see: Luhmann 1971, where the concept is developed from the perspectives of Parsonsian, "classical systems theory." Regarding the new concept of world society, based on the theory of autopoietic social systems, see Luhmann 1997: 145.

4   About the influences and consequences of the processes of privatization on the transformation of the modern social system: Teubner 1998, 2000.

demonstrates the contrary: the emergence of constitutional processes within different sectors of modern society. For the scientific analysis of the above-mentioned processes, where conventional jurisprudence, with its contradictory principles and dogmatic methodology, is helpless, modern social theory and interdisciplinary legal studies really do have something to say. Thus, legal sociology, as an interdisciplinary discourse about the mutual interaction and interdependence of law and society, is the branch of science that is able to identify and analyze the process of constitutionalization within global society, on the basis of deep theoretical reconsideration and empirical verification.

The aim of the present chapter is, along with a review of some basic trends in the development of constitutional theory, to identify the basic gaps within classical constitutional theory, to offer a critique of "constitutional monism" as an influential ideology, and to attempt to develop the concept of "constitutional pluralism." The concept of *societal constitutionalism* will also be discussed: Due to the increasing processes of globalization, self-regulation, and privatization, changes within classical constitutional theory are unavoidable, which requires, in the circumstances created by the deconstruction of state-centered constitutionalism, the development of the idea of "societal constitutionalism." (Sciulli 1992, Teubner 2004). According to the main argument of the present chapter, the differentiation of the modern global legal space within the *local, national, international, supranational*, and *transnational* legal levels, presupposes internal constitutionalization within each of the mentioned legal levels, which implicitly opposes the ideal of constitutional monism and establishes the idea of constitutional pluralism—*individual constitutional processes intrinsic to each legal level*. Thus, the constitution, as "the basic law of the State," is not an all-encompassing concept and avoids the most important constitutional processes, which occur without the states, beyond their formal regulation. All that underlines the development of the concept of "societal constitutionalism," thereby supporting the idea of plural constitutionalism: the existence of constitutional elements, but also of pure, genuine constitutions, beyond the basic laws of the state. In the analytical sense, this chapter is based on the perspectives of the deconstruction[5] and the theory of *autopoietic social systems*.[6] By way of empirical verification for these arguments, the chapter will discuss the emerging processes of constitution-building beyond the boundaries of the nation-state, occurring within the European Union and other supranational entities, as well as within the United Nations and the World Trade Organization. In addition, the processes of *private constitutionalism* within the transnational level of the modern legal system will be discussed. However, before we turn to the basic arguments of this chapter, the concept of legal pluralism itself has first to be briefly reviewed.

---

5   On the deconstruction in the field of law in general, and especially the deconstruction of the hierarchy of the legal system, see Derrida 1992, Teubner 1997a.

6   On the theory of autopoietic social systems in general, see Luhmann 1984.

Development of the Idea of Legal Pluralism

Legal pluralism is recognized as one of the most important concepts within legal sociology and anthropology.[7] As indicated earlier in the title of the concept, it opposes the basic principle of the legal doctrine—legal monism, which reduces the notion of law only to the set of "official," state laws. In general, legal pluralism, along with and parallel to state law, recognizes as law the alternative forms of social control, as well as legal orders existing "out of the state," and accepts the coexistence of different "legal spaces" within one social environment as a necessary reality.

The grounds for the idea of legal pluralism can be detected as early as the writings of classical sociolegal scholars (though the term "legal pluralism" was established later). Eugen Ehrlich distinguished the forms of State Law and "Living Law" (*lebendes Recht*) (Ehrlich 1989: 419). Leon Petrazycki developed the theory of differentiation of official and intuitive law (Petrazycki 1955). And the founder of the French sociolegal school, Georges Gurvitch, identified different layers of law emerging in a society (Gurvitch 1942: 221). Also, the founder of the modern legal anthropology, Leopold Pospísil, makes a distinction between different legal orders and maintains the idea of multiplicity of legal systems (Pospísil 1974: 99 and 1978: 52). Thus, the idea of legal pluralism presupposes the coexistence of several (more than one) legal orders, spaces, or levels in a concrete society that excludes the very monopoly of the state law – law is what the society itself conceives, uses, and elaborates as law and not merely the official normative order established and enforced by the state, which, in most cases, cannot reach, that is "enter" within, the society and is socially denied as a mechanism for societal guidance.

The emergence of the concept of legal pluralism was supported by the development of the postcolonial legal anthropology (Hooker 1975: 55; Merry 2004: 569), which studied the coexistence of transplanted legal institutions and norms along with the indigenous, local, traditional, legal orders in postcolonial societies (such as in India, Latin American, and African states), and their cultural–historical grounds and trends of development. Later, after the "rediscovery" of the works of classical sociolegal theorists, legal pluralism appeared as a central concept within the empirical sociology of law, when the accent was shifted from local, traditional, customary regimes to the parallel existence of legal systems within the industrial societies, to the coexistence of state and church law, to the infra-legal mechanisms within the specific social groups (professional, political, criminal unities), to the alternative forms of dispute resolution, and—finally—to the emergence of global legal regimes.[8]

---

7   Due to the concrete aims of this chapter, the concept of legal pluralism will be dealt with only in general. For more extensive discussion of the subject, see Merry 1988 and Griffiths 2002 and 1986.

8   For the reformulation of the concept of legal pluralism, see, notably, Galanter 1981, Macaulay 1987, Moore 1978, and Greenhouse and Strijbosch 1993.

Theoretical and empirical surveys on legal pluralism are mostly directed toward the discovery and explanation of the coexistence of different parallel legal orders within a certain nation-state. Thus, in classical sociolegal writings, the "center" of the existence and acting area of legal pluralism is a territory of a nation-state, populated by certain social groups. This is also quite explicit in the research conducted in the realm of legal anthropology, which tries to "read" the local, traditional legal space. The important exception is the perspective in the sociology of law, based on social criticism and importantly on the autopoietic systems theory, analyzing the emergence of transnational legal regimes through the processes of globalization.[9] But the concepts of "global legal pluralism," detached from the local spaces, are also exaggerated and oversimplified, indicating the processes of legal pluralization only within the transnational orders and thus paying little attention to the regional, supranational, and local legal orders, and the paradox of pluralism among the legal orders.

As the main sense of the idea of legal pluralism is the recognition of independent, alternative legal orders within a society, the crucial question has to be answered, namely: Which society is under consideration as the realm, or space for existence of legal pluralism? Traditionally, in classical anthropology and sociology of law, the unit of society of a certain nation-state is used, where colonial, transplanted, and received laws coexist with the indigenous, local, infra-state law. But in modern conditions, due to the globalization of social communications and functional differentiation of the world society, the "unit" of the existence of legal pluralism has to be shifted from infra-state, local, national societies to global society, and accordingly, as the only possible, all-encompassing space of existence of legal pluralism has to be admitted to world society itself, where, on the basis of social interactions and productive irritations, local and global discourses coexist and benefit for their mutual coevolution.

Thus legal pluralism can be defined as the coexistence of different levels of legal communications in world society, and their internal fragmentation into independent regimes, due to the different logic of social differentiation.[10] Classical sociolegal and anthropological theories are focused on the pluralism *within* certain (basically, national) legal orders, though pluralism can also be detected *among* the legal orders when the very different-level legal regimes coexist. Law, on any level of world society, exists solely in the form of legal communications. The nature and purely legal essence of the given social communications are determined by the binary code (legal/illegal) and the universal function of the law, which consists in the stabilization of normative expectations and distinguishes the legal

---

9   Important works in this respect include: Teubner 1992, Santos 2002, Twining 2000, Perez 2003, and Günther 2001.

10   Compare this with Teubner's definition: "Legal Pluralism is ... defined no longer as a set of conflicting social norms in a given social field but as a multiplicity of diverse communicative processes that observe social action under the binary code of legal/illegal." Teubner 1992: 1451.

subsystem from the other functionally differentiated subsystems of the world society (Luhmann 1993: 124).

According to the above definition of legal pluralism, local, national, international, supranational, and transnational legal levels can be differentiated, which together constitute the global legal field and, without looking at the different levels of their validity and their internal fragmentation into autonomous regimes, coexist in the global society as legal communications, governed by different logics of social differentiation.

The Differentiation of Legal Levels within the World Society

Classical legal education and legal doctrine are traditionally concerned with the study and theoretical/practical elaboration of two legal levels: *national* and *international* laws. This is understandable, as the given levels represent an "official law" and are normative systems based on the political order of the certain nation-state. However, it must be mentioned here that the indicated levels cover only the minor part of the modern global legal field, which encompasses widely divergent and disparate sectors of the world society.

Given the era of legal globalization, following the increasing functional differentiation and fragmentation of global social communications, through the interactions of global and local processes, and parallel to the national and international orders, three independent legal levels are being developed and (re-)emerging on the basis of spontaneous and self-regulated norm-production: supranational, transnational, and local. Consequently, local, supranational, and transnational legal orders are presented alongside national and international laws as independent legal levels.

The best way to identify and analyze the emerging legal orders within global society might be through the concept of living law developed by the founder of legal sociology, Eugen Ehrlich (Ehrlich 1989).[11] Ehrlich makes a sharp distinction between an "official law", enforced by state authority, and spontaneous legal orders —"living law," which develops within society and controls everyday social interactions, thereby maintaining the social integration, conflict resolution, and unity of the society. Ehrlich points out that every social group is characterized by a firm system of values and "living law" that determines the identity of a certain group and its social stability. The state law remains as a "written document," the factual effect of which attains only a formal, symbolic importance. The society itself determines and establishes the valid law, not the state.

---

11 Some earlier, shorter essays by Ehrlich also contain valuable information and can be found in Ehrlich 1967. With reference to "early legal pluralism," important works from this book (published by Ehrlich at different times and edited by Manfred Rehbinder) include: "Die Erforschung des lebenden Rechts" (1911): 11–27; "Ein Institut für lebendes Recht" (1911): 28–42; "Das lebende Recht der Völker der Bukowina" (1912): 43–60.

The indicated legal levels, local, supranational, and transnational, are maybe less attractive for classical jurisprudence because of the impossibility of incorporating those alternative levels of law within the elementary internal differentiation of the legal system into national and international law. It must be noted that some problems also arise while differentiating the mentioned legal levels from the national and international legal systems, as the given legal levels (but not the local law!) are continuously emerging as independent regimes at the present time. Their emergence is determined by modern social transformation—that is, globalization!

Local law is constructed by the "living law" regimes, acting within certain social groups, which are characterized by informal, though nonetheless quite effective, validity and enforcement mechanisms. Within every social group, such as professional, creative, religious, political, or even criminal unions, a certain normative order is enacted, maintained by group members and their elaborated practices, standards, repetitive actions, and traditions. The functioning of each social group is based on the system of certain basic principles, unwritten (but quite often written as well) "laws," fundamental rights, and duties of members of a concrete group. Overall, this determines the establishment and development, the construction and constitution (in its both meanings!), of the given group. Within such social groups the level of social enforcement is rather high; sometimes even higher than that of state enforcement. The local law and its validity solely depend on local traditions and local authority.

Supranational law, like national and international legal orders, also belongs to the category of "official" law, though its study and theoretical/practical elaboration is less intensive. Supranational (*supra*—above, over, up) orders exist on a higher, upper level than the nation-state regimes, but in contrast with traditional international law they are characterized by specific features that necessitate their differentiation as an independent legal level. The first basic distinction between international and supranational legal levels is the fact that supranational regimes, while transcending nation-state boundaries and attaining an "above-national" character, are still determined by certain regional boundaries, or certain supranational regimes are valid only within certain geopolitical regions. The law of the European Union can serve as the best example of supranational legal regimes—though operating "above" state level, it is reduced, limited to a certain geographical, regional validity (none of the African states, for example, can be admitted as a EU member and use the EU legal system, simply because they cannot be located within the geographical area of this regime; whereas for traditional international organizations, like the United Nations, the geographical location of a certain nation-state has no importance!). Another example of a supranational legal regime is the North American Free Trade Agreement (NAFTA), which operates only between the states located on the North American continent—USA, Canada, and Mexico—and regulates trade relationships among those states. One more divergent feature of supranational regimes can be found in their institutional independence—the existence of independent mechanisms for dispute settlement, substantial legislation, and adjudication which regulate disputes arising within certain spheres and at the "above-national" level and regulate the relationships only for the states comprising the supranational unity and their citizens (for example, the judicial system of the European Union and the development of EU substantive law, and private mechanisms of dispute settlement within the NAFTA regime and internal laws regulating the trade issues only among the member states of NAFTA). Supranational regimes are characterized by their own, internal processes of constitutionalization and constitute their supranational constitutions.

Transnational law represents the legal level existing beyond (*trans*—beyond, on the other side) and independent of the states' legal order with global validity, free from subordination to the public sphere, engaged in the process of social evolution through private autonomy and self-regulation. Transnational law can also be termed "global private law." *Lex mercatoria* can serve as the colorful example of transnational legal order: a global commercial law existing beyond the official laws of nation-states and independent of their intervention. *Lex mercatoria* has been operating as a set of basic principles and usages for centuries and regulates effectively disputes arising in the fields of international commerce and global private transactions. *Lex mercatoria* ("merchant law") is a kind of mechanism that stimulates flexible regulation and is most attractive for parties involved in transnational commercial relations; it is also a kind of "soft law" and is, at the same time, neutral, based on usages and private initiative, and, most importantly, independent of the control mechanisms of political regimes. Another example of transnational law is "Internet law"—an autonomous normative order, established and practiced by the Internet Corporation for Assigned Names and Numbers (ICANN), as the mechanism for private norm-making and dispute settlement beyond states, regulating conflicts arising in cyberspace.[12] World Trade Organization law can also be admitted as a transnational legal order, which, while it bears some signs of politicization, on the basis of private standards and without political pressures determines (or should determine!) the dynamics of world trade. The basic feature of the transnational legal level is that it consists of fragmented, independent regimes that are characterized by *autonomous constitutionalization* and which operate everywhere in the world, but outside and beyond national and international legal orders. The disputes, emerging in the realm of transnational law, are regulated solely by private mechanisms—by *transnational private arbitration*, without any reference to certain national or international legislation, using the soft forms of "private justice," on the basis of "global private constitutions."

---

12 ICANN is a nonprofit, transnational corporation that manages and controls the distribution of Internet addresses, monitors organizational issues connected with Internet Protocol (IP), controls top-level domain (TLD) general and country codes, and on the basis of private principles, legislation, and "private constitutionalization" resolves emerging conflicts within cyberspace.

The Post-national Constellation and the Transformation of the Form of Constitution

After the identification of genuine legal orders beyond state regimes, a logical question arises: Can there be a constitution without the state, a basic law outside of the political space of the state? However, is the constitution not one of the most important legislative acts associated with a certain unitary national legal system, establishing the sense of legal unity? What are the important changes, challenges, and unpredicted transformations for modern constitutional theory, determined by the processes of globalization and privatization in the world society? Do the role, function, and form of the constitution change due to the social transformations?

In order to answer these questions, the concept of constitution itself and the basic trends of classical constitutional theory must first be analyzed. What is more, a critical reconsideration of the classical constitutional doctrine from the standpoint of post-national transformations is necessary.

The emergence of the modern, state-centered form of constitution was caused by revolutionary changes; the formation of the United States of America and the French Republic became possible only after revolutions and the adoption of the first constitutions that officially enabled newly emerged political regimes to be established as states on given territories. Thus, the first constitutions were foundational documents. Such a constitutional model was rapidly adopted as this innovation was consistently domesticated within the "new states" of the "old Europe." After these processes, the constitution was established as a basic law of certain, sovereign, nation-states; but also sub-state (interstate) forms of constitution emerged with the validity limited to certain federal units, autonomous republics or states, though of course under the principle of legal centralism subordinated to the "central constitution" of the state. In 1989, after the dissolution of the Soviet Union, as German constitutionalist Peter Häberle remarks, the "global hour of the constitutional state" emerged, when the states of the "new democracy" engaged in the transplantation of Western constitutional models (Häberle 1997: 101). Accordingly, constitutional processes have covered the whole geopolitical space of the globe.

In modern constitutional theory *empirical* and *normative* concepts of constitution are distinguished. The empirical concept of constitution, introduced within classical political thought from the perspective of the description of nature (*Naturbeschreibung*), described the general characteristics of the territory of a certain state and its population, political regimes, and the mechanisms of authority (Grimm 2005: 448), in sum, the social and political *construction* of the state. If the concept of constitution was still used with a normative meaning, it supposed a system of "laws," enforced by a certain authority, and not the *basic statute* that regulates how and on which bases the concrete state functions (Grimm 1995: 582). And the normative concept of constitution presupposes the shift from descriptive toward prescriptive point—constitution, after the adoption of the French and the US constitutions became the highest statute that establishes the nation-state and legitimizes a state authority. Thus constitution appeared to be a mechanism for *juridification of power* and *politicization of law*. According to liberal legalism, the main function of constitution is the *limitation of politics*.

The representative of classical constitutional theory, Carl Schmitt, distinguishes the following concepts of constitution:

1. the absolute concept of constitution (*absoluter Verfassungsbegriff*), which defines the constitution as a whole unity;
2. the relative concept of constitution (*relativer Verfassungsbegriff*), which defines the constitution as a set of certain statutes, the totality of constitutional laws;
3. the positive concept of constitution (*positiver Verfassungsbegriff*), which defines the constitution as a common decision about the form of political unity;
4. the ideal concept of constitution (*Idealbegriff der Verfassung*), which defines the constitution as a basic law due to its specific, unique content (Schmitt 1993: 1–44).

The eminent representative of the normative school in jurisprudence, Hans Kelsen, while defining the constitution as the supreme normative act of a certain sovereign nation-state, distinguishes *formal* and *material* concepts of constitution (Kelsen 1925: 248–54 and 1960: 228–30). In the formal sense, the constitution is an important, fundamental document, and its norms can be changed only through established procedures and norms. In the material sense, the constitution represents the totality of those general norms that determine and regulate the specific rules for the elaboration and functioning of certain statutes and legal norms. Finally, the validity of the constitution is determined by the *basic norm* (*Grundnorm*), and, according to Kelsen, all positive legal orders are based on it, as on the universal, abstract category.

Within modern constitutional discourse three types of constitutions are also distinguished: *legal*, *real*, and *ideal* constitutions (Allott 2001: 135–6). The legal constitution is a special statute which regulates the division of power and determines the limits and the essence of social authority. The real constitution is *constitution in action*, the system and structure of power involved in current social processes. The ideal constitution constructs the views of social integration, of how society should be organized, and determines the boundaries of an ideal, hypothetical order.

Joseph Raz, a modern legal philosopher and follower of the positivist school, points out the following seven basic features of the constitution:

1. the constitution has a fundamental, *constitutive* character, constructing the legal and the political systems;
2. without looking at the special possibilities of amendment or change, the constitution, as a basic law, is prone to maintaining a stable political–legal

structure and preserves stability and continuity in the basic principles, thus the constitution is *stable*;
3. the constitution, as a canonical document, exists in a *written* form. This is why the constitution exists in the form of one or a small number of documents
4. the constitution is the *superior law*: laws conflicting with the constitution are invalid;
5. the constitution is *justiciable*, since all the laws that do not fit with the constitution are declared as invalid and the validity of constitution is protected by specific procedural rules;
6. the constitution is *entrenched*: While the special mechanisms for amending or changing the constitution exist, amendments are more difficult to secure compared with the ordinary legislation;
7. the constitution has significance not only as a "lawyer's law," but also as the "people's law." Thus it determines the basic interests of the population and protects social values, constructing a *common ideology* (Raz 1999: 153–4).

Of course, for classical constitutional theory, the idea of constitution without the state is unimaginable. According to the conventional view within constitutional theory, one of the most important functions of the constitution is the construction of the public sphere (Frankenberg 1997: 35). The given point excludes explicitly the idea of "private constitutionalism." According to Carl Schmitt: "If we would like to catch the essence of the word "constitution", its use has to be reduced solely to the concept of the constitution of *state*, or people's political union" (Schmitt 1993: 1, own translation).

Though constitutional theory excludes the possibility of constitutionalism without the state, the idea of legal pluralism—according to which there are emerging alternative constitutional processes (and even genuine constitutions!) in different sectors of world society, within the legal orders of different levels—breaks this dogma. The theory of *autopoietic social systems* which interprets the notion of constitution as a form of structural coupling between legal and political subsystems of world society, and the advancement of this idea by Teubner who advocates the idea of societal constitutionalism introduced by David Sciulli, demonstrates well the emergence and establishment of transnational constitutional discourse beyond the state.

Conclusion

One more provocative and paradoxical category—"impossible necessity"—has been used by Luhmann to describe the consequence orientation (*Folgenorientierung*) in the legal system as the mode of reasoning and justification. He originally describes consequence orientation in legal practice as impossible and necessary at the same time (Luhmann 1986: 30). Criticizing the favored trend of modern legal regulation, Luhmann states: "... the theoretical principle that justification can ultimately be sought only in consequences, leads back to the paradox that impossible is postulated as necessary" (Luhmann 1988: 33).

The idea of emerging constitutional forms beyond the state is another example of *impossible necessity*. Observing from the formalized, dogmatic standpoint of orthodox jurisprudence, constitutional processes beyond state controlled? mechanisms are totally unthinkable. Such innovation could even demolish the conceptual unity of public law discourse and normative jurisprudence in general. However, after taking into consideration the evolutionary processes underlying modern world society, it becomes evident that such constitutional transformations are required and even necessary for modern social dynamics. Auto-constitutional regimes beyond the state, based on spontaneous legal communications in transnational spaces, are already empirical, observable facts occurring in different sectors of modern world society.

The category of *impossible necessity* attributed to polycontextural constitutionalism—the multiple coexistence of binary code constitutional/ unconstitutional in different sectors of the global legal subsystem (local, national, international, supranational and transnational spaces)—does not really deny the empirical fact of emerging new constitutional forms and regimes beyond the nation-state. On the contrary: impossible necessity is the very condition of the paradoxical existence of societal constitutional forms beyond the state. The idea of polycontextural constitutionalism beyond the state is impossible, but is nonetheless necessary.

References

Allott, P., *Eunomia: New Order for a New World* (Oxford: Oxford University Press, 2001).
Derrida, J., "Force of law: the 'mystical foundation of authority'," in D. Cornell, M. Rosenfeld, and D. G. Carlson (eds), *Deconstruction and the Possibility of Justice* (New York: Routledge, 1992), 3–67.
Ehrlich, E., *Recht und Leben: Gesammelte Schriften zur Rechtstatsachenforschung und zur Freiheitslehre* (Berlin: Duncker & Humblot, 1967).
____, *Grundlegung der Soziologie des Rechts*, 4th edn. (Berlin: Duncker & Humblot, 1989).
Febbrajo, A., "From hierarchical to circular models in the sociology of law," *European Yearbook in the Sociology of Law* (Milan: Giuffrè, 1988), 3–21.
Foerster, H. von, *Observing Systems* (Seaside: Intersystems Publications, 1982).
____, *Understanding Understanding: Essays on Cybernetics and Cognition* (New York: Springer, 2003).
Frankenberg, G., *Die Verfassung der Republik: Autorität und Solidarität in der Zivilgesellschaft* (Frankfurt am Main: Suhrkamp, 1997).

Galanter, M., "Justice in many rooms: courts, private ordering, and indigenous law," *Journal of Legal Pluralism* 19 (1981), 1–47.
Greenhouse, C. J., and F. Strijbosch, "Legal pluralism in industrialized societies" *Journal of Legal Pluralism* 33 (1993), 1–9.
Griffiths, A., "Legal pluralism," in R. Banakar and M. Travers (eds), *An Introduction to Law and Social Theory* (Oxford: Hart, 2002), 289–310.
Griffiths, J., "What is legal pluralism?" *Journal of Legal Pluralism* 24 (1986), 1–55.
Grimm, D., "Braucht Europa eine Verfassung?" *Juristenzeitung* 50/12 (1995), 581–91.
____, "The constitution in the process of denationalization," *Constellations* 12/4 (2005), 447–63.
Günther, K., "Rechtspluralismus und universaler Code der Legalität: Globalisierung als Rechtstheoretisches Problem," in L. Wingert und K. Günther (eds), *Die Öffentlichkeit der Vernunft und die Vernunft der Öffentlichkeit: Festschrift für Jürgen Habermas* (Frankfurt am Main: Suhrkamp, 2001), 539–67.
Gurvitch, G., *Sociology of Law* (New York: Alliance Book Corporation, 1942).
Häberle, P., "Verfassungsentwicklungen in Osteuropa—aus der Sicht der Rechtsphilosophie und der Verfassungslehre," in P. Häberle, *Europäische Rechtskultur* (Frankfurt am Main: Suhrkamp, 1997), 101–48.
Hooker, M. B., *Legal Pluralism: An Introduction to Colonial and Neo-colonial Laws* (Oxford: Clarendon Press, 1975).
Kelsen, H., *Allgemeine Staatslehre* (Vienna: Springer, 1925).
____, *Reine Rechtslehre,* 2nd edn. (Vienna: Deuticke, 1960).
Luhmann, N., "Die Weltgesellschaft," *Archiv für Rechts- und Sozialphilosophie* 57/1 (1971), 1–35.
____, *Soziale Systeme: Grundriß einer allgemeinen Theorie* (Frankfurt am Main: Suhrkamp, 1984).
____, *Die soziologische Beobachtung des Rechts* (Frankfurt am Main: A. Metzner, 1986).
____, "The sociological observation of the theory and practice of law," *European Yearbook in the Sociology of Law* (Milan: Giuffrè, 1988), 23–42.
____, "Operational closure and structural coupling: the differentiation of the legal system," *Cardozo Law Review* 13 (1992), 1418–41.
____, *Das Recht der Gesellschaft* (Frankfurt am Main: Suhrkamp, 1993).
____, *Die Gesellschaft der Gesellschaft* (Frankfurt am Main: Suhrkamp, 1998).
Macaulay, S., "Images of law in everyday life: the lessons of school, entertainment and spectator sports," *Law & Society Review* 21/2 (1987), 185–218.
Merry, S. E., "Legal pluralism," *Law & Society Review* 22/5 (1988), 869–96.
____, "Colonial and postcolonial law," in A. Sarat (ed.), *The Blackwell Companion to Law and Society* (Oxford: Blackwell, 2004), 569–88.
Moore, S. F., "Law and social change: the semi-autonomous social field as an appropriate subject of study," in S. F. Moore, *Law as Process* (London: Routledge and Kegan Paul, 1978) 54–81.

Perez, O., "Normative creativity and global legal pluralism: reflections on the democratic critique of transnational law," *Indiana Journal of Global Legal Studies* 10 (2003), 25–64.

Petrazycki, L., *Law and Morality*, trans. W. H. Babb (Cambridge: Harvard University Press, 1955).

Pospísil, L., *Anthropology of Law: A Comparative Theory* (New Haven: HRAF Press, 1974).

____, *The Ethnology of Law,* 2nd edn. (Menlo Park: Cummings, 1978).

Raz, J., "On the authority and interpretation of constitutions: some preliminaries," in L. Alexander (ed.), *Constitutionalism: Philosophical Foundations* (Cambridge: Cambridge University Press, 1999), 152–93.

Santos, B. de S., *Toward a New Legal Common Sense: Law, Globalization, and Emancipation*, 2nd edn. (London: Butterworths, 2002).

Schmitt, C., *Verfassungslehre*, 9th edn. (Berlin: Duncker & Humblot, 1993).

Sciulli, D., *Theory of Societal Constitutionalism: Foundations of a Non-Marxist Critical Theory* (Cambridge: Cambridge University Press, 1992).

Teubner, G., "The two faces of Janus: rethinking legal pluralism," *Cardozo Law Review* 13 (1992), 1443–62.

____, "The king's many bodies: the self-deconstruction of law's hierarchy," *Law & Society Review* 31/4 (1997a), 763–87.

____, "Global Bukowina: legal pluralism in the world society," in G. Teubner (ed.), *Global Law Without a State* (Aldershot: Dartmouth, 1997b), 3–28.

____, "After privatization? The many autonomies of private law," *Current Legal Problems* 51 (1998), 393–424.

____, "Contracting worlds: the many autonomies of private law," *Social & Legal Studies* 9/3 (2000), 399–417.

____, "Societal constitutionalism: alternatives to state-centred constitutional theory?" in C. Joerges, I. Sand and G. Teubner (eds), *Constitutionalism and Transnational Governance* (Oxford: Hart, 2004), 3-28.

Twining, W., *Globalisation and Legal Theory* (London: Butterworths, 2000).

Chapter 15
Legal Pluralism as a Form of Structural Coupling[1]

Gunther Teubner

> Et enfin: les phrase de régime ou de genre hétérogène se "rencontre" sur les noms propres, dans les mondes determines par les réseaux de noms
>
> (Jean-Francois Lyotard)[2]

I

Looking at the "dark side" of the majestic rule of law, legal pluralism rediscovers the subversive power of suppressed discourses. Plural, informal, local quasi-laws are seen as the "supplement" of the official, formal centralism of the modern legal order.

It is the ambivalent, double-faced character of legal pluralism that is so attractive to postmodern jurists. Like the old Roman god Janus, guardian of gates and doors, beginning and ends, with two faces, one on the front and the other at the back of his head, legal pluralism is at the same time both: social norms *and* legal rules, law *and* society, formal *and* informal, rule-oriented *and* spontaneous. And the relations between the legal and the social in legal pluralism are highly ambiguous, almost paradoxical: separate but intertwined, autonomous but interdependent, closed but open. Boaventura de Sousa Santos, one of the protagonists of postmodern legal style declares the program:

> Legal pluralism is the key concept in a postmodern view of law. Not the legal pluralism of traditional legal anthropology in which the different legal orders are conceived as separate entities coexisting in the same political space, but rather the conception of different legal spaces superposed, interpenetrated and mixed in our minds as much as in our actions, in occasions of qualitative leaps or

---

1 Slightly abridged version of the article "The Two Faces of Janus: Rethinking Legal Pluralism," in *Cardozo Law Review* 13 (1992), 1443–62, published in: J. Uusitalo, Z. Bankowski and K. Tuori (eds.), *Law and Power: Critical and Socio-legal Essays* (Liverpool: Deborah Charles, 1998), 119–40, and in H. Stuart (ed.), *Social Control: Aspects of Non-State Justice* (Aldershot: Ashgate, 1994).

2 Jean-François Lyotard, *Le différend* (Paris: Minuit) 1986, at 51.

sweeping crises in our life trajectories as well as in the dull routine of eventless everyday life.[3]

The crucial question of how to reconstruct, in postmodern architecture, the connections between the social and the legal finds a highly vague answer interpenetrating, intertwined, integral, superposed, mutually constitutive, dialectical. We are left with ambiguity and confusion. After all, this is the very charm of postmodernism.

II

Does autopoiesis lead us any further here? Can we understand legal pluralism's interwovenness of the social and the legal better via "operational closure and structural coupling"? Legal autopoiesis and postmodern jurisprudence have several things in common: the linguistic turn away from positivist sociology of law, the dissolution of social and legal realities into discursivity, the image of fragmentation and closure of multiple discourses, the non-foundational character of legal reasoning, the decentering of the legal subject, the eclectic exploitation of diverse *différance* and *différends* over unity, and most important the foundation of law on paradoxes, antinomies, and tautologies. But here the bifurcation begins.

While postmodernists are obviously satisfied to deconstruct legal doctrine and are joyfully playing with antinomies and paradoxes, legal autopoiesis poses the somewhat sobering question: After the deconstruction? Creative use of paradox is the message that moves autopoiesis beyond deconstructive analysis into reconstructive practice. It is the experience of real life, the experience that discursive practices "know" how to overcome the blockage of paradoxes and antinomies that does not allow autopoiesis theory to remain in the comforting twilight of closure and openness, separation and interwovenness, autonomy and interdependence in legal pluralism. Paradoxes, tautologies, contradictions, and ambiguities in discursive practice are not the end of autopoietic analysis; they are seen as the starting point, as the very foundation of self-organizing social practices.

At the same time legal pluralism can be seen as a kind of test case for autopoiesis theory, since even for sympathizing observers this latter theory seems to have "tended towards a too radical separation between law and society."[4] Can a theory that stresses operational closure of social systems take sufficient account

---

3   Boaventura de Sousa Santos, "Law: A Map of Misreading. Toward a Postmodern Conception of Law," *Journal of Law and Society* 14 (1987), 293.

4   David Nelken, "Review Essay: Beyond the Study of 'Law and Society': Henry's Private Justice and O'Hagan's The End of the Law," *American Bar Foundation Research Journal* (1986), 323–38, at 338.

of "intersecting bodies of expertise"?[5] While it may be plausible to describe the official law of the centralized state as autonomous, self-referential, and self-productive, this becomes highly questionable in the "fleeting ambivalence" of legal pluralism[6] where the legal merges into the social and vice versa.

This problem has to do with autopoietics' own history. In regard to operational closure—which was the broadside on open systems theory—the theory is well developed. However, autopoiesic theory is rather underdeveloped when it comes to spelling out the logics of informational openness and structural coupling. Up to now autopoiesic theory has quite successfully transformed the theory of open systems into a theory of operationally closed systems without at the same time falling back into old ideas of a system without an environment.[7] Indeed, the reformulation of basic concepts of systems theory from input–conversion–output into operational closure entails a fully fledged change of paradigm. System, function, structure, process, double contingency, communication, action, and, above all, meaning—all these notions find a new conceptualization in the world of autonomy and closure, self-reference and autopoiesis. However, this is the point where new problems emerge: How can one cope with the paradox that the closure of cognizing systems is the basis for their openness? How can one on the basis of operative closure construct an openness which is different from input–output relations? How does autopoiesis theory solve the self-imposed enigma: "L'ouvert s'appuye sur le fermé"?[8]

The metaphor is "order from noise." Perturbation, structural coupling and coevolution are the key concepts.[9] This can be misunderstood as an easy compromise between operative closure and input–output relations, a "middle path" between two extremes.[10] However, what it really does is to radicalize simultaneously both closure and openness. To make cognition possible at all, systems need to develop operative closure and at the same time open up toward

---

5   Peter Miller and Michael Power, "Accounting, Law and Economic Calculation," in *Accounting and the Law*, ed. M. Bromwich and A. Hopwood (London: Prentice Hall, 1992), 230–53.

6   Stuart Henry, "The Construction and Deconstruction of Social Control: Thoughts on the Discursive Production of State Law and Private Justice," in *Transcarceration: Essays in the Sociology of Social Control*, ed. J. Lowmann, R. Menzies, and T. Palys (Aldershot: Gower, 1987), 89–100, at 98.

7   Niklas Luhmann, *Social Systems* (Palo Alto: Stanford University Press, 1995).

8   Edgar Morin, *La Méthode: 3. La Connaissance/1* (Paris: Seuil, 1986), 203ff.

9   Humberto R. Maturana and Francisco J. Varela, *Autopoiesis and Cognition* (Boston: Reidel, 1980), 102ff., and Humberto R. Maturana and Francisco J. Varela, *Tree of Knowledge: Biological Roots of Human Understanding* (Boston: Shambhala, 1988), ch. 6, and Heinz von Förster, *Observing Systems* (Seaside, CA: Intersystems Publications, 1981), 274ff., and Luhmann, *supra*, at ch. 5.

10   Francisco J. Varela, "Living Ways of Sense-making: A Middle Path for Neuroscience," in *Disorder and Order: Proceedings of the Stanford International Symposium,* ed. P. Livingstone (Saratoga, CA: Anma Libri, 1984), 208.

their environment in a new and different way, not via input–output, but via perturbation and structural coupling. The difference is subtle but important. "Open systems" receive informational input from the environment and convert it through internal processes into informational output which may be used as new input in a feedback loop.[11] By contrast, an operationally closed system is structurally coupled to its niche when it uses events in the environment as perturbations in order to build or to change its internal structures. From external noise it creates internal order.[12] The contact between the system and its niche are real; however, the environmental constraints are not defined externally by spatiotemporal reality.[13] Rather, it is the system itself that defines its environmental constraints by projecting expectations on perturbating events. The perturbatory event, then, is interpreted as the expectation's fulfillment or its disappointment. And this bifurcation decides how to continue internal operations. Thus, a system that disposes of the internal distinction between self-reference and hetero-reference makes itself dependent upon the environment using external events as conditions of its own operations, as irritations as well as opportunities for structural change.[14] The multiplication of such singular micro-synchronizations of system and niche then leads to a common path of development, to structural drift and coevolution.[15]

This seems a promising set of ideas to rethink the relations between the legal discourse and other social discourses, especially under the challenge of legal pluralism. It helps to understand the "relative autonomy" of law better than the simple distinction of internal and external causes of legal change would allow for.[16] It promises to clarify the obscure metaphor of "interwovenness" of the legal and the social and to replace it by a genuine theoretical construction that makes us see more clearly which aspects are responsible for the openness of law and which for closure, even in the twilight of legal pluralism. However, in spite of all its innovative potential, the concept of structural coupling developed in general systems theory is not complex enough to cope with the special problems of law and society. After all, the relations between law and other social fields result from internal differentiation of one and only one society. Thus, in spite of all their autonomy, they belong to the same comprehensive social system and cannot simply be conceptualized according to the model of two independent autopoietic

---

11   E.g. Walter Buckley, *Sociology and Modern Systems Theory* (Englewood Cliffs, NJ: Prentice Hall, 1967).

12   Forster, *supra*, n. 8, at 15.

13   Michael A. Arbib and Mary B. Hesse, *The Construction of Reality* (Cambridge: Cambridge University Press, 1986), 3.

14   Niklas Luhmann, *Die Wissenschaft der Gesellschaft* (Frankfurt: Suhrkamp, 1990), 29ff., 163ff.

15   Maturana and Varela 1988, *supra* n. 8, at ch. 5.

16   Cf. the debate between Lempert (Richard Lempert, "The Autonomy of Law: Two Visions Compared," in *Autopoietic Law: A New Approach to Law and Society*, ed. G. Teubner (Berlin: de Gruyter, 1980), 152–90), and Niklas Luhmann, "Closure and Openness: On Reality in the World of Law," at 335–48).

systems. The vexing conundrum of "autopoiesis within autopoiesis" which poses itself for autonomous sectors within society[17] presses for modifications of the general concept: Is not law in relation to other cultural provinces such as politics, science, economy, religion, culture much more "open" than the general concept of structural coupling would allow for? Is not "interdiscursivity"[18] in law and society much more dense than mere transitory perturbations could ever produce? And do we not find in the coevolution of law and society significantly more elective affinities than the mere co-existence of structural drift would provide for? To use our metaphor as a theme with variations: "Order from music" instead of "order from noise"?

In order to do justice to interdiscursive relations in law and society I suggest modifying the idea of structural coupling:

1. *Productive misreading*: Since interdiscursivity means structural coupling in a situation of autopoiesis within autopoiesis, mere perturbation does not suffice to grasp the specific closure/openness of social subsystems. In the relations between social discourses, I suggest replacing perturbation by productive misreading. In legal pluralism the legal discourse is not only perturbated by processes of social self-production, but law productively misreads other social discourses as "sources" of norm production.

2. *Linkage institutions*: Structural coupling depends on specific institutions of linkage that shape its duration, quality, and intensity. While in "old" legal pluralism the main institutional link was the legal formalization of diffuse social norms, the "new" legal pluralism is characterized by specialized institutions that bind law to a multitude of functional subsystems and formal organizations.

3. *Responsiveness*: Coevolution leads to mere viability of internal constructs of law. In contrast, social responsiveness comes about when linkage institutions connect law more tightly to other autonomous social discourses. Legal pluralism makes law more responsive to society, not by increasing explicit social and economic knowledge of law but by using the synchronicity of legal and social operations as the law's tacit knowledge.

III

The new legal pluralism moves away from questions about the effect of law on society or even the effect of society on law toward conceptualizing a more complex and interactive relationship between official and unofficial forms of ordering.

---

17 Gunther Teubner, *Law as an Autopoietic System* (London: Blackwell, 1993), ch. 3.
18 Bernard S. Jackson, *Law, Fact and Narrative Coherence* (Liverpool: Deborah Charles, 1988).

Instead of mutual influences between two separate entities, this perspective sees plural forms of ordering as participating in the same social field.[19]

Indeed, this new view concisely conceptualized by Griffiths[20] means considerable progress, primarily as against a legalistic view of legal pluralism that defined it as a problem of state law's "recognition" of subordinate normative orders like regional or corporate regimes. It successfully moves away from hierarchical concepts of legal pluralism that tended to identify "legal levels" with a hierarchical stratified structure of society ignoring legal phenomena outside the hierarchy.[21] And it liberates itself from the heritage of old-style institutionalism that "reified" the social locus of legal pluralism in formally structured institutions, corporations, and organizations.[22] The new legal pluralism is non-legalistic, non-hierarchical, and non-institutional. It focuses on the dynamic interaction of a multitude of "legal orders" within one social field.[23]

There is a price to be paid for progress. As a consequence of its own construction, the new legal pluralism is confronted with the disquieting question: "Where do we stop speaking of law and find ourselves simply describing social life?"[24] Two things have been lost in the course of progress, in the move from spatial separation to discursive interwovenness: (1) the notion of what is distinctively "legal" in the new legal pluralism as well as (2) a clear-cut concept of the interrelations between the social and the legal.

---

19   Sally E. Merry, "Legal Pluralism," *Law & Society Review* 22 (1988), 873.

20   John Griffiths, "What is Legal Pluralism?" *Journal of Legal Pluralism* 24 (1986), 1–55.

21   Leopold Pospisil, *The Anthropology of Law: A Comparative Theory of Law* (New York: Harper & Row, 1971), 125.

22   Michael G. Smith, *Corporations and Society* (London: Duckworth, 1974).

23   Sally F. Moore, "Law and Social Change: The Semi-Autonomous Social Field as an Appropriate Object of Study," *Law & Society Review* 7 (1973), 719–46; Mark Galanter, "Justice in Many Rooms," in *Access to Justice and the Welfare State*, ed. Mauro Cappelletti (Florence: Le Monnier, 1981), 147–81; Francis Snyder, "Colonialism and Legal Form: The Creation of 'Customary Law' in Senegal," *Journal of Legal Pluralism and Unofficial Law* 19 (1981), 79; Boaventura de Sousa Santos, "Modes of Production of Law and Social Power," *International Journal of the Sociology of Law* 13 (1984), 299–336; Santos, *supra* n.2; Peter Fitzpatrick, "Law and Societies," *Osgoode Hall Law Journal* 22 (1984), 115–38; Stuart Henry, *Private Justice* (Boston: Routledge and Kegan Paul, 1983); Stuart Henry, "Community, Justice, Capitalist Society, and Human Agency: The Dialectics of Collective Law in the Cooperative," *Law & Society Review* 19 (1985), 303; Henry, *supra* n.5, at 89–108; Stewart Macaulay, "Private Government," in *Law and the Social Sciences*, ed. L. Lipson and S. Wheeler (New York: Russell Sage, 1986), 445–518; Griffiths, *supra* n. 19; Merry, *supra* n. 18, at 869–901.

24   Merry, *supra* n. 18, at 878.

If we take a concrete market as our "semi-autonomous social field,"[25] what counts as one among many "legal orders"? Antitrust rules, consumer protection laws, and the contract law of the courts are easy cases since they have the stamp of official law. The written agreements of the parties to the transaction and the rules of adhesion contracts clearly belong to the competing "private" legal orders as well as the unwritten customary rules of the trade and the disciplinary rules within a firm. But what about the demands from informal exchange relations, the gifts, loans, and favors that dominate the day-to-day relations? What about the emerging habits in an ongoing contractual relationship, what about informal rules within the firms and organizational patterns and routines, what about economic trust relations in the market? What about the exigencies of rational economic calculation? And what about power pressures from an oligopolist in the market or "tax" rules of a local mafia? Structuralist solutions seem to me as unsatisfactory as functionalist ones. The usual structuralist solution is normativity; it includes within legal pluralism normative expectations of any kind, but excludes merely cognitive expectations as well as purely economic or political pressures. However, normative expectations as such (in a sociological, not in a legal. sense of course) are not sufficient to grasp the distinctively legal in legal pluralism. It is not only the age-old problem of how to delineate rules of non-State law from moral, social, and conventional norms, but also its inherently static, non-dynamic, non-processual character that speaks against such a structuralist solution.

Therefore, new legal pluralists tend to replace "law" by social control.[26] They would include all the phenomena mentioned in our example within legal pluralism, even purely economic exigencies and sheer power pressures. If legal pluralism entailed anything that serves the function of social control, it would be identical with a comprehensive pluralism of social constraints of any kind. Cohen probably exaggerates in calling social control a "Mickey Mouse concept, used to include all social processes ranging from infant socialization to public education, all social policies whether called health, education or welfare."[27] But he has a point. Why should it be just the function of "social control"[28] that defines law in legal pluralism and not the function of "conflict resolution" as theories of private justice would suggest?[29] But then we would have to include different social phenomena in legal pluralism and exclude others. Why could

---

25   Moore, *supra* n. 22, at 719–46.
26   Moore, *supra* n. 22, at 719–46; explicitly Griffiths, *supra* n. 19, at 50 n. 41: "more or less specialized social control,"
27   Stanley Cohen, "Social-Control Talk: Telling Stories about Correctional Change," in *The Power to Punish: Contemporary Penality and Social Analysis*, ed. D. Garland and P. Young (London: Heinemann, 1983), 101–29.
28   Griffiths, *supra* n. 19, at 50.
29   Galanter, *supra* n. 22, at 147–81; Henry, *supra* n. 22.

it not be the function of "coordinating behaviour,"[30] the function of "securing expectations"[31] or the function of "social regulation" which theories of private government would underline?[32] And why not "discipline and punish" which would tend to include any mechanism of disciplinary micro-power that permeates social life?[33] Each of these functions would bring rather diverse social mechanisms into the realm of legal pluralism.[34] Functional analysis of this kind, which occurs because of today's fashions in a hidden form rather than an overt one, is certainly fruitful for comparing functional equivalents of law. However, it is not at all suitable to provide criteria for the delineation of the legal and the nonlegal in legal pluralism.

Now, let us follow the linguistic turn. The decisive move—it seems to me— is from structure to process, from norm to action, from unity to difference and, most important for the legal proprium, from function to code.[35] This move brings forward the dynamic processual character of legal pluralism, and at the same time delineates clearly the "legal" from other types of social action. Legal pluralism is then defined no longer as a set of conflicting social norms in a given social field but as a multiplicity of diverse communicative processes that observe social action under the binary code of legal/illegal. Purely economic calculations from our example are excluded from its ambit as are sheer pressures of power, merely conventional or moral norms, and organizational routines. But whenever such non-legal phenomena are communicatively observed under the *distinction directrice* legal/illegal,[36] they become part of the game of legal pluralism. It is the implicit or explicit invocation of the legal code which constitutes phenomena of legal pluralism, ranging from the official law of the State to the unofficial laws of markets and mafias. To avoid misunderstanding, I should hasten to add: The binary code legal/illegal is not peculiar to the law of the State. This is not at all a view of

---

30 Theodor Geiger, *Vorstudien zu einer Soziologie des Rechts* (Neuwied: Luchterhand, 1987, 4th edn; Berlin: Duncker & Humblot, 1964), 48.

31 Niklas Luhmann, *A Sociological Theory of Law* (London: Routledge, 1985), ch. 3, 6.

32 Macaulay, *supra* n. 22, at 445–518.

33 Michel Foucault, *Discipline and Punish* (New York: Vintage/Random House, 1979); Peter Fitzpatrick, "The Desperate Vacuum: Imperialism and Law in the Experience of Enlightenment," *Droit et Société* 13 (1989), 347–58.

34 Joseph Raz, "On the Functions of Law," in *Oxford Essays in Jurisprudence* (Second Series), ed. A.W.B. Simpson (Oxford: Clarendon Press, 1973), 278–304; Klaus F. Röhl, *Rechtssoziologie* (Cologne: Heymanns, 1987), §26,5; Michel van de Kerchove and François Ost, *Le Système juridique entre ordre et désordre* (Paris: Presses universitaires de France, 1988), 161ff.

35 See Niklas Luhmann, "Operational Closure and Structural Coupling: The Differentiation of the Legal System," *Cardozo Law Review* 13 (1992), 1419–41, and Teubner, *supra* n. 16, at ch. 3.

36 Niklas Luhmann, "The Coding of the Legal System," in *State, Law and Economy as Autopoietic Systems*, ed. A. Febbrajo and G. Teubner (Milan: Giuffrè, 1992), 145–85.

"legal centralism."[37] It refutes categorically any hierarchically superior position of the official law of the State, but invokes rather the imagery of a heterarchy of diverse legal discourses. "Tax laws" of a local mafia which grants its "protection" to the merchants are the case in point. Clearly, in their "illegality," they are excluded from any "recognition" by the official law of the State. Nevertheless, mafia rules are an integral part of legal pluralism in our semiautonomous social field insofar as they use the binary code of legal communication. They belong to the multitude of fragmented legal discourses, be they State law, rules of private justice, regulations of private government, or outright "illegal" laws of underground organizations, that play a part in the dynamic process of mutual constitution of actions and structures in the social field. The multiple orders of legal pluralism always produce normative expectations in the sociological sense, excluding, however, merely social conventions and moral norms since they are not based on the binary code legal/illegal. And "law" in this broad sense may serve many functions (of the Mickey Mouse type): social control, conflict regulation, securing expectations, social regulation, coordination of behavior, or disciplining bodies and souls. It is neither structure nor function but the binary code which defines what is "legal" in legal pluralism.

Why is it so important to be meticulous in defining the legal proprium? Should we not be more interested in a theory of law than in a mere concept of law?[38] And is the definition of law not something which varies according to the research interests involved? Sure, any observer may draw the lines between law and non-law according to the concrete cognitive interests. But there is one privileged delineation: the line that the discursive practice of law draws between itself and its environment. If we are interested in a theory of law as a self-organizing social practice, the boundaries of law are not something which is up to the arbitrary research interests to define. Boundaries of law are one among many structures that law itself produces under the pressures of its social environment. And only a clear delineation of the self-produced boundaries of law can help to clarify the interrelations of law and other social practices.

IV

Now, if law and other discourses close their boundaries via the use of binary codes, how is "interdiscursivity"[39] nevertheless feasible? How does legal autopoiesis

---

37 Griffiths, *supra*, n. 19, at 2ff.; Franz von Benda-Beckmann, "Unterwerfung oder Distanz: Rechtssoziologie, Rechtsanthropologie und Rechtspluralismus aus rechtsanthropologischer Sicht," *Zeitschrift für Rechtssoziologie* 12 (1991), 97–119, at 106ff.

38 Philippe Nonet and Philip Selznick, *Law and Society in Transition: Toward Responsive Law* (New York: Harper & Row, 1978), 10.

39 Jackson, *supra* n. 17.

answer Lyotard's challenge of fragmented discourses: "il faut bien qu'elles aient ensemble des propriétés commune, et que la 'rencontre' ait lieu dans un même univers, sinon il n'y pas de rencontre du tout."[40]

In the case of legal pluralism, what about the relations between unofficial and official legal discourses? What about the relations between them and other social discourses? The formulas of neopluralism—interwoven, integral, dialectical, superimposed—are suggestive metaphors but they lack analytical power.[41] "Mutually constitutive"[42] is by far the most powerful image, but how does mutual constitution work? Fitzpatrick explains what he calls "integral pluralism": Custom supports law, but law transforms the elements of custom that it appropriates into its own image and likeness. Law, in turn, supports other social forms but becomes, in the process, part of the other form. How separate are they in their interwovenness? After all, "talking of intertwining, interaction or mutual constitution presupposes distinguishing what is being intertwined."[43] I propose to analyze "interdiscursivity" in terms of a clear-cut separation of autonomous (not semiautonomous) discourses and, at the same time, in terms of their structural coupling. In our example of market transactions, we have a simultaneous, but causal, parallel processing of diverse legal and non-legal communicative chains that are operationally closed to each other. Each of them builds up structures of its own: concrete day-to-day interaction of the transacting parties, communication within formalized contracts and organizations, economic transactions as part of the larger economic system, and claims and counterclaims within diverse and competing legal discourses, official and unofficial. All these discursive processes interfere in one and the same social situation. And one and the same concrete communicative event will be processed in these different discourses which in spite of this "overlapping membership" (of a communicative event, not of a person) remain closed to each other. Over time, these discourses coevolve in relations of structural coupling. They do not causally influence each other, rather they use each other as *chocs exogènes*,[44] as perturbations to build up their own internal structures.

This is the point where "productive misunderstanding" comes in to explain in more detail what could be meant by "mutually constitutive" relations between social and legal forms and between different legal discourses.[45] In a firm, hierarchical patterns of decision-making, roles of supervision and control, and rules of competence are law-free organizational routines that guide the self-production

---

40 Lyotard, *supra* n. 2, at 51.
41 Cf. the critique by Nelken, *supra* n. 3.
42 Fitzpatrick, *supra* n. 22, at 9.
43 Benda-Beckmann, *supra* n. 36, at 898.
44 Kerchove and Ost, *supra* n. 33, at 151.
45 See also Gunther Teubner, "Autopoiesis and Steering: How Politics Exploits the Normative Surplus of Capital," in *Steering: Autopoiesis and Configuration Theory*, ed. R.J. in't Veld, L. Schaap, C.J.A.M. Termeer, and M.J.W. van Twist (Dordrecht: Kluwer, 1991), 127–41.

of ongoing social processes. Whenever, for example in an internal disciplinary action, the *quaestio iuris* is raised, a subtle but decisive shift of meaning occurs. The firm's internal legal process, the system of "private justice"[46]—not the official law of the State—rereads, reinterprets, reconstructs, reobserves these routines under the code legal/illegal and constitutes them anew as integral part of intra-organizational law. This is a mere fiction because organizational routines were meant as something else. The intra-organizational legal discourse misreads organizational self-production as norm production and thus invents a new and rich "source" of law. And it is the famous "legal affinity" of formal organizations[47] that supports law's subtle misreading of law. Since organizational routines tend to be "formalized"—i.e. they shift from a mix of cognitive and normative expectations to purely normative expectations—it needs only a minute shift of meaning to read them as legal norms that had already existed before.

Vice-versa, a similar misreading occurs when the organization reincorporates legal rules developed and refined in the firm's disciplinary proceedings and makes use of them to restructure the firm's decision-making process. These originally legal norms are "decoded"—i.e. observed no longer under the code legal/illegal—stripped of their legal connotations of valid/non-valid and of their structural context of disciplinary rules, and are reconstituted as power bases in the micropolitical games of the organization. The mutual constitution of law and organization turns out to be a mutual misreading, a reciprocal construction of fictitious realities, a mutual distortion which, however, works for practical purposes.

A similar constructive distortion takes place in the case of economic transactions. The structures of economic transactions are essentially non-legal: They build on factual chances of action and create new chances of action or on trust in future changes of chances. In ongoing business relations it is wise to keep the lawyers out. They will distort business realities.[48] Why? They misread factual chances of action as legal "property," and they misunderstand mutual trust in future behavior as contractually binding "obligations," as "rights" and

---

46 Henry, *supra*, n. 22.

47 Philip Selznick, *Law, Society and Industrial Justice* (New York: Russell Sage,1969), 32ff.; Renate Mayntz, "Politische Steuerung und gesellschaftliche Steuerungsprobleme: Anmerkungen zu einem politischen Paradigma," *Jahrbuch zur Staats·und Verwaltungswissenschaft* 1 (1987), 89–110, at 103; Fritz Scharpf, "Grenzen der institutionellen Reform," *Jahrbuch zur Staats und Verwaltungswissenschaft* 1 (1987), 111–51, at 117ff.; Fritz Scharpf, "Politische Steuerung und politische Institutionen," *Politische Vierteljahresschrift* 30 (1989), 10–21, at 16; Franz-Xaver Kaufmann, "Steuerung wohlfahrtsstaatlicher Abläufe durch Recht," in *Gesetzgebungstheorie und Rechtspolitik*, ed. D. Grimm and W. Maihofer (Opladen: Westdeutscher Verlag, 1988), 65–108, at 82ff.; Lauren B. Edelman, "Legal Environments and Organizational Governance: The Expansion of Due Process in the American Workplace," *American Journal of Sociology* 95 (1990), 1401–40, at 1406ff., 1435ff.

48 See Stewart Macaulay, *Law and the Balance of Power: The Automobile Manufacturers and Their Dealers* (New York: Russell Sage Foundation, 1966).

"duties." And if their rigid and formalist claims and counterclaims are reread in the ongoing transaction relation they will destroy precarious trust relations. The difference between economic chances of action and legal property and between trust and obligations is again due to the difference in coding. The lawyers observe economic action under the code legal/illegal and misread economic processes and structures as sources of law. Vice-versa, clever economic actors misread legal norms under the economic code as bargaining chips, as new opportunities for profit-making. Again, we have a symbiosis of mutual distortion. In Lyotard's words, the isolated discourses which are not translatable into each other "meet" in the "reseaux de noms."[49]

Note that in both our examples the State and its official law were not relevant. The juridification of social phenomena, in our words, the legal distortion of social realities, happens independently of the "recognition" of this law by? the State and the courts. Within the regimes of "private government,"[50] "private justice,"[51] and "private regulation"[52] one should distinguish carefully between

1. phenomena like micropolitical power structures and economic exigencies and moral or social conventional expectations, which are essentially non-legal;
2. their reconstruction within genuinely legal processes of non-State character like private agreements, intra-organizational disciplinary procedures, inter-organizational regimes of oligopolist market regulations;
3. their legislative, administrative or judicial "recognition" which produces new rules of State law.

Thus, interdiscursivity occurs in two diverse forms: between legal discourses (State law vs. "private law" and mafia law) and between legal and non-legal discourses (legal vs. moral, economic, political phenomena). This is due to the difference between "binary codes" which are stable and "programs" which are historically contingent.[53] In both cases one can speak about recontextualization, in the first case between legal and non-legal discourses as decoding and recoding, in the second case between different legal discourses as deprogramming and reprogramming.

But one has to free one's mind of any idea of information transportation.[54] After all these distortions, the original normative meaning will not be recognizable

---

49 Lyotard, *supra* n. 2, at 10–51.
50 Macaulay, *supra* n. 31, at 445–518.
51 Henry, *supra* n. 22.
52 Brian Bercusson, "Juridification and Disorder," in *Juridification of Social Spheres*, ed. G. Teubner (Berlin: de Gruyter, 1987), 49–90.
53 For this distinction, see Luhmann, *supra* n. 35.
54 Klaus Krippendorf, "Eine häretische Kommunikation über Kommunikation über Kommunikation über Realität," *Delfin* 13 (1990), 52–67.

anymore. In any case, interdiscursivity in legal pluralism is a conspicuous case of systematically distorted communication. One cannot simply speak of a "transfer" of constructs from one normative order to the other as in older theories of legal pluralism. Neither is "interaction," "negotiation," or "interpenetration" of diverse legal orders the adequate metaphor. "Mutual constitution" comes close, however only under three conditions. First, against all recent assertions on blurring the "law/society" distinction,[55] the boundaries of meaning that separate closed discourses need to be recognized.[56] Second, mutual constitution cannot be understood as a transfer of meaning from one field to the other but needs to be seen as an internal reconstruction process. Third, the internal constraints that render the mutual constitution highly selective must be taken seriously. The constraints that are responsible for systematic distortion are not something that could be avoided by rational argument. It is not just the local specialities of the diverse discourses involved but basic requirements of their self-reproduction including the resistance of presently existing structures that necessarily lead to the mutual misreading of discourses.

Unavoidably, this leads us back to closure, to the separation of intertwined systems, to the *différend* of heterogeneous discourses, to "the necessarily unbridgeable gaps (*sic!*) between law and other social forms."[57] The dynamics of legal pluralism cannot be understood by a common logic of the discourses involved, be it the transaction economics of law and organization, the politics of omnipresent micro-power, the socio-logics of social control, or yesterday's political economy. Rather, it is the radical diversity of discourses—the internal rationality of the organization, the exigencies of the market, the idiosyncrasies of personal interaction, and the intrinsic logics of diverse public and "private" legal orders—that are responsible for distorted communication in legal pluralism.

V

The shift from old to new legal pluralism is often described as a conceptual expansion from colonial domination of the indigenous population to the modem State's domination of a variety of groups. Legal pluralism has expanded from a concept that refers to the relations between colonized and colonizer, to relations between dominant and subordinate groups, such as religious, ethnic, or cultural minorities, immigrant groups, and unofficial forms of ordering located in social networks of institutions.[58] In my view, such a perspective of "internal colonialism" that focuses on the modern State dominating the "laws" of diverse groups misses

---

55 Robert W. Gordon, "Critical Legal Histories," *Stanford Law Review* 36 (1984), 57–125, at 102ff.
56 Lyotard, *supra* n. 2, at 12ff.
57 Fitzpatrick, *supra* n. 22, at 126.
58 Merry, *supra* n. 18, at 872ff.

crucial aspects of modernity. As a consequence, it unduly restricts the scope of the new legal pluralism. "Old" legal pluralism, be it in Europe or in the colonies, had to do with the legal formalization of social norms that are the product of general coordination of behavior in diffuse processes of social reproduction. The "new" legal pluralism needs to shift emphasis and to focus on the fragmentation of social self-production in a multiplicity of closed discourses. "Standard setting" is the new paradigm and no longer "social customs"! Today we face an immense pluralization of legal pluralism which is due not just to the pluralization of groups and communities, but to the fragmentation of social discourses. There is a danger that legal pluralism will be marginalized if the idea of "internal colonialism" draws attention only to diverse groups, communities, and networks and their social norms instead of looking to social discourses and their diverse rationalities.

Ubi societas, ibi ius. This old juridical wisdom has undergone a dramatic shift of meaning. In traditional societies it meant the emergence of legal phenomena in different clans, groups, castes, strata, or classes according to the prevailing principle of differentiation.[59] In modern societies it means the emergence of legal phenomena in the context of highly specialized discourses that are the new sources of social self-reproduction which the law then misreads as sources of norm production. This changes the character of legal pluralism, its content and its dynamics. To put it into Gurvitch's imagery of "vertical" and "horizontal" relations between law and society,[60] the main question for legal pluralism is no longer how in the "vertical" dimension of law and society informal and diffuse social norms are gradually "formalized" into more specific legal norms. Rather it is in the "horizontal" dimension, in the relation of law to a variety of other language games, that we today observe pluralist norm production processes. The problem has changed from a "translation" of social norms of groups into legal norms to the "recoding" of a bewildering multitude of otherwise coded communication in the code of the law. And in this process, I submit, the linkage institutions of legal pluralism have also changed their character— from concept and structure to process and transformation.

What are linkage institutions? I propose to distinguish between structural coupling and linkage institutions.[61] Structural coupling as such leads only to transitory structural changes. Legal misreading of other discourses happens only at random—as tangential responses, as it were—whenever social communications are observed under the code legal/illegal. The misreading becomes epidemic when linkage institutions are evolving that are responsible for the duration, intensity, and quality of structural coupling. Roman law's *boni mores*, but also classical formulas of *bona fides* and *bonus pater familias*, are the paradigms of the legal

---

59   Otto von Gierke, *Die Genossenschaftstheorie und die deutsche Rechtsprechung* (Berlin: Weidmann, 1863).

60   Georges Gurvitch, *The Sociology of Law* (London: K. Paul, Trench, Trubner & Co., 1947), 181.

61   See also Teubner, *supra* n. 44.

tradition. It is their very ambiguity that makes them the institutional links between legal and social processes. They represent, at the same time, social norms and legal norms, "standards" as well as "directives."[62] Like the old Roman god Janus, they have a double-faced character. While the concept is identical in law and in society, it is nevertheless different: If you look at it from society "outside," it is different from what you see if you look at it from law "inside.".

In modern terminology the old *boni mores* and other institutional links between law and society would have to be called "essentially contested concepts."[63] They have no fixed reference and take on a different meaning according to the context of the relevant discourse. They have no determined content but are loci for the sociolegal debate. These concepts are "essential" because they reflect the very intrinsic logic of the discourses involved. And they are "contested" because they reflect the basic discursive differences. They do not create a new unity of the separate discourses involved; they only link them, transcending the boundaries but respecting, even reaffirming, them. In spite of their identical *nom propre*, they are purely internal constructs of each discourse involved. Linking institutions do not have an interdiscursive common meaning; they are internal constructs, separate but complementary. "Et enfin: les phrases de régime ou de genre hétérogène se 'rencontrent' sur les noms propres, dans les mondes déterminés par les réseaux de noms."[64] Now, if it is true that the new legal pluralism "juridifies" specialized discourses instead of diffuse social norms in the lifeworld of groups and communities, we should also expect the linkage institutions to change. Indeed, in relation to economic processes "contracting" has emerged as the modern linkage institution,[65] "standard setting" in relation to technical, scientific, and medical processes.[66] The legal discourse, including "private government," "private justice," and "private regulation," constructively misreads economic or technical processes of social reproduction and turns them into new and rich "sources" of law. Certainly, one could interpret this as a specialization of institutional links and still adhere to the model of *boni mores* with the only difference that their content varies from field to field. But there is more to it. Our "essentially contested

---

62   Gunther Teubner, *Standards und Direktiven in Generalklauseln: Möglichkeiten und Grenzen der empirischen Sozialforschung bei der Präzisierung der Gute-Sitten-Klauseln im Privatrecht* (Frankfurt; Athenaeum, 1971).

63   William B. Connolly, *The Terms of Political Discourse*, 2nd edn. (Princeton: Princeton University Press, 1983).

64   Lyotard, *supra* n. 2, at 51.

65   Teubner, *supra* n. 44.

66   Giandomenico Majone, "Science and Trans-science in Standard-setting," *Science, Technology & Human Values* 9 (1984), 15–22; Giandomenico Majone, *Evidence, Argument and Persuasion in the Policy Process* (New Haven: Yale University Press. 1989); Loria Salter, "Science and Peer Review: The Canadian Standard-Setting Experience," *Science, Technology & Human Values* 10 (1985), 37–46; Christian Joerges, "Quality Regulation in Consumer Good Markets: Theoretical Concepts and Practical Examples," in *Contract and Organisation*, ed. T.C. Daintith and G. Teubner (Berlin: de Gruyter, 1986), 142–63.

concepts" have become "essentially contested processes." The legal discourse no longer "incorporates" results by misreading social norms as legal norms; today it "incorporates" processes misreading economic or technical production as law production.

VI

Now we can see more clearly why legal pluralism represents the "openness" of the law toward society. The legal system's boundaries, to repeat, are not defined by the official law of the State. Rather, any communication that observes action under the legal code constitutes an integral part of the legal discourse, including communication among laypeople that invokes claims against each other. It is not the distinction legal/illegal that separates the State's law from the "law" of organizations and groups but the different use of the operative symbol of "validity." And it is within the overarching legal discourse that we can observe secondary differentiation processes that separate center and periphery.[67] The center is not as one would expect in old-European traditions of thought political legislation. Legislative law is peripheral law! Rather, the center is represented in the hierarchy of courts. They produce law in its most autonomous form. They celebrate the central function of law, using the occasion of conflicts to create congruently generalized expectations. Contemporary law's real dynamism, however, takes place in the "legal peripheries," as the dynamism of social life takes place in the peripheries of the grand metropolis. Peripheral law constitutes those parts of official and unofficial law that are structurally coupled to other social discourses. Here, we find the linkage institutions that participate in legal processes as well as in economic, technical, scientific, and cultural processes. Thus, legal pluralism makes the law "responsive" toward society by transforming social self-production processes into sources of law production. Responsiveness is not identical to viability. The distinction coupling/binding forces us to distinguish between the mere viability of social structures (knowledge, law, policies) and their responsiveness. Viability means survival of structures under conditions of "structural drift."[68] Indeed, if social systems coevolve under conditions of transitory structural coupling, the result is mere survival of certain structures which have proved resistant to environmental perturbations. Of course, this provides the system with a certainty of reality. If the system is capable of maintaining its own autopoiesis via highly specified structures, it disposes of an internal indication

---

67 Niklas Luhmann, "Die Stellung der Gerichte im Rechtssystem," *Rechtstheorie* 21 (1990), 459–73, at 466ff.

68 Ernst von Glasersfeld, "An Epistemology for Cognitive Systems," in *Self-Organizing Systems. An Interdisciplinary Approach*, ed. G. Roth and H. Schwegler (Frankfurt: Campus, 1981), 121–31; Ernst von Glasersfeld, *Wissen, Sprache und Wirklichkeit: Arbeiten zum radikalen Konstruktivismus* (Braunschweig: Vieweg, 1987).

that it is "on the right track, even without knowing where and how."[69] Viability, however, has two problems. First, there will usually be a whole variety of similarly viable solutions which poses the question of how to select among them. Secondly, mere viability says nothing about ecological compatibility, about the suitability with social, psychic, and natural environments. Usually, there are more or less ecologically suitable solutions.

Thus mere viability of systemic eigenvalues does not tell very much about their responsiveness. It is the introduction of linkage institutions that changes the situation drastically. If such institutions permanently link parallel processes of social self-reproduction to each other, the number of possible viable eigenvalues will decrease since they are exposed to increased perturbation under which they have to endure. But at the same time their ecological responsiveness is increasing. Such a responsiveness may become stable if linkage institutions squeeze structural coupling into a direction such that systems act upon each other in a cyclical fashion. We then have the interesting case in which processes of self-reproduction would, without the systems involved losing their autopoietic closure, take place outside the boundaries of autopoietic systems. This would be the case of ecological (not systemic!) recursiveness.

The autopoiesis of the systems involved is not impaired; instead, it is being exploited to build up ecological cycles that respect system boundaries even as they cross them. This would indicate the direction in which we would have to search for "responsive law."[70] The usual recommendation is: politicize formal law! The open acknowledgment of the political character of law and the change of its conceptual apparatus in the political direction, the governance of "purpose," "policies," and "interests", all this would make the law more responsive to political needs. This is the message of "political jurisprudence" from Jhering to Habermas. To be sure, this strategy has made law more responsive to institutionalized politics. However, at the same time it has subordinated law to political reality constructs. This raises the question of whether such a politicization would not remove law even further away from other social discourses instead of bringing it closer to them.

Importing social science knowledge into law is the other recommendation for making law more responsive. Instead of using the artificial reasoning of law, we should use the theoretical insights, empirical experience, and policy recommendations of the social sciences. But again: What gives us the reassurance that scientific constructs make law more responsive to social needs?

Legal pluralism—as understood in this text—may be more promising. Linkage institutions that bind law to diverse social discourses much more closely than politics or social science suggest a "resonance" of law with civil society. The institutions of legal pluralism may become a source for the law's "tacit knowledge"[71] about

---

69   Luhmann, *supra* n. 12. at 317.
70   Nonet and Selznick, *supra* n. 37, at 73ff.
71   Michael Polanyi, *Personal Knowledge: Toward a Post-critical Philosophy* (Chicago: Chicago University Press, 1958), 69ff.

its social ecology. Rethinking legal pluralism in the end could open an "ecological approach" to law and legal intervention."[72] Indeed, the intellectual tradition of "private law" which paved the way for law's historical extraordinary responsiveness to the economic system via the institutions of property, contract, and organization needs to be generalized. Social autonomy is the key word:

> Taking autonomy seriously means to rely on self-determination and at the same time on inevitable externalization (outside control), not understood as hetero-determination but as a potential outside support in situations of impossible self-help. It would be similar to therapeutical help and to supportive structures outside of the law.[73]

If private law's reliance on social autonomy and structural coupling is applied not only to the economic system but to the multiplicity of social discourses,[74] it may become a model for new ways in which law, instead of relying solely on its political legitimation and its economic efficiency, opens up to the dynamics of "civil society."[75]

---

72 Karl-Heinz Ladeur, "Flexibilisierungsstrategien: Alternativen zum 'Steuerungsstaat'—'Reflexives Recht'— 'Prozeduralisierung'—'Okologisches Recht'," in *Workshop zu Konzepten des postinterventionistischen Rechts*, ed. G. Bruggemeier and C. Joerges (Bremen: ZERP Materialien), 311–99; Karl-Heinz Ladeur, "The Law of Uncertainty," in *Critical Legal Thought: An American–German Debate*. ed. C. Joerges and D. Trubek (Baden-Baden: Nomos, 1989) 567–90; David Nelken. "Law in Action or Living Law? Back to the Beginning in Sociology of law," *Legal Studies* 4 (1984), 157–74 at 171 n. 54.

73 Rudolf Wiethölter, "Zum Fortbildungsrecht der (richterlichen) Rechtsfortbildung: Fragen eines lesenden Recht-Fertigungslehrers," *Kritische Vierteljahreszeitschrift für Gesetzgebung und Rechtswissenschaft* 3 (1988), 128, at 27f.

74 Rudolf Wiethölter, "Zur Regelbildung in der Dogmatik des Zivilrechts," *Archiv fur Rechts- und Sozialphilosophie. Beiheft* (Stuttgart: Steiner, 1992).

75 Lyotard, Jean-François, *Le différend*, Ed. de Minuit, Paris 1986.

Index

abortion 59n16, 290, 294, 295, 298, 299–300, 302, 303–4
administrative revolution 78–79
Albert, M. 102n3, 107
Andersen, N.Â. 11, 68
appeals *see* criminal appeals
Arnaud, A.-J. 10, 51–52, **52**, 55, 57, 59
autopoiesis 1–2, 38n13, 57–58, 60–61, 71, 102, 203n8, 344–45, 346–47, 359
    organisations 168, 169
    social systems theory 3, 5, 6, 171, 257–58, 259–61, 262–63, 284, 338

Baghai, K. 13
Baumann, Z. 36–37
behaviors 21, 55, 197, 218
Berman, H. 75
Bourdieu, P. 76, 78n9, 84, 271n25
Bowers v. *Hardwick* (U.S.1986) 295, 306–7, 308
Bregvadze, L. 13
Broquet, J. 11
business organisations *see* organisations

Campbell, D. 135, 136
CDS (credit default swap) 157, 160–61, *161*, 162, *163*, 164, *166*, 166–67, 169–70
codes 68–69, 71–72, *73*, 73–74, *74*, 78–79, 80, 90, 165, 212
coevolution 5, 6–7, 97, 100, 106, 258, 347
Collins, H. 135, 136
communication 1, 5, 67, 69, 202, 238, 259, 283
community of practice 242–43
company interest 167–68, *168*
complexity 25–26
consciousness 9–10, 12, 13, 198–200, 202, 208, 218, 278
    Luhmann 257–64, 265–66, 267–68

constitutional theory 330, 336–38
constitutions 8, 13, 208, 309, 327–28, 329–30, 335, 336–38, 339
contracts 6, 11, 83, 129–30, 131–38, *139*, 139–41, *141*, 147–49, **149**, 150, 151, 172
    CDS 157, 160–61, *161*, 162, *163*, 164, *166*, 166–67, 169–70
    corporate bonds 157, *161*, 162, *162*, 163, 169–70
    derivative financial instruments 155–56, 157–58, 159–60
    structural coupling 12, 141–42, *142*, 146–47, *147*, 148
contractual fragmentation 12, 174
convergence theories 40–41, 42–43, 44, 45
convictions *see* criminal convictions
corporate bonds 157, *161*, 162, *162*, 163, 169–70
corporate organisations *see* organisations
Cotterrell, R. 10, 51–52, **52**, 55, 57, 59
courts 13, 237–38, 240–41, 243, 244–45, 248–49
credit default swap *see* CDS
credit systems 83–84
criminal appeals 320–24, 325
criminal convictions 318, 319–20, 321–23, 324–25
culture 21, 41, 57

d'Aguesseau, H.-F. 75, 76
de Grauwe, P. 120
de Sousa Santos, B. 18–19
decision-making 21, 25–26, 27–30
democracy 8–9
derivative financial instruments 155–56, 157–58, 159–60
    CDS 157, 160–61, *161*, 162, *163*, 164, *166*, 166–67, 169–70
distinctions, functionalism of 1, 2, 3, 6, 14

EAW (European Arrest Warrant) 246
ECB (European Central Bank) 114, 115, 118, 119, 122
ECJ (European Court of Justice) 108, 239n17, 239n18, 246
Economic Intelligence 27, 28
economic system 7–8, 9, 111, 112, 113–14, 148, 360
efficiency 9, 53–54, 57
Ehrlich, E. 18, 53–54, **56**, 57, 232, 331, 333
Elias, N. 68
empires 45, 86
EMU (European Monetary Union) 114, 118, 120, 121, 122
equality, right to 296, 297
Eurogroup 117–18, 119, 120, 122
European Union 37, 39–40, 106–8, 121–23, 239–40, 334
    ECB 114, 115, 118, 119, 122
    EMU 114, 118, 120, 121, 122
    Eurogroup 117–18, 119, 120, 122
    financial crisis 119–20, 121
    governance 97–98, 108–15, 116–17, 120–21, 122–23
    SGP 115–16, 117, 120, 122
exchange contracts 132–33, 147–48
expectations 3, 215, 216, 218, 219, 220, **221**, 222, 223

Fact dimension 210, **211**, 215–17, **221**
Febbrajo, A. 11
financial contracts *see* contracts
financial crisis 119–20, 121, 155–56, 159–61, 171
financial regulation 12, 159–60, 170–73, 174–75
Fisher-Lescano, A. 241
Foucault, M. 79, 90
fragile states 84, 85–86, **87–89**
France 75–76, 83, 84
Fukuyama, F. 40
function systems 84–85, 142–43, **144**, 146, 147–49, **149**, 150, **150**
functional adequacy 54, 55
functional differentiation 73, *73*, 74, *74*, 76–77, 84, 142–49, **144**, *147*, 268, 276, 297, 310

Gamble, A. 111
Geiger, T. 18, 54–55, **56**, 57
generalizations 3, 4, 215, 219
globalization 22, 26, 57, 329, 332
governance 11, 26, 97, 98–100, 104–6
    European Union 97–98, 108–15, 116–17, 120–21, 122–23
Gros, D. and Mayer, T. 120
Guibentif, P. 13
Gurvitch, G. 18, 42, 331, 356

harmonised law 40, 41, 43
Harste, G. 11
Herbst, P.G. 236–37
historical sociology 70, 80
homosexuality 290, 294, 295, 298, 299, 300, 302, 303, 304
    Bowers v. *Hardwick* 295, 306–7, 308
    Lawrence v. *Texas* 295, 306, 307, 308
human rights 244, 245, 246, 277, 284
hypercycle 58

'impossible necessity' 338–39
incommensurate values 42, 43–44
independent agencies 113–14, 115
institutional linkages 347, 356–58, 359
interaction systems 79, 83, 85, 183
internal differentiation 61, 122, 165, 170
international law 45–46, 333
interpenetration 202–6, 212, 213, 215, 218, 220, 222
intersystemic communication 5–6, 7, 8, 9–10, 61

Jessop, B. 99, 102n2, 117
judicial dialogue 237, 238, 242, 244, 245, 246
judicial review 290–91, 292–94, 298, 302, 309–10
judiciary 58, 233–35, 237–38, 240, 244, 248–49

Kant, I. 76–77, 81
Kelsen, H. 337

Laflamme, D. 12
language 205–6, 267, 280, 281
Lasswell, H.D. 40

law 4, 5, 12–13, 21, 24–25, 32, 44, 47, 57, 61–62, 351
  sociology of 10–11, 18–19, 21, 22, 23, 25, 26–27, 46, **57**, 289
Lawrence v. *Texas* (U.S. 2003) 295, 306, 307, 308
legal evolution 74–77
legal instrumentalism 37–39, 42
legal orders 2, 61, 233, 234, 235, 331, 332, 333–34, 349
legal pluralism 14, 20, 33–34, 62, 231–33, 248–49, 331–33, 343, 344–45, 347–51, 355–56, 358, 359–60
legal positivism 17, 240–41, 328
legal regulations 8–9, 34–35, 44, 51, 53–54, 55, 57
legal system of communication 5, 143
legal systems 4, 58, 60, 61, 74–77, 238, 243
  media 318, 319, 320–24, 325
legal transnationalism 10, 31–32, 33, 35–36, 39–40, 44, 45, 46–47
Legrand, P. 42
Levine, F.J. 19–20
liberalism 42, 45
links, functionalism of 1, 2, 3, 6, 14
Living Constitutionalism 290, 301, 303–4, 305, 306, 309
'living law' 53–54, 55, 60, 333, 334
local law 334
Luhmann, N. 3, 19, 58, 67, 69, 106, 165, 201, 245, 256–57, 283, 289
  autopoiesis 171, 257–58, 259–61, 262–63
  communication 5, 209, 259, 263
  consciousness 257–64, 265–66, 267–68
  meaning-constituting systems 198–201, 202–6, 207–8, 209, 210–11, 213–14, 220
  modern society 98, 99, 100
  morality 197–98, 212, 213
  rights 255, 268–77, 278, 283–84
  social systems theory 2–3, 5–6, **6**, 52–53, 61, 255, 283, 338
  steering 90, 100, 102, 103–4, 105–6, 213–14

structural coupling 6–7, 8–10, 101–2, 203–4, 264–68, 274–75, 284
subjective rights 255, 269, 270–71, 272, 273, 275, 277, 278

Macaulay, S. 131, 133–35, 137
Macneil, I.R. 131–33, 135, 137, 147
markets 9, 82–83, 112–13
Mather, L. 39, 41
Mayntz, R. 98–99
meaning 207, 208, 209–10, **211**, 222, 223, 240, 267
  Fact dimension 210, **211**, 215–17, **221**
  Social dimension 12, 210, 211, **211**, 219, **221**
  Temporal dimension 12, 210–11, **211**, 218–19, **221**
meaning-constituting systems 198–201, 202–6, 207–8, 209, 210–11, 213–14, 220, 222–23
media 13, 281, 317–18
  criminal appeals 320–24, 325
  criminal convictions 318, 319–20, 321–23, 324–25
memory 317–18, 319, 320–22, 324
military organisational system 79, 80, 81–82, 86
modern society 98, 99, 100
Modern Systems Theory *see* MST
money 7, 9, 82–84, 113–14
Montesquieu, C. 76
morality 197–98, 205, 212–13, 214–15, 219, 220, **221**, 222, 223
MST (Modern Systems Theory) 11, 97, 98–100, 102, 104, 105, 106–7, 121
multiculturalism 44
music 12–13, 229–30
mutual constitution 355

NAFTA (North American Free Trade Agreement) 334–35
Nobles, R. and Schiff, D. 13
nonhierarchical communication 239, 248
normative system 3–4, 59–60, 61, 232
norms 8, 55, 58, 218, 219, 239, 328, 337, 356
North American Free Trade Agreement *see* NAFTA

observation 180–81, *181*, *182*, 182–83, *184*, *186*
Offe, C. 120
OMC (Open Method of Coordination) 116–17, 118, 120, 122
organisational evolution 77–79
organisational systems 74, *74*, 79, 84–85, 86, 90–91, 101–2, 352–53
organisations 11, 12, 168, 169, 183, *186*, 187–88, *189*, 235–37
  company interest 167–69, *168*
  value communication *182*, 182–83, 186–87, 188–89, 190–91, *191*, 192–93
  values 179, 184–85, 186, 188–89, 191–92, *192*, 193
Originalism 290, 301–3, 305, 309

Paterson, J. 12
persons 143, 183n5, 201–2, 216, 217, 223, 267–68, 270–71, 280
perspectivism 133–35, 137
Pirandello, L. 60
Poland 232, 247, 248
Policy Intelligence 27, 28–29, 30
political systems 1, 8, 9, 90, 97, 102–4, 108–9, 110, 148–49, 241, 318
polycontextuality 99, 100, 102, 103, 106, 111, 122, **145**, 339
Pound, R. 42–43
privacy, right to 13, 297, 304n60
private constitutionalism 330, 338
private law 136, 230, 335, 360
privatisation 297, 329
procedures 4, 5, 9, 281
promises 131–33, 137, 147–48
psychic systems 9, 13, 199, 200, 201, 206, 210, 257–58, 263, 266, 284
  interpenetration 204, 205, 212
Puetter, U. 117, 118

rationality 9, 21, 54, 55, 99
Rawls, J. 45
Raz, J. 337–38
reflexive contracting 135–37
reflexive governance 104–5, 106, 109–10, 111–12, 121–22, 123
reflexive law 105, 171, 173

regulations 3, 20–21, 23, 51, 53–54, 57, 58
relational contracts 131, 133, 137
rights 255, 268–77, 278, 283–84
roles 216, 217, 223, 270
Roman Empire 72, 75
rules 3, 4, 115–16

Sand, I.-J. 107, 239–40
Schmitt, C. 45–46, 72, 337
selective indifference 149, 296
self-constituting systems 199, **199**, 200, 203–4
self-correction 1, 5–6, 7, 58, 60, 61
self-descriptions 58n10, 71, 72, 90, 102, 103–4, 109
self-observation 4, 5–6, 58, 60, 61, 70, 71, 102, 262, 318
self-organisation 71–72, 76, 351
self-reference 71, 75, 76, 77, 105–6, 239
SGP (Stability and Growth Pact) 115–16, 117, 120, 122
Simmel, G. 41, 82
Social dimension 12, 210, 211, **211**, 219, **221**
social regulation 197, 201, 205, 206, 213, 216, 217, 223
social systems 6–7, 14, 183, 199–200, 204, 210, 358–59
social systems theory 1, 2–6, **6**, 61, 70, 86, 89, 90–91, 156–57, 171, 185, 245
  autopoiesis 3, 5, 6, 171, 257–58, 259–61, 262–63, 284, 338
  company interest 167–68, *168*
  contracts 140, *162*, 162–67, *163*, *166*, 172
  rights 255, 268–77, 278, 283–84
sociolegal studies 17, 18–21, 26–30, 38, 39, 44–45, 61–62
sodomy laws *see* homosexuality
Stability and Growth Pact *see* SGP
state-building 70, 71, 76, 89, 90–91
states 35–36, 71–72, 74, *74*, 84–86, **87–89**, 89, 90–91
steering 90, 100, 102, 103–4, 105–6, 213–14, **221**
Stichweh, R. 90
structural coupling 6–7, 8–10, 11, 13, 14, 62, 101–2, 203–4, 264–68, 345–46, 347, 356

contracts 141–42, *142*, 148
rights 274–75, 284
subjective rights 13, 255, 269, 270–71, 272, 273, 275, 277, 278
Supreme Court 290–94, 295–96, 297, 298–300, 301, 306, 309–10
   abortion 290, 294, 295, 298, 299, 303–4
   Bowers v. *Hardwick* 295, 306–7, 308
   homosexuality 290, 294, 295, 298, 299
   Lawrence v. *Texas* 295, 306, 307, 308
systems analysis 67–68, 68

Tamanaha, B. 37, 38, 42
technologies 217, 242, 243
Temporal dimension 12, 210–11, **211**, 218–19, **221**
territorial differentiation 103, 115, 116, 117
Teubner, G. 14, 58, 71, 105, 171, 175, 327n2, 338
   company interest 167, 168
   contracts 129–30, 139, 172, 173, 174
Tilly, C. 69
Tocqueville, A. 78
transnational law 31–32, 39–40, 46, 310, 335
Treves, R. 18

United States 37, 171, 172–73, 296, 297–98, 308
   abortion 290, 294, 295, 298, 299–300, 302, 303–4
   Bowers v. *Hardwick* 295, 306–7, 308
   homosexuality 290, 294, 295, 298, 299, 300, 302, 303, 304
   Lawrence v. *Texas* 295, 306, 307, 308
   Living Constitutionalism 290, 301, 303–4, 305, 306, 309
   Originalism 290, 301–3, 305, 309
   Supreme Court 290–94, 295–96, 297, 298–300, 301, 306, 309–10

validity 55, 59, 271, 300–301, 329–30, 334, 358
value communication 12, 179–80, *182*, 182–87, 188–93, *191*, 192–93
values 12, 43–44, 179, 180, 184–85, 186, 198, 217
   organisations 179, 184–85, 186, 188–89, 191–92, *192*, 193
Veitch, S. 42, 43
Vincent-Jones, P. 135, 136
von Clausewitz, C. 80, 90
von Groddeck, V. 12
Voß, J.-P. and Kemp, R. 104–5

war 11, 72, 79, 80–82, 83, 84, 86, 90
Weber, M. 18, 42, 54, **56**, 57, 84, 236
Weiler, J.H.H. 107–8
well-formed states 85, 86, **87–89**
Westphalian nation-state 33, 37, 39
Williams, G. 115
Winczorek, J. 12–13
world society 12, 102, 106–7, 278, 284, 327–28, 329, 332–33, 338, 339
Wróblewski, B. and Świda, W. 232